Canadian Families Today:
New Perspectives

Edited by
David Cheal

OXFORD
UNIVERSITY PRESS

OXFORD

UNIVERSITY PRESS

70 Wynford Drive, Don Mills, Ontario M3C 1J9
www.oup.com/ca

Oxford University Press is a department of the University of Oxford.
It furthers the University's objective of excellence in research, scholarship,
and education by publishing worldwide in

Oxford New York

Auckland Cape Town Dar es Salaam Hong Kong Karachi
Kuala Lumpur Madrid Melbourne Mexico City Nairobi
New Delhi Shanghai Taipei Toronto

With offices in

Argentina Austria Brazil Chile Czech Republic France Greece
Guatemala Hungary Italy Japan Poland Portugal Singapore
South Korea Switzerland Thailand Turkey Ukraine Vietnam

Oxford is a trade mark of Oxford University Press
in the UK and in certain other countries

Published in Canada
by Oxford University Press

Copyright © Oxford University Press Canada 2007

The moral rights of the author have been asserted.

Database right Oxford University Press (maker)

First published 2007

Library and Archives Canada Cataloguing in Publication

Main entry under title:
Canadian families today : new perspectives / edited by David Cheal.

Includes bibliographical references and index.

ISBN-13: 978-0-19-542294-8
ISBN-10: 0-19-542294-5

1. Family–Canada. I. Cheal, David J

HQ560.C3586 2007   306.85'0971   C2006-905969-1

Cover Image: John Foxx/Getty Images: Stockbyte
Cover design: Joan Dempsey
Text composition: Valentino Sanna, Ignition Design & Communications

1 2 3 4 – 10 09 08 07

This book is printed on permanent (acid-free) paper ∞.
Printed in Canada

Contents

Contributors

PATRIZIA ALBANESE is Associate Professor of Sociology at Ryerson University and author of *Mothers of the Nation: Women, Families and Nationalism in Twentieth-Century Europe* (2006). She is currently doing research and writing on family policies and practices. These include a research project assessing the impact of Quebec's $7/day child-care program on families living in an economically disadvantaged region in Quebec, and a project (with Margrit Eichler) on household work and lifelong learning. She is co-director of the Centre for Children, Youth and Families at Ryerson University.

RACHEL ARISS teaches law and society and family sociology in the Department of Sociology at Lakehead University. Currently, she is researching and writing on the treatment of common-law spouses in pension and workers' compensation law, socio-legal recognition of parentage involving new reproductive technologies, accessibility and care after the legalization of midwifery, and the legal requirement for respectful treatment of dead bodies.

LORI D. CAMPBELL is Assistant Professor of Sociology and Gerontology at McMaster University. Her primary research interests centre on aging families. She has published research on sibling ties in middle and later life, intergenerational family transfers, and men's experiences in filial caregiving. She is currently lead investigator on a study exploring the experience and meaning of inheritance within families.

MICHAEL P. CARROLL is Professor of Sociology at the University of Western Ontario. Although most of his published research to date has been concerned with the sociology of religion, he has a long-standing interest in feminist theory and the study of gender. An article on the meaning of masculinity among male caregivers, co-authored with Lori Campbell, will shortly be coming out in *Men and Masculinities*.

DAVID CHEAL is Professor of Sociology at the University of Winnipeg. His current areas of specialization are sociological theory and family studies. Professor Cheal is the author of *Sociology of Family Life* (2002) and the editor of the four-volume work, *Family: Critical Concepts in Sociology* (2003), as well as other books and numerous articles and chapters.

PAULA CHEGWIDDEN recently retired from the Department of Sociology at Acadia University, where she was an associate professor for 30 years. Her research interests include sociology of food, family studies, and the women's movement.

ANDREA DOUCET is Associate Professor of Sociology at Carleton University. She has published many articles and book chapters on fathering, masculinities, gender and domestic life, methodologies and epistemologies in Canadian and international journals. She is the author of *Do Men Mother?* (2006) and co-author (with Janet Siltanen) of *Gender Relations: Intersectionality and Beyond* (forthcoming).

MARGRIT EICHLER is Professor of Sociology and Equity Studies at the Ontario Institute for Studies in Education at the University of Toronto. She has published widely in the areas of family policy, sexist, racist, and ableist biases in research, women's studies, and feminist eco-sociology. She is a member of the Royal Society of Canada and a Past President of the Canadian Sociology and Anthropology Association and the Canadian Research Institute for the Advancement of Women.

J.S. FRIDERES has taught at a number of universities, both in Canada and abroad—University of Manitoba, Dalhousie University, McQuarie University, University of Hawaii, and the Arctic College. He has published several books, the best known being *Aboriginal Peoples in Canada* (7th edition, with R. Gadacz, 2005). He is currently the Director of the International Indigenous Studies program at the University of Calgary. He also has worked with community groups as a volunteer and supported their efforts to enhance the quality of life for immigrants and minority ethnic groups in Canada.

DOREEN FUMIA is Assistant Professor of Sociology at Ryerson University in Toronto. Her community work has focused on issues of equity and anti-homophobia in Toronto schools and neighbourhoods. Her current research project, 'Honey I'm Home! Sexual Citizenship, Gentrification, and Queer Homeownership in Cabbagetown', examines how different groups of people—in a particularly diverse neighbourhood in Toronto—make use of race, sexuality, class, and geographic location to stake claims to legal and social citizenship.

DON KERR is an Associate Professor of Sociology at King's University College, affiliated with the University of Western Ontario. He is also a research associate at the Population Studies Centre at Western. He was previously a population analyst in the Demography Division at Statistics Canada, and has worked on several projects for Indian and Northern Affairs Canada and the Royal Commission on Aboriginal Peoples, as well as for Justice Canada.

KAREN M. KOBAYASHI is an Assistant Professor in the Department of Sociology and a Research Affiliate with the Centre on Aging at the University of Victoria. Her research interests include health and aging in visible minority immigrant families, intergenerational relationships over the adult life course, and social isolation in later life. Recent research appears in the *Canadian Journal on Aging, Canadian Ethnic Studies*, and the *Journal of Cross-Cultural Gerontology*.

CATHERINE KRULL is an Associate Professor in the Department of Sociology at Queen's University. Her research interests include reproductive politics, family policy, social movements, and development. Recently, she has been conducting focus group interviews with women living in Havana, Cuba, on generation, participation, strategies of resistance, and community development. She continues to write on the efficacy of Canadian family policies, particularly those adopted in Quebec.

CRAIG MCKIE is a retired Associate Professor of Sociology at Carleton University and formerly Editor-in-Chief of *Canadian Social Trends*, Statistics Canada's social statistical quarterly.

JOSEPH H. MICHALSKI is an Associate Professor in the Department of Sociology, King's University College, University of Western Ontario. His research focuses on family violence, conflict management, crime, poverty, and household coping strategies. During the 1990s, he helped launch the Centre for Applied Social Research and the Centre of Excellence for Research on Immigration and Settlement at the University of Toronto, followed by two years as a Senior Policy Analyst for the Canadian Policy Research Networks.

MICHELLE K. OWEN is an Associate Professor in the Sociology Department at the University of Winnipeg. Her primary research interests are gender, sexuality, family, and disability. In 2003–4 she was selected to serve as Royal Bank Research Chair in Disability Studies at the Canadian Centre on Disability Studies. Current projects include a longitudinal study into intimate partner violence for women with disabilities and an edited anthology on women with chronic illnesses.

GILLIAN RANSON is an Associate Professor in the Department of Sociology at the University of Calgary. Her research interests are in the interwoven fields of gender, families, and work. Currently, she is working on a book about couples who confound gender stereotypes in the ways they share paid work, child care, and other family responsibilities. She is also a co-investigator on an international, multi-disciplinary study of employment relations in information technology workplaces.

AYSAN SEV'ER is Professor of Sociology at the University of Toronto. Her current research focuses on extreme forms of violence against women in India and in southeastern Turkey. She is the founding editor of the journal, *Women's Health & Urban Life*, and the recipient of the Canadian Women's Studies Book Award for 2004 for her *Fleeing the House of Horrors: Women Who Have Left Abusive Partners*. Currently, she is serving as the Special Advisor to the Principal on Equity Issues at the University of Toronto at Scarborough.

Preface

Canadian Families Today is an introduction to the sociology of family life that draws on a wide range of materials, but the focus is specifically on families in Canada. It is a multi-authored textbook that covers a wide range of topics. Seventeen experts in the field were asked to write 15 chapters, and they have responded in fine style.

The book is organized into five parts, reflecting its main themes. Part I contains two introductory chapters: Introduction to Canada's Families: Variations in Definitions and Theories by Patrizia Albanese, and Families in Historical and Cross-Cultural Context by Paula Chegwidden. The first chapter provides an introduction to the sociology of family life that shows the changing and diverse definition of families, presents multiple perspectives on family issues, and provides data on Canadian demographic trends. The second chapter presents a broad overview of historical and cross-cultural diversity in family life, and stresses the changing nature of family.

Part II provides information about various stages and events in the life course. In Chapter 3, Rachel Ariss examines how people form relationships, some of which result in marriage. Gillian Ranson, in Chapter 4, discusses the ideological context of parenting and examines parenting in practice in different types of families. Craig McKie, in Chapter 5, studies how families fragment through separation or divorce, some of them becoming lone-parent families, which often reformulate themselves within the context of a new marital union. After reviewing events that may occur in the life course, the book then turns to a consideration of two life stages: middle age and old age. In Chapter 6, Karen Kobayashi focuses on the relationships and transitions that mark mid-life families (e.g., the 'empty nest', caregiving) and are triggered by the occurrence of life events in

families (e.g., adult children leaving home, care for aging parents). This chapter also examines some of the diversity of mid-life families by describing patterns of separation and divorce, remarriage, same-sex relationships, and childlessness. Aging in Canadian families is discussed by Lori Campbell and Michael Carroll in Chapter 7, in which they look at the specific family issues affecting older people. This chapter describes the marital statuses and life experiences of the elderly, examines intergenerational exchange, and considers the caregiving support that younger family members provide to older family members.

In Part III, the economic aspects of family life are examined. Chapter 8, by Andrea Doucet, concerns paid and unpaid work, both of which she describes as being gendered. In Chapter 9, Don Kerr and Joseph Michalski explore the relevance of family and demographic changes to recent poverty trends, while also considering some of the broader structural shifts in the Canadian economy and in government policies. Kerr and Michalski also discuss the coping strategies that poor families use to survive and examine the evidence on the consequences of poverty for poor people's lives.

The chapters in Part IV look at the experiences of families that live outside the mainstream. Chapter 10, by Doreen Fumia, focuses on the experiences of individuals who differ from the heterosexual norm. In Chapter 11, James Frideres considers the family patterns of Aboriginal Canadians, immigrants, and visible minorities, including the social significance of intermarriage and mixed unions. Michelle Owen, in Chapter 12, seeks to understand the impact that disability has on families and on individuals within families.

Finally, Part V of the book looks at issues that, if not unique to families, are endemic to the contemporary family: violence, shifts in public policy, and questions regarding the future. Chapter 13, by Aysan Sev'er, analyzes how power differences in the family can lead to mental, physical, or sexual abuse. Catherine Krull, in Chapter 14, discusses government policies affecting families in Canada, which she believes have a great impact on family life. In the concluding chapter, Margrit Eichler discusses what predictions of the future of the family have been like in the past and also ventures her own predictions.

Acknowledgement

Statistics Canada information is used with the permission of Statistics Canada. Users are forbidden to copy this material and/or redisseminate the data, in an original or modified form, for commercial purposes, without the expressed permission of Statistics Canada. Information on the availability of the wide range of data from Statistics Canada can be obtained from Statistics Canada's regional offices, its World Wide Web site at http://www.statcan.ca, and its toll-free access number 1-800-263-1136.

Part I   Conceptualizing Family

The first two chapters of this book provide an introduction to the sociology of family life, review the major issues in the study of families, with a special focus on Canada, and present a broad overview of historical and cross-cultural diversity in family life. Multiple perspectives on family issues are presented, and the complexity of family life is stressed. The contributors argue that change always has been, and continues to be, a normal part of family life.

In Chapter 1, Patrizia Albanese discusses the diversity of family forms existing in Canada today, reviews different definitions of the family, and considers how the changing definition of this concept has had policy implications for access to programs and privileges or status within society. Albanese also introduces different theories of family life and discusses the influence that theoretical assumptions have on ways of seeing the world. Recent changes in family life in Canada are also considered. She concludes the chapter by noting that today, as in the past, Canadian families take on a number of diverse forms. The changing definition of family simply reflects a reality that change has been, and continues to be, a normal part of family life.

Paula Chegwidden, in Chapter 2, examines families in historical and cross-cultural context. She notes that one of the major criteria that people have used to organize their relationships is kinship, understood as the cultural meanings attached to networks of genealogical relationships. Differing cultures emphasize different features of kinship, and as a result there are many kinds of kinship groups. Marriage and sexual relations are discussed next, and the point is made that in small societies marriage was important as a means of tying together kinship groups. The economic context of family life is noted, and it is suggested that women and men have a more equal relationship in cultures where each gender has critical economic functions.

In regard to Canadian family history, Chegwidden stresses that industrialization transformed family life in the nineteenth century. Relationships between spouses took on new emphases and children took on a different kind of importance to parents. Chegwidden also discusses twentieth-century changes, including the trends of declining fertility and two-breadwinner families. She concludes that family life is always changing and adapting and will continue to do so.

CHAPTER 1

Introduction to Canada's Families: Variations in Definitions and Theories

Patrizia Albanese

Learning Objectives

- To discover that Canadian families take diverse forms.
- To see that definitions of 'family' have changed and are continuing to change.
- To recognize the implications for defining family in certain ways—restricting who has access to programs, policies, and privileges and who does not.
- To learn about some of the theories that guide our understanding of families.
- To understand that theoretical orientations guide what we study and how we study it.
- To gain an overview of some changing Canadian demographic trends.

Introduction: Changing and Diverse Family Forms

In 2001, in Canada there were 8,371,000 families, up from 7,838,000 in 1996 (Statistics Canada, 2002a). Of these, 41.4 per cent were married couples with children (in single and dual-earner households; and in first, second, or subsequent marriages), 29 per cent were married couples without children; 6.3 per cent were common-law couples with children (in same-sex and hetero-sexual unions), 7.5 per cent were common-law couples without children (in same-sex and hetero-sexual unions), and 15.7 per cent were lone-parent (mostly female-headed) families (see Vanier Institute of the Family, 2006).

Clearly, Canadian families come in a plurality of forms, with no one family portrait capturing this diversity. Instead, to get a comprehensive picture of Canadian families, a composite or collage or whole scrapbook of family photos would have to be used, because like in any individual family, no single photo would accurately capture the changing lives and experiences of all involved. Below are examples of four diverse families that make up a small part of Canada's large and growing family scrapbook/photo album.

CANADIAN FAMILY PORTRAIT 1

My partner and I have been together 11 years. We live in Winnipeg with our daughter, who is five, and our son, four. . . . We have spent a lifetime building relationships and family privately, 'in the space between the laws' to quote poet Alice Bloch. . . . My beloved and I feel extraordinarily blessed to have found one another and to have brought children into our family. In deciding to marry, we have the blessing of our friends, our families and our faith communities. We feel privileged to live in a culture and a country that step by small step has recognized and redressed many of the injustices we have faced in our individual and family lives for no reason other than that we are lesbians. Our wedding day will be both a celebration of this era of extraordinary change and the embodiment of it. (Stevens, 2006, on-line)

After decades of political mobilizing and many legal battles, same-sex families in Canada have gone from being illegal, to being invisible, to being recognized and counted as marriages and families in the 2006 Canadian census (see Chapter 10). While it surely underestimates the actual number of same-sex families in Canada, the 2001 census revealed that a total of 34,200 couples identified themselves as same-sex common-law couples (Statistics Canada, 2002a). The 2001 census also revealed that some 3,000 same-sex couples are raising children, with the majority of these children being born in mother–father unions that ended in divorce (Ambert, 2005). As a result, some same-sex families are then also bi-nuclear, step-, or blended families.

CANADIAN FAMILY PORTRAIT 2

Only a few weeks before Francois Cantin married Louise Theriault last August, Cantin reached an agreement with his first wife that gave him custody of their two young children. Louis-Philippe, 8, and Maude, 6, moved from their mother's place in the country to the Cantin-Theriault household in Quebec City. 'It's been quite an eye-opener', says Theriault, a 30-year-old graphic designer with no children of her own. 'Francois has to work a lot of overtime and I work at home, so I find myself almost like a single mother sometimes.' Theriault took on much of the responsibility for the children. (Webb et al., 1994: 34)

Following divorces and other breakups, we are seeing many second and subsequent unions (in the form of remarriages and common-law unions). This has amounted to an increase in the number of stepfamilies in Canada today. In 2001, Canada had 503,100 stepfamilies, up from 430,500 in 1995 (Statistics Canada, 2002b). Almost 12 per cent of all Canadian couples with children were stepfamilies. Five out of 10 contained only the female spouse's children, one in 10 contained only the male spouse's children and the rest, four out of 10, were blended families, with 81 per cent of these composed of a child born to the couple, in addition to children born from a previous union of one of the two spouses. Nineteen per cent of blended families consisted of children born from previous unions of both spouses (ibid.). Like Louise Theriault, many stepparents face a number of unique challenges and experiences. At the same time, they have much in common with other families today.

CANADIAN FAMILY PORTRAIT 3

My mother was living in Ottawa, and she applied for me to come [to Canada, from Guatemala] with my daughter only, so my two other sons stayed there. Since my mother had already put in the application for me as a single (not married) applicant, she was afraid that they would reject me or that it would take a much longer time, and she thought she would have to pay a fortune to request me with all of the children. So she said to me, 'you come first with the girl, and in less than a year you can bring the boys' [she was separated from her male children for six years]. (Bernhard et al., 2005)

Recent years have seen an increase in interest, research, and information on **transnational, multi-local families** (ibid.; Burholt, 2004; Waters, 2001). Interest in transnational families has been sparked by the growing awareness of some of the challenges faced by immigrant families, refugee claimants, foreign domestic workers from the Caribbean and Philippines, migrant workers, visa students, and individuals and families with 'less-than-full' legal status (for more on immigrant families, see Chapter 11). Thousands of people living in Canada currently find themselves (temporarily) separated from their children and spouses as part of a strategy to secure a better economic future and opportunities for their family. Some have been called **'satellite' families** (satellite children), a term first used in the 1980s to describe Chinese children whose parents were immigrants to North America (usually from Hong Kong or Taiwan) but who have returned to their country of origin after immigration and left children, and sometimes spouses, in Canada (Tsang et al., 2003). Researchers studying transnational families have been documenting the changes and challenges that arise from parent-child separations (for more on parenting, see Chapter 4), long-distance relationships, extended family networks providing child care, and the often emotionally charged reunifications that follow the multi-local family arrangements (Bernhard et al., 2005; Burholt, 2004; Tsang et al., 2003; Waters, 2001).

While some families find themselves living between and across households and borders (multi-local), others, particularly younger Canadians, find themselves increasingly unable to leave their parental homes and establish independent households.

CANADIAN FAMILY PORTRAIT 4

Dave Walsh never expected to be living with his parents, never mind his in-laws, at the age of 25. But after graduating from the University of Alberta in Edmonton with a civil engineering degree last year, he faced the bleakest job market since the 1930s. Unemployed and burdened with hefty student loans, Walsh and his new wife, Carolin Henry—who earns only a modest income as a social worker—moved in with her parents in Hamilton after their marriage last July. 'I was brought up to believe that when you get married, you have your own place', says Walsh. 'But it was simply not possible.'

'We asked them to stay here because we knew that they couldn't manage on their own', says Carolin's mother, Aldith Henry. (Webb et al., 1994: 34)

In 1981, about 28 per cent of Canadians between the ages of 20 and 29 lived with their parents. By 2001, this increased to 41 per cent (Beaujot, 2004). Because of changing economic circumstances and difficulty in finding stable, long-term, decent-paying work (see Chapter 8 on work and families, and Chapter 9 on poverty), coupled with increasing demand for post-secondary education and large debt loads, we have seen the postponement of home-leaving or a delayed **child launch** (see Chapter 6). Linked with this is an increase in the number of 'boomerang children' or 'velcro kids' (Tyyskä, 2001; Mitchell, 1998), or people like Dave Walsh and Carolin Henry, who leave their parental homes for work or school, only to return

due to large debt loads, shifting employment prospects, or changing marital status (unions and breakups—see Chapter 5).

While Dave Walsh may never have expected to live with his in-laws at the age of 25, for many new immigrants to Canada, older Canadians (see Chapter 7), or Canadians with disabilities (see Chapter 12), the extended family model and the pooling of family resources in multi-generational households is nothing new, unexpected, or alarming (Che-Alford and Hamm, 1999). In fact, many of Canada's 'new' family forms have always existed, only some have done so in the margins, in the shadows, or during specific historical and economic contexts. For example, lone-parent families and stepfamilies/remarriages are not new on the Canadian landscape. Nor are same-sex families or transnational families, for that matter.

My great-grandfather was a sojourner or migrant worker to Canada in the early part of the twentieth century, working on Canada's western railroads. Like many migrant and temporary workers to Canada, he was separated from his wife and child for years, with the goal of improving his family's economic prospects (also see Knowles, 1992). Despite differences, this was not unlike some of the experiences of the many Latina, Filipina, and Caribbean immigrants and their families today.

Not long before my great-grandfather's temporary arrival in Canada, high mortality rates, particularly among women during childbirth, resulted in a large number of lone-parent families. Subsequent remarriages and the formation of stepfamilies, where most family members worked, were a necessity for basic survival, particularly in pre-industrial, agriculturally based communities across Canada (Bradbury, 1993; Janovicek and Parr, 2003). In sum, while diversity seems to best characterize Canadian families today, diversity, adaptability, and change have been a fact of life for Canadian families in the past as well (for more on Canadian family history, see Chapter 2). What seems to have changed dramatically are the number of variants within each type and the types we have come to accept or legally define as family. Closely linked with these changes is how researchers have theorized and studied families.

Contemporary Canadian Family Studies

Today, studying Canadian families requires students and researchers to stay on top of legal, political, social, and economic changes, and all this at the community, sub-national/provincial, national, and international levels (see Chapter 14). Studying Canadian families often includes understanding and studying aspects of the Canadian economy, policy shifts, changes to health care and longevity, the Internet (see Chapter 3), poverty, immigration, environmental issues (see Chapter 15), globalization, war/genocide/ethnic conflict, violence (see Chapter 13), taxation, legal changes, human rights issues, etc. And much of this has been sparked by what some have called the 'big bang' (Cheal, 1991) in family theorizing. Before exploring the 'big bang' let us first turn to what we mean by 'family' and how the changing definition of this concept has had profound implications on access to programs, policies, and privilege in this country.

CHANGING DEFINITIONS OF FAMILY

The definition of 'family' continues to go through many changes (see Box 1.1), so that today one will have a difficult time identifying one conventional definition of family accepted within and across academic research and disciplines and formal or informal organizations. In fact, the adjectives used with the term 'family' find more consensus on their definitions. For example, most agree on the definition of a nuclear family, which typically includes a couple and their children, sharing the same household, but may also define one parent and his/her child(ren) (Ambert, 2006). Today, with divorce and remarriages, we are also seeing an increase in the number of **bi-nuclear families**—where children of divorced parents move and live across households. For children, the family they 'belong to' or originate in is called their 'family of origin' or 'orientation' (Ambert, 2006). There is also the **extended family**, in which several generations (grandparents, aunts, uncles, cousins) share a household. This has also come to be called a 'multi-generational household'. Terms like **household**, a set of related and unrelated individuals who share a dwelling, are also relatively easily defined (also see Chapter 2).

Box 1.1 Evolving Definitions of 'Family'—Is Everyone Accounted For?

Do any of the following definitions exclude your own family? Who else is excluded from the following definitions? Can you spot any other changes to the definition?

Murdock (1949): . . . a social group characterized by common residence, economic co-operation and reproduction. It includes adults of both sexes, at least two of whom maintain a socially approved sexual relationship, and one or more children, own or adopted, of the sexually cohabiting adults.

Stephens (1963): . . . a social arrangement based on marriage and the marriage contract, including recognition of the rights and duties of parents, common residence for husband, wife, and children and reciprocal economic obligations between husband and wife.

Box 1.1 Evolving Definitions of 'Family' — Is Everyone Accounted For? (cont.)

Coser (1974): . . . a group manifesting the following organizational attributes: it finds its origin in marriage; it consists of husband, wife, and children born in their wedlock, though other relatives may find their place close to this nuclear group, and the group is united by moral, legal, economic, religious, and social rights and obligations.

Eichler (1983): A family is a social group which may or may not include adults of both sexes (e.g., lone-parent families), may or may not include one or more children (e.g., childless couples), who may or may not have been born in their wedlock (e.g., adopted children, or children by one adult partner of a previous union). The relationship of the adults may or may not have its origin in marriage (e.g., common-law couples), they may or may not share a common residence (e.g., commuting couples). The adults may or may not cohabit sexually, and the relationship may or may not involve such socially patterned feelings as love, attraction, and awe.

Goode (1995): Doubtless the following list is not comprehensive, but it [family] includes most of those relationships: (1) At least two adult persons of opposite sex reside together. (2) They engage in some kind of division of labor; that is, they do not both perform exactly the same tasks. (3) They engage in many types of economic and social exchanges; that is, they do things for one another. (4) They share many things in common, such as food, sex, residence, and both goods and social activities. (5) The adults have parental relations with their children, as their children have filial relations with them; the parents have some authority over children, and share with one another, while also assuming some obligations for protection, co-operation, and nurturance. (6) There are sibling relations among the children themselves, with, once more, a range of obligations to share, protect, and help one another.

Mandell and Duffy (2000): . . . a social ideal, generally referring to a unit of economic co-operation, typically thought to include only those related by blood, but revised by feminists to include those forming an economically co-operative, residential unit bound by feelings of common ties and strong emotions.

The difficulty comes in the definition of 'family' itself. This difficulty partly stems from the fact that there are legal/formal definitions (census family), social definitions (for different organizations and social groups, see Box 1.2), and personal definitions (created by individuals and families themselves) of families that are created for different purposes and in different contexts. We are perhaps most familiar with personal definitions, which in themselves are widely diverse. Because of the very personal nature of families, many of us have come up with our own definitions of who is and is not family. For example, when my stepson was eight, he had a difficult time explaining to others his relation to one of my two brothers. Cleverly, my stepson described my brother to others as 'step-uncle John'. The terms aunt/auntie and uncle are commonly used across cultures to selectively include some close friends or frequent visitors to one's home as kin. They are commonly referred to as **fictive kin**.

Box 1.2 Department of National Defence/Canadian Forces Definition of Family

Question: Why is the definition of a family member restricted to 'a relative of a member of the CF, by blood, marriage or adoption, who normally is resident with that member and who is not a member of the CF'? (CFAO 56–39)

By this definition, I am not entitled to deployment support from the Military Family Resource Centre because although I am a spouse, I am also a member of the military. It also means that single members' parents, and children of non-custodial parents, are not entitled to MFRC support (i.e., warm calls, access to postage, etc.).

I believe the definition of family needs to be revised.

Answer: You will find, depending on the DND/CF organization involved, that definitions of what constitutes 'family' vary. The definition is often about eligibility for benefits and services as much as anything else. Currently, Director Quality of Life is formulating a definition of 'family' for the CF, but that definition is not yet finalized.

We can, however, offer a definition of 'family' as it applies to the services provided under the Military Family Services Program (MFSP) and available through your MFRC.

With respect to your specific question, you are most definitely entitled to services from your MFRC. For the purposes of the MFSP on a national basis, the Assistant Deputy Minister (Human Resources— Military), through Director Military Family Services, provides funding to MFRCs to support the delivery of services to:

- married or common-law full-time serving CF members and their spouses (with 'spouse' broadly interpreted—CF policy recognizes common-law and same-sex partners);
- children (17 and younger) of full-time serving CF members (the residence or custodial situation of the children is not a consideration, providing the children are within the proximity of an MFRC);
- full-time serving CF members who are single parents with children (17 and younger); and
- Class 'A' Reservist families, before, during and after deployment.

Populations served by the MFRCs as listed above are consistent with CFAO 56–40.

- At this time, funding is not provided to MFRCs for the support of parents of single Regular Force members (although, depending on the MFRC, the service is provided regardless). There is limited funding.

For more information or clarification: visit Director Military Family Services at www.cfpsa.com/en/psp/dmfs/ or e-mail Thompson.CA@forces.gc.ca; and/or visit Quality of Life at www.forces.gc.ca/hr/qol/ or e-mail Armstrong.HJ@forces.gc.ca.

SOURCE: Department of National Defence website, at: <www.forces.gc.ca/hr/cfpn/engraph/6_04/6_04_qa-definition-cf-family_e.asp>.

The legal definition of family has been changing rapidly following court challenges and legislative changes over the past decade or so. The transformation of the definition of family can be traced through the changing description of the **census family** (see Box 1.3). Since 1871, Canadians have been legally obliged to complete a census (for example, in 1996, 2001, and 2006), a detailed survey of Canadian households. In it, Canadian residents are asked, among other things, about their family composition, dwelling, household finances, their paid work, and, since 1996, their unpaid work.

How we define family has profound implications for who is actually counted as a family. Census data, for example, actually reflect and are constrained by which families are measured and how. As a result, we only know about the types of families we have defined, asked about, and counted. In other words, if we do not include or ask about same-sex couples, census data (and/or other quantitative studies) mask their actual existence. With each census, and especially since 1996, we have seen changes in those who have been legally entitled to call themselves families. That is, before the 2001 census, same-sex families were completely excluded from the definition. In many cases, while same-sex partners may have lived together, they were not counted as families. Instead, a lesbian couple with children would often be counted as a female-headed, lone-parent family (the biological mother and her children, excluding her female partner). The 2001 census was the first in Canada to allow same-sex couples to self-identify as common-law couples. The 2006

Box 1.3 Definition of Census Family, 1996, 2001, 2006

1996: Refers to a now-married couple (with or without never-married sons and/or daughters of either or both spouses), a couple living common-law (with or without never-married sons and/or daughters of either or both partners) or a lone parent of any marital status, with at least one never-married son or daughter living in the same dwelling.

2001: Refers to a married couple (with or without children of either or both spouses), a couple living common-law (with or without children of either or both partners), or a lone parent of any marital status with at least one child living in the same dwelling. A couple living common-law may be of opposite or same sex. 'Children' in a census family include grandchildren living with their grandparent(s) but with no parents present.

2006: Refers to a married couple and the children, if any, of either or both spouses; a couple living common law and the children, if any, of either or both partners; or, a lone parent of any marital status with at least one child living in the same dwelling and that child or those children. All members of a particular census family live in the same dwelling. A couple may be of opposite or same sex. Children may be children by birth, marriage, or adoption regardless of their age or marital status as long as they live in the dwelling and do not have their own spouse or child living in the dwelling. Grandchildren living with their grandparent(s) but with no parents present also constitute a census family.

SOURCES: Statistics Canada, at: <www.statcan.ca>, Census Dictionary 1996, Census Dictionary 2001, and for 2006, personal e-mail correspondence (12 June 2006) with Shirley Li, Statistics Canada.

census allowed same-sex partners to self-identify as married couples.

Eichler (2005: 53), writing on the definition of family, noted that 'who is included in the definition of family is an issue of great importance as well as great consequence', because who we include in our definition will determine who is eligible to claim tax benefits, sponsor family members in immigration (see Box 1.4), claim insurance benefits, claim Indian status, etc. Eichler challenges us to move beyond 'who' definitions of family, which focus on group membership and family structure (a mom and a dad

---

Box 1.3 Definition of Census Family, 1996, 2001, 2006 (cont.)

2006 Census—'About Question 6'

The 2006 Census is the first Canadian census where same-sex married couples can indicate their relationship. The census thus continues to keep in step with societal and legal realities. Results of the 2006 Census will be used to provide Canadian citizens and institutions with accurate data needed for decision-making.

Statistics Canada 's goal is to provide the most accurate count possible of opposite-sex and same-sex married couples. Testing by Statistics Canada prior to the 2006 Census determined that the most accurate information on same-sex married couples is obtained when they directly report their relationship by using the write-in space provided. While same-sex married couples can also indicate their relationship by checking the 'husband or wife' box, testing to date has shown the results have data quality problems. In this case, the gender variable must be used to distinguish between opposite-sex and same-sex married couples. Because the number of same-sex married couples is relatively small compared to all married couples, a very small level of misreporting of gender leads to an overestimation many times over of the number of same-sex married couples.

This variable like all other census variables will be subject to a rigorous data quality assessment. The release of information on married couples will include a quality assessment of the data for same-sex married couples obtained from the write-in space and the 'husband or wife' box.

Statistics Canada also tested a number of options including using the expression 'same-sex spouse' or 'opposite-sex spouse'. The expression 'spouse' was confusing for many respondents. Statistics Canada also found that 'husband or wife' was not used by all gay and lesbian married couples to describe their relationship. It is, therefore, because of its desire to produce the most accurate statistics possible that Statistics Canada encourages same-sex married couples to report their relationship by using the write-in space provided.

As we prepare for the 2011 Census, consultation will be held with the Gay and Lesbian community on this matter as well as further testing with same-sex married couples to review wording and options for this question.

SOURCE: Statistics Canada, 2006, at: <www22.statcan.ca/ccr_r016_e.htm>.

and their children, for example) towards a 'what definition of family', which focuses on the services and supports provided by various members. One such definition is provided by the Vanier Institute of the Family (2006), which defines family as:

> any combination of two or more persons who are bound together over time by ties of mutual consent, birth, and/or adoption or placement and who, together, assume responsibilities for variant combinations of the following:
>
> - physical maintenance and care of group members
> - addition of new members through procreation or adoption
> - socialization of children
> - social control of members
> - production, consumption, distribution of goods and services, and
> - affective nurturance—love.

In accepting a 'what' definition of family, we would then recognize, reward, and legitimize families for what they do together and for each other, rather than recognize and privilege only those who take the 'proper' form, regardless of what happens behind closed doors.

Box 1.4 Citizenship and Immigration Family Class Sponsorship Guide

You can use this application package to sponsor your spouse, common-law partner or conjugal partner, and your dependent children, who live outside Canada and meet the requirements defined for members of the family class.

Spouses, common-law partners and conjugal partners

You can sponsor a person as your spouse if that person is married to you and the marriage is a legally valid civil marriage. If your spouse is of the

- opposite sex and your marriage took place outside Canada, the marriage must be valid both under the laws of the jurisdiction where it took place and under Canadian law;
- same sex, your marriage must have taken place in Canada and be recognized by the authorities of the province where it took place. Note: A marriage between two persons of the same sex will be recognized for immigration purposes only if one of these persons is a citizen or a permanent resident of Canada and the marriage was performed in a Canadian province in which marriages between same-sex persons are legally recognized. For additional information on same-sex marriages, consult our web site.

You can sponsor a person as your **common-law partner** if

- that person is of the opposite or same sex,
- you and that other person have cohabited in a conjugal relationship for a period of at least one year, and
- your relationship with that person is continuing, even though you are temporarily living apart.

Box 1.4 Citizenship and Immigration Family Class Sponsorship Guide (cont.)

You can sponsor a person as a **conjugal partner** (1) if

- that person is of the opposite or same sex,
- that person is residing outside Canada (that is, has, for legal purposes, a fixed, permanent and principal home outside Canada), and
- you have maintained a conjugal relationship with that person for at least one year, that is, you have been in a committed and mutually interdependent relationship of some permanence where you have combined your affairs to the extent possible.

(1) This last category is intended for partners of Canadian sponsors who would ordinarily apply as

- common-law partners but cannot meet the definition, that is, were not able to live together continuously for one year with their sponsor, or
- spouses, but marriage to their sponsor is usually not an available option to them, usually because of marital status or sexual orientation, combined with an immigration barrier (for example, rules preventing partner and sponsor of long stays in one another's countries).

If your sponsorship is successful, your conjugal partner becomes a permanent resident of Canada but cannot exercise any rights or privileges associated with common-law status until you have cohabited for at least one year.

Note: There is no provision for fiancé(e)s in Canada's immigration legislation. If you are the fiancé(e) of a Canadian citizen or permanent resident, you must marry before the immigration process takes place. Conjugal partners are not fiancé(e)s and are not fiancé-like (that is, intending to live together and begin a conjugal relationship).

Excluded relationships

You cannot sponsor a person as your spouse, common-law partner or conjugal partner if

- that person is under 16 years of age;
- you are a permanent resident or a naturalized citizen of Canada and at the time you made your application for permanent residence, that person was a non-accompanying family member, former spouse or common-law partner and was not examined; or
- you previously sponsored another spouse, a common-law partner or a conjugal partner and three years have not passed since that spouse, common-law partner or conjugal partner became a permanent resident.

Further, you cannot sponsor a person as your spouse

- if you or this person were the spouse of another person at the time of your marriage, or
- if you have lived separate and apart from this person for at least one year and

Box 1.4 Citizenship and Immigration Family Class Sponsorship Guide (cont.)

A. you are the common-law or conjugal partner of another person, or

B. the person you want to sponsor is the common-law partner of another person or the conjugal partner of another sponsor.

Dependent children

Your child or a child of the person you are sponsoring will be considered a dependent child if that child

A. is under the age of 22 and not married or in a common-law relationship; or

B. married or entered into a common-law relationship before the age 22 and, since becoming a spouse or a common-law partner, has

- been continuously enrolled and in attendance as a full-time student in a post–secondary institution accredited by the relevant government authority and

- depended substantially on the financial support of a parent; or is 22 years of age or older and, since before the age of 22, has

- been continuously enrolled and in attendance as a full-time student in a post-secondary institution accredited by the relevant government authority and

- depended substantially on the financial support of a parent; or

C. is 22 years of age or older, has depended substantially on the financial support of a parent since before the age of 22 and is unable to provide for him/herself due to a medical condition.

Adopted children

A permanent resident visa cannot be issued to a child as a member of the family class if that child is the adopted dependent child of the sponsor unless the sponsor demonstrates he or she has obtained information concerning the medical condition of the child. This is one of the measures the government has taken to ensure that the child's best interests are protected.

If your sponsorship application includes a child described above, complete and sign the *Medical Condition Statement* and include it with the other documentation supporting your application.

If the adoption process of your adopted dependent child was completed while you were living in Canada as a citizen or permanent resident of that country or will be completed in Canada, do not use this kit.

SOURCE: Citizenship and Immigration Canada (2006a: 5–6).

Theoretical and Methodological Approaches to Studying Families

Theories are not fixed or complete or 'once and for all' explanations of how things work or are expected to work. They neither emerge as 'complete theories, nor remain "the same"' because theory and research are intertwined (Ingoldsby et al., 2004: 2). As our understanding or theory changes, so do our research questions. Likewise, as we do research and come up with new observations that run counter to existing theories, our theories change. Even the seemingly unchanging or indisputable theories in the natural sciences are constructed in cultural contexts and so are influenced by social change (for example, there was Galileo's challenge to the widely accepted idea that the earth was flat, and the Catholic Church's profound disapproval of his work, resulting in his arrest). Paradigm shifts, or radical shifts in scientific views, occur after significant data have been collected that do not fit the existing theory so that a new theory is needed to fit the data. This is clearly the case in theorizing on/about families, as family theories have undergone a number of significant shifts and modifications, resulting from challenges and social change.

Theories provide us with a lens through which we look at the social world. With a shift in theory, we take on a different lens through which we try to understand the social world in general and families in particular. Theories then suggest *what* we look at and *how*, because each theory contains underlying assumptions about how the social world works—which in turn guide our research questions and methods. For example, some assume human behaviour is biologically based, and so things like the gender division of labour are not only justified and necessary, but natural, inevitable, and unchanging or unalterable. Others assume our behaviour is learned and so can be unlearned, relearned, or learned differently as products of the culture in which we live, and therefore patterns of behaviour can be constructed to support specific groups and interests, at the expense of others. For the first group of theorists, certain kinds of social change are viewed as problematic or dysfunctional, and so they seek to preserve particular existing structures and relations—to prevent certain kinds of change. Others, like those in the second group, recognize power struggles and inequities in existing structures and relations, and so seek change.

Although some approaches seemingly lend themselves to certain methods, as we will see below,

it is important to note that sociologists a[nd] family researchers *within* each theoretical tra[dition] can and do use multiple types of methods ([both] qualitative and quantitative, at times), and theorie[s] and methods do not always 'line up' exactly.

Researchers may use seemingly similar methods but with different theoretical approaches, and so come to very different results. For example, anthropologists have been studying families in cross-cultural contexts (and comparative **case studies**) for a relatively long time. Within the discipline there has also been considerable variation in theorizing. For example, George Murdock (1949), who surveyed 250 human societies, concluded that the nuclear family was universal and served four basic social functions: sexual, economic, reproductive, and educational. According to Murdock, a man and woman constitute an efficient co-operating unit, whereby a man's 'superior physical strength' (and ability to 'range further afield' to hunt and trade) complements a woman's 'lighter tasks' performed in or near the home. He noted that all known societies work this way because of innate and inevitable biological facts and differences (Murdock, 1949: 7).

In contrast, Margaret Mead's comparative ethnographic research (which is **qualitative** and descriptive in nature) in the South Pacific, at approximately the same time, identified considerable variation across cultures. She stressed that the division of labour in every known society rests firmly on learned behaviour and not simply on biological differences. For example, she noted that if and when men went away to work in large cities, women were left behind to do the farm labour (which, by Murdock's biological explanation, would be considered heavy male labour requiring 'superior male strength'). She did not dismiss or even minimize biology, but instead argued that 'human beings have learned, laboriously, to be human' (Mead, 1949: 198).

Clearly, two seemingly similar cross-cultural studies of societies from around the world have come to different conclusions about family life because of differing theoretical orientations. Let us explore some of these differences.

al functionalist theories are ... a of organic ontology, which ... ciety is like a living organism or ... p of a series of interrelated parts, ... ether for the good of the whole. Each ... institution or subsystem, like parts of the organism/body, serves specific functions, keeping society in a state of equilibrium. Individuals within the institutions, like cells in a body, fill specific and prescribed roles, again, for the proper functioning of the institution and society. From a functionalist point of view, families are institutions that serve specific functions in society, and family members are expected to fill prescribed roles within the institution for the good of society as a whole. Social change, or a challenge to the existing order, is then undesirable, at best. Murdock's work exemplifies this approach. He believed we can best understand 'the family' by examining what it does and how it functions for and within society. Talcott Parsons (1955) also studied the functions of family by looking at the roles men and women fill within them. According to Parsons, men were biologically better suited to fulfill instrumental functions, that is, tasks that needed to be performed to ensure a family's physical survival—providing for the material needs of the family by earning an income, for example (Parsons and Bales, 1955). Women were believed to be better suited to performing expressive functions—the tasks involved in building emotionally supportive relationships among family members—that are needed for their psychological well-being (the nurturing role).

Those researchers who begin with a functionalist theoretical orientation are likely to look for cultural universals and aspects of dominant family forms and ask 'what purpose do they serve?' They are also likely to look negatively upon rapid social change that could challenge or disrupt the existing social order.

MARXISM

The functionalist approach to the study of families was particularly popular in North America throughout the 1940s and 1950s. However, competing views also existed and some researchers studying families turned to the work of Friedrich Engels, who provided a very different explanation and approach to the study of families in *Origin of the Family, Private Property and the State* (1972 [1884]). Engels, like Marx, argued that a number of distinct phases in human history shape, alter, and constrain human relations. He explained that the mode of production, or the way we organize economic life—whether the hunting and gathering (foraging) in primitive communism, land-based (agrarian) feudalism, or modern industry and profit-driven capitalism—affects the way we organize social life and experience family relations. He noted in the shift away from primitive communism (characterized by a foraging/nomadic existence) the absence of the notion of private ownership and relative equality between the sexes. Then, with land-based feudalism came a reorganization and privatization of family life and a change in power relations between the sexes. With the advent of the notion of private ownership and male control of land and other property, women lost power and control both within and outside of families. Ideally, for Marxists, the social goal is to abolish private property, re-establish communism, and return to more equitable relations between the sexes. Thus, unlike functionalists, for Marxists, gender differences in power and status, and the domination of men over women, within and outside families, is neither natural nor inevitable, but rather a product of the (re)organization of economic life. This approach, again unlike functionalism, implies that social change is a normal, and at times desirable, part of social life. For family researchers who embrace a Marxist approach, a likely goal would be to identify power relations within the home and connect them to inequities in economic relations outside it.

SYMBOLIC INTERACTIONISM

While Marxists looked outside of families to economic forms and relations to understand what was happening within them, others have looked instead within families at social relations and interactions.

That is, while Marxists saw economic forces acting on individuals and families, others, like George Herbert Mead, assumed that individuals were active agents or 'doers' of social life. In other words, if you want to understand social life in general and family life in particular, you should examine how individuals construct meaning through their daily interactions with others. For example, according to Mead, understanding family involves understanding parent–child relations and 'the relationship between the sexes' (Mead, 1967 [1934]: 238). Exchanges or interactions between them lead to the organization of the family and society. That is, he explained that 'all such larger units or forms of human social organization as the clan or the state are ultimately based upon, and (whether directly or indirectly) are developments from or extensions of, the family' (ibid., 229). Therefore, in contrast to Marxism, this approach implies that the individuals and interactions within families shape the organization of family life, which in turn helps shape larger organizations like the state. Thus, if one were to do research using this theoretical approach, it is very likely that one would conduct in-depth, qualitative interviews with family members and/or observe individuals and interactions within families as they happen.

Family Systems Theory

Influenced by symbolic interactionism, family systems theory assumes that a family is a relatively closed system of social interactions, or a site of interacting personalities. According to this theory, which happens to be especially popular among family therapists and social workers, an individual's problems and behaviour are best understood in the context of families, because it is believed that the locus of pathology is not within the person but in a system dysfunction. In other words, the family is more than a collection of individuals or interactions, it is a natural social system, 'with its own rules, roles, communication patterns, and power structure' (Ingoldsby et al., 2004: 168).

Urie Bronfenbrenner's ecological theory of human development uses a systems approach to understanding family life by looking at how the home environment (or microsystem) affects child development. Bronfenbrenner's ecological model, however, explains child development as a multi-level interactive process, requiring multi-level analysis of a number of interconnected systems. His bioecological paradigm stresses the importance of reciprocal interactions between individuals and their micro- (family environment), meso- (e.g., school), exo- (institutions beyond a child's immediate environment, like a parent's workplace), and macro systems (customs, values, and laws of the culture in which we live) on developmental and socio-emotional outcomes (Bronfenbrenner, 1977). Bronfenbrenner argued that a child's immediate family environment (one system) and larger social environment (other systems and institutions) shape development. All of these interacting systems, taken together, provided an understanding of child development.

Doing research from this theoretical perspective would require the researcher to study interactions at multiple levels, modelled like a series of circles, one inside the other. One may first study a child's interactions within the home (the first and smallest circle), then the child's interactions at school (the next and slightly larger circle), then the child's neighbourhood (the next and larger circle), etc. One would try to understand how the child is affected by and affects relations within each environment or circle.

Developmental Theories

In the 1940s, some family researchers noted that, like individuals, families were influenced by developmental processes, or experienced life cycles, with clearly delineated stages (Ingoldsby et al., 2004). In a report created for the 'First National Conference on the Family' (called together by US President Truman), Duvall and Hill (1948) outlined a relatively new and interdisciplinary approach to the study of families. Evelyn Millis Duvall, a specialist in human development, teamed up with Reuben Hill, a family sociologist, to create the family development theory. Using the work of Freud, on psychosexual development, Erikson on psychosocial development, Piaget on cognitive development, and Kohlberg on moral development, along with demographic and **longitudinal** research on families, Duvall and Hill argued that families go through a series of eight sequential or developmental stages in the family life cycle (Duvall, 1988). At each life stage(marriage, child-bearing, preschool, school, teen, launching centre, middle-aged, and aging), family members, depending on their physical maturation, are challenged by different developmental tasks (like roles) and normative events, which can, at times, result in stress, crises, and critical transitions.

Duvall noted that 'although the timing and duration of family life cycle stages vary widely, families everywhere try to conform to norms present in all societies in what is expected at each life cycle's stage' (ibid., 130). She explained that the family development theory was unique among theoretical frameworks because:

(a) its family life cycle dimension provides the basis for study of families over time;

(b) its emphasis on the developmental tasks of individual family members and of families at every stage of their development;

(c) its built-in recognition of family stress at critical periods in development; and

(d) its recognition ever since 1947 of the need for services, supports, and programs for families throughout their life cycles. (Ibid., 133)

More recent research using a life-course approach has attempted to capture life-course complexity and gender-specific experiences and trajectories, which were somewhat lacking in the original approach (see Krüger and Levy, 2001).

BIASES IN TRADITIONAL APPROACHES/ THEORIZING

Within many of the family theories popular throughout the first half of the twentieth century, the family was conceptualized as an important but relatively isolated unit 'whose internal structures resulted mainly from negotiated action of adult members' (Krüger and Levy, 2001: 149). Most of these theories tended to treat all or most families as homogeneous, and questions about gender differences affecting experiences within families, and inequality, generally remained unasked and unanswered. Writing about this, Eichler (1997) noted that, in fact, a great deal of theorizing about families in the past contained a number of hidden assumptions and biases. She identified seven biases in past family literature and theorizing: monolithic, conservative, sexist, ageist, microstructural, racist, and heterosexist. She noted that a number of theories tended to treat family as a monolithic structure by emphasizing uniformity of experience and universality of functions (*monolithic bias*). In other words, theories tended to under-represent the diversity of family forms that actually existed in any given society. She identified a *conservative bias*, where theorists tended to provide only a romanticized view of the nuclear family and regarded recent changes as ephemeral. A *sexist bias* was manifested in a number of ways, including the assumption that there is a 'natural' division of functions between the sexes. Theorists also almost exclusively talked about families as involving exchanges between two middle-aged adults, largely excluding children and the elderly in their analysis, producing an *ageist bias*. She identified a *microstructural bias*, a tendency to treat families as encapsulated units, typically ignoring extraneous/external factors. Theories also often devalued or outright ignored families of culturally or ethnically non-dominant groups (*racist bias*) and treated the heterosexual family as 'natural', denying family status to lesbian and gay families (*heterosexist bias*). A large number of these biases have since been addressed by feminist theorizing on families.

THE 'BIG BANG'—FEMINIST THEORIES

Feminism is not a new paradigm, and in fact has existed for as long as, if not longer than, sociology itself (for example, Mary Wollstonecraft,

1759–97). But what is new is the force with which feminism was able to challenge existing family theories in the period following the 1960s—a period that David Cheal (1991) called 'the big bang'. Since then, feminist scholarship and feminist questions have charted a different course for theorizing families. Feminism 'is not only an academic school of thought, it is also a broad movement for change' (Cheal, 1991: 9). Feminism took what, for a long time, have been considered intimate or 'private' matters (sexuality, violence, child-rearing and care, domestic division of labour, etc.) and made them public, social, and political issues—not only worthy of study, but in need of change.

Feminist theorizing on families generally challenges the apparently gender-neutral assumptions about family life and roles—often found in other family theories—that mask or ignore inequalities and result in negative outcomes for women. Feminists typically seek to determine who does what, for whom, and with what consequences, often assessing the differential distribution of activities, resources, and power (see Saul, 2003). Second, feminists believe that gender relations in the home and in other institutions are neither natural nor immutable, but rather historical and socio-cultural products, subject to reconstruction (Elliot and Mandel, 1998). Typically, feminists subject marriage and family to a series of profound and critical questions, challenge myths about women's abilities, and advocate for change.

Having said this, there is considerable variation within feminism, as feminists themselves depart from, or have developed in response to, different intellectual traditions, for example, Marxism, symbolic interactionism, phenomenology, and psychoanalysis. These traditional approaches were 'sooner or later all reflected in feminist analysis of family life, and they were in turn transformed by it' (Cheal, 1991: 2). As a result, within feminism there are liberal feminists, Marxist feminists, radical feminists, socialist feminists, psychoanalytic feminists, post-structural feminists, post-colonial feminists, anti-racist feminists, etc. Each focuses

on a somewhat different aspect of inequality, often identifying a different source of the problem, and therefore proposing different solutions. The authors of the chapters that follow reflect some of this diversity.

Queer theory has provided some additional stimulus in rethinking family theories, because most feminist approaches have failed to provide an adequate analysis of lesbian and gay family experiences. For example, while feminists have done important work on family violence and on the subordination of women of different races, classes, and other diverse backgrounds, most have failed to note that for lesbian families, 'it is not their powerlessness *within* the family that marks their subordination, but rather their denial of access *to* a legitimate and socially instituted sphere of family, marriage, and parenting' (Calhoun, 2000: 139). This more critical theorizing and activism has resulted in legal and attitudinal changes; on the other hand, much remains to be done.

Changing Canadian Demographic Trends

Quantitative research indicates that due to changing economic trends and social attitudes, an increasing number of Canadians postpone marriage or choose not to marry. The number of marriages in Canada in 2002 was the lowest in several decades, and part of a steady downward trend since the 1990s (Statistics Canada, 2003a). The average age of first marriage has risen from 22.1 for women and 24.4 for men in 1971, to 28.0 for women and 30.0 for men in 1997 (Statistics Canada, 2000). Quebec has continued to have a crude marriage rate significantly lower than that of other provinces, but it is also the province with the highest rates of cohabitation/common-law unions (Statistics Canada, 2003a). The Canadian census has been asking about common-law status since 1991. By the 2001 census, it was discovered that almost 2.3 million Canadian women and men were in a common-law relationship (Statistics Canada, 2003b).

Table 1.1 Average Age of Mothers and Total Fertility Rate,[1] 2003

	Average Age[2] in Years		Total Fertility Rate[3]
	All Mothers	First-time Mothers	Per Woman Aged 15–49
Canada[4]	29.6	28.0	1.5
Newfoundland and Labrador	28.6	26.9	1.3
Prince Edward Island	28.6	26.6	1.6
Nova Scotia	29.1	27.4	1.4
New Brunswick	28.3	26.6	1.4
Quebec	29.2	27.7	1.5
Ontario	30.3	28.7	1.5
Manitoba	28.2	26.3	1.8
Saskatchewan	27.6	25.3	1.9
Alberta	29.0	27.3	1.7
British Columbia	30.2	28.8	1.4
Yukon	28.7	26.7	1.5
Northwest Territories	28.1	26.2	2.0
Nunavut	25.3	21.7	3.1

1. Excludes births to non-residents of Canada, with unknown age of mother, and stillbirths.
2. To estimate mid-year average age, 0.5 has been added to the mother's age at her last birthday preceding the birth of her child.
3. Total fertility rate is an estimate of the average number of children women aged 15–49 will have in their lifetime.
4. Canada total includes births with unknown province or territory of residence of mother.

SOURCE: Statistics Canada, 2005, at: <www.statcan.ca/Daily/English/050712/d050712a.htm>.

Many Canadians are also postponing child-bearing or choosing not to have children. We have seen an increase in the average age of first-time mothers, which has contributed to declining fertility rates across the country. Only two decades ago, the average age of women giving birth was 26.9. By 2003, the average age was 29.6, with the average among women giving birth for the first time being 28.0 (Statistics Canada, 2005). As a result, the total fertility rate, which estimates the average number of children women aged 15 to 49 will have in their lifetime, is about 1.5 children per woman (ibid.; see Table 1.1). This has remained fairly stable since about 1997 (Statistics Canada, 2003a). Interestingly, contrary to popular belief, divorce rates have remained relatively stable, an average of approximately 23 divorces per 1,000 marriages since 1997 (ibid.).

With the postponement of marriage, increased longevity, and changes in the state provision of social services, we have also seen the rise of the 'sandwich generation', people caught between the demands of raising children and caring for aging parents. Almost three in 10 Canadians between the ages of 45 and 64 with children under 25 in their home were also caring for a senior (Statistics Canada, 2004a). The majority of those doing this care work are women, many of whom also work for pay.

Today, the proportion of dual-earner families is on the rise (Morissette and Picot, 2005). This, too, has contributed to declining birth rates, but, at the same time, an increased need for non-parental child care for young children (Bushnik, 2006). That is, in 2003, 54 per cent of children aged six months to five years were in some form of child care, up from 42 per cent in 1995, with most of these in three forms of care—about 30 per cent in daycare centres, 30 per cent in care outside the home by a non-relative, and 30 per cent in care by a relative either inside or outside the home (ibid.). In sum, Canadians are having fewer children, but a large proportion of them need to be cared for by someone other than a parent/parents, which in turn affects household relations and finances.

To offset the decline in population from lower birth rates, Canada is increasingly relying on immigration in order to maintain population growth—a perceived need in a liberal capitalist state to keep the engines of economic growth and profit humming. Since 2000, between approximately 221,000 and 262,000 immigrants have entered Canada each year—the vast majority from parts of Asia (China and India), South America, and Africa, resulting in an increase in the number of visible minority families, particularly in larger urban centres (Citizenship and Immigration Canada, 2006b). While unions involving partners of different ethnic origins, religions, or members of visible minority groups still represent a small proportion of all unions in Canada (we still tend to practice **endogamy/homogamy**), there has been a notable increase in inter-ethnic marriage between 1991 and 2001 (Statistics Canada, 2004b). Between 1991 and 2001, there was a 35 per cent increase in the number of 'mixed' unions in Canada. This represented 3.2 per cent of all people living as couples in Canada in 2001, up from 2.6 per cent in 1991 (Statistics Canada, 2004b).

While immigration, divorce, remarriage, lone-parenthood, stepfamilies, and same-sex families are not new on the Canadian landscape, they are certainly increasingly important in the study of Canadian families.

Conclusion

Today, as in the past, Canadian families take on a number of very diverse forms, which, in relation to other social institutions, both aid and constrain individual family members. That is, while a variety of family forms have existed in the past, our changing definitions of family are now making it possible for us to identify, count, and validate a variety of diverse forms. At the same time, our current definitions, theories, and measurement tools are likely to miss or mask a number of family forms that actually exist but remain unrecognized and uncounted, and these family forms may become part of future definitions of family.

Our current and shifting definitions reflect changing social attitudes, economic trends, laws, and policies. At the same time, changing economic trends and social attitudes have changed the age of first marriage, the duration of a marriage, whether marriage occurs at all, family size, the sequence and spacing of life-cycle events, where families live (together or apart, across households and/or borders, etc.), and how they live.

With changing definitions and trends there have been shifts in how family theorists and researchers study and try to understand family life. Some are critical of change, while others actively seek it. Some look within families to understand them, some look outside them, and still others look at a combination or variety of contexts. Some take a qualitative and descriptive approach, some a quantitative one, and others use both. The chapters that follow will reflect some of this diversity in approaches, as they map out and critically assess some of the trends and changes that, for better or worse, are part of the complex collage that makes up Canadian family life.

Study Questions

1. Find one of your own family photos that best captures or characterizes what you would consider your family. What is it about that particular photo that makes it the best? Does it capture who and what makes up your family today? Five years ago? Ten years ago? Who or what is still excluded? Who or what else would have to be included to make it a better representation of your family?
2. What would you consider the 'best' definition of family? Why?
3. Select any two theories. How do you think they would compare in their approach to and study of non-parental child care (daycare)?
4. Why do you think Canadians are postponing marriage and childbirth? What do you think is an ideal age (if any) to marry? To have children? Why?
5. If you wanted to study the domestic division of labour within families, how would you study it? Which theoretical orientation would best suit/guide your approach?

Glossary

Bi-nuclear family A family consisting of children and their parents who live in two households, usually following a divorce.

Case study research/case studies A qualitative method of inquiry that investigates a contemporary phenomenon within its real-life context; it helps provide in-depth or detailed contextual analysis of a limited number of events or relationships.

Census family One of the formal and changing definitions of 'family' as outlined in the Canadian census. In the 2006 census, it refers to a married couple and the children, if any, of either or both spouses; a couple living common law and the children, if any, of either or both partners; or, a lone parent of any marital status with at least one child living in the same dwelling and that child or those children. All members of a particular census family live in the same dwelling. A couple may be of opposite or same sex. Children may be children by birth, marriage, or adoption regardless of their age or marital status as long as they live in the dwelling and do not have their own spouse or child living in the dwelling. Grandchildren living with their grandparent(s) but with no parents present also constitute a census family.

Child launch Refers to one of the 'early adult transitions', the point at which children leave their parental home. This has been increasingly delayed over the past decade or so, resulting in 'cluttered' or 'crowded' rather than the 'empty nests' of the past.

Endogamy/homogamy The tendency for people to partner with/marry someone within their own social group (*endo*—within) or with similar (*homo*—same) characteristics.

Extended family/multigenerational household A family in which two or more generations (e.g., grandparents, aunts, uncles, cousins) share a household.

Fertility rate A measure that estimates the average number of children women aged 15 to 49 will have in their lifetime.

Fictive kin Non-related friends/individuals who, because they offer services, support, and goods to a family, come to be considered part of that family.

Household A group of people who occupy the same dwelling/housing unit.

Longitudinal studies A study that shows changes over time, usually by tracking a particular group of people or by taking snapshots of different groups at different points in time.

Qualitative research/approach A non-numeric analysis of data intended to discover underlying meaning and explore relationships.

Transnational, multi-local family/satellite family A family that finds itself (temporarily) separated and living across borders, in multiple locations.

Further Readings

Eichler, Margrit. 1997. *Family Shifts: Families, Policies, and Gender Equality*. Toronto: Oxford University Press. While it may be considered an 'older' text, this work is still a major contribution to the study of Canadian families because it both traces shifts in Canadian family composition and gender roles and identifies important theoretical and policy implications.

Ingoldsby, Bron, Suzanne Smith, and J. Elizabeth Miller. 2004. *Exploring Family Theories*. Los Angeles: Roxbury. This book provides a reader-friendly and relatively detailed introduction and overview of family theory and research. Following each chapter that presents an overview of a particular theory, the book includes a 'sample reading' or application of the theoretical approach.

Janovicek, Nancy, and Joy Parr, eds. 2003. *Histories of Canadian Children and Youth*. Toronto: Oxford University Press. This collection of readings pro-vides valuable insight into the life of Canadian families in the past by looking at the lives of children and youth in various contexts. It not only shows us some of the diversity that existed in Canadian families in the past, but also shows us how far we have come in recognizing children and youth as important to understanding Canadian families.

McQuillan, Kevin, and Zenaida Ravanera, eds. 2006. *Canada's Changing Families*. Toronto: University of Toronto Press. This collection of studies looks at the changing composition and role of Canadian families in a broader economic context and in light of social changes.

Saul, Jennifer Mather. 2003. *Feminism: Issues and Arguments*. New York: Oxford University Press. A good overview of feminist theorizing is presented through an analysis of selected contemporary issues ranging from work and family to abortion, sexual harassment, feminine appearance, etc.

Websites

www.equal-marriage.ca

Canadians for Equal Marriage is an organization that pursues a nationwide, bilingual campaign for rights for same-sex families. Its partners include Egale Canada, PFLAG Canada, the Canadian Federation of Students, the Canadian Labour Congress, the Canadian Psychological Association, and the Canadian Association of University Teachers, among others. It works at the grassroots level, in the media, and in Parliament, with the goal of per-suading MPs to oppose any measures to take away equal marriage by channelling grassroots web-based lobbying, directly lobbying MPs, encouraging gay and non-gay organizations and individuals to speak out, and main-taining a strong voice in the media.

http://dsp-psd.pwgsc.gc.ca/Collection-R/Statcan/ 11-008-XIE/11-008-XIE.html

Canadian Social Trends is an on-line publication of Statistics Canada that discusses the social, economic, and demographic changes affecting the lives of Canadians. It contains the latest figures for major social indicators and articles written by Statistics Canada researchers on social situations in Canada. Individual issues released since January 1990 have been indexed.

http://ceris.metropolis.net/frameset_e.html

The Joint Centre of Excellence for Research on Immi-gration and Settlement, Toronto (CERIS) is a consortium of Toronto-area universities and community partners. It is one of five such research centres across Canada. CERIS goals include: promoting research about the impact of immigration on the Greater Toronto Area and on the integration of immigrants into Canadian society; providing training opportunities; disseminating policy and program relevant research information. The site has an extensive virtual library which includes research projects, research reports, public policy discussion papers, etc.

www.un.org/esa/socdev/family

This United Nations Program on the Family site con-tains an overview of major trends affecting families worldwide, including changing family structure, aging families, and the rise of migration. It also includes infor-mation on the International Year of the Family, access to reports of the Secretary-General and UN General Assembly resolutions, and 'Family Matters', a bimonthly circular letter with information about activities related to the family from around the globe.

References

Ambert, Anne Marie. 2005. 'Same-sex couples and same-sex parent families: Relationships, parenting and issues of marriage'. Vanier Institute of the Family, at: <www.vifamily.ca/library/cft/samesex_05.html>.

Beaujot, Roderic. 2004. 'Delayed life transitions: Trends and implications', *Contemporary Family Trends* (Vanier Institute of the Family).

———. 2006. 'Delayed life transitions: Trends and implications', in Kevin McQuillan and Zenaida Ravanera, eds, *Canada's Changing Families*. Toronto: University of Toronto Press, 105–32.

Bernhard, Judith, Patricia Landolt, and Luin Goldring. 2005. 'Transnational, multi-local motherhood: Experiences of separation and reunification among Latin American families in Canada', Latin American Research Group, at: <www.ryerson.ca/~bernhard/pdf/Transnational_Families_LARG_May_05.pdf>.

Bradbury, Bettina. 1993. *Working Families: Age, Gender, and Daily Survival in Industrializing Montreal*. Toronto: McClelland & Stewart.

Bronfenbrenner, Urie. 1977. 'Towards an experimental ecology of human development', *American Psychologist* 32: 513–31.

——— and Stephen Ceci. 1994. 'Nature-nurture reconceptualized in developmental perspective: A bioecological model', *Psychological Review* 101: 568–86.

Bushnik, Tracey. 2006. *Child Care in Canada* (Catalogue no. 89–599–MIE–No. 003). Children and Youth Research Paper Series. Ottawa: Statistics Canada.

Calhoun, Cheshire. 2000. *Feminism, the Family and the Politics of the Closet*. New York: Oxford University Press.

Campbell, Marie. 2003. 'Dorothy Smith and knowing the world we live in', *Journal of Sociology and Social Welfare* 30, 1: 3–22.

Cheal, David. 1991. *Family and the State of Theory*. Toronto: University of Toronto Press.

Che-Alford, Janet, and Brian Hamm. 1999. 'Under one roof: Three generations living together', *Canadian Social Trends* 53: 6–9. At: <http://dsp-psd.pwgsc.gc.ca/Collection-R/Statcan/11-008-XIE/0019911-008-XIE.pdf>.

Citizenship and Immigration Canada. 2006a. 'Family class—Sponsorship of a spouse, common-law partner, conjugal partner or dependent child living outside canada, Part 1: Sponsorship Guide', Catalogue no. IMM 3900E (05–2006). At:
<www.cic.gc.ca/ english/pdf/kits/guides/3900E.pdf>.

———. 2006b. 'Facts and figures 2005: Immigration overview'. At: <www.cic.gc.ca/english/pub/facts2005/overview/1.html>.

Coser, Rose Laub. 1974. *The Family: Its Structure and Functions*, 2nd edn. New York: St Martin's Press.

Duvall, Evelyn Millis. 1988. 'Family development's first forty years', *Family Relations* 37, 2: 127–34.

——— and Ruben Hill. 1948. *Reports of the Committee on the Dynamic of Family Interaction*. Washington: National Conference on Family Life.

Eichler, Margrit. 1983. *Families in Canada Today: Recent Changes and Their Policy Consequences*. Toronto: Gage.

———. 1997. *Family Shifts: Families, Policies, and Gender Equality*. Toronto: Oxford University Press.

Elliot, Patricia, and Nancy Mandell. 1998. 'Feminist theories', in Nancy Mandel, ed., *Feminist Issues: Race, Class and Sexuality*. Toronto: Prentice-Hall Allyn and Bacon Canada, 2–21.

Engels, Friedrich. 1972 [1884]. *The Origin of the Family, Private Property and the State*. New York: Pathfinder.

Goode, William. 1995. 'The theoretical importance of the family', in Mark Robert Rank and Edward L. Kain, eds, *Diversity and Change in Families: Patterns, Prospects and Policies*. Englewood Cliffs, NJ: Prentice-Hall, 1–14.

Ingoldsby, Bron, Suzanne Smith, and J. Elizabeth Miller. 2004. *Exploring Family Theories*. Los Angeles: Roxbury.

Janovicek, Nancy, and Joy Parr, eds. 2003. *Histories of Canadian Children and Youth*. Toronto: Oxford University Press.

Knowles, Valerie. 1992. *Stranger at Our Gates: Canadian Immigration and Immigration Policy, 1540–1990*. Toronto: Dundurn Press.

Krüger, Helga, and René Levy. 2001. 'Linking life courses, work, and the family: Theorizing a not so visible nexus between men and women', *Canadian Journal of Sociology* 26, 2: 145–66.

Mandell, Nancy, and Ann Duffy. 2000. *Canadian Families: Diversity, Conflicts and Change*, 2nd edn. Toronto: Nelson Thomson Learning.

Mead, George Herbert. 1967 [1934]. *Mind, Self and Society*. Chicago: University of Chicago Press.

Mead, Margaret. 1949. *Male and Female: A Study of the Sexes in a Changing World*. New York: Dell Publishing, Laurel Editions.

Mitchell, Barbara. 1998. 'Too close for comfort? Parental assessments of "boomerang kid" living arrangements', *Canadian Journal of Sociology* 23, 1: 21–46.

Morissette, René, and Garnett Picot. 2005. 'Low-paid work and economically vulnerable families over the last two decades' (Catalogue no. 11F0019MIE-No. 248). Analytical Studies Branch Research Paper Series. Ottawa: Statistics Canada. At: <www.statcan.ca/english/research/11F0019MIE/11F0019MIE2005248.pdf>.

Murdock, George P. 1949. *Social Structure*. New York: Macmillan.

Parsons, Talcott, and Robert Bales. 1955. *Family, Socialization and Interaction Process*. New York: Free Press of Glencoe.

Saul, Jennifer Mather. 2003. *Feminism: Issues and Arguments*. New York: Oxford University Press.

Statistics Canada. 1996. *1996 Census Dictionary*. (Catalogue no. 92–351–UIE). At: <www.statcan.ca/english/freepub/92-351-UIE/04fam.pdf>.

———. 2000. *Women in Canada: A Gender-Based Statistical Report*. (Catalogue no. 89–503–XPE). Ottawa.

———. 2001. *2001 Census Dictionary*. (Catalogue no. 92–378–XIE). At: <www12.statcan.ca/english/census01/Products/Reference/dict/index.htm>.

———. 2002a. '2001 census: Marital status, common-law status, families, dwellings and households', *The Daily*, 22 Oct.

———. 2002b. 'Changing conjugal life in Canada', *The Daily*, 11 July.

———. 2003a. 'Report on the demographic situation in Canada—2003' (Catalogue no. 91–209–XIE). At: <www.statcan.ca/english/ads/91-209-XPE/highlights.htm>.

———. 2003b. 'Marital status of Canadians, 2001 census: Common-law status, age group and sex' (Catalogue no. 95F0405XIE). At: <www.statcan.ca/bsolc/english/beolc?catno=95F0405X>.

———. 2004a. 'The sandwich generation', *The Daily*, 28 Sept. At: <www.statcan.ca/Daily/English/040928/d040928b.htm>.

———. 2004b. 'Mixed unions', *The Daily*, 8 June. At: <www.statcan.ca/Daily/English/040608/d040608b.htm>.

———. 2005. 'Births', *The Daily*, 12 July. At: <www.statcan.ca/Daily/English/050712/d050712a..htm>.

Stephens, William. 1963. *The Family in Cross-Cultural Perspective*. New York: Holt, Rinehart and Winston.

Stevens, Noreen. 2006. 'The brides of Stephen Harper', *Winnipeg Free Press*, 30 Apr. Available at: <www.equal-marriage.ca/resource.php?id=488>.

Tsang, A. Ka Tat, Howard Irving, Ramona Alaggia, Shirley B.Y. Chau, and Michael Benjamin. 2003. 'Negotiating ethnic identity in Canada: The case of "satellite children"', *Youth & Society* 34, 3: 359–84.

Tyyskä, Vappu. 2001. *The Long and Winding Road: Adolescents and Youth in Canada Today*. Toronto: Canadian Scholars' Press.

Vanier Institute of the Family. 2006. 'Family facts'. At: <www.vifamily.ca/library/facts/facts.html>.

Waters, Johanna L. 2001. *Migration Strategies and Transnational Families: Vancouver's Satellite Kids*. Working Paper Series, No. 01–10. Vancouver: Vancouver Centre of Excellence, Research on Immigration and Integration in the Metropolis. At: <http://ceris.metropolis.net/frameset_e.html>.

Webb, Adrienne, Sharon Doyle Dreidger, and Mark Cardwell. 1994. 'A new diversity', *Maclean's* 107, 25: 34.

Wollstonecraft, Mary. 1988 [1792]. *A Vindication of the Rights of Women*. New York: Norton.

CHAPTER 2

Families in Historical and Cross-Cultural Context

Paula Chegwidden

Learning Objectives

- To understand how the concept of kinship is used for social organization in human cultures.
- To understand that the institution of marriage seems to be universal, yet what a marital relationship is in any particular culture varies widely.
- To learn that the concept of family may mean many different things and is not the same thing as the concept of household.
- To see how household life can be examined from a political economy perspective.
- To discover what the dominant models of family life in Canada have been and what makes these European.
- To understand how industrialization changed family life.
- To learn how family life continued to change through the twentieth century.

Introduction

Understanding contemporary Canadian family life fully is not possible without a cross-cultural and historical perspective on families. Looking at the broadest possible context will give one a better idea of why family life changes over time and place and what the effects of those changes might be. The information needed to provide this context is primarily found in cultural anthropology and history, rather than in sociology.

Although cultural anthropologists do use documents, questionnaires, and analysis of artifacts, human remains, and cultural texts, most of the data relevant to the study of family life come from participant observation or fieldwork. The anthropologist lives within a particular culture, participating as much as possible, while observing as an outsider, and learning from members of the culture. Much of our information about variations in family structure comes from observations of small-scale traditional cultures, which by the twenty-first century have been absorbed into nation-states, so much of the relevant participant-observation data comes from the recent past, the twentieth century before the 1960s.

Social historians study how particular social units change over time. Most historical data come from analysis of documents, whether government records such as tax assessments or censuses, personal diaries and letters, or other written records. Some historians do study other kinds of cultural artifacts, such as the artwork of an era or the material remains left by a social unit. Family history is a well-established subfield within the field of history. However, not all families of the past are represented in written records; the poor and illiterate or members of minority groups are often missing. For this reason, family historians are continually searching for new sources of data, e.g., folk music or grave markers, to get at the subtleties of daily life in the past.

Anthropologists, like sociologists, attempt to generate theory from their data to develop explanations for why cultures differ from each other and why some cultures share particular features. Historians tend to have a different view of grand theory. They are aware that social phenomena are systemically related; causes and effects are multiple and mutually interactive. They concentrate on understanding the complexities of a particular social situation, rather than developing abstract generalizations. The Canadian family historian Bettina Bradbury (1993) likens historical scholarship to putting together a jigsaw puzzle that is never quite complete.

One aspect of participating in a culture is being ethnocentric, assuming that one's own cultural patterns are the only ones that are desirable. Family relationships, among the most intimate that humans experience, may lend themselves to feeling 'natural' rather than being a product of a particular cultural perspective. Hence, many North Americans (and others) may feel that their own behaviours and feelings about family life are the only ones that are normal or acceptable because they are experienced as right and inevitable. One of the tasks of cultural anthropologists is to document the differences among human cultures, showing that each pattern makes a kind of sense for a particular time and place. Further, any particular culture is not static. Cultural ideas and practices are always changing and adapting as social contexts and environments change. So family life can exist in a variety of forms and still meet basic human needs.

Historians also have to deal with the limited perspective of much of the public. North Americans (and others) tend to project onto the past particular ideas about how family life must have been in order to make statements about what is wrong with contemporary family life. Many social historians describe contemporary people as having 'myths' about how families used to be. As the historian John Gillis puts it: 'Families past are presented to us not only as more stable but as more authentic than families present. . . . Don't confuse the family past we live by with the families that previous generations actually lived with' (Gillis, 1996: 8). For this reason, family historians have spent a good deal of time evaluating the accuracy of popular contemporary assumptions, e.g., that elders were treated with more respect in the past or that families routinely lived in multi-generational households.

Kinship

Human beings are adapted to survive primarily by relying on culture, which in anthropology is a term referring to the set of behaviours and ideas learned from other members of their social group. Culture exists in the form of specific cultures—a variety of ways of thinking and behaving, each characteristic of a particular social group. As the anthropologist Clifford Geertz has put it:

> Human beings are incomplete or unfinished animals who complete themselves through culture —not culture in general, but specific forms of it: Balinese, Italian, Ilongot, Chinese, Kwakiutl, American, and so on. When people share the meanings they give to experiences, they share and participate in the same culture. (Geertz, cited in Robbins, 1993: 5)

All human groups need organization in order to continue, but many living and work arrangements are compatible with a society's capacity to meet basic social needs. Sooner or later in their histories, particular societies make choices among available alternatives. Within a culture, a variety of criteria may be used to assign people to roles, categories, and groups. Among these are gender, age, ability, ethnic origin, and preference. Some cultures highlight some criteria more than others.

A major criterion used to sort people out is kinship, one of the factors that human groups have used to establish social organization, creating rights and obligations among individuals and forming social groups. Kinship exists in all societies to some degree, but societies usually described as small-scale by anthropologists may use it as the major criterion for assigning people their rights and duties and group memberships.

But what do anthropologists mean by kinship? All human groups recognize the biological practices of mating, birth, and nurturance. They take their own culturally specific perceptions of these biological processes and elaborate them into complex social relationships, based on concepts such as marriage, descent, and parenting. Everyone is connected to a genealogy, a vast network of individuals (kin) through ties of descent from a common ancestor or ties created through marriage. These individuals become potential social resources. The cultural meanings attached to these networks of genealogical relationships are what is referred to as kinship.

Differing cultures emphasize some features of kinship and downplay others. For example, relationships traced through women might be more important in a particular culture than relationships traced through men, and the seniority in age of some kin to other kin might be important or not. Some biological connections may not be recognized as kin relations; other non-biological connections may be recognized as kin, through what anthropologists call 'fictive kin'. For example, one's social parents may not correspond with one's genetic parents, as in the case of adoption in Canada, so that people in one's genealogy are those people recognized socially as kin but not necessarily all of one's genetic relatives.

In some cultures, kinship has not been merely the basis of providing individuals with a network of relationships; it has also been the criterion used to assign people into specific social units rather than collections of individuals. Depending on the time and place, groups based on kinship criteria may have names, control property in common, act as a political unit, and have their own particular religious observances. Euro-Canadians may have difficulty understanding a society in which kinship groups are major social institutions, since families are the only kinship groups that are common in Euro-Canadian society. But for cultures that lacked centralized governments, kinship group membership was often the major determinant of an individual's rights, obligations, and opportunities. How membership was determined, relationships among kinship groups, and what kinship groups actually did varied enormously from culture to culture, and

studying their complexities has been a major part of cultural anthropology.

There are many kinds of kinship groups. Many are unilineal descent groups; that is, all the descendants of one particular ancestor belong to a social unit. Until the early twentieth century, about 60 per cent of cultures traced descent unilineally. A person affiliates to one descent group, that of one's father or mother, depending on the culture. Two common types of unilineal descent groups are clans, where the founding ancestor is a mythological being, and lineages, where the founding ancestor is a historically existing named person. Kinship groups have had the widest range of uses in cultures often called **tribes and chiefdoms**. These societies are large enough in population so that individual kinship connections are not sufficient to organize the entire society, but they lack the organization provided by centralized governments.

The most common form of unilineal descent is **patrilineality**, where children affiliate to the kinship group of the father. A smaller percentage of human cultures are matrilineal, with people assigned to groups on the basis of their descent through female relatives. There are many theories about why unilineal descent should be important in particular kinds of cultures. The most important of these theories link the way descent is traced to the mode of production of a society. Descent rules organize people into groups who are likely to be able to work together. Matrilineal descent seems to have been important in areas where women did critical productive labour and controlled property; production of food was horticultural, using gardening techniques, in these societies. Patrilineal descent characterizes societies with plough agriculture, where male labour was most important (Goody, 1976). This kind of observation points out the importance of having a political economy perspective on kinship. Households and families and kinship groups and networks organize and respond to meet the economic needs of a society.

Over human history, larger-scale societies, usually called states by anthropologists, developed and tended to displace smaller-scale, less central-ized societies. In larger societies, political power is more centralized and access to economic resources is restricted to the upper social strata. As well, in many cases, the central authority has its own religious practices. Thus, the religious, economic, and political functions of kinship groups are less important. However, kinship continues to be important as a criterion establishing networks tying together individuals. By the twenty-first cen-tury, virtually all the geographical territory of the world was divided up into nation-states. Smaller-scale cultures had been absorbed into these large units. But enough of their traditional life remains or at least was recorded in the recent past by anthropologists for us to understand how kinship could be used to organize an entire society.

MARRIAGE

All human cultures have some version of an incest taboo, a rule that sexual relationships should not occur between individuals who are kin. What the exact function of the incest taboo is has been a matter of great anthropological debate (Wolf, 1993). The range of kin with whom sexual contact is forbidden varies considerably cross-culturally, but the incest taboo in some form is one of the few human universals.

One kind of culturally approved sexual rela-tionship is through marriage, which in effect cre-ates kinship ties between individuals who were not previously related, since people who are already kin are not supposed to mate. All known cultures seem to have some version of what could be called marriage, but finding a truly cross cultural defini-tion is rather more difficult than what a North American might expect. One introductory cultural anthropology text defines marriage as 'a socially approved sexual and economic union, usually between a woman and a man' (Ember and Ember, 2004: 145). However, two people may well be regarded as married in Canadian society who do not have a sexual relationship and/or do not pool economic resources.

Another introductory text, in response to this, came up with this non-committal definition: 'Marriage: a more or less stable union, usually between two people, and who are likely, but not necessarily co-resident, sexually involved with each other, and procreative with each other' (Miller et al., 2001: 203).

What we can say is that every culture studied has developed particular expectations about mat-ing and reproduction. 'Every society favours forms of union that conform to its ethical standards and needs' (Borneman and Hart, 2004). Other than the general concept that people who are already kin should not mate, everything else about these rules varies. The number of mates, whether mates are restricted to opposite gender, and whether the relationship begins or ends with ritual all vary with different cultural traditions.

In all cultures, most marital relationships have been between men and women. However, in con-temporary North American society, where many gay people are demanding the right to marry, it is useful to keep in mind that marriages between peo-ple of the same gender have been quite acceptable in some historical cultures. One well-known exam-ple is Evans-Pritchard's account of woman–woman marriage among the Nuer, a tribal society in what is now Sudan. In traditional Nuer culture, it was important that everyone have children. After death, one continued to be part of one's lineage by being remembered through ritual by one's descendants. Not everyone, however, produced offspring through a man–woman link. In some cases, for example, a man might have died before producing children. In that case, the younger brother of the deceased would marry someone in the name of the dead older brother. The children of this marriage would have the 'ghost' father as their legally recognized father, even though the biological father would be the younger brother. For equivalent reasons, a woman who was barren could change her social role to that of man and marry another woman. The female husband would have all the legal and social rights of a male husband. The female wife would have sexual relations with an unrelated male in order to produce children, but the female husband would be the social and legal father. Children would affiliate to her patrilineage. Further, if a woman died before producing children, she could become a 'ghost husband' by having a younger kinsman marry in her name (Evans-Pritchard, 1951). Nuer woman–woman and ghost marriages are examples of relationships that seem to be marriage, yet are not based on the criterion of the partners having a sexual relationship.

Of course, the kind of same-sex marriage that North Americans are coming to recognize is based on the criterion of a sexual union. These, too, exist in some traditional cultures, although not in the same way that they exist in contemporary Canada. Some cultures recognize more than two genders. A few of the individuals who are considered to be something other than male or female have ambiguous biological sex but most do not. Assignment to a third gender is most often based on personal preference or the perception by others of one's special qualities. A member of a third gender might well have a marital relationship with someone assigned to the male or female gender by their culture (Nanda, 2000).

Further, sexual practices in some cultures have not necessarily been as tied to marriage as they have been in the Judeo-Christian traditions that have so influenced Canadian patterns. Cultural rules about sexuality vary from what North Americans would see as extremely restrictive to what they might consider extremely permissive. Kinship is about relationships created through the reproduction of new generations. Sexual practices not intended to produce offspring might be considered quite a different kind of activity. For example, Gilbert Herdt (1996) has written extensively about male ritual homosexual activity among the Sambia, a tribal group of New Guinea. This was a normal part of masculine ritual life for all men, but so was marriage to a female in order to reproduce.

In small societies, marriage was important as a means of tying together kinship groups. It functioned as a connection between two groups, not just two individuals. Choice of whom one could marry was directed by the rules of the kinship system. There might be rules of exclusion, categories of people who were not 'marriageable', and rules of preference—categories of people preferred as spouses. One typical restriction is exogamy: an individual would be required to select a spouse from outside his/her own kinship group. The size of the group within which one could not marry varied with the particulars of the kinship system. For example, a person of the Navajo culture, a large tribal society of the American Southwest, could not marry anyone from his or her mother's or father's clans, which might exclude a quarter of the population (Kluckhohn and Leighton, 1962). Another restriction is endogamy: one would be required to marry within a defined social group. Larger-scale societies tend to have social strata; one typically is expected to marry within one's social class, which is a way of keeping the classes separate.

Marriage is not always the intimate romantic tie that Canadian popular culture portrays in never-ending variation. In many cultures, marriage may be a fairly formal relationship and intense personal feelings may be stronger for one's siblings (as Burch, 1968, described for North Alaskans) or one's co-wives (as Fernea, 1969, showed for rural Iraqi women). The Western concept of romantic love developed with the chivalric age in medieval Europe. In its original manifestation it concerned the idealized love of a knight for his lord's wife, to whom he might dedicate poetry or a heroic performance at the joust. Marrying for romantic love becomes a central motive for Europeans and Euro-North Americans only in the nineteenth century as the economic functions of marriage become less important with industrialization (Lindholm, 1998).

The sheer variety of arrangements regarded as marriage by cultural groups—some same-sex, some non-sexual—has led many anthropologists to comment about the gay marriage debate in the United States. Roger Lancaster notes:

> Leaders often make global pronouncements about 'marriage', as though it were a self-evident

institution. Depending on its cultural context, marital unions can involve a host of different persons in a number of possible combinations. People are inventive and creative about the way they create kinship networks. (Lancaster, 2003)

FAMILY AND HOUSEHOLD

Family is another concept that is difficult to define in a cross-cultural context. English-speakers routinely use the word to refer variously to relatives sharing a household, a circle of close kin, some of whom live elsewhere, or an extensive network of relatives. 'Family' might refer to a group of relatives one shared a household with as a child (what anthropologists call one's family of orientation) or a group of relatives one shares a household with as an adult (what anthropologists call one's family of procreation). In a culture where people live and share with kinship groups, including a variety of relatives Canadians would regard as 'distant', it is difficult to find an equivalent term. One introductory text gives this necessarily general definition of a family as 'a social and economic unit consisting *minimally* of one or more parents and their children' (Ember and Ember, 2004: 160).

Historically in Canada the term 'family' often refers to the **nuclear family**, a group comprised of mother, father, and children. Anthropologists have debated whether the nuclear family is universal, i.e., recognized as a social group for at least some purpose in all cultures (Spiro, 1954). What we do know is that other small kinship groups may be much more important than the nuclear type. In polygynous societies, where men have more than one wife, in many respects the group formed by a wife and her children is the basic kinship unit—what Canadians might call a family. In other cultures, the extended family, consisting of more than two generations and more than one marital pair, might be the smallest kinship unit that has any social meaning.

It is important to distinguish families from households, although the terms are often used synonymously. Cross-culturally, close kinship ties are the most common reason for people to live in the same household, sharing a living space. However, other social ties may be relevant as well. University students frequently share a household with friends. In communes, several families may share a household. In some traditional societies, men spent most of their time together in their own households, away from women and children. In tribal cultures where **age sets**—groups of community members of the same generation and gender—were important, young men might spend several years together, living separately from the rest of the community.

What can be recognized about households cross-culturally is their importance as units of production. Until the changes in production that came with industrialization, most economic activity took place in households. Members of households worked together to produce and distribute the goods and services needed for survival. Larger units of people also worked together as needed—often they belonged to the same kinship group, which might have owned common property—or because any kin had the duty to help another member of an individual's kinship network.

Since kinship groups, whether small family-based households or larger units, have important functions as organizers of economic life, it is not surprising that family life itself and the relationships among close kin cannot be understood without looking at the economic context of families. For example, attitudes and practices of child-rearing often reflect the differing economic roles that children, either when young or as adults, must learn to fill. An extensive analysis of children from six cultures conducted by Whiting and Whiting (1975) found a strong correlation between child-rearing and children's personalities in relationship to the tasks that children and, later, adults are expected to carry out in their respective cultures.

Relationships between male and female spouses are often shaped by the economic roles that they play. Gender is a major criterion used by traditional cultures to assign work, although the strictness of the rules about men's versus women's work varies considerably. Many anthropologists argue that women and men have a more equal relationship in cultures where each gender has critical economic functions (Ward, 1999).

Canadian Family History

Although Canadians come from an ever-increasing diversity of ethnic backgrounds, the dominant models of family life in Canada came from Europe. That is, the expectations about kinship institutionalized into legal, educational, and religious mores and eventually into the conventions of popular culture have been European ones. Ideas about family life were brought into Canada with its colonization by France and England, and these ideas continue to be influential. Such contemporary situations as the size and design of housing, immigration rules about who can be sponsored, and marketing of household goods still reflect European models of family and household.

Kinship patterns in Europe were themselves variable over time and from place to place. However, some generalizations are possible about the pre-industrial family life typical of those French and English settlers who immigrated to Canada and how it compares to other cultural patterns. European kinship patterns were male-dominant. Authority in the family rested with the husband/father of the nuclear unit. Both wives and children were to be controlled by the male family head. This emphasis on male authority had deep historical roots in both the Greco-Roman and Judeo-Christian traditions that shaped European culture. This male right to authority sometimes balanced precariously with the important economic roles of wives, which created mutual dependence between spouses (Sampson, 1977). Although kinship was reckoned bilaterally, recognizing both maternal and paternal relatives, there was a bias towards patrilineality. It was considered normal that last names came from the father's side, a wife would indicate her absorption into her husband's family by taking his last name, and real property primarily belonged with the sons.

Households were the basic economic unit; they were primarily composed of nuclear family groups, unattached relatives, and other non-kin such as servants and apprentices. (Many historians have pointed out that the English term 'family' was not confined to kin, but referred to everyone in the household before the eighteenth century.) Residence was neolocal; that is, most children moved out of the family home on marriage. This meant that marriage tended to be postponed until both husband and wife had the economic resources to start a separate household (Sampson, 1977).

Kinship networks, but not kinship groups, had some importance, depending on one's social class. Being a distant relative of a member of the nobility could be a useful social tie, while being a distant relative of another peasant farmer would not necessarily have any particular social importance. In fact, Adams (2001) argues that evidence suggests even adult siblings, once they established separate households, did not interact with each other frequently in medieval England. In comparison to a tribal society, such as the Nuer, where kinship was central to social organization, the range of genealogical relationships recognized as kin in England or France was fairly narrow.

Canada, of course, was occupied before European colonization. Canada's Native peoples were dispersed into many cultures living in relatively small-scale social systems. Although each had its own kinship norms, there were basic differences between all Aboriginal kinship patterns and those of the French and English (Bradbury, 2001).

1. Aboriginal cultures were organized around extended family networks and, in some cases, such as in the Northwest Coast cultures, elaborate systems of unilineal descent.
2. Child-rearing practices were permissive by European standards. Children were granted a high level of autonomy, a practice fairly typical for hunters and gatherers, the productive system of most Canadian Aboriginal peoples. European ideas about the nature of children

were complex, but actual practices tended to be highly authoritarian, involving strict imposition of authority through physical punishment.

3. Both Europeans and Aboriginal peoples had a highly gendered division of labour. Both men's and women's work was vital for a household to survive. However, First Nations societies were not nearly as organized around male authority over women. Aboriginal women had a fair amount of autonomy in comparison to European women.

4. Land tenure adhered to large kinship groups or whole communities. A particular family was not owner or tenant on a particular plot of land, as was the European practice.

Europeans arrived in Canada with a built-in set of assumptions about their superiority over the Native peoples they sought to control. They were quite ethnocentric about their own family patterns, as well as every other aspect of their culture, assuming that these were morally superior. Consequently, a significant part of the colonization process involved restraining First Nation family life to bring it into conformity with European ideas, whether this involved curbing women's autonomy, maintaining children's obedience, or establishing individual land tenure.

Before we consider the effect of industrialization on households in the nineteenth century, it is important to keep in mind how much households before this time were units of economic co-operation. The European pattern emphasized a gendered division of labour, so it is not surprising that the earliest colonists, who were largely men, needed to recruit women as economic partners. We can see this strategy in two different historical setting, the frontier fur trade and the agricultural and urban settlement of New France.

Early fur traders often took First Nations women as 'country wives'. The women provided them with companionship on the frontier, but also had important economic functions as links to the Aboriginal groups with furs to trade. These marriages 'à la

façon du pay' involved a blend of European and Aboriginal marriage customs, but no Church sanction. As trading became more institutionalized around Hudson's Bay posts, a new culture of mixed-blood (Métis) offspring of these marriages developed around these settlements. A new generation of Hudson's Bay factors then formed further country marriages with the daughters of this group. Most of these relationships did not survive when the fur traders had to return to Europe or to the European-settled parts of Canada, as Canadians of Aboriginal or mixed ancestry were not accepted away from the frontier (Van Kirk, 1992).

As New France became settled with European immigrants, the importance of having a mate was so central that single women were recruited in France and brought over as 'filles des Roi' to provide spouses for male colonists. Some 700 women from poverty-stricken backgrounds were brought over between 1663 and 1673 to become the wives of farmers, artisans, and merchants. This total represented half of the female immigrants to New France from its earliest settlement up until the mid-eighteenth century. Most were able to choose among a variety of marriage offers and established a more prosperous family life than they would have been able to in France (Landry, 1992).

Industrialization and Family Life

Industrialization transformed family life in nineteenth-century North America. As an economic system changes, social institutions have to adapt and family life is no exception. Eighteenth-century Canada was a society in which most people participated in a family economy; family-based households worked as a group to produce goods and services. By the end of the nineteenth century, a majority of Canadians lived in households where people left home to work elsewhere for wages. Work came to be defined as something one got paid to do; domestic work was not thought of as 'real' work until the emergence of the second-wave of the women's movement in the 1960s.

'Industrialization' or 'industrialism' is a term that refers to the application of machine technology powered by inanimate sources of energy (e.g., coal, electricity) to the production of goods. Changes in social organization are necessary to facilitate the use of this kind of technology; most economic production takes place away from the home. Eighteenth-century Great Britain is usually considered the first economy to make extensive use of industrial technology, and one of the sources of the wealth needed to change the technological basis of the British economy came from the development of overseas trade in the seventeenth century and even earlier. The desire to develop this trade, in both England and France, was a primary reason for Europeans beginning to settle in Canada.

The presence of Europeans on the frontier was largely dictated by the demands of international commerce, in particular the trade in furs. But by the eighteenth century, a majority of Canadians lived on farms, where each family member had work to do for the survival of the household. Although farms were self-sufficient in many respects, farmers did sell surpluses in order to purchase some necessities, such as tea and sugar. Male and female household work tasks were distinct and ideas about the gendered division of labour were brought by settlers to Canada. However, women stepped in to do men's work when men were away doing supplementary wage work or helped do what was still thought of as men's work when male children were not available (Cohen, 1988). Family work was not confined to adults; the family enterprise required the work of everyone. Family size continued to be high by modern standards as children had economic value as workers (Gaffield, 1992).

Pre-industrial urban families also were characterized by a family economy. Craft production or retail trade took place in the same buildings where families lived. Men were generally responsible for the main revenue-generating activity, but women and children organized domestic work and found supplementary sources of income. Beginning at age eight or earlier, children helped with the upkeep of the house, gathered fuel, and fetched water. They cultivated gardens and provided care to younger siblings and sick family members (Bullen, 1986). Historians often use the term **family strategy** to refer to the variety of ways in which a family-based household may allocate its members to meet the needs of production and reproduction. Each strategy will vary with the material resources available to a household and the gender and age composition of its members (see, e.g., Wilson, 1998).

Canada began to industrialize in the nineteenth century. Changes in production occurred rapidly in some economic sectors but happened much later in others, and thus the situation confronting families varied considerably from place to place. Even within the city of Montreal itself, artisanal home-based work in sections of the economy existed simultaneously with factory work in others (Bradbury, 1993).

The historian Bettina Bradbury (1993) has reconstructed the daily life of working-class Montrealers between the 1860s and 1890s, as the city economy gradually became dominated by wage work and industrial technology. She found that waged work was primarily available to males and so adult women needed access to marriage in order to survive economically. Men needed women as well. The amount of domestic labour necessary just to feed, clothe, and look after a worker made living alone impractical (Bradbury, 1993: 53). Neolocal residence patterns continued, although extended kin might well live nearby. The age at marriage varied with the state of the economy in any decade, as couples waited to be able to afford their own household.

Parents continued to need their children as workers. 'The work they expected of sons and daughters ranged from odd jobs to formal full-time waged labour' (ibid., 188). Older boys had the most access to waged work, although some factories did employ girls. Girls were more apt to do piecework in clothing manufacture at home or to work as domestic servants. Female white-collar occupations, such as retail sales and later clerical work, expanded. Access to waged work before marriage did give some young women a new kind of independence and worried social reformers, who thought that young women needed special protection (Light and Parr, 1983). Some historians have used the term 'family wage economy' to describe this period when the family strategy was to have more than one wage earner, since working-class wages were very low (Gaffield, 1992). This pattern emerged again in the last third of the twentieth century, except that the extra wage earner was usually the wife rather than children. Industrial production began to affect rural life as well. Cohen (1988) describes the gradual replacement of women's small-scale production of dairy products on Canadian farms with factory-based manufacture during the same time period Bradbury describes for Montreal.

The effects of industrialism on family life were not confined to changing work patterns. As the wider economy changed, the significance of family ties changed as well. Relationships between spouses took on new emphases and children took on a different kind of importance to parents.

So far this discussion of industrialism has focused on ordinary working people. However, social elites were affected as well. Changes in the values attached to spouses and children began at this social level and eventually became ideals for lower classes. The economic growth of the industrial era resulted in the expansion of the middle class. The relatively well-off professionals and merchants who existed in pre-industrial Canada were joined by the developing ranks of business management. Neither children nor spouses needed to contribute their labour to the economic well-being of these families. Household work was accomplished by servants, with supervision from wives. Boys received an education suitable to obtain high economic status as adults and girls were trained to make a suitable marriage. Many historians see the

nineteenth century as the era in which **companionate marriage** became important. As the economic functions of the wife in middle-class homes were less critical to family survival, a romantic emotional bond between spouses became more central. W. Peter Ward (1990) has traced the courtship patterns of several nineteenth-century middle-class Ontario men and women through their love letters. Although people thought about finding a wife who would be a social asset or a husband who was a good provider, the process of 'falling in love', so familiar to contemporary Canadians through popular culture, was a feature of what they described. Various writers have suggested that 'love' in the sense of idealized attraction occurs in many cultures, but its centrality as a motive for marriage is unusual. With minimal obligations to extended kin and wealth less tied to the inheritance of property in the industrializing economy of the nineteenth century, obeying one's parents and their choice of a suitable mate was less critical for one's economic success. Consequently, free choice of spouse and romantic courtship took on a new significance (Goode, 1959; Lindholm, 1998).

As most upper-class men, along with working-class men, began to spend their working hours away from their homes, home life took on a different significance. Wives were increasingly cut off from the working life of their husbands. Most historians describe this change as the development of the concept of **separate spheres**. Home was increasingly pictured in popular advice, religious tracts, songs, and novels as a refuge from the outside world of business, which was the sphere of men. Wives' primary family role changed from contributing to the family economy to making the home a peaceful sanctuary filled with love and warmth. The middle-class household lost economic functions but gained emotional and symbolic significance. Gillis (1996) suggests that many of the family rituals that North Americans find 'timeless'—Christmas customs, Sunday dinner, family memorabilia, white weddings—date from this period of the sentimentalizing of family life (see Box 2.1).

Box 2.1 'Home, Sweet Home': Family Life as Sentimentality

'Mid pleasures and palaces, though we may roam,
   Be it ever so humble, there's no place like home;
   A charm from the skies, seems to hallow us there,
   Which, seek through the world, is ne'er met with elsewhere.

Home, home, sweet, sweet home,
   There's no place like home.

I gaze on the moon, as I trace the drear wild,
   And feel that my parent now thinks of her child;
   She looks on that moon from our own cottage door,
   Through woodbines whose fragrance shall cheer me no more.

Home, home, sweet, sweet home,
   There's no place like home.

SOURCE: Library of Congress, American Song Sheets.

During the same time period, ideas about the nature of children were changing. Margolis (1984) looks back to the late eighteenth century as the beginnings of the concept of children as 'blank slates' whose nature could be wholly determined by their environment, especially the social environment created by their parents. As men's work increasingly took them away from the home and wives had less economic production to do in the home, mother's importance as child nurturer was emphasized in advice literature and popular culture. Margolis calls this the development of the 'cult of motherhood'. The growing centrality in the nineteenth century of the responsibility of the mother—and responsibility of children to the mother—is tied to the changing economic context of family life. As adolescent apprentices and domestics joined the industrial workforce and men left the house to go to a workplace, fewer people were present in the household to share child-rearing with the mother. Mothers took on new importance as the sole nurturers of the next generation.

The 'Angel in the House'—the idealized role as guardian of love and teacher of morality assigned to middle-class wives and mothers—referred to women's separate place in the home. Ironically, this image became a motivating force encouraging women to leave the home to participate in movements of social reform. The philosophy of maternal feminism argued that it was women's duty to better society because they were specially equipped to improve the lives of others (Roberts, 1979). Middle-class women were a dominant component of the movements for social change that developed in the late nineteenth century in Canada.

Much of the impetus for social reform concerned alleviating the impoverishment of the working classes that characterized early industrialization. Women were active in improving public health, food safety, housing, and education and in curbing the sale of alcohol. Maternal feminists thought that public life would benefit from the essential qualities of womanhood. As Mrs Doctor Parker expressed it in 1890:

The qualities of womanhood which revere purity and chastity, embodied in the national laws, would rid us of evils under which we groan. . . . That quality of womanhood which shrinks from the spilling of blood, woven into national law, will make for the triumph of conscience, intellect, and humanity, over the mere brute force which men call war. (Parker, 1890: 465)

This urge to reform also turned to improving the status of women. The legal status of women in nineteenth-century Canada reflected the country's European roots. A wife could not make contracts, control any wages she might earn, or own property. The Married Women's Property Act of 1884 finally created legal equality between husbands and wives after decades of political agitation (Chambers, 1997). Women also became active in the struggle to gain access to higher education and, eventually, the right to vote (Bradbury, 2001).

Towards the end of the nineteenth century, more public attention was given to the exploitation of children and youth in the industrial system. The developing trade union movement joined with middle-class movements for social reform to restrict the use of children as workers. In the 1880s, a series of **Factory Acts** restricted children's access to factory work and limited women's employment in ways seen as protecting their 'natural' status as child-bearers and homemakers (Ursel, 1988) (see Box 2.2). At the same time, changing technological complexity meant that there were fewer uses for unskilled workers in the economy. The idea that children needed training and education to have a place in the economy became widespread. Gradually, each province passed legislation requiring children to be in school for much of their youth.

Social reformers agitated for the institution of a **family wage**, a wage sufficient for a male worker to support a wife and children without other family members having to be employed. Although this social goal was never attainable for the poorest Canadians, who continued to need more than one wage per household, the model of the male breadwinner, with dependent wife and children, had been established. Eventually the ideal of companionate marriage with a female housewife and small numbers of children became a central value in North American popular culture. The 1950s are often singled out as having the most heightened

Box 2.2 Inquiry into Industrial Disputes in the Cotton Factories of Quebec, 1909

In determining what the maximum number of working hours should be, economic considerations alone demand that a full regard should be had for the effects of long and continuous employment, whatever its nature upon the constitution of women, and their place in the social economy of a nation. Excessive work bequeaths a legacy of weakness or disability to those who directly or indirectly are affected by it. In the upbuilding of a nation, this is a factor which cannot be too constantly kept in mind. If Canada is to have a hardy and intelligent body of producers, on which primarily her industrial position among the nations of the world will depend, she cannot view with too much caution all those factors which go into the making of a nation's manhood, and of these none are of like importance of the health and well-being of the mother and the child.

SOURCE: Royal Commission to Inquire into Industrial Disputes in the Cotton Factories of the Province of Quebec, *Report*, Canada, *Sessional Paper*, No. 39, 1909, 16–18.

portrayal of this kind of family in North American novels, films, television drama, advertising, and many other mass media images (Leibman, 1995).

The Twentieth Century

Canadian family history did not stop at 1900. The next century saw a number of changes that made family life different by 2000. Causes of some of these changes were ideological, cultural, and demographic, but once again many of them were tied to the changing wider economic context.

Two continuing demographic trends began well before 1900: Canadians live longer and longer and have fewer and fewer children. Life expectancy increased in all industrialized countries, primarily because of improvements to public health. Infectious disease ceased to be the primary cause of death. One consequence of this was that people did not feel the need to have so many children in order to be sure that some survived into adulthood.

Economic factors also accounted for the fall in the birth rate. Children's economic value as workers continued to decline. Given high cultural standards for what is needed to raise competent and self-supporting adults, raising children is now more expensive than ever before. A virtual industry of experts offers advice about how to manufacture the best possible child. By 2000, Canada was not replacing its native-born population. A consequence of the drop in fertility is the aging of the Canadian population. The average age of Canadians continues to rise as younger people become a smaller proportion of the population. The implications of this for family relations and for family policy are of ongoing interest to sociologists.

An exception to this pattern was the period 1945–60, often called the 'baby boom'. North American births increased during those years, as more people married and more married people had children than earlier in the century. By 1960, the dominant trend of lower births returned, and this trend has continued to the present. The existence of this population bulge resulting from the baby boom meant that North America has confronted the implications of an aging population later than the countries of Europe.

Canada became a more ethnically diverse country in the twentieth century, a trend that accelerated in the 1990s, which saw Canada with the second highest proportion of foreign-born residents in the world (Statistics Canada, 2003b). Beginning in the late nineteenth century, demands of the developing Canadian and global economies brought new kinds of settlers to Canada. Each ethnic group has its own particular family history. For example, Chinese-Canadian men were legally prevented from bringing their wives and children to Canada for decades, while the Canadian government actively recruited Mennonite families from Eastern Europe to farm on the Prairies (Knowles, 1992).

Despite this diversity, Nancy Howell's study of recent immigrants to Canada found that they have tended to adopt Euro-Canadian family norms. She argues this has not been so much from a desire to assimilate to Canadian culture as from the need to adapt to the realities of the Canadian economy. Immigrant wives are likely to be in the labour force and much of family resources go into providing educational opportunities for children. Children spend great amounts of time away from the home in school, develop real independence from their parents, and socialize with contemporaries from other ethnic groups. Neither Canadian immigration rules nor the available housing stock make living in extended families viable for many. Howell (2001: 141) concludes: 'Canada seems to be in the process of becoming a country with people of ethnically distinctive identities . . . but with the same kinds of family behaviour.'

Two other major changes in Canadian family life began after 1960: the most common type of Canadian household now has two breadwinners and Canadian marriage practices are changing rapidly. As is the case with increased longevity and declining births, these trends are shared with all other wealthy industrialized countries.

Women began to join the paid labour force in large numbers in the second half of the century. In 1901, only 14.4 per cent of women were in the paid labour force; by 2003, 61.6 per cent were (Wilson, 1991; Statistics Canada, 2003a). Some of this change reflected ideas from the women's movement, especially the restlessness of the traditional home-bound housewife that Betty Friedan described as 'the problem that has no name' (Friedan, 1963: 32). However, much of it was also related to rising costs of living and the inability of families to economize through intensifying domestic work, as had been possible in earlier decades. The family wage was less and less accessible in the second half of the century. By the 1990s, even mothers of young children were more apt to be in the labour force than not. As well, the industrial economy continued to develop and the demand for women to fill typical female jobs, in services, sales, and clerical work, burgeoned (Connelly, 1978). Balancing employment and family responsibilities has become a problem for Canada's two-breadwinner families of the twenty-first century.

As the economic family has changed, so have marriage practices. Divorce has become socially acceptable and common. The stress put on the ideal of companionate marriage once people began to live longer is one factor cited by family sociologists. The ability of some women to survive economically on their own without finding a male breadwinner is another (ibid.). Cohabitation is now common and relatively socially acceptable. For most Canadians, cohabitation is still a prelude to marriage, but LeBourdais and Lapierre-Adamcyk (2004) argue that it is now a substitute for marriage in the province of Quebec. Most Canadians continue to live in family-based households, but they are, as noted earlier, 'creative and inventive about the way they create kinship networks' (Lancaster, 2003).

Conclusion

The information presented here comes from the study of anthropology and history. Both of these disciplines have different techniques for gathering information and distinctive ways of thinking about it. What both of these disciplines show is that kinship is a central method by which people organize themselves everywhere and family life adapts to changes in cultural, demographic, and economic contexts.

This chapter has emphasized one theoretical perspective, usually called political economy. Families are organized to meet the economic needs of their members and changing economic structures require changing family structures. Scholars with different theoretical perspectives might pay attention to somewhat different aspects of family life and offer a somewhat different explanation for why families change.

Family life is experienced at an intimate level; it is not surprising that many people assume that their own experiences of family life are natural and inevitable rather than cultural. Anthropology shows that kinship is an organizational tool, but what kinship means varies considerably from culture to culture. Family relationships among the Nuer felt as inevitable to a Nuer as Canadian family life does to a Canadian.

Family life in Canada has gone through a number of changes in the twentieth century. Many North Americans find these changes disturbing and mistakenly assume that family life in some distant past was the way 'real' family life is supposed to be. What we can assume on the basis of what anthropologists and historians have shown is that family life is always changing and adapting and will continue to do so. In a sense, every Canadian family is a 'new' Canadian family.

Study Questions

1. Do you think that you might have misunderstandings about what family life was like in the past? What are they? Why do you think you acquired these beliefs?
2. Marriage is an elusive concept. Fewer and fewer Canadians marry. Do you think marriage will continue to exist or not? Why?
3. In what ways is kinship still important in your life? Try to be specific. Compare and contrast with other students' experiences.
4. What does the political economy perspective leave out of the study of family life?

Glossary

Age set A group formed by members of the same age cohort, who move through life stages together. An age set may have a name, may hold meetings, and may have specific social responsibilities to the wider society.

Companionate marriage A marital relationship emphasizing the close companionship of husband and wife. This ideal is usually thought of as becoming widespread in the later nineteenth century in industrializing countries.

Ethnocentrism The assumption that one's own cultural patterns are the only appropriate way to behave.

Factory Acts Legislation passed in the 1880s to restrict the use of female and child labour in Canadian factories.

Family strategy Decision-makers within a family unit may allocate different economic and social roles to family members in order to allow the family unit to survive.

Family wage A wage that is large enough to allow a man to support a wife and children. A family wage became a social ideal in Canada at the end of the nineteenth century, but the poorest Canadian families were never able to achieve it and had to rely on other family members earning wages as well.

Nuclear family A type of family consisting of a mother and father and their children.

Patrilineality A form of organizing people into kinship groups based on common descent from a male ancestor.

Separate spheres The idea that men and women are inherently designed to occupy separate areas of social life. Men make decisions in public—in economic and political life—while women focus their attention on private family life.

Tribes and chiefdoms Societies with populations in the thousands and many local communities but lacking centralized government.

Further Readings

Bradbury, Bettina. 1993. *Working Families: Age, Gender, and Daily Survival in Industrializing Montreal*. Toronto: McClelland & Stewart. Bradbury reconstructs the lives of working-class families in nineteenth-century Montreal. She shows how work varied with gender and age and how women without spouses eked out a living.

Evans-Pritchard, E.E. 1951. *Kinship and Marriage among the Nuer*. Oxford: Clarendon Press. Based on the author's long-time fieldwork, this is a classic anthropological study of kinship and marriage in a patrilineal tribal society.

Gillis, John. 1996. *A World of Their Own Making: Myth, Ritual, and the Quest for Family Values*. Cambridge, Mass.: Harvard University Press. Gillis emphasizes the mythical nature of beliefs that contemporary North Americans have about family life in the past and makes the claim that family rituals are a product of the changes in family life brought about by industrialization

Nanda, Serena. 2000. *Gender Diversity: Crosscultural Variations*. Prospect Heights, Ill.: Waveland Press. Nanda provides an overview of many cultures that recognize more than two gender categories.

Ward Peter. 1990. *Courtship, Love, and Marriage in Nineteenth-Century English Canada*. Montreal and Kingston: McGill-Queen's University Press. Primarily through analysis of love letters, Ward documents the evolution of companionate marriage among the middle and upper classes of English Canada in the nineteenth century.

Websites

www.umanitoba.ca/faculties/arts/anthropology/tutor/index.html
Brian Schwimmer of the University of Manitoba has provided this Kinship Tutorial, a comprehensive guide to traditional kinship systems. This site includes a close look at Ju/'hoansi kinship.

http://genealogy.allinfoabout.com/countries/canada.html
Many Canadians enjoy researching their own family history. The Canadian Family History Research Primer is a guide to getting started.

http://collections.ic.gc.ca/blackloyalists/blhs/genealogy.htm
Every Canadian ethnic group has its own distinctive history. Black Loyalists: Our History, Our People is a look at African-Canadian experiences.

http://web.uvic.ca/hrd/cfp/
A group of Canadian family historians has organized as the Canadian Families Project to develop reliable historical research on family life in Canada using Canadian census data.

www.watchoutforchildren.org/html/maternal_feminism.html
The Motherhood Project looks at the continuing influence of maternal feminism in North American society.

References

Adams, Tracy. 2001. 'Women, men, and the family in Medieval England', in Fox (2001).

Bornemann, John, and Laurie Kain Hart. 2004. 'An elastic institution', *Washington Post*, 14 Apr. 2004.

Bradbury, Bettina, ed. 1992. *Canadian Family History: Selected Readings*. Toronto: Copp Clark.

———. 1993. *Working Families: Age, Gender, and Daily Survival in Industrializing Montreal*. Toronto: McClelland & Stewart.

———. 2001. 'Social, economic, and cultural origins of contemporary families', in Maureen Baker, ed., *Families: Changing Trends in Canada*, 4th edn. Toronto: McGraw-Hill Ryerson.

Bullen, John. 1986. 'Hidden workers: Child labour and the family economy in late nineteenth century urban Ontario', *Labour/Le Travail* 18: 163–87.

Burch, Ernest. 1968. 'Marriage and divorce among the North Alaskan Eskimo', in Paul Bohannon, ed., *Divorce and After*. Garden City, NY: Anchor Books.

Chambers, Lori. 1997. *Married Women and Property Law in Victorian Ontario*. Toronto: University of Toronto Press.

Cohen, Marjorie Griffen. 1988. *Women's Work, Markets and Economic Development in Nineteenth-Century Ontario*. Toronto: University of Toronto Press.

Connelly, Patricia. 1978. *Last Hired, First Fired: Women and the Canadian Work Force*. Toronto: Women's Press.

Ember, Carol, and Melvin Ember. 2004. *Cultural Anthropology*, 11th edn. New York: Prentice-Hall.

Evans-Pritchard, E.E. 1951. *Kinship and Marriage among the Nuer*. Oxford: Clarendon Press.

Fernea, Elizabeth Warnock. 1969. *Guests of the Sheik: An Ethnography of an Iraqi Village*. New York: Anchor Books.

Fox, Bonnie, ed. 2001. *Family Patterns, Gender Relations*, 2nd edn. Toronto: Oxford University Press.

Friedan, Betty. 1963. *The Feminine Mystique*. New York: Norton.

Gaffield, Chad. 1992. 'Canadian families in cultural context: Hypotheses from the mid-nineteenth century', in Bradbury (1992).

Gillis, John. 1996. *A World of Their Own Making: Myth, Ritual, and the Quest for Family Values*. Cambridge, Mass.: Harvard University Press.

Goode, William. 1959. 'The theoretical importance of love', *American Sociological Review* 24: 811–23.

Goody, Jack. 1976. *Production and Reproduction: A Comparative Study of the Domestic Domain*. New York: Cambridge University Press.

Herdt, Gilbert. 1996. *Third Sex: Crosscultural Variations*. Prospect Heights, Ill.: Waveland Press.

Howell, Nancy. 2001. 'Ethnic families', in Maureen Baker, ed., *Families: Changing Trends in Canada*, 4th edn. Toronto: McGraw-Hill Ryerson.

Kluckhohn, Clyde, and Dorothea Leighton. 1962. *The Navaho*. New York: Doubleday.

Knowles, Valerie. 1992. *Stranger at Our Gates: Canadian Immigration and Immigration Policy*. Toronto: Dundurn Press.

Lancaster, Roger. 2003. *The Trouble with Nature: Sex in Science and Popular Culture*. Berkeley, Calif.: University Press Books.

Landry, Yves. 1992. 'Gender imbalances, les filles du roi, and choice of spouse in New France', in Bradbury (1992).

LeBourdais, Celine, and Evelyne Lapierre-Adamcyk. 2004. 'Changes in conjugal life in Canada: Is cohabitation progressively replacing marriage?', *Journal of Marriage and Family* 66: 929–42.

Library of Congress. 2004. *America Singing: Nineteenth-Century Song Sheets*. At: <http://lcweb2.loc.gov/ammem/amsshtml/>; accessed 13 Dec. 2004.

Lindholm, Charles. 1998. 'Love and structure', *Theory, Culture, and Society* 15: 243–63.

M. 1879. 'The Woman Question', *Rose-Belford's Canadian Monthly and National Review* 3, 2: 568–79.

Margolis, Maxine. 2001. 'Putting mothers on the pedestal', in Fox (2001).

Miller, Barbara, Penny Van Esterik, John Van Esterik. 2001. *Cultural Anthropology*, Canadian edn. Toronto: Allyn and Bacon.

Nanda, Serena. 2000. *Gender Diversity: Crosscultural Variations*. Prospect Heights, Ill.: Waveland Press.

Parker, Mrs Dr. 1890. 'Woman in nation-building', in Rev. B.F. Austin, ed., *Woman: Her Character, Culture, and Calling*. Brantford, Ont.: n.p.

Robbins, Richard. 1993. *Cultural Anthropology: A Problem-Based Approach*. Itasca, NY: Peacock.

Roberts, Wayne. 1979. '"Rocking the cradle for the world": The new woman and maternal feminism, Toronto, 1877–1914', in Linda Kealey, ed., *A Not Unreasonable Claim: Women and Reform in Canada, 1880s–1920s*. Toronto: Women's Press.

Royal Commission to Inquire into Industrial Disputes in the Cotton Factories of the Province of Quebec. 1909. *Report*. Canada, *Sessional Paper*, No. 39.

Sampson, Margaret. 1977. 'The woe that was in marriage: Some recent work on the history of women, marriage and the family in early modern England and Europe', *Historical Journal* 40, 3: 811–23.

Spiro, Melvin. 1954. 'Is the nuclear family universal?', *American Anthropologist* 56: 839–46.

Statistics Canada. 2003a. *Labour Force, Employed and Unemployed, Numbers and Rates, by Provinces*. At: <www.statcan.ca/english/Pgdb/labor07a.htm>; accessed 17 Dec. 2004.

———. 2003b. *Canada's Ethno-cultural Portrait: The Changing Mosaic*. At: <www12.statcan.ca/english/census01/products/analytic/companion/etoimm/canada.cfm>; accessed 23 Feb. 2005.

Ursel, Jane. 1988. 'The state and the maintenance of patriarchy: A case study of family, labour, and welfare legislation in Canada', in Arlene Tigar McLaren, ed., *Gender and Society: Creating a Canadian Women's Sociology*. Toronto: Copp Clark.

Van Kirk, Sylvia. 1992. '"The custom of the country": An examination of fur trade marriage practices', in Bradbury (1992).

Ward, Martha. 1999. *A World Full of Women*, 2nd edn. Boston: Allyn and Bacon.

Ward, W. Peter. 1990. *Courtship, Love, and Marriage in Nineteenth-Century English Canada*. Montreal and Kingston: McGill-Queen's University Press.

Whiting, Beatrice, and John W.M. Whiting. 1975. *Children of Six Cultures: A Psycho-Cultural Analysis*. Cambridge, Mass.: Harvard University Press.

Wilson, Catharine Anne. 1998. 'Tenancy as a family strategy in mid-nineteenth century Ontario', *Journal of Social History* 31, 4: 875–96.

Wilson, S.J. 1991. *Women, Families, and Work*. Toronto: McGraw-Hill.

Wolf, A.P. 1993. 'Westermarck redivivus', *Annual Review of Anthropology* 22: 157–75.

Part II   The Life Course

Family life changes over time as people have new experiences, such as the birth of a child, and as they undergo the changes associated with aging. Of course, not everyone experiences the same changes. Some people have children whereas others do not; some people who get married later get divorced, whereas other married couples remain together; and some people live long into old age while others die young. The chapters in Part II, therefore, do not pretend that everyone follows a predictable life cycle. Rather, the contributors here set out some of the common changes that occur in family life and some of the stages of the life course, in order to give a sense of how family experiences may differ at different times of life.

In Chapter 3, Rachel Ariss focuses on how people form relationships, some of which result in marriage. This chapter discusses theories and ideologies of intimacy; the role of romance; how people meet and establish intimate relations, both heterosexual and same-sex; gender roles and socio-cultural variations in dating practice; and the relationship between intimacy and commitment. Ariss also examines how new families are sometimes formed through marriage and sometimes they are formed through people simply moving in together, that is, cohabiting. The number of people cohabiting has increased in Canada in recent years, and Ariss therefore pays special attention to this pattern. Another trend described here has been for people who are divorced to form new families through remarriage. Where there are children involved, the children of both partners may be brought into the marriage to form blended families.

Gillian Ranson continues the theme of children in families in Chapter 4, which starts with a discussion of the ideological context of parenting. Ranson traces the social and historical origins of the ideologies of motherhood and fatherhood that are most influential in contemporary Canadian society, including the ideology of 'intensive mothering', and explores beliefs about parenting, which are closely connected to views about the needs of children. A more concrete examination of parenting in practice includes a look at how it is shaped by class differences, by parents' access to financial, educational, and other resources, and by family form, such as stepfamilies and same-sex couples with children. From an examination of parents and parenting practices, Ranson looks more closely at some of the different ways Canadian children experience childhood. The chapter concludes with a brief consideration of public policy and the future of child-rearing in Canada.

In Chapter 5, Craig McKie studies how families fragment through separation or divorce, some of them becoming lone-parent families, which often reformulate themselves within the context of a new marital union. The chapter begins by reviewing the legal context for divorce and presents statistics on divorce. However, McKie notes that these statistics can be misleading as a picture of relationship dissolution in contemporary Canada because many cohabiting relationships end without legal or statistical consequences. The economic and social effects of divorce and separation have been the subject of great interest and are also discussed here. McKie concludes that accounts of post-separation hardships must be weighed against the real risks of physical and emotional trauma in relationships that are full of conflict, which are greatly diminished by separation. Separation is not necessarily the end of family life, however. The chapter considers how separation and divorce are often followed by the formation of new families, either lone-parent families or families that are reconstituted through new relationships, and closes with a discussion of recent developments in divorce and family law.

Two stages of the life course—middle age and old age—are considered in Chapters 6 and 7. Karen Kobayashi, in Chapter 6, focuses on the transitions that mark middle age (e.g., the 'empty nest', care-giving) and are triggered by the occurrence of life events in families (e.g., adult children leaving home, care for aging parents). Home-leaving by adult children, Kobayashi notes, has been taking longer in recent years, and in many instances adult children return to their natal home after having left. Support for elderly parents is becoming a significant issue in Canada as a result of population aging. Of course, the experience of such life events as taking care of elderly parents varies according to individuals' situations, and these can be quite various. The chapter therefore examines some of the diversity of mid-life families by describing patterns of separation and divorce, remarriage, same-sex relationships, and childlessness. The chapter concludes with a discussion of the relationship between mid-life families and social policy.

Finally, in Chapter 7, Lori Campbell and Michael Carroll consider family life in old age. The authors begin by looking at various marital statuses that older adults occupy, including marriage, widowhood, divorce, and lifelong singlehood. They then look at two common experiences of older people—retirement, and recreation and leisure—with a special focus on how these are affected by family relationships. For example, there is some evidence that married couples tend to retire at the same time. Campbell and Carroll emphasize the importance of intergenerational exchange, that is, the exchange of support between older and younger generations. This support flows both ways, but over the life course older people provide significantly more support to their children and grandchildren than they receive, including grandparenting, financial assistance, and inheritance. Younger family members, on the other hand, often provide caregiving support to older family members. To round out the picture of family caregiving, the authors also examine spousal care. The chapter closes by considering a dark side that exists in some families—the abuse of older people.

CHAPTER 3

Intimacy, Commitment, and Family Formation

Rachel Ariss

Learning Objectives

- To learn that there are various theories of the role of intimacy in Western culture.
- To discover that 'dating' is a Western socio-cultural phenomenon.
- To understand why cohabitation is increasing and becoming more acceptable in Canada.
- To recognize that legal structures of marriage have historically excluded some Canadians based on ethnicity, 'Indian status', and sexual orientation.
- To understand that legal recognition of same-sex marriage is part of a recent societal approach to marriage as social acceptance of a committed relationship.
- To identify and understand many diverse pathways to family intimacy.

Introduction

Family formation is a significant topic within the sociology of the family. What is a 'new' family? Why and how do people create them? What individual factors and social structures encourage or discourage people from marrying or having children? How do ways of forming families vary across cultures and across time?

Families are formed in many different ways. Some people see moving in together as becoming a family. Others may not consider that a new family has formed until a first child is born to a married couple. Adults may bring children and former in-laws, as well as their own siblings and parents, into blended family formations. Finally, some may see new births as extensions of ancestral families—the idea of 'newness' has little significance in this understanding of 'family'.

In Canada, as in most Western societies, there is a social expectation that emotional and sexual intimacy between a couple and their commitment to caring for each other is a central aspect of new family formation (Langford, 1999: xi). But before we can ask questions about the roles that intimacy and commitment might play in family formation, we have to recognize that there are broad and diverse understandings of these concepts among individuals and within and across cultures, societies, and time. For some people, a commitment such as marriage cannot even be contemplated without first developing emotional and sexual intimacy. For others, emotional intimacy is expected to grow out of a formal commitment to each other through marriage. Some people have significant emotional and time commitments to children while they simultaneously are developing intimacy with a new partner. Finally, living together without the social expectations built into marriage may be seen as the best way to experience continued emotional closeness. This chapter recognizes the diversity of individual experience and cultural norms surrounding intimacy, commitment, and family formation. There are, however, patterns to be found through studying family formation, such as increasing rates of cohabitation, which allow us to understand commonality of experience.

This chapter discusses theories and ideologies of intimacy; the role of romance; how people meet and establish intimate relations, both heterosexual and same-sex; gender roles and socio-cultural variations in dating practice; dating violence; and the relationships between intimacy and commitment.

A commitment of some sort to care seems to be necessary before people think of each other as family members. Various ways of expressing commitment, ranging from living together to formal marriage to becoming parents, and the social norms and legalities surrounding these family commitments will be discussed.

Defining 'family formation' depends, in part, on defining family. This chapter will not focus on any single definitive point at which a family forms, but rather, on the combined elements of commitment and social structures that shape a group of people into a family.

Intimacy: Meanings and Theories

What do we mean when we talk about intimacy? The word 'intimate' is used to describe close emotional relationships, such as those between friends or siblings, as well as sexual relationships that may or may not include emotional closeness (Cheal, 1991: 139). The experience of intimacy, whether emotional or sexual or both, is subjective: intimacy is felt primarily between two people or among a small group of people. Because intimacy is something people experience individually, there will be many understandings of what 'real' intimacy is, and many different expressions of what people desire in 'intimate' relationships.

Recently, there has much discussion of intimacy in sociology centred on the idea of the 'pure relationship' as developed by British sociologist Anthony Giddens. The **pure relationship** is 'entered into for its own sake, what can be derived by each person from a sustained association with another; and which is continued only in so far as it is thought by both parties to deliver enough satisfaction for each individual to remain in it' (Giddens, 1992: 58). The pure relationship is based in the search for self-development and identity. It becomes possible in an age of 'plastic sexuality' where sexual activity can be separated from reproduction (ibid., 2). The pure relationship encourages 'confluent love', which is based in equality of emotional exchange—only where both

partners are prepared to be open with and vulnerable to each other will love grow (ibid., 62). Negotiation, rather than the socio-cultural institution per se, such as marriage, is key to the continuation of pure relationships (ibid., 190). Giddens derives his theory in part from the equality he saw in studies of lesbian relationships. Giddens believes that pure relationships and confluent love can be developed within both same-sex and heterosexual relationships, although he briefly states that this change in heterosexual relationships requires adjusting the power imbalance between the sexes, which has been so much a part of traditional romantic notions of love (ibid., 62).

The pure relationship centralizes intimacy for both partners and is detached from the institutionalized, gender-bound aspects of both romantic love and companionate marriage as they developed through the late 1800s to mid-1900s. Marriage became understood during that time as more than an economic partnership; it was an institution of companionship—if not quite intimacy—and gender complementarity (Bittman and Pixley, 1997: 51–2). The inward-looking, abstracted nature of the pure relationship is transformative in that it is seen as freeing relationships from social (particularly gender-based) conventions. Women's changing economic and social positions, and the erosion of the sexual double standard for women, Giddens argues, both encourage and are supported by the development of the 'pure relationship'.

Giddens's ideas about the role of intimacy in society have been both accepted and critiqued. Recent qualitative studies confirm the significance of 'equality' for those in intimate same-sex relationships, particularly as opposed to institutionalized (i.e., married) heterosexual relationships (Weeks et al., 1999: 113, 118–19). Respondents' descriptions and valuation of same-sex relationships prompted Weeks to note a connection with the self-development aspects of Giddens's pure relationship: 'Affirmation through involvement in a democratic, egalitarian relationship appears to be the dominant non-heterosexual norm' (ibid.,

114). Weeks et al. argued that the concepts of equality, democracy, and 'mutual trust' are strongly present in same-sex relationships (ibid., 124). Hall used the idea of the 'pure relationship' to develop a hypothesis that couples in egalitarian relationships (married or cohabiting) would desire fewer or no children. Using the 1995 Canadian General Social Survey, Hall did find a tendency for more egalitarian couples to be more uncertain about having children (Hall, 2003: 54, 61). Hughes's study of adults who had experienced divorce as children found that they experienced relationships as contributing to personal growth and expected that most relationships would prove transitory (Hughes: 2005: 74, 77). These adult children of divorce imagined that future families would stretch intimacy outside nuclear family boundaries, with more adults becoming involved in children's lives. Family membership would be fluid and determined 'more by the quality of the relationships of those who consider themselves part of a family' (ibid., 83). Indeed, recent focus on intimate relations as a place of equality, democracy, support, and self-development is acclaimed as a positive social change. And there may be many in agreement with this: the 'pure relationship' and the ideal intimacy it reflects 'generally, accurately describes contemporary *expectations* about intimacy' (Bittman and Pixley, 1997: 70, emphasis added).

Giddens has been criticized for not paying sufficient attention to current power imbalances based on gender in intimate relationships. Some claim he downplays the role of 'public' and 'private' in the construction of intimacy (Jamieson, 1999: 481), and how responsibilities for children affect the pure relationship (Smart and Neal, 1999: 12). Some researchers have suggested that studies showing the inequality in gender-based divisions of household and emotional labour reflect that intimate relations in heterosexual couples have not been transformed (Jamieson, 1999: 484–5; Langford, 1999: 14). The concern is that the celebration of the ideals of equality and democratization carried in the mutual self-disclosure of

intimacy hides the reality of unequal, non-negotiable partnerships. Jamieson brings the everyday world of intimacy into focus, emphasizing that: 'Matters ranging from who last cleaned the toilet to how the insurance claim was spent become means of communicating care or neglect, equality or hierarchy, unity or division. Actions can speak louder than words and perhaps the important words, if men and women are to live together as equals, may be sorting out fair ways to get things done rather than purer forms of mutual self-disclosure' (Jamieson, 1999: 490).

Social expectations of intimacy shape our experiences of it. In the modern, nuclear family, sexual intimacy plays a significant role: 'the sexual life of married couples is assumed to be a litmus test of the health of the marriage' (Bittman and Pixley, 1997: 52; also see Langford, 1999: 3). Conjugal intimacy, despite the prevalence of divorce, is expected to extend to all aspects of the partnership. Beyond conjugal relationships, society expects us to feel close to family members (Cheal, 2002: 37; Pahl and Spencer, 2004: 212–13). Indeed, families are often close—in a British study family members were predominant in personal networks (Cheal, 2002: 36). And we seek intimacy throughout much of our lives, whether within one sexual relationship, in a series of sexual relationships, or within friendships and non-sexual family relationships. Theories of intimacy may seem distant from individual relationship experiences. Ways of thinking about intimacy matter, however, because they frame the questions that sociologists continue to ask about how intimate relations are structured: how they begin and end, and how they are celebrated and condemned.

Getting to Know You: 'Dating'

Emotional closeness and sexual fulfillment are now seen as significant aspects of dating relationships, cohabitation, and marriage. How do such relationships begin?

It all starts with meeting people. While the specifics vary from town to city and province to region, opportunities to make friends and meet potential dating partners are found in schools, sports teams, religious organizations, work, bars, dance clubs, and other places where people engage in shared activities or interests. An American study found that, over time, the majority of women continue to meet their eventual male spouses directly, and that work organizations, dances, and parties are becoming more common meeting places (Whyte, 1990: 32). Personal ads, through traditional print and newer digital media, are commonplace. Matchmaker services are also offered through classified ads and on the Internet (see Box 3.1). The growing availability and use of the Internet, ranging from real-time chat rooms to bulletin board services (Parks and Roberts, 1998; Correll, 1995) to personal ads specifically looking for dates (Phua and Kaufman, 2003a, 2003b), offer new avenues for getting to know people. The youth subculture of 'rave' combines real and virtual

meetings: it relies on electronic communication to publicize and discuss rave events, as well to facilitate individuals' on-line participation in rave parties (Wilson and Jette, 2005: 79).

North America has had a **dating culture** since the early twentieth century (Whyte, 1990: 17). Currently, the dominant dating culture approves and facilitates romantic heterosexual relationships between young people, without assuming that those relationships will lead to marriage or to other long-term commitments (ibid.). In the nineteenth century, socializing between young men and women was supervised by adults and was more definitely seen as a prelude to marriage (ibid.). Dating culture in North America seems to have arisen with increased affluence, longer periods of education, and the increase of youth-focused social activities. As with companionate marriage and the image of the family as private, dating culture seems to be part of modernization and individualism.

Box 3.1 Speed-dating

Speed-dating is a service offered through Internet-based companies. Speed-dating involves signing up and paying for the opportunity to meet people. Single in the City explains that 'When you date with speed, you get to meet the large quantities of people you wouldn't meet in a normal dating night. Dating is a numbers game, the more dates you go on, the more chances of meeting someone. . . . Generally, people who attend Single in the City events have little time to go out and meet people, are sick of the bar scene, or they're just looking for something to do. It's a great experience!' (www.singleinthecity.ca). This organization conducts speed-dating as follows: events are organized at bars or clubs, for groups of 15–25 people in specific age ranges. Participants sit across from each other and 'Every 4 minutes a bell will sound, take a few seconds to indicate yes or no on your match card and move to the next person. This continues to half-time' (www.singleinthecity.ca). Within two days, the name and e-mail address of any matches—where both speed-daters said yes to contact information—will be sent to participants. This kind of service is marketed at 'professionals' through ideas of quantity, efficiency, and the time crunch. As well as using economic terms to sell their services, speed-dating relies on the romantic ideal of 'love at first sight'. No need for long walks on the beach at sunset—you should know within four minutes if this is the person for you.

Recent changes in dating culture appear to reflect more group-focused (rather than pair-focused) outings (ibid., 18; Bibby, 2001: 175). This can be seen in rave culture, which, in contrast to many dance clubs, emphasizes group participation in the rave event, thus decentralizing pair-focused activities (Wilson and Jette, 2005: 78). There is also wider social acceptance of sexual intercourse as part of dating, compared to the pre-war and baby-boom generations (Whyte, 1990: 18).

Most studies of dating or 'courtship' have focused on heterosexual couples (Klinkenberg and Rose, 1994: 23; Whyte, 1990). Several recent studies consider same-sex dating culture (Hatala et al., 1998; Klinkenberg and Rose, 1994), while others specifically compare heterosexual men and gay men in their attitudes towards age and race when looking for partners (Phua and Kaufman, 2003a, 2003b). Although social and legal acceptance of gay and lesbian relationships has certainly increased, there is still social hostility towards same-sex couples (Adam, 2004: 272; Calhoun, 1997). Gay and lesbian youth experience isolation and prejudice, especially in the form of verbal harassment, in high school (Elze, 2003: 226). This occurs at the same time as their heterosexual peers are beginning to 'date' (Bibby, 2004: 11). Gay and lesbian bars have been historically, and continue to be, spaces free of social prejudice where gays and lesbians can look for friendship, community, sex, and dating partners (Correll, 1995: 272).

Some researchers use **script theory** to try to determine the degree of convergence and prevalence of specific expectations of behaviour in social settings: for example, going on a first date. There is a 'public and well-defined cultural script' for heterosexual first dates (Klinkenberg and Rose, 1994: 24), including actions such as organizing a date, preparations, interactions with partner, and ending the date. Gender roles are a significant, convergent aspect in the construction of this dating script, with social expectations of men as the initiators, planning and paying for a date as well as beginning sexual contact. The woman is expected to be a reactor, responding to a request for a date, think-

ing about her appearance, and containing sexual activity (ibid., 2). This reflects women's cultural roles as sexual 'gatekeepers', as well as differences in heterosexual men's and women's expectations around sexual activity and dating. Less than 40 per cent of Canadian female teens, but approximately 70 per cent of male teens, say that sexual intercourse is acceptable after a few dates (Bibby, 2001: 95). These differing expectations of when sex is acceptable are more than just interesting examples of gender-based attitudes towards sex. Such different expectations, feelings of male heterosexual entitlement, and real or deliberate miscommunication may contribute to sexual abuse in dating relationships. A study conducted at the University of Alberta in 1992 found that of women reporting an unwanted sexual experience, 44 per cent said that the perpetrator was a 'romantic acquaintance' and for 18 per cent it was a 'casual or first date' (as cited in DeKesedery and Kelly, 1993: 141).

According to Klinkenberg and Rose, there are several points of convergence on a first date script that are common to same-sex (at least the white, well-educated, middle-class gays and lesbians in this study) and heterosexual couples (who were younger than the gays and lesbian studied). First dates are expected to conform to a culturally strong script. There are some gender differences between gay first dates and lesbian first dates, with gay men more likely to engage in sexual activity and lesbians focusing on emotional connections. This reflects gendered social constructions of women and men. But within lesbian and gay pairs, heterosexual division into 'initiator' and 'reactor' were not played out—planning a date, encouraging conversation, and initiating sexual contact were conducted by both dating partners (Klinkenberg and Rose, 1994: 33).

Not all cultural groups approve of 'dating culture'. Two recent studies of young South Asian women living in Canada and the US found that dating was neither approved of nor allowed by most parents (Zaidi and Shuraydi, 2002: 506; Talbani and Hasanali, 2000: 620). Dating is seen as a possible threat to family honour, which often rests in women's chastity (Zaidi and Shuraydi, 2002: 496; also see Talbani and Hasanali, 2000). Yet, young men were allowed to date (Zaidi and Shuraydi, 2002: 507; Talbani and Hasanali 2000: 620). Most young Pakistani Muslim women living in Canada and the US interviewed in one study, however, wanted a chance to get to know a prospective husband prior to marriage (Zaidi and Shuraydi, 2002: 506)—and a few had dated young men (ibid., 500–2).

Although it is not part of socio-cultural expectations of a date, the experience of abuse in heterosexual dating relationships is all too common in Canada. Same-sex domestic violence is severely under-reported, and this likely applies to same-sex dating abuse as well. DeKesedery and Kelly, in a random sample study of university and college students, found that, since leaving high school, 45 per cent of women said they had been sexually assaulted, and 19 per cent of men said they had abused a woman in this way. The most common experience of sexual assault for women was engaging in unwanted sexual activity 'because you were overwhelmed by a man's continual arguments and pressure' (DeKesedery and Kelly, 1993: 148–50). In addition, 35 per cent of women report being physically assaulted since leaving high school (ibid., 152). Psychological abuse, ranging from insults to accusations of flirting to threats of violence, was very prevalent, with over 80 per cent of men engaging in this type of abuse (ibid., 153). Other research has shown a correlation between psychological abuse and later physical violence in marriage (ibid., 147).

Personal Ads and Electronic Communication

Personal advertising to meet people is found both in traditional print sources, such as daily newspapers, and on Internet sites. Sociologists find personal ads interesting for several reasons: advertisers are not responding to a survey about expectations in relationships, rather, they are actually looking for a partner, and sociologists can directly analyze any patterns in the ads (Hatala et al., 1998: 269). The dating and sexual values of a particular time period can be deduced from these ads and comparisons can be made across time (ibid.).

Such advertising may be attractive to users for several reasons: increased working hours across North America may make it difficult to find social time; the Internet makes ad use fast and convenient; ads allow both advertiser and respondent to 'pre-screen' dates, and using ads avoids facing rejection in person (ibid.; Phua and Kaufman, 2003a: 981). At the same time, advertisers have to balance being direct about what they want—friendship, sex, romance, a longer-term commitment, marriage—while avoiding risks (Phua and Kaufman, 2003a: 981).

Not surprisingly, most analyses of personal advertising have focused on heterosexual dating. **Social exchange theory** has been the frame for several heterosexual and same-sex personal ad studies from the 1970s into the twenty-first century, as well as comparisons between them (Hatala et al., 1998: 269; Phua and Kaufman, 2003a: 982). Social exchange theory posits that people commodify social characteristics—including physical attractiveness, youth, wealth, and education—and then offer their best traits in trade for traits they see as socially desirable (Phua and Kaufman, 2003a: 982–3). For example, Hatala et al. found that gay men who advertised their HIV negative status were more likely than those who advertised being HIV positive to ask for physical attractiveness, specific age ranges, a photo, and a specific type of relationship (1998: 274). It appeared that being HIV negative reflected a sense of being able to choose among a wider range of possible partners.

Much research on personal ads has found that traits appropriate to stereotypical gender roles are offered and sought by heterosexual personal advertisers. Heterosexual men are more likely to advertise for physical attractiveness and youth in women, while offering financial security, height, and status (ibid., 269: Phua and Kaufman, 2003a: 982). An ad placed by an attractive woman in a lower socio-economic bracket gains more responses than an ad placed by an 'average-looking professional woman' (Phua and Kaufman, 2003a: 982). In societies that base their social hierarchies at least partly on race, such as the US and Canada, race as well as ethnicity is likely to become a commodified social trait. Phua and Kaufman (2003a, 2003b) have engaged in a series of analyses of race, ethnicity, and age in Internet personal ads placed by gay and heterosexual men. Their finding that black men were most likely overall to mention a racial preference or, specifically, no preference supports their theory that those who have experienced racism in society are more likely to be specific about race or mention that race is 'not important' (2003a: 985, 989, 991). They also point out, however, that specific requests about race were often couched in stereotypical racialized sexual images, suggesting links between some specific requests for race and racism in personal ads (ibid., 992).

Before widespread use of the Internet, most sociologists assumed that intimacy required face-to-face communication, and some found that computer-based communication was less likely to encourage personal relationships (Parks and Roberts, 1998: 519–20). Communication clues such as facial expression and tone of voice are absent from screen-based communication, prompting one researcher to note that it 'requires people to be very creative in conversing' (Correll, 1995: 275–6). People do, however, develop both 'romantic' and friendship relationships through computer use (Parks and Roberts, 1998; Correll, 1995).

Currently, several services are offered through the Internet for people to meet others by describing themselves, who they want to meet, and what kind of a relationship they prefer. Subscribers can meet anonymously on-line, through internal e-mail, instant messaging, and even instant messaging with video. Contact information is provided by the service if people mutually request it. The availability of Internet services to meet people on-line and in person reflects the work-focused, fast pace of urban, middle-class culture.

People develop on-line relationships for a variety of reasons. Many of the participants in the elec-

tronic Lesbian Café were from smaller towns or centres that did not have lesbian community structures, like bars or bookstores, to serve as meeting places (Correll, 1995: 282). Parks and Robert (1998: 531) suggest that the prevalence of cross-sex relationships on-line shows that electronic communication may 'reduce the perception of risk associated with cross-sex relationships in the physical world (e.g., unwanted physical sexual advances and social censure)'. People tend to move slowly from on-line to face-to-face meetings (ibid., 533). For cultural groups that disapprove of North American dating culture, the Internet may allow people to meet without directly violating cultural norms. A study of young Pakistani Muslim women living in North America noted that some used chat lines to meet people (Zaidi and Shuraydi, 2002: 500, 503), presumably including young men.

Some researchers suggest that even though dating is less directly focused on marriage than it was in the nineteenth century, 'the primary goal of this activity—to find a suitable mate—has not changed, although the rules about what one may do along the way have clearly been modified' (Whyte, 1990: 40). Supporting this assumption are studies that conceive of 'dating' relationships in terms of satisfaction, commitment, and stability, which is further defined as 'relationship happiness and success' (Sprecher, 2001: 600). Of the five 'Success Stories' featured on the Lavalife website the week of 13 December 2004, three explained that they had married or were engaged to a person they met through Lavalife (www.lavalife.com). Another study found that several of those living in blended families (families where at least one partner brings children to the partnership) saw the 'new' family as beginning sometime during the dating relationship between the parental couple (Braithwaite et al., 2001: 243). In contrast, Giddens's ideas of the 'pure relationship' do not include commitment and stability as indicators of success; rather, commitment reflects current satisfaction. For young adults 'having relationships' is of much more concern than getting married (Cheal, 2002: 33–4). For Canadian teens, noticeably fewer are significantly concerned about not having a boyfriend or girlfriend in 2001 compared to 1992 (Bibby, 2001: 180). Establishing intimacy, however, is often a significant part of committing to long-term relationships, such as cohabitation or marriage, and this chapter now turns to these.

Intimacy and Commitment

What does commitment mean? And how is it related to intimacy? For a majority of Canadians, marriage is important because it signifies commitment—ideally, for a lifetime (Bibby, 2004: 28, 30). A recent discussion on CBC radio's *The Current* about same-sex marriage introduced the topic by saying that people marry because they feel it is 'the ultimate commitment'. The cultural association between marriage and commitment is strong, even though Canadians are well aware of the rising divorce rate and increase in cohabitation. Many researchers comment that the meaning of 'marriage' changes and is constructed in a variety of ways according to social, cultural, religious, and legal perspectives (Langford, 1999: 3; Holland, 2000: 125; Auchmuty, 2004; Eichler, 1997; also see *Halpern v. Canada*). But before we discuss marriage, let's think about what commitment might mean.

Commitment to people who may or may not become part of one's family can be understood in various ways. Commitment to a conjugal partner can be expressed privately, simply by living together and sharing each other's lives, as well as publicly, through wedding ceremonies, some of which are large and elaborate. Some commitments are legally recognized and encouraged—governments recognize heterosexual marriage commitments people have made to each other through recognizing the rights of spouses to make medical decisions for each other, as well as their right to financial support from each other. Other commitments, such as a same-sex partner's commitment to the other's biological child, have been legally ignored and overtly discouraged until very recently. Some commitments, such as the relationship between a step-parent and his or her partner's biological child, are legally ambiguous (Jones, 2003: 231). Small reciprocal acts of kindness over several years may lead to commitment between neighbours who may not see each other as 'family', but who help each other in practical ways that are often associated with family caring, responsibility, and commitment.

Nuclear families are assumed to be a place of commitment, as much as they are assumed to be a place of intimacy, for both the conjugal couple and, especially, any children. But nuclear families are not the only place where commitment is found. Blended families often acknowledge and accom-

Box 3.2 Friendship

Is friendship an expression of intimacy and commitment? What are **friends**? According to Pahl and Spencer, friendship has been understudied in sociology (2004: 203). They studied personal communities in Britain to determine levels of commitment in friendship and what roles friends played in individual lives. They found that some people strongly distinguished between family and friendship roles, while others saw them as suffused or blurred. Pahl and Spencer concluded in their study that 'people are often embedded in a highly complex set of relationships within and between generations' (ibid., 218). The connections between family, intimacy, care, and commitment are likely more complex individually than has been accounted for.

modate children's 'old' family relationships, while developing a strong sense of solidarity within the 'new' family (Braithwaite, 2001: 230–3). 'Families of choice' are 'flexible but often strong networks' of relationships that include friends, lovers, former lovers, and perhaps members of a family of origin, emphasized as an important part of gay and lesbian culture (Weeks et al., 1999: 111–12). In Weeks et al.'s study, commitment meant 'a willingness to work at difficulties', which implies a constant process of mutual negotiation; and a responsibility to care, and 'emotional labour' (ibid., 124). Most of the respondents for the Weeks et al. study avoided the connection between commitment and concepts of duty, explaining that their commitments were 'not dependent on any institutional backing' (ibid., 124).

In some cultures, members of the extended family are held to higher standards of commitment than is usually expected in mainstream society. Many First Nations cultures understand raising and caring for children as an obligation that stretches beyond parents. Grandparents, aunts, and uncles are expected to participate in child-rearing to an extent that dominant North American society sees as reserved for parents (Castellano, 2002: 12; Ing, 1991: 81).

Social expectations, ideals, and definitive social structures (like religion and law) affect and confound individuals' conduct in committed relationships. The rest of this chapter will discuss socio-cultural expectations and patterns in different forms of commitment.

Family Formation, Social Structures, and Commitment

How do families form? In this section, we will think about families forming as commitment develops, is expressed, and is socially recognized.

About 36 per cent of Canadians under age 35 understand a cohabiting couple with no children as a family (Bibby, 2004: 1). **Cohabitation** (also known as **common-law** or **consensual unions**) has become a common experience for younger Canadians over the last 25 years. Only approximately 6 per cent of couples cohabited in 1981 (Turcotte and Goldscheider, 1998: 146); by 2001, 16 per cent of all Canadian couples were cohabiting (Ambert, 2005b: 7). This recent increase in cohabitation rates is 'most likely unprecedented in any historical period in Canada' (Wu, 2000: 42). The numbers of cohabitants vary widely with region: 22 per cent of Quebec adults are currently cohabiting, while only 4 per cent of adults in the Atlantic provinces cohabit (Bibby, 2004: 19). About 40 per cent of Canadians say that 'they have lived with a non-marital sexual partner' (ibid., 20). Cohabitation has also increased significantly in the US (Forste, 2002: 589) and in Europe during the same time period (Blossfeld and Mills, 2001: 419, 423).

But those are just the numbers. This increase represents a dramatic cultural shift in attitudes towards and experiences of forming couples: 'While the decision to cohabit may not be as difficult to make as the decision to marry, "moving in together" is an important step in development of coupling relationships: it entails the sharing of a common residence, usually a pooling of financial resources, and generally involves the obligation of exclusive sexual intimacy' (Wu, 2000: 72). Living with a heterosexual partner is becoming more socially acceptable—approximately half of Canadians accept and approve of heterosexual cohabitation (Bibby, 2004: 16). Younger people and those in Quebec express the highest rates of approval (Wu, 2000: 57–8). Cohabiting is understood by many people, especially those under 35, as making for a better marriage although the statistics do not support that belief. Almost half of Canadians think that cohabitation does not involve sexual fidelity to the same extent as marriage; and almost two-thirds believe that cohabitation has a lesser level of commitment than marriage. But there are notable differences here between young men and young women: young women are more likely to see cohabitation as a substitute for marriage; and young men are more likely to feel that cohabitation involves less sexual fidelity than marriage (Bibby, 2004: 19).

Why do people choose cohabitation rather than marriage? About two-thirds of cohabiting Canadians say they see no need to marry (ibid., 32). Not seeing a need to marry appears to be related to having little religious involvement (ibid., 27; Wu, 2000: 61). In Quebec, where cohabitation appears to be an alternative to marriage, people feel less social and financial pressure to marry (Bibby, 2004: 28).

Other studies have posited that women's changing roles and attitudes affect decisions to cohabit. One found that women and men with egalitarian attitudes were more likely to cohabit (Kaufman, 2000: 130), while Kaufman's own study found that egalitarian men were more likely to cohabit. Education appears not to have an effect on which women choose cohabitation (Wu, 2000: 80; Turcotte and Goldscheider, 1998: 158). Some researchers have argued that women's increasing ability to earn their own living has made it less necessary for them to enter into undesirable marriages or cohabitation. On the other hand, women's workforce participation may make marriage more feasible as both partners contribute to earnings (Turcotte and Goldscheider, 1998: 148). Wu's Canadian study found that employment appeared to coincide with women choosing to cohabit (2000: 79), and Wu argues that employment may make women feel freer to choose cohabitation instead of marriage. On the other hand, newspaper columnist Leah McLaren suggests that young working women may be less willing to cohabit with their boyfriends because it involves giving up their independence simply for convenience and lower living costs (McLaren, 2003: F8).

Some studies have found that women who start their first unions in a cohabiting situation are twice as likely to separate as those who began with marriage (Statistics Canada, 2002: 5). But in Quebec, where cohabitation as both a first and a lifelong union is more common, it is more stable than in the rest of Canada (ibid., 4, 6).

Why is Quebec so different from the rest of Canada in beliefs about and rates of cohabitation? Statistically, cohabiting became more common at an earlier time period in Quebec than in the rest of the country (ibid., 4), so it has perhaps become more culturally acceptable, more 'normal', and perhaps viewed more like marriage. This makes sense when we consider the stability of first cohabitation unions in Quebec and that younger people across Canada are more likely to see cohabitation as a committed and loyal relationship (Bibby, 2004: 19). It is possible that as cohabitation becomes more common it is absorbed into standard cultural expectations of co-residential relationships as committed relationships. Perhaps family and friends surrounding the couple take cohabitation as seriously as marriage and more actively support the couple than in the past. The rise of cohabitation in Quebec followed the Quiet Revolution of the 1960s, a time of great cultural shifting away from the predominantly religious, rural, and collective norms that dominated Quebec from the 1600s to the 1950s (ibid., 4). This cultural shift away from the Roman Catholic Church as a significant aspect of everyday life appears to have reached into norms about marriage and cohabitation. Changes in gender ideologies may also be proceeding differently in Quebec from the rest of Canada: Quebec was the first province to stop automatically changing women's surnames to those of their husbands when they married (Eichler, 1997: 49). All Canadian provinces have now followed Quebec's lead.

Bibby argues that cohabitation is seen as 'complementary' to but not a substitute for marriage for most Canadians. In Quebec, however, cohabitation is becoming more stable as a lifelong commitment, and may be better described as an 'alternative' to marriage (Wu, 2000: 49). Common-law unions were once seen as immoral; now they are viewed almost on par with marriage. Overall, there are growing similarities in social structures surrounding marriage and cohabitation, especially legal structures.

Marriage: Ceremonies, Legal Structures, and Cultural Privilege

The most significant aspect of marriage for Canadians is that it is seen as a commitment. Secondarily, marriage is viewed as an expression of moral values and the belief that children should have married parents (Bibby, 2004: 28). But it is an institution with deep historical, religious, and legal roots. It has been a place of maintenance of patriarchal authority and direct control over women and children (Langford, 1999; Eichler, 1997). Marriage as a social institution, a legal status, and a religious duty has often been given much more privilege and social support than the individuals, especially the women, actually living in the marriage.

Marriage is socially and legally recognized as a commitment between two people expressed through sexual exclusivity and, most often, making a home together. Marriage gives two people the legal status of **spouses** (Holland, 2002: 121–2). Getting married is definitely a change in social status, and, for many communities, it is how one becomes an adult.

Changing social status from a single person to a married person is often marked by a widely recognized set of ceremonies in dominant North American culture, including weddings and pre-wedding events (Tye and Powers, 1998: 552; Whyte, 1990: 56–7). Pre-wedding events include traditional wedding showers for the bride and 'stag' or 'bachelor' parties for the groom. 'Stags' often involve heavy drinking, sexual crudeness, and sexual objectification of women through pornography, hiring a stripper, or going to strip clubs (Tye and Powers, 1998: 555). Traditional wedding showers are aimed at turning the bride into a homemaker, and focus her attention to her upcoming status as a wife. They include female family members of the bride and groom of all ages and household gifts are central to a shower (ibid., 556; Whyte, 1990: 56). Both of these events appear to be increasing in popularity (Whyte, 1990: 57).

Recently, researchers studied 'stagette' or 'bachelorette' parties, which are organized by women friends of the bride as her 'last night of freedom'. The bride's friends, on their night out, create a safe space for the bride where she has both 'freedom and safety to engage in clearly bounded sexual banter', while she is somewhere between being a single woman and part of a committed couple (Tye and Powers, 1998: 558). The parties celebrate heterosexuality, yet offer a subtle critique of the patriarchal aspects of marriage. 'Stag-and-doe' parties are a gender-neutral version of 'bachelor' and 'bachelorette' parties. They are known by different terms: 'Jack-and-Jill' in Atlantic Canada, 'social' in Manitoba, and 'shag' ('shower' + 'stag'?) in north-western Ontario. One woman in Atlantic Canada commented that the men and women separate into groups at these parties, with the men getting rowdy and the women rather subdued. She thought that these parties were not as much fun as 'stagettes' (ibid., 559).

Broad recognition of these ceremonies, however, does not mean that they are compulsory, and the extent of participation in them varies. Some common patterns are found in wedding ceremonies. For most Canadians, whether or not they attend weekly religious services, religion-based wedding ceremonies remain popular—87 per cent of those currently married had religious ceremonies. But the trappings that people commonly associate with 'traditional' weddings, such as religious ceremonies, fancy dresses, special bridesmaids' outfits, and large receptions are not necessarily traditional. Whyte found in his Detroit study that weddings have become increasingly more elaborate and costly since the 1930s, with increasing numbers of guests (1990: 57). This is echoed in the Atlantic Canada study, where researchers note that the grandmothers of today's brides may not even have had a new dress for the ceremony (Tye and Powers, 1998: 552). Civil wedding ceremonies were also much more common in the early 1900s (Whyte, 1990: 56). The popularity of religious ceremonies appears to be slowly declining: 63 per cent of Canadians who expect eventually to marry would like religious ceremonies (Bibby, 2004: 26).

Today, being a spouse means being assigned a long list of legal rights and obligations that most people only vaguely understand (Auchmuty, 2004: 112). These include: sharing property, financial support of each other and of any children of the marriage, changes in taxation status, rights as next-of-kin in medical decision-making and inheritance, and rights to occupy and jointly own the family home.

Cohabitation is becoming more like marriage, 'with social change and legal change being mutually reinforcing' (Bala and Bromwich, 2002: 157). Illegitimacy—the concept that a child born to an unmarried woman has a different legal status from one born to a married couple—has been abolished in all provinces (Eichler, 1997: 50). Ontario has been extending spousal rights to cohabitants since 1986, and common-law spouses now share most of the legal rights of married spouses, such as financial support, inheritance and next-of-kin rights, custody rights, and rights to occupy the family home across the country (Holland, 2000: 127–9; Eichler, 1997: 49). All provinces now recognize cohabiting parties as spouses after they have cohabited for between two and three years, depending on the province, or are the parents of a child while living in a relationship of some permanence (or, in some provinces, for a minimum of one year). According to the Supreme Court of Canada, cohabiting or **conjugal relationships**, generally, share a household, sexual relations, financial support, responsibility for children, and a social understanding of the couple as 'a couple'. The Court has also explained that not all of these elements are always present to the same degree and relationships may be defined as conjugal without all of the above elements being fulfilled (*M v. H.*, 1999: 59). Cohabiting spouses are recognized for several different government benefits ranging from spousal pension allowances to insurance and employment benefits. What common-law spouses do not share with married spouses are rights to an equal division of property if the couple breaks up—rather, a common-law spouse has to prove how she or he has contributed to

property maintenance and development to such an extent that it would be unfair to exclude him or her from at least partial ownership rights (Bailey, 2004: 155, 170 n. 11).

The Canadian state has historically both promoted and ignored marriage rights and tied other rights to marital status in order to further its own interest in nation-building. The earliest example of this is the *filles du roi*, poor women sent to New France in the 1600s to marry voyageurs and populate the new colony for the King. The Canadian state privileged marriages between European people. During the early 1900s, Canada tried to deport the married wives and children of several Punjabi-Canadian men, who had worked in Canada and then brought their wives from India. Although a wife's citizenship usually followed that of her husband in those days, Canada tried to overrule the marriage-based citizenship rights of Punjabi women (Buchignani and Indra, 1985). Canada's imposition of a head tax on Chinese immigrants similarly prevented family reunification.

Marriage has also been denied to people based on their race and ethnicity. Black slaves were not allowed to marry in Canada (Calliste, 2003: 202). From the late 1800s to 1985, status Indian women who married non-status men lost their rights to live on reserve, any education or treaty rights they might have had, and the right to pass their status to their children, even if the marriage later dissolved. In making marriage so costly for many First Nations women, the Canadian government encouraged cohabitation. For most of this time period cohabitation left women with no rights to financial support for themselves or their children should the relationships end, and children of the unions were illegitimate. Without Indian status, First Nations women had no right to return to their home communities (Bear and Tobique Women's Group, 1991). Although marriage as an institution has supported patriarchy, it is still socially valued and some privileges accompany it. Excluding people from marriage, or making it costly in other ways for them to marry, is a significant form of discrimination.

Same-Sex Marriage

The provinces of Nova Scotia, Saskatchewan, Quebec, and Manitoba allow same-sex couples to register **civil unions**, which provide rights very similar to those under marriage; overall, civil unions have not caused controversy (Bailey, 2004: 162–3). The problem appears to be in applying the term 'marriage' to same-sex commitments. Significant political and legal debate has arisen over same-sex marriage, although nearly half of Canadians approve of it, particularly younger people (Bibby, 2004: 31). Justice Blair wrote in *Halpern v. Canada*, the trial decision that permitted same-sex marriage in Ontario, that approval of same-sex marriage is usually related to what people see as the purpose of marriage. He explained that there are three different models of marriage in Western society: the classical, choice, and commitment models.

The historical classical model focuses on biological and social complementarity between the sexes as the basis of marriage and the best social situation in which to raise children. Heterosexuality and commitment have been integral to this model since the writings of St Augustine in the fourth century.

The choice model sees marriage as a private agreement between individuals. Sexuality is considered to be about self-expression and not limited to heterosexuals (*Halpern v. Canada*, 2002: para. 53–4).

In the commitment model, marriage begins with individuals, but the relationship between them is central. Marriage is an intimate, committed relationship centralizing emotional support. It recognizes individual choice, but focuses on community and the values of being connected within a long-term relationship. There is no reason to limit it to heterosexual partners (ibid., para. 55).

Justice Blair stated that the current institution and social norms of marriage were best reflected in the commitment model. Marriage is important in its economic and emotional interdependence, obligations of mutual support, and shared social activities. It is more important as a place to rear

children than simply to biologically produce them (ibid., para. 70–1). The judge stated that marriage is the highest social recognition of a relationship between two people in society (ibid., para. 83; also Auchmuty, 2004: 102). The exclusion of same-sex couples from recognition through the institution of marriage was, according to Justice Blair, a violation of their equality rights. Blair's assessment of the commitment model is reflected in Bibby's study of what marriage means to Canadians: marriage is understood primarily as a serious commitment, and the best thing about marriage, for Canadians, is the relationship.

Excluding gays and lesbians from marriage is discriminatory: 'If marriage is regarded as a desirable and privileged institution, as it appears to be in our society, the exclusion from it constitutes a significant penalty' (Auchmuty, 2004: 105). Gay and lesbian activists seek equal rights to marriage as part of an overall goal of achieving equality and expanding social understandings of 'family' (Bala and Bromwich, 2002: 166). Importantly, gay and lesbian activists seek the right to define their own families as 'real families', whether conventionally married or uniquely structured (Calhoun, 1997: 146–7). There is concern in the gay and lesbian community that marriage, as a patriarchal institution that has been the site of oppression for women, should be approached with caution (Bala and Bromwich, 2002: 166; Auchmuty, 2004: 104).

Arranged Marriage

There are varying cultural perspectives on marriage in Canada. In many South Asian cultures, which presume that commitment should precede intimacy, arranged marriages are the norm (Zaidi and Shuraydi, 2002: 496).

The term 'arranged marriage' includes several practices in which marriage is not left to two young people alone, but requires some participation or control by parents and extended families. These practices range from community elders making the decision to children making the decision but only with parental consent (Talbani and

Hasanali, 2000: 617). Sometimes, parents are fully in control and the couple may not meet until the wedding day. Sometimes parents ask their children about their expectations of a marriage partner and try to find someone who fits those desires (Zaidi and Shuraydi, 2002: 496). In a third approach, both parents and children participate in finding a spouse for the young person. These latter two approaches may include chaperoned interaction or dating (ibid.).

Many children who have grown up in Canada see marriage quite differently from the view of their parents. Parents may value arranged marriage because it tends to preserve group cultural identity and cohesion (Talbani and Hasanali, 2000: 618, 625). Arranged marriages in North America usually include children in the planning and grant them some freedom of choice (Zaidi and Shuraydi, 2002: 498). Almost half of unmarried South Asian-Canadian women in one study believed that their parents would ask their opinions of prospective marriage partners and take those opinions into account (Talbani and Hasanali, 2000: 621). But a significant majority of unmarried South Asian women in each of two studies believed that love should come before marriage (ibid., 617; Zaidi and Shuraydi, 2002: 506). Pre-marriage intimacy appears to become more valued by those who have grown up in individualized, Western culture.

Pregnancy, Birth, and Family Formation

Children define a family for many Canadians—slightly more are likely to see a single parent with a child as a family than are likely to see an unmarried or married heterosexual couple without children as a family (Bibby, 2004: 1). Planning for children is relatively easy for fertile, heterosexual couples. For infertile heterosexual couples and for same-sex couples, having children involves active planning and extra effort.

Many cohabiting relationships in Canada eventually become marriages, and pregnancy plays a role in this shift. The majority of Canadians—77 per cent overall, but only 63 per cent in Quebec—believe that children should be born into married relationships (Bibby, 2004: 28). Complementing this social belief are statistics showing that among cohabiting couples marriage rates are higher during than before a pregnancy, drop around the time of birth, rise again for about six months following a birth, and then drop to pre-pregnancy levels. Although there are variations in the precise timing of marriage during pregnancy, this general pattern holds true in Germany, Canada, the Netherlands, and Latvia (Blossfeld and Mills, 2001: 425). Turcotte and Goldscheider (1998: 158, 160) further explain that, in Canada, a partner's pregnancy has a strong effect on men's entry into both cohabitation and marriage, although it is noticeably stronger for marriage.

Other researchers understand the maintenance of non-residential, income-pooling relationships between parents as a significant way of expressing family connection and commitment (Mincy and Dupree, 2001: 578). This study provides a good example of looking beyond the structures of marriage and cohabitation to how people actually form family connections. Non-residential unions or 'visiting' unions are an accepted cultural tradition in the Caribbean, especially for younger women. Visiting unions begin while each partner is living in the parental home, are publicly recognized, and are considered 'a legitimate sphere of procreation' (Ariza and de Oliviera, 2001: 48). Non-residential unions, or partial cohabitation, have recently become more common in Europe—both for younger people before they marry as a test of the relationship, and for couples over age 50 in a second union (ibid., 49). Marriage does confer social status in the Caribbean, and remains widely practised in Europe. But marriage does not appear to be held as central to living a 'good' or 'moral' life in those cultures as it is in most of North America.

Blended Family Formation

In Canada, blended families make up about 12 per cent of all couples with children (Ambert, 2001: 10). Blended families currently develop most often after divorce—in the early 1900s blended families usually arose following the death of a parent: 'Loss is [an] important theme in stepfamilies; stepfamilies are formed after the loss of at least one relationship' (Church, 1999: 5). Building intimacy in a 'new' blended family always includes dealing with the loss of the 'old' family structure.

The diversity of blended family structures means that there is no single pathway to family cohesion. Although research in the area is limited, several researchers agree that open communication is particularly important while blended families negotiate new roles and new relationships, adapt and continue 'old' relationships, and form a new solidarity (Portrie and Hill, 2005: 449, Braithwaite et al., 2001: 222). One study showed that adapting 'old' family rituals and creating 'new' rituals built family solidarity and encouraged communication (Braithwaite et al., 1998). One blended family in this study had a board game night—they often did not finish the game, as it led them to discuss and resolve family issues. The adaptation of 'old' rituals to new family settings was also a way to show respect to the 'old' family and to the memories that children brought with them (ibid., 110).

Blended families must also overcome cultural myths and stereotypes about blended families. One such myth, strongly supported by folktales from many cultures (and the popular Disney movies based on them), is that of the evil, jealous stepmother (Jones, 2003: 230; Church, 1999: 2). According to one small Canadian study, stepmothers who experienced jealousy while adjusting to a 'new' family felt ashamed and wicked (Church, 1999: 13). This prevented some stepmothers from talking about these feelings—yet when they were able to talk with their partners about feeling jealous they found those feelings evaporate (ibid., 14). Another powerful myth is 'instant love' (Jones, 2003: 230). This myth raises expectations for one big happy family without allowing for feelings of loss and jealousy or recognizing the communicative effort that adaptation to a new family structure (and new family members) involves. Further, it creates the expectation that a blended family is just like any nuclear family (ibid.). This myth is reflected in TV shows like *The Brady Bunch* (see Box 3.3). An American study showed that blended families that started with 'the myth of instant love' had trouble developing family cohesion (Braithwaite et al., 2001: 234, 243).

Blended families require boundaries that are 'permeable enough to allow access to outside family members and non-kin, but firm enough to protect developing relationships' (ibid., 225). Many blended families are quite fluid, with children residing in two different blended family structures as their parents establish relationships with new partners (Baxter et al., 1999: 297, 299). The emphasis on open communication, role negotiation, permeable boundaries, and diversity (and de-emphasis of biological, nuclear family ties) in blended families is quite reflective of Giddens's theory of intimacy. Blended families may be one family form in which Giddens's emphasis on communication in intimacy is manifest.

Box 3.3 The Brady Bunch

The Brady Bunch was a 1970s sitcom telling the story of a widowed man (with three sons) and widowed woman (with three daughters) who married and formed a new family. The Bradys represented a traditional, nuclear, middle-class family in every way except their original formation. The show ran for five years, then went into syndication and has not been off-air since. It had several spinoffs, including a variety TV show involving the Brady children, a theatre production, and a movie in the 1990s (see Griffin, n.d.).

Conclusion

Intimacy and the cultural practices that accompany it, such as dating, cohabitation, and marriage, are intensely personal experiences. But it is important to consider intimacy from a sociological perspective, because social expectations and ideologies about intimacy shape individual experiences. Seeing dating, for example, through the ideology of heterosexual romance may make it difficult for society to accept that dating violence does occur. Myths of 'instant love' may prevent the open communication necessary to build intimacy in blended families. Definitive social structures, such as law and religion, preclude people from expressing intimacy and commitment in some ways while rewarding other expressions of commitment. Marriage, for example, has been a patriarchal and exclusive institution. Although marriage today retains some of these qualities, it has been opened to same-sex couples and the costs of marriage for First Nations women with Indian status have been reduced. This will change individual decisions about marriage.

It is also important to consider commonality of experience. 'Dating' has clearly defined cultural parameters. Growing rates of cohabitation and long-term cohabitation encourage legal changes in cohabitants' rights, while changes in those rights make cohabitation more secure. Social approval increases with both experience of and fewer legal sanctions attached to cohabitation.

Family formation is not a simple or straightforward process. Ideologies about intimacy and social structures affect patterns, changes, and individuals' experiences of family formation.

Study Questions

1. Why are feminists concerned about ideologies and theories of intimacy?
2. Do new communication technologies change 'dating culture'?
3. What do same-sex and heterosexual dating and marriage have in common?
4. To what extent have legal structures of marriage been used as a political tool by the Canadian state?
5. What are the roles of ceremonies relating to commitment, such as 'bachelor' and 'stagette' parties and weddings?
6. How do blended families create intimacy in 'new' family structures?

Glossary

Arranged marriage Arranged marriages generally involve some participation or control in selection of marriage partners by parents, extended family, and, sometimes, community members.

Civil unions (registered partnerships) A civil union is a legal procedure through which same-sex and/or heterosexual couples can register their partnerships, thus receiving most of the public and private obligations and rights as married partners.

Cohabitation (common-law and consensual unions) These terms describe an emotional, sexual, and (usually) residential relationship between two people that is not legalized through marriage. Historically, they described heterosexual relationships, but are now also used to describe same-sex relationships.

Conjugal relationship This relationship often includes sharing a household, sexual relations, shared financial support, the raising of children as well as a social perception of the couple as 'a couple'. It is assumed that married people are in a conjugal relationship; but a conjugal relationship has to be shown before a couple is seen as being in a common-law relationship.

Dating culture This is a culture where romantic heterosexual relationships between young people are encouraged and expected. Dating culture does not assume that those relationships will lead to marriage or other long-term commitments.

Friends Friends are neither family nor do they fit a specific status category, like neighbour or colleague. The term 'friend' best describes some degree of developed, mutually achieved relationship.

Pure relationship Giddens's 'pure relationship' describes an ideal relationship based in emotional and sexual intimacy, begun and continued for as long as it satisfies both partners. It relies on sexuality freed from reproduction, intimacy as central to love, and egalitarianism between partners.

Script theory Script theory states that there are sets of stereotypical actions expected in certain social situations. Scripts help people organize the world around them, providing predictability to social interactions.

Social exchange theory Social exchange theory posits that people commodify a range of social characteristics, including physical attractiveness, youth, wealth, education, gender role, and social status and then offer their best traits in trade for traits they desire. This theory is used in studies of dating, cohabitation, and marriage partner choices.

Spouse Legal definitions of spouse vary among provinces. Ontario defines spouses as married, opposite-sex couples and opposite-sex couples who have cohabited for three years and/or are the parents of a child in a relationship of some permanence. Ontario does not include same-sex couples as spouses, but defines them as similar to cohabitants. Saskatchewan defines spouses as married spouses, or two people who have cohabited continuously for two years, or parents of a child. Saskatchewan makes no reference to the sex of spouses.

Further Readings

Backhouse, Constance. 1991. 'The Ceremony of Marriage', in Backhouse, *Petticoats and Prejudice: Women and Law in Nineteenth-Century Canada*. Toronto: Women's Press. This chapter discusses two legal decisions about the validity of specific marriage ceremonies in the 1800s, explaining the relations between law and social customs around marriage.

Hogben, Susan, and Justine Coupland. 2000. 'Egg seeks sperm. End of story? . . . Articulating gay parenting in small ads for reproductive partners', *Discourse & Society* 194: 459–85. The authors analyze gay and lesbian classified ads for reproductive partners. They consider the construction of identities, role, and commitment expectations in terms of donor, mother, father, and co-parents in these ads.

Langford, Wendy. 1999. *Revolutions of the Heart: Gender, Power and the Delusions of Love*. London: Routledge. Langford analyzes feminist critiques of ideologies of romance and theories of intimacy. The author conducted interviews with 15 heterosexual women in Britain to support her conclusions, persuasively demystifying 'love'.

Sanchez, Laura, Steven L. Nock, James D. Wright, and Constance T. Gager. 2002. 'Setting the clock forward or back? Covenant marriage and the "divorce revolution"', *Journal of Family Issues* 23, 1: 91–120. In 20 American states, couples may choose a 'covenant marriage', which requires premarital counselling and permits only fault-based (adultery or abuse) divorce. This article analyzes attitudes to covenant marriage, in terms of political discourses around feminism, family values, and the practical difficulties of poverty.

Wu, Zheng. 2000. *Cohabitation: An Alternative Form of Family Living*. Toronto: Oxford University Press. Wu's book provides an extensive range of statistics regarding cohabitation and attitudes towards it in Canada. He addresses the effects of regionalism, child-bearing in cohabitation, and various theoretical approaches to 'mate selection'.

Websites

www.egale.ca
EGALE—Equality for Gays And Lesbians Everywhere—provides information about gay and lesbian struggles for equality, ranging from anti-discrimination efforts in high school to same-sex marriage.

www.cwhn.ca
The Canadian Women's Health Network site has articles about and links to sites on sexuality, sexual health, and relationship issues from a feminist perspective.

www.mencanstoprape.org
Men Can Stop Rape provides programs for male high school and university students about ending dating violence and sexual assault.

www.theory.org.uk
This website focuses on social theory and popular culture. Commentary on various social theorists and articles about the media, sexuality, identity, and gender roles can be found here.

References

Adam, Barry D. 2004. 'Care, intimacy and same-sex partnership in the 21st century', *Current Sociology* 52, 2: 265–79.

Ambert, Anne-Marie. 2005a. *Divorce: Facts, Causes and Consequences*, rev. edn. Ottawa: Vanier Institute of the Family. Available at: <www.vifamily.ca>.

———. 2005b. *Cohabitation and Marriage: How Are They Related?* Ottawa: Vanier Institute of the Family. Available at: <www.vifamily.ca>.

Ariza, Marina, and Orlandina de Oliveira. 2001. 'Contrasting scenarios: Non-residential family formation patterns in the Caribbean and Europe', *International Review of Sociology* 11, 1: 47–61.

Auchmuty, Rosemary. 2004. 'Same-sex marriage revived: Feminist critique and legal strategy', *Feminism & Psychology* 14, 1: 101–26.

Bailey, Martha. 2004. 'Regulation of cohabitation and marriage in Canada', *Law & Policy* 26, 1: 153–75.

Bala, Nicholas, and Rebecca Jaremko Bromwich. 2002. 'Context and inclusivity in Canada's evolving definition of the family', *International Journal of Law, Policy and the Family* 16: 145–80.

Baxter, Leslie A., Dawn O. Braithwaite, and John H. Nicholson. 1999. 'Turning points in the development of blended families', *Journal of Social and Personal Relationships* 16: 291–313.

Bear, Shirley, with the Tobique Women's Group. 1991. 'You can't change the Indian Act?', in Jeri Wine and Janice Ristock, eds, *Women and Social Change*. Toronto: James Lorimer.

Bibby, Reginald W. 2001. *Canada's Teens: Today, Yesterday and Tomorrow*. Toronto: Stoddart.

———. 2004. *The Future Families Project: A Survey of Canadian Hopes and Dreams*. Ottawa: Vanier Institute of the Family. Available at: <www.vifamily.ca>.

Bittman, Michael, and Jocelyn Pixley. 1997. *The Double Life of the Family: Myth, Hope and Experience*. St Leonard's, Australia: Allen and Unwin.

Blossfeld, Hans-Peter, and Melinda Mills. 2001. 'A causal approach to interrelated family events: A cross-national comparison of cohabitation, nonmarital conception and marriage', *Canadian Studies in Population* (special issue) 28, 2: 409–37.

Braithwaite, Dawn O., Leslie A. Baxter, and Anneliese M. Harper. 1998. 'The role of rituals in the management of the dialectical tension of "old" and "new" in blended families', *Communication Studies* 49: 101–20.

———, Loreen N. Olson, Tamara D. Golish, Charles Soukup, and Paul Turman. 2001. '"Becoming a family": Developmental processes represented in blended family discourse', *Journal of Applied Communication Research* 29: 221–47.

Buchignani, Norman, and Doreen M. Indra. 1985. *Continuous Journey: A Social History of South Asians in Canada*. Toronto: McClelland & Stewart.

Calhoun, Cheshire. 1997. 'Family outlaws: Rethinking the connections between feminism, lesbianism and the family', in Hilde Lindemann Nelson, ed., *Feminism and Families*. New York: Routledge.

Calliste, Agnes. 2003. 'Black families in Canada: Exploring the interconnections of race, class and gender', in Marion Lynn, ed., *Voices: Essays on Canadian Families*, 2nd edn. Toronto: Thomson Nelson.

Castellano, Marlene Brant. 2002. 'Aboriginal family trends: Extended families, nuclear families, families of the heart', *Contemporary Family Trends Series*. Ottawa: Vanier Institute of the Family.

CBC Radio. 2004. *The Current*, 10 Dec. At: <www.cbc.ca/thecurrent/2004/200412/20041210.html>; accessed 11 Dec. 2004.

Cheal, David. 1991. *Family and the State of Theory*. Toronto: University of Toronto Press.

———. 2002. *The Sociology of Family Life*. Houndmills, Basingstoke, Hampshire: Palgrave.

Church, Elizabeth. 1999. 'The poisoned apple: Stepmothers' experience of envy and jealousy', *Journal of Feminist and Family Therapy* 11: 1–18.

Correll, Shelley. 1995. 'The ethnography of an electronic bar: The Lesbian Café', *Journal of Contemporary Ethnography* 24: 270–98.

DeKesedery, Walter, and Katherine Kelly. 1993. 'The incidence and prevalence of woman abuse in Canadian university and college dating relationships', *Canadian Journal of Sociology* 18, 2: 137–59.

Eichler, Margrit. 1997. *Family Shifts: Families, Policies and Gender Equality*. Toronto: Oxford University Press.

Elze, Diane. 2003. 'Gay, lesbian and bisexual youths' perceptions of their high school environments and comfort in school', *Children and Schools* 25: 225–39.

Family Law Act, R.S.O. 1990 c. F.3, s. 29 (as amended) (Ontario).

Family Property Act, c. F-6.3 S.S. 1997, s. 1 (as amended) (Saskatchewan).

Forste, Renata. 2002. 'Where are all the men? A conceptual analysis of the role of men in family formation', *Journal of Family Issues* 23: 579–600.

Giddens, Anthony. 1992. *The Transformation of Intimacy: Sexuality, Love and Eroticism in Modern Societies*. Stanford, Calif.: Stanford University Press.

Griffin, Sean. n.d. 'The Brady Bunch', The Museum of Broadcast Communications, Chicago. At: <www.museum.tv/archives/etv/B/htmlB/bradybunch/bradybunch.htm>; accessed 7 Apr. 2006.

Hall, David R. 2003. 'The pure relationship and below replacement fertility', *Canadian Studies in Population* 30, 1: 51–69.

Halpern v. *Canada (A.G.)*, [2002] O.J. No. 2714 (Ont. Sup. Ct. Blair, J.) [QL].

Hatala, Mark Nicholas, Daniel W. Baack, and Ryan Parmenter. 1997. 'Dating with HIV: A content analysis of gay male HIV-positive and HIV-negative personal advertisements', *Journal of Social and Personal Relationships* 15, 2: 268–76.

Holland, Winifred. 2000. 'Intimate relationships in the new millennium: The assimilation of marriage and cohabitation?', *Canadian Review of Family Law* 17: 114–50.

Hughes, Kate. 2005. 'The adult children of divorce: Pure relationships and family values?', *Journal of Sociology* 41: 69–86.

Jamieson, Lynn. 1999. 'Intimacy transformed? A critical look at the "pure relationship"', *Sociology* 33, 3: 477–94.

Jones, Anne C. 2003. 'Reconstructing the stepfamily: Old myths, new stories', *Social Work* 48: 228–36.

Kaufman, Gayle. 2000. 'Do gender role attitudes matter? Family formation and dissolution among traditional and egalitarian men and women', *Journal of Family Issues* 21: 128–44.

Klinkenberg, Dean, and Suzanna Rose. 1994. 'Dating scripts of gay men and lesbians', *Journal of Homosexuality* 26, 4: 23–35.

Langford, Wendy. *Revolutions of the Heart: Gender, Power and the Delusions of Love*. London: Routledge.

Lavalife. www.lavalife.com. Accessed 13 Dec. 2004.

M. v. *H.*, [1999] 2 S.C.R. 3 (S.C.C.).

McLaren, Leah. 2003. 'The new traditionalists', *Globe and Mail*, 14 June, F8.

Mincy, Ronald B., and Allen T. Dupree. 2001. 'Welfare, child support and family formation', *Child and Youth Services Review* 23, 6 and 7: 577–601.

Pahl, Ray, and Liz Spencer. 2004. 'Personal communities: Not simply families of "fate" or "choice"', *Current Sociology* 52, 2: 199–221.

Parks, Malcolm R., and Lynne D. Roberts. 1998. '"Making MOOsic": The development of personal relationships on line and a comparison to their off-line counterparts', *Journal of Social and Personal Relationships* 15, 4: 517–37.

Phua, Voon Chin, and Gayle Kaufman. 2003a. 'The crossroads of race and sexuality: Date selection among men in Internet "personal" ads', *Journal of Family Issues* 24, 8: 981–94.

——— and ———. 2003b. 'Is ageism alive in date selection among men? Age requests among gay and straight men in Internet personal ads', *Journal of Men's Studies* 11, 2: 225–35.

Portrie, Torey, and Nicole R. Hill. 2005. 'Blended families: A critical review of current research', *Family Journal* 13: 445–51.

Single in the City. At: <www.singleinthecity.ca>. Accessed 13 Dec. 2004.

Smart, Carol, and Bren Neale. 1999. *Family Fragments?* Malden, Mass.: Polity Press.

Sprecher, Susan. 2001. 'Equity and social exchange in dating couples: Associations with satisfaction, commitment, and stability', *Journal of Marriage and the Family* 63: 599–613.

Statistics Canada. 2002. *Changing Conjugal Life in Canada*. Ottawa: Statistics Canada, Housing, Family and Social Statistics Division.

Talbani, Aziz, and Parveen Hasanali. 2000. 'Adolescent females between tradition and modernity: Gender role socialization in South Asian immigrant culture', *Journal of Adolescence* 23: 615–27.

Turcotte, Pierre, and Frances Goldscheider. 1998. 'Evolution of factors influencing first union formation', *Canadian Studies in Population* 25, 2: 145–73.

Tye, Diane, and Ann Marie Powers. 1998. 'Gender, resistance and play: Bachelorette parties in Atlantic Canada', *Women's Studies International Forum* 21, 5: 551–61.

Weeks, Jeffrey, Brian Heaphy, and Catherine Donovan. 1999. 'Partners by choice: Equality, power and commitment in non-heterosexual relationships', in Graham Allen, ed., *The Sociology of the Family: A Reader*. Oxford: Blackwell.

Whyte, Martin King. 1990. *Dating, Mating and Marriage*. New York: Aldine de Gruyter.

Wilson, Brian, and Shannon Jette. 2005. 'Making sense of the cultural activities of Canadian youth', in Nancy Mandell and Ann Duffy, eds, *Canadian Families: Diversity, Conflict and Change*, 3rd edn. Toronto: Thomson Nelson.

Wu, Zheng. 2000. *Cohabitation: An Alternative Form of Family Living*. Toronto: Oxford University Press.

Zaidi, Arshia U., and Muhammad Shuraydi. 2002. 'Perceptions of arranged marriages by young Pakistani Muslim women living in a Western society', *Journal of Comparative Family Studies* 33, 4: 495–514.

CHAPTER 4

'Bringing Up' and 'Growing Up': Parents, Children, and Family Life

Gillian Ranson

Learning Objectives

- To introduce students to dominant understandings of motherhood and fatherhood in Canada.
- To help students appreciate the extent to which parenting practices are shaped by family structure and social and economic contexts.
- To demonstrate the linkages between changing understandings of children's needs and parenting practices.
- To introduce the idea of childhood as socially constructed and historically situated.
- To explore the implications of different parenting styles.
- To highlight differences among children in their experience of parenting and family life.

Introduction

Fertility rates in Canada are declining, as they are in much of the industrialized world. But though people are having their children later, and having fewer of them, reproduction continues to be both an expectation and an outcome for most adults. The transition to parenthood is an important marker of culturally recognized adulthood, signalling the achievement not only of full adult status but also (especially for women) the fulfillment of widely held gender expectations.

The average age of women at first birth has increased from 23.4 in 1976 to 27.6 in 2001. In 2001, 34 per cent of first-time mothers were aged 30 or more, compared to only 9 per cent in 1976 (Beaujot, 2004: 10). So today's children are likely to be born to parents who are on average a little older—and, on average, a little better educated.

Children today are also likely to have fewer siblings. Those living in families with two parents (still the majority, though a declining one) are likely to be supported financially by two incomes and to experience parenting organized around the demands of paid work (Beaujot, 2004). But despite changes in the 'culture of parenting' (Daly, 2004) and the demographic evidence that women are putting off childbirth till they are older, the having and raising of children continue to be a significant part of adult life for most Canadians.

Its significance becomes apparent in the context of research on adoption, until recently the main recourse for individuals unable to become biological parents. Miall and March (2003) point out that in North American culture the kinship system has traditionally been based on the bond of blood, with family scholars tending to assume a biological connection between parents and their children, and with adoptive (i.e., social) parenthood viewed as second-best. This research illuminates the extent to which *biological* parenthood—and particularly biological motherhood—is culturally preferred.

But as Miall and March go on to point out, 'the distinction between biological and **social parenthood** has never been so blurred' (ibid., 8). The development of new reproductive technologies, designed mainly to help infertile couples, has challenged many of the old assumptions. The use of donor sperm and ova, or surrogate mothers to gestate children for other couples, raises questions about the meaning of 'biological' parenthood. At the same time, the increase in other family forms, like blended families with step-parents, is showing the importance and prevalence of social parenthood without a biological basis (ibid.).

The ideological superiority of biological parent-hood in Canadian society links to a web of often deeply held beliefs about mothering and father-ing. These beliefs, in turn, are informed by chang-ing views about how childhood should be viewed and what children need to become competent and independent adults. Contemporary scholars inter-ested in childhood are coming to see that children are not just passive recipients of adult activity or objects to be 'socialized' in order to enter civilized society. They are individuals in their own right, interested and active players in their own families, with distinct perspectives and the capacity to shape family life according to their own interests.

This chapter explores in detail the way Canadian women and men go about the job of parenting. As well as being concerned with what they do as parents, it looks at *why* they do what they do. It also examines childhood, not only as a universal stage in human development, but more importantly from the perspective of children whose diverse social and cultural experiences make them 'worth listening to' (James and James, 2001: 26).

The next section discusses the ideological con-text of parenting. It traces the social and histori-cal origins of the ideologies of motherhood and fatherhood that are most influential in contem-porary Canadian society. These beliefs, as noted above, are intricately connected to changing views about the needs of children, which are discussed in the section that follows. From the abstract realm of ideology, the chapter then moves to a more concrete examination of parent-ing in practice, looking at how it is shaped by parents' access to financial, educational, and other resources. This section also looks at class differences in parenting styles. From an exami-nation of parents and parenting practices, we then move to a closer look at some of the different ways Canadian children experience childhood. The chapter concludes with a brief consideration of public policy and the future of child-rearing in Canada.

The Ideological Context of Parenting

The Canadian sociologist Dorothy Smith has argued that an ideological 'code' organizes the activities of individuals in North American families. She calls this code SNAF, for 'Standard North American Family'. Smith describes SNAF as follows:

> It is a conception of the family as a legally married couple sharing a household. The adult male is in paid employment; his earnings provide the economic basis of the family house-hold. The adult female may also earn an income, but her primary responsibility is to the care of husband, household and children. (Smith, 1993: 52)

Smith argues that SNAF describes the way families are *supposed* to run; it's the model by which, in North American society, all families are judged. This code suggests that mothers, though they may have paid employment, are ultimately responsible for the practical care of children. And fathers, though they may also get involved with child care, are helpers rather than family managers; their main family responsibility is to provide adequate financial support

The strong ideological connection between mothers and nurture, and fathers and breadwin-ning, is often traced back to the effects of industri-alization. As this economic form gradually replaced agricultural economies in Europe and North America from the early nineteenth century onward, so the basis of family financial support shifted to wages earned in industrial workplaces. As work-places increasingly became separated from the homes and family holdings of an earlier era, and were populated largely by a male workforce, they came to be constructed symbolically as the domain of men, while homes—and the daily care of children—were the symbolic domain of women.

This symbolic allocation of family roles corre-sponded to middle-class social reformers' fears, at the end of the nineteenth century, about the stability of working-class families in the wake of major social and economic change. In Canada, concern about women in industrial workplaces was based on fears for their health, their safety, and their virtue, which stemmed from deeply held moral beliefs about the sanctity—and the responsibilities—of motherhood. Concerns about child labour were linked to middle-class views of childhood as a period of dependency, separate from the responsibilities—and freedoms—of adult life. Mothers and fathers were believed to have 'biologically prescribed roles within the domestic unit' (Chunn, 2003: 191).

The model of motherhood that has emerged from this history establishes one woman (the biological mother) as primarily responsible for mothering during her children's formative years, with the children constructed reciprocally as needing her constant care and attention (Glenn, 1994; Wearing, 1984). Men as fathers are also reciprocally constructed as breadwinners, discharging their family responsibilities primarily by financial provision. This ideological construction of mothers and fathers was based on the situation of the white, middle-class family; it never reflected the family experiences of working-class or ethnically more diverse families. But as Smith noted, this construction became ideologically dominant, shaping the way people behave in families and how they make sense of what they do.

FATHERHOOD AND FATHERING

To consider first the case of fatherhood, current research confirms the 'breadwinner' or 'good provider' model as both durable and pervasive in North America. Men are expected to provide for their families, no matter how else they are involved as fathers (Daly and Palkovitz, 2004; Doucet, 2004; LaRossa, 1997, Wilkie, 1993). But current scholarly work on fatherhood is raising some interesting questions about what it means to be a 'good provider', and whether this role is the best way to represent what contemporary fathers do for and with their children.

As Christiansen and Palkovitz (2001) point out, there are some negative connotations attached to the traditional provider role. Historically, the separation of homes and workplaces as a consequence of industrialization took fathers away from their families. As providers, they were required to be good workers, so their primary commitment was to their jobs. Christiansen and Palkovitz cite studies showing breadwinner fathers labelled as 'distant, strict, harsh, authoritarian and incompetent' (Christiansen and Palkovitz, 2001: 88).

Christiansen and Palkovitz argue that these negative connotations detract from the significant contribution fathers make to their families by their financial provision. Indeed, others (e.g., Walker and McGraw, 2000) have argued that this may be the best thing fathers *can* do for their families. Most labour markets are characterized by significant job segregation by gender. Men tend to have jobs that pay better, so their generally superior earnings may influence their standing as primary breadwinners. Christiansen and Palkovitz point out that, when couples first become parents, many mothers cut back on or quit their paid employment. Since this is also a time when household expenses mount, many men commit more time to work to compensate (see also Fox, 2001; Walzer, 1996). In many working-class families, fathers work two jobs to help families make ends meet. To label such fathers as distant and uninvolved in their families does them a grave injustice (Christiansen and Palkovitz, 2001).

But research also indicates that the identification of fathers with financial support has a moral dimension, closely linked to understandings of appropriate masculinity. Men see breadwinning as something they must do to fulfill their responsibilities not only as fathers but as men. Studies in Canada (e.g., Luxton and Corman, 2001) and the US (e.g., Roy, 2004; Townsend, 2002) suggest that a man who is not a breadwinner may feel that his masculinity is being judged and found wanting. Townsend (2002), in an **ethnographic** study of fathers in a northern California town, found that they tended to view economic provision as part of a 'package deal' in which having children, being married, holding down a steady job, and owning a home were interconnected elements. Roy (2004) examined how the provider role was understood by men in low-income and working-class families, where well-paying jobs were scarce. He gave the example of Tony, a 24-year-old father of an infant and two non-biological children, who 'flipped burgers and laid pipe to make ends meet'. When he was laid off, he turned to illegal sources of income:

> I got to do what I got to do, gotta provide; that's what led up to [dealing drugs] right there . . . laid off, no unemployment, no [cheque] coming, so hey, gotta do what I gotta do, gotta provide. Dealing paid real nice, but it wasn't my cup of tea. (Roy, 2004: 262)

While the continuing expectation is that fathers will provide, this demand has been tempered by the recognition that, these days, most families have two adult incomes. Since the 1960s, increasing numbers of mothers have entered the workforce. The fact of mothers contributing to their families' financial support has led to questions about fathers sharing the hands-on caregiving long considered to be mothers' responsibility. Several scholars have commented on the changing image of fathers, suggesting that the 'distant breadwinner' is giving way to a new image, the 'new father', described by Pleck (1987) as follows:

> This new father differs from older images of involved fatherhood in several key respects: he is present at the birth; he is involved with his children as infants, not just when they are older; he participates in the actual day-to-day work of child care, and not just play; he is involved with his daughters as much as his sons. (Pleck, 1987: 93)

In the years since Pleck provided this description, several other, roughly similar versions have appeared in the literature on fathering. For example, 'generative fathering' describes a form of fathering focused on children's needs, fathers' spe-

cial strengths as parents, and the ethical obligation of fathers to support the next generation (Brotherson et al., 2005). 'Responsible fathering' (Doherty et al., 1998) also focuses on fathers' ongoing commitment to their children's financial support, physical care, and emotional nurture. Marks and Palkovitz (2004) point out that these and other variants on new, involved fatherhood may not be as new as we think. Fathers in earlier generations may not have changed as many diapers, but there is historical evidence of emotionally involved fathers who spent considerable time with their children (see also LaRossa, 1997).

Attention to changing images of good fathering and the emergence (or re-emergence) of the new involved father raises questions about what this involvement actually means in practice. Writing about fathering in the US in the late 1980s, sociologist Ralph LaRossa contended that there was a lag between the *culture* and the *conduct* of fatherhood. Because the image of the new father was so pervasive, people assumed that, as mothers' paid work drew them away from their family responsibilities, fathers must be picking up the slack. But there is some debate about how much more domestic work—including child care—fathers really are picking up (LaRossa, 1988).

The consensus from many research studies is that fathers are certainly doing more than their own fathers did, but not as much as the mothers of their children—even those mothers in full-time paying jobs (Beaujot, 2000; Daly, 2004; Silver, 2000). There are also important class differences. For example, a common strategy in dual-earning working-class families is to have parents work alternating shifts so that outside child care and its attendant costs are minimized. This positions fathers to share both caregiving and breadwinning with their partners on a much more equal basis. Yet studies show that this non-traditional behaviour is usually accompanied by traditional gender ideologies in which the father is still framed as the breadwinner (Deutsch and Saxon, 1998; Hochschild, 1989).

If fathers have been slower to assume domestic responsibility than mothers have been to take up paid work, one reason may be that they are still expected to be financial providers as well. So they may have less freedom to choose work situations that will accommodate family responsibilities. The influx of women into paid employment has led to greater awareness of the need for **work-family balance**. But this is mainly because women, unlike men, are assumed to have family responsibilities that are not discharged by financial provision. Organization-level policies like parental leave or flexible schedules are designed to make workplaces more 'family-friendly' and to help workers with 'work-life balance'. They are generally framed in **gender-neutral** terms, which suggest that men, as well as women, might be interested in taking them up. But the extent to which men take advantage of such policies remains extremely limited, often because they are discouraged from doing so (Daly and Palkovitz, 2004; Rapoport and Bailyn, 1996; Hochschild, 1997). Organizational expectations about men as workers who do not experience work-family conflict and therefore do not need special accommodation remain entrenched. This creates tensions for men who want to be more involved with their children as well as good providers.

MOTHERHOOD AND MOTHERING

The perceived cultural superiority of biological parenthood has already been noted. But the association of fatherhood with its biological base is not nearly as strong as with motherhood. Where fathering is understood as needing to be learned, mothering is still often recognized as instinctual. One young mother, interviewed in a Canadian study, put it this way:

> I think more than anything it's your instinctive mothering or your mothering instincts or whatever, because they're primal and they're first and foremost. It doesn't matter if anything else is going on in the world, you're going to protect and look after your child before anything. . . . I feel very— not possessive, but I think very close. I could be one of those African women that carry their babies around all the time. (Ranson, 2004: 93)

Biology is obviously implicated in the processes of pregnancy, birth, and lactation. But what is implied in the interview excerpt above is a similarly biological basis for *mothering*, the practices of child care and nurture associated with being a mother. From this perspective, the next logical step is to see these practices as somehow universal, a bond that joins all mothers. Motherhood, furthermore, has historically been understood as women's destiny and the core of their identity as women. The symbolic assignment of women to the sphere of home and children in the wake of industrialization, as described earlier, was based on just such common-sense understandings of women's 'nature'.

It was also based on a particular set of social and economic events at a particular point in time and in particular parts of the world, which positioned the biological mother as the sole caregiver and nurturer of children (Ambert, 1994). The current cultural dominance of this ideological construction of mothering masks significant class, race, and ethnic differences in the way mothering is practised. For example, in the US context, Collins (1999) describes the importance of African-American women in a family's social and community network who act as 'other mothers' in the raising of children. Ambert (1994) cites examples in the anthropological literature of communities in which children are cared for by multiple 'mothers', and some where mothers are not found to be particularly nurturing. This cross-cultural evidence leads Ambert to argue that one mother is not 'a necessity of human nature', even though 'it may be that mothers are indeed the most important persons and parents in a majority of children's lives in modern, urban and technological societies' (ibid., 530).

In North American society, the heyday of stay-at-home mothers managing the households and children of breadwinner fathers was during the post-war economy of the 1950s, when many families could survive on one income and when the demographic phenomenon of the **baby boom** was beginning. This period is viewed nostalgically by some as representing an ideal form of family life, which is reflected today in **neo-liberal** political policies formulated around 'traditional family values'. This is the era the US sociological theorist Talcott Parsons was describing when he theorized a woman's family role (based on the primacy of the mother–child bond) as the *expressive* leader, responsible for the emotional nurture of family members, and a man's as the *instrumental* leader, responsible above all for financial support (Parsons, 1955). Other commentators point out that the period of the 1950s was an anomaly, produced by a number of factors—economic growth, suburbanization, a strong collective desire for the life-affirming comfort of marriage and family life after the years of war. In North America, other forces for change were soon to reorganize family life once again.

The most important of these changes, as mentioned in the discussion on fathering, was the movement of women into the paid labour force, particularly in the 1960s and 1970s. In Canada, for example, women's labour force participation rate moved from 29.1 per cent in 1961 to 51.8 per cent in 1981 (Beaujot, 2000: 136). Over the decades, their work histories have become much more similar to men's. Where once childbirth signalled the end of paid employment and a turn to full-time child-rearing, mothers began to take temporary maternity leaves and then return to paid work. In 2002, 62 per cent of mothers whose youngest child was under three were in paid employment; 68 per cent of those whose youngest child was aged three

to five also had paying jobs (Statistics Canada, 2003; see Table 4.1 for more information).

These mothers face what US sociologist Sharon Hays (1996) calls 'cultural contradictions'. On the one hand, they must confront the expectations of the workplace—rational, efficiency-oriented, the domain of the 'instrumental' (in other words, male) worker. On the other hand, they must conform to prevailing ideological expectations about mothering and motherhood, which require them to be devoted, selfless nurturers with primary responsibility for their children

Hays has labelled the dominant contemporary ideology of mothering as 'intensive mothering'. She describes it by drawing on the practices and beliefs of Rachel, one of the mothers she interviewed for her study. Rachel is a married professional woman with a two-year-old daughter, Kristin. According to Hays, Rachel believes that as the mother she must be the central caregiver (even though Kristin is also cared for by her emotionally involved father and by qualified child-care providers). Rachel also believes she must put her child's needs before her own, and must attend to all those needs at all the different stages of Kristin's emotional and intellectual development. This in turn requires her to draw on expert knowledge about child development so she will know what to do. And Rachel also understands that this is an emotionally demanding task, since the foundation of this kind of mothering is love.

TABLE 4.1 Percentage of Women Employed, by Age of Youngest Child, Selected Years, 1980–2002

	Youngest child under 3	Youngest child aged 3–5	Youngest child aged 6–15	Total with children under age 16
1980	37.1	45.3	53.5	47.1
1985	46.9	52.1	59.0	54.0
1990	53.8	59.8	70.2	63.2
1995	56.7	60.7	70.0	64.2
2000	60.9	67.8	74.5	69.5
2001	62.0	67.4	75.3	70.3
2002	62.4	68.4	76.9	71.5

SOURCE: Statistics Canada, *Women in Canada: Work Chapter Updates*, 2003.

In sum, says Hays, intensive mothering calls for methods of child-rearing that are 'child-centered, expert-guided, emotionally absorbing, labor-intensive, and financially expensive' (Hays, 1996: 8).

Intensive mothering, like breadwinning for fathers, has a moral dimension as well. It acts as a measuring stick, or a template, for what mothers *should* do. The fact that many mothers are not in a position to engage in mothering that is expert-guided or labour-intensive or financially expensive does not diminish its ideological power. Hays included working-class and poor mothers in her study, and found that they had different standards for what good mothers should provide, as well as different ideas about how to meet children's needs. But, Hays argues, 'all these mothers share a set of fundamental assumptions about the importance of putting their children's needs first and dedicating themselves to providing what is best for their kids, as they understand it' (ibid., 86).

Perspectives on the Needs of Children

Ideas about appropriate mothering and fathering are intricately connected to and, indeed, follow from ideas about children and their needs. Some of the shifts in thinking, as noted above, have resulted from economic and other social change. But they have also followed from changes in expert opinion about child development and, more fundamentally, the moral nature and value of children. These changes, in turn, are linked to changing understandings of *childhood* as both a developmental stage and a socially constructed space (see Box 4.1).

Box 4.1 The Creation of Childhood

The French historian Philippe Ariès is generally credited with introducing a 'paradigm shift' (Cook, 2004) in scholarly circles in the 1960s with his assertion that childhood was a relatively recent invention. Ariès's most widely cited claim, based largely on paintings dating back to the twelfth century, is that childhood as a separate, segregated stage of human development did not exist until around the seventeenth century. Ariès notes that children in medieval art were portrayed simply as miniature adults. He cites other sources, along with his analysis of paintings, to show that children's dress and their games and stories were modelled on those of adults—as if, at an age hardly past infancy, they were full inhabitants of the adult world. While our modern world is 'obsessed by the physical, moral and sexual problems of childhood', this was not a problem in the Middle Ages, because on or soon after weaning 'the child became the natural companion of the adult.' This was the case, Ariès concluded, because medieval civilization 'had no idea of education' (Ariès, 1962: 411). It was only with the revival of interest in education, gathering apace in the seventeenth and eighteenth centuries, galvanized by religious reformers and **Enlightenment** scholars, that children came to be seen as needing preparation for adult life. This recognition constructed childhood itself as a distinct phase in individual development.

There is scholarly disagreement about the details of these claims (for discussion, see Cook, 2004; Pollock, 1983). But as James and James (2001) point out, the broad framework of Ariès's argument remains 'foundational'. First, Ariès forces us to see childhood as a 'particular cultural phrasing of the early part of the life course, historically and politically contingent and subject to change'. Second, the way we see and behave towards children of necessity shapes children's experiences of being a child and also 'their responses to and engagement with the adult world' (James and James, 2001: 27).

In seventeenth- and eighteenth-century Western Europe, for example, recognition of childhood as a special and valuable period of life corresponded to views emerging during the same period of children as precious and innocent, in need of protection and preparation for the challenges of adult life, and as possessors of souls in need of saving. The philosophers John Locke and Jean-Jacques Rousseau both wrote treatises on child-rearing, which may well have influenced middle-class and aristocratic families in particular.

Ehrensaft (2001) claims that understandings of childhood throughout history have moved between two poles of a continuum. At one end is the child as miniature adult, at the other the child as 'innocent cherub'. Each historical era develops an image of childhood and children that fits the context in which those children must grow. In earlier historical time periods, but also in other parts of the contemporary world, children's early independence and their economic contributions to their family's support have been, and continue to be, essential to family survival. In the context of contemporary industrialized societies, children are better placed to be 'innocent cherubs' (Ehrensaft, 2001: 308).

One factor that could certainly explain parental indifference to the needs of children *as children* in earlier historical periods is high infant mortality. Parents could hardly be expected to make a significant sentimental investment in children until they could be more assured of their survival. (An excellent contemporary example of this argument is found in the work of Nancy Scheper-Hughes, discussed in Box 4.2.) On the other hand, scholars such as Shorter (1977) argue that more parental love and concern might have ensured that more babies did survive. Shorter's views are generally disposed of by other historical evidence clearly demonstrating parental concern and affection for their children and grief over their deaths (e.g., Pollock, 1983). The fact that some parental practices may have harmed children could be attributed to a lack of knowledge, but not necessarily to a lack of love.

THE CANADIAN CONTEXT

In Canada, infant mortality in the late nineteenth and early twentieth centuries was the issue that first mobilized experts to provide advice for mothers. Mothers, as noted above, had clearly been positioned as those most responsible for their children's welfare, and they had already been the focus of social reformers' concerns about family life.

Especially in urban areas, infant mortality rates were a legitimate source of concern. In 1901, for example, the City of Toronto reported that 160 of every 1,000 babies died before their first birthday. In 1907 that rate climbed to 197. In Montreal, about one-third of all infants died (Arnup, 1994: 14–15). But while reformers had been putting pressure on governments to recognize the scale of the problem, Arnup notes that infant mortality began to receive serious government attention when it was viewed in the context of the nation's health. A significant number of potential Canadian recruits for military service during World War I had to be turned away because of ill health. National health concerns were compounded by the effects of the war (Canada sustained some 250,000 casualties, 60,681 of them fatal). Some 50,000 Canadians also died from the post- war Spanish influenza epidemic. This damage, in a population just over eight million, was serious indeed. Arnup cites a 1922 editorial in the *Canadian Medical Association Journal* calling for 'a more careful medical oversight of all children during their early years of growth' (ibid., 19).

Arnup's 1994 book, *Education for Motherhood: Advice for Mothers in Twentieth-Century Canada*, goes on to document the way concerns about infant health were taken up. She notes that while departments of health and divisions of child welfare were established at every level of government, in practice little was done to address the poverty, malnutrition, and poor housing that were the root causes of much infant ill health. Instead, responsibility was placed squarely on mothers, and an elaborate educational campaign was mounted to train mothers in their proper duties. The campaign was conducted through well-baby clinics, lectures

Box 4.2 The Social Conditions of Motherhood

Motherhood as a biological phenomenon is the basis for powerful cultural understandings about how mothers are supposed to behave as mothers. Mothers' practices are often seen as instinctual, universal, and 'natural'. Mothers are supposed to know what to do with their babies, just as the 'maternal instinct' is supposed to ensure that they will love their babies unconditionally. Because of this love, they are also assumed to be totally invested in their babies' survival.

But scholars point out that far from being 'natural' and 'universal', mothering practices are shaped by the social and economic context in which mothers live (Glenn, 1994; Ambert, 1994). How a very different environment can produce very different mothering practices is vividly shown in the work of anthropologist Nancy Scheper-Hughes, who worked in the 1960s as a medic among desperately poor mothers in an urban slum community in Brazil.

Scheper-Hughes found that in an environment of poverty and high infant mortality, mothers developed differential patterns of nurturing, distinguishing infants likely to thrive, and therefore considered 'keepers', from those they thought of as having been born 'already wanting to die'. Keepers were tended in the careful, committed way associated with Western 'mother love'. Babies in the second category were left for nature to take its course. Scheper-Hughes reports that these babies were often carefully washed, combed, and powdered—but not fed. When they died, they usually did so 'with candles propped up in tiny waxen hands to light their way to the afterlife' (Scheper-Hughes, 1999: 258). They were considered little angels, returning to the place from which they had just come. Scheper-Hughes argues that a high expectancy of infant death is 'a powerful shaper of maternal thinking and practice'. She adds:

> I am *not* arguing that mother love, as we understand it, is deficient or absent in this threatened little human community but rather that its life history, its course, is different, shaped by overwhelming economic and cultural constraints. (Ibid., 257)

in department stores, radio programs, and columns in women's magazines, as well as in the informational material produced by the professionals in the child health bureaucracy.

Arnup shows how, over the decades of the twentieth century, the advice changed as physicians and other professionals changed their views about what children needed. Concerns about infant mortality in the early decades of the century led to a preoccupation with feeding and a focus on schedules and regimentation. After World War II, concern about rigidly training children to develop good habits gave way to a new maturational-developmental approach to child development, represented most prominently by Arnold Gesell at the Yale Clinic of Child Development. This new approach was reflected in the advice manual first published in 1946 by Dr Benjamin Spock. Spock's *Baby and Child Care* offered a more relaxed, permissive, and child-centred approach to child-rearing.

Baby and Child Care has enjoyed enormous popularity, in Canada and elsewhere. (It is reported to have been translated into 38 languages and to have sold some 50 million copies worldwide at the time of Spock's death in 1998.) It characterized a trend in the advice literature to emphasize children's needs, and mothers' responsibility to meet them. Like Hays, who sees current advice manuals as 'fully elaborated models of intensive mothering' (Hays, 1996: 51), Canadian sociologist Glenda Wall (2004) points to the increased responsibility placed on mothers for their children's cognitive and emotional well-being. Wall considers research and theories in developmental psychology that have been crucial to this shift, and cites a variety of developmental psychology known as 'new brain research' as the latest example.

Advice literature informed by this 'new brain research' tells parents that children need early and appropriate stimulation—before they turn six—to ensure optimal brain development. If they don't get it, they will experience a deficit that can't easily be made up. Wall notes that, though the 'facts' of this research are not universally accepted in the scientific community, they have been taken up enthusiastically in Canada and elsewhere. Foundations like the Canadian Institute of Child Health and the Invest in Kids Foundation have organized educational campaigns and achieved a wide distribution of resource kits and literature to new parents. In Ontario, following the 1999 Early Years Study commissioned by then Premier Mike Harris, the provincial government initiated plans for a network of Early Years Centres across the province. By early 2003, there were 42 such centres, with 61 more scheduled to open during the year (Wall, 2004: 42).

Wall argues that advice based on 'new brain research' builds on earlier (and now largely discredited) theories of developmental psychology stressing the importance of mother–infant bonding. These theories resonate with the dominant ideology of mothering. So does the advice based on 'new brain research'. In fact, it extends the requirements of intensive mothering already discussed. Wall considers it also conforms to a trend in child-rearing ideology towards perfecting children, at a time of

rapid social and economic change and uncertainty about the future. At the same time, the tendency is to privatize child-rearing responsibilities even as, with the 'new brain research' initiatives, those responsibilities become more burdensome. The focus of programs and policies like Ontario's Early Years Centres is to provide parents with information and leave them to raise perfect children without further support (ibid.).

Parenting in Practice

Advice to parents, based on expert opinion about what children need, ties in to dominant ideologies of mothering and fathering like those described earlier. These shape not only what people do, but how they make sense of what they do and what they think they ought to do. The 'ought' is important, because in practice many people do not conform to the ideal. Dominant images of mothering and fathering may work in the 'Standard North American Family' described by Smith (1993), but are much more difficult to conform to in non-SNAF families.

For example, in 2001 about 16 per cent of Canadian families were single-parent (predominantly single-mother) families. Conforming to a dominant image of mothering (or fathering) can't be managed easily when the other parent is absent, or even present but not resident in the household. There are different complications when parents separate or divorce, then form new relationships. This often has the effect of introducing new adult relationships—which may or may not be considered 'parental'—into children's lives. If both of the new partners bring children into the relationship, the complications redouble.

STEPFAMILIES AND 'BLENDED' FAMILIES

Statistics Canada defines a stepfamily as one in which at least one of the children in the household is from a previous relationship of one of the parents. In a 'simple' stepfamily, the children of only one of the spouses live in the household. In a 'blended' family, there are children of both partners from one or more previous relationships, or children from the current union and at least one prior one. According to General Social Survey data, Canada had 503,100 stepfamilies in 2001, compared to 430,500 in 1995. This represented almost 12 per cent of all Canadian couples with children in 2001, compared with 10 per cent in 1995 (Statistics Canada, 2002a). About 50 per cent of stepfamilies contained only the children of the female partner. About 10 per cent contained only the male partner's children. The remainder, about 40 per cent, were 'blended'. In most of these cases (81 per cent) they were formed after the birth of a child to the couple. The other 19 per cent included children from previous relationships of both partners (Statistics Canada, 2002b).

Juby (2003–4) notes that these statistics suggest stepfamilies are still a minority family type. She argues that the stepfamily experience is in fact much more widespread than cross-sectional survey data (like those derived from the General Social Survey) indicate. Such data, she points out, show the prevalence of the stepfamily experience at a given point in time but are unable to show how common it is over the lifetime of the population. Juby adds that another reason survey statistics underestimate the extent of the stepfamily experience is that family statistics are usually based on families as *residential* units. This means, for example, that situations where children live mostly with one parent (in one 'residential unit'), while the other parent has formed a new relationship and had other children in another 'residential unit', are not counted in the stepfamily statistics. Juby cites the conjugal history of Martin and Louise to make her point. They lived together for a couple of years, then married when their son Thomas was conceived. Later they had a second child, Laura. When Laura was four, they separated. Martin later moved in with Marie, and two years later, Martin and Marie had a baby, Jessica. Because Thomas and Laura lived mostly with their mother, their step-parent relationships through their father's family didn't 'count', statistically speaking. Juby feels strongly that they *should* count.

Juby and her colleagues have attempted to overcome the shortcomings of cross-sectional data in their study of stepfamily and blended family networks by using data from the children being followed through the National Longitudinal Study of Children and Youth. Their findings strikingly illustrate the extent to which Canadian children are likely to experience stepfamily relationships in the course of their lives. For example, of the children included in the study whose parents had separated, one-third of the fathers and a quarter of the mothers had remarried or started living with someone other than the child's other parent within three years of separation. Close to half the new relationships formed by separated parents were with people who already had children from a previous relationship. Overall, almost one in five children aged between birth and 13 years in 1996–7 had at least one stepsibling or half-sibling in their family network (Juby et al., 2005).

The study by Juby et al. also noted some other interesting characteristics of stepfamilies. For example, since children most often live with their mothers after separation and divorce, the children in their study sample were much more likely to be living with mothers and stepfathers (84 per cent) than with fathers and stepmothers. For the same reason, the study also found that stepsiblings rarely shared the same residence. In fact, Thomas and Laura, described above, are quite characteristic of the study findings. But for Juby, the fact that they don't share a permanent residence with their father and his new family does not diminish the significance of the stepfamily experience in their lives.

The reality is that these relationships *are* of great importance, at many different levels. Even though Thomas and Laura spend only weekends and holidays with their father and his new family, there are important implications for them all. For Martin, being a part-time Dad to Thomas and Laura involves frequent emotional adjustments as his children come and go. He's also affected financially, since he needs a bigger house with separate bedrooms for Laura and Thomas, and he contributes to the cost of Louise's house through monthly child support payments. Marie has to deal with the challenges of being a part-time stepmother, and Thomas and Laura with having two 'mothers'. Once Jessica comes along, Thomas and Laura also have to cope with the potential threat to their father's affection posed by the new baby, who, unlike them, lives with him all the time. As for Jessica, she must learn to negotiate the complicated universe into which she was born. She will never be the oldest or the only child in the family network . . . she has to shift back and forward between the positions of younger half-sibling when Thomas and Laura are in the house, and only child when they leave. (Juby, 2003: 5–6)

The complexities of separations and new unions have given rise to the phenomenon of the 'new extended family' (Cherlin and Furstenberg, 1994) whose boundaries are ambiguous and in which family roles are not always clear. Cherlin and Furstenberg note that, in a marriage following divorce, a step-parent does not replace the step-child's non-resident parent, as was usually the case in earlier generations when remarriages followed the death of a spouse. The lack of norms and guidelines available to step-parents suggest that the step-parent role is 'incompletely institutional-ized'. What also seems to be the case, as step-parents discover in practice, is that 'they have been issued only a limited license to parent' (ibid., 367). Step-parents, like the adoptive parents discussed earlier in the research by Miall and March (2003), experience all the difficulties of social parenting, often in situations where biological parents may also be in the picture.

This is challenging for all concerned. Cherlin and Furstenberg cite research suggesting that the adjustment can take years to complete. The situation is particularly tricky for stepmothers, who typically don't live with their stepchildren but must establish a connection to them on visits.

A stepmother is also competing with the children's biological mother, with whom they usually have a closer connection. As one stepmother put it, 'When they come back from their mom's on Sunday night, I want to cry. They treat me differ-ent[ly]. They want me to know I am not their real mom' (Mason et al., 2002: 514). Stepfathers, on the other hand, may be competing with non-cus-todial fathers, many of whom see little of their chil-dren. In this context stepfathers may be able to fill a vacuum (Cherlin and Furstenberg, 1994).

In spite of the challenges, evidence suggests that step-parents make a significant difference to the families they join. In an extensive study of stepfamily fucntioning in the US, Mason et al. (2002) found that step-parents served as primary caregivers. They also performed the 'yeoman work' of helping with homework and shuttling the chil-dren back and forth, just as biological parents do. The researchers found that, 'on the more delicate issues of giving advice and setting and enforcing rules', stepparents were less often the leaders but still participated actively. They also made a major difference to the economic well-being of their stepchildren (Mason et al., 2002: 518).

SAME-SEX FAMILIES

Stereotypical expectations about 'mothering' and 'fathering', based on the dominant ideologies described earlier, also do not work well for same-sex couples with children. About 15 per cent of the 15,200 female same-sex couples counted for the first time in the 2001 Canadian census had children living with them, as did about 3 per cent of the 19,000 male same-sex couples. In cases where these children were born to prior hetero-sexual relationships, biological mothers and fathers may still be present and active in the child's family network. In cases where two women, or two men, each with children, form a new partner-ship, the step- or blended-family dynamics just described are also characteristic.

Increasingly, however, children are being born or adopted into same-sex families. While adoption is an option for gay men, it is not yet widespread in Canada, and information about gay adoptive fathers is almost non-existent. The situation is different for lesbian mothers. Because of the possibility for women to make use of donor insemination (DI) using either known or unknown donors, increasing numbers of children are being born within lesbian relationships. Known donors, as biological fathers, may have a role in the child's life, but more often as 'kindly uncles' than as fathers (Dunne, 2000). The major challenge in such families is to accommodate two mothers, one of whom gave birth to the child, the other of whom is a 'social' rather than a biological mother. Reimann (1997), in a study of US lesbian families, concluded that the distinction between the biological mother and the non-biological mother affected couples in three main areas: *public* motherhood, which is concerned with how motherhood is defined through the law and social customs; *relational* motherhood, which refers to the definition of motherhood shared by parents and their children in the family; and *personal* motherhood, which links to the idea of motherhood as personal identity (Reimann, 1997: 164–5). Studies suggest that while co-mothers confront challenges in all three domains, lesbian couples work hard, and with some success, to achieve a more egalitarian sharing of parenting and household work than that often found in the households of heterosexual couples. Based on her Canadian study of lesbian families, Nelson (1996) comments:

> Lesbian D.I. couples . . . present a substantial challenge to established maternal culture by demanding that they (both partners) not be differentiated on the basis of having given birth or not. By insisting that non-biological mothers are mothers too, these women have the potential to alter the understanding mothers have of motherhood. In this sense, lesbian motherhood through donor insemination can be seen as a revolutionary activity. (Nelson, 1996: 101)

Research information is lacking for gay adoptive fathers. But it is easy to see that the need to accommodate two fathers, while probably not involving a comparison of biological and non-biological fatherhood, would still require negotiation in the public, relational, and personal domains identified by Reimann.

OTHER CHALLENGES TO 'IDEAL' MOTHERING AND FATHERING

Even among two-parent heterosexual couples raising their own biological children, parenting practices are shaped by factors that make ideal mothering and fathering hard to achieve. Poverty, ill health, unemployment, and the presence of children with special needs all pose challenges for parents. Most parents 'share in the cultural mandate to support their children, attend to their physical well-being, help them stay out of trouble and push them to achieve' (Daly, 2004: 1). But they differ in their interpretation of all these parenting responsibilities and their capacity to fulfill them.

Socio-economic class and the concomitant level of access to material and cultural resources are major influences on parenting. In an ethnographic study of middle-class, working-class, and poor families in the US, Lareau (2002) found that middle-class families (both white and black) engaged in what she called 'concerted cultivation' of their children. In part, this involves the kind of financially expensive, labour-intensive promotion of their children's talents and abilities (through a variety of organized extracurricular activities) covered in Hays's (1996) description of intensive mothering. These parents also stressed language use and the development of reasoning, with talking as the major means of disciplining their children. In contrast, the working-class and poor parents emphasized the 'accomplishment of natural growth'. Lareau commented: 'These parents believe that as long as they provide love, food and safety, their children will grow and thrive' (Lareau, 2002: 748–9). Working-class parents involved their children in fewer organized activities; they used language less in disciplining their children; they were more directive; and they placed more emphasis on physical discipline than did the middle-class parents. Lareau found that the middle-class pattern of 'concerted cultivation' produced an emerging sense of entitlement in children, who were confident about speaking up and asking questions. In contrast, the working-class pattern of the accomplishment of natural growth seemed to produce an attitude, in both parents and children, of outward deference and compliance to authority (ibid., 749).

The need in most families to organize family responsibilities around paid work is stressful for parents. In working-class families, long hours of work, occasionally at more than one job, may be necessary to make ends meet. In middle-class families, especially in times of economic uncertainty and restructuring, the expectations placed on professional jobs often expand as organizations downsize. Long hours may be necessary both to keep up and to stay hired. Employers are only slowly becoming aware of the need for 'work–family balance', and have been equally slow to offer programs that would help (Duxbury and Higgins, 2002).

At the same time, the 'concerted cultivation' in parenting identified by Lareau, the time- and labour-intensive implications of intensive mothering, and the pressures on breadwinner fathers to be more involved in their families put other time pressures on families. In a book appropriately titled *The Time Bind*, US sociologist Arlie Hochschild describes the time pressures many parents face at home as a consequence of long hours at work. Hochschild (1997) argues that there is now a need to strive for workplace-like efficiency at home as well, as parents schedule and multi-task to get everything done. In an earlier (1989) study, Hochschild identified the 'second shift' that mothers put in at home on top of their regular working day. Now, she argues, parents need to do a 'third shift' of emotional work to compensate children for the time-crunched second shift.

Parenting organized around paid work and the worker-like, rational efficiency required of time-stressed parents at home are elements of what Daly (2004) calls the current 'culture of parenting'—the 'background undercurrents that guide what seem right, natural or appropriate' (Daly, 2004: 1). So are the ideologies of mothering and fathering already discussed, along with their implications, as Daly notes, for gender practice. Daly points out that parenting today also takes place in a culture of consumption, in which children's needs and wants exert a powerful influence on how time and money are spent. Finally, Daly notes that parenting takes place in a media culture, in which children are at the centre of a highly politicized debate about the effects of media technology—including, increasingly, computer technology. Daly concludes:

> For all parents, this is an environment that requires the ongoing refinement of navigation skills that will take them through uncharted waters. The culture of parenthood is a culture without prescription where knowledge of the traditional rules of the game is less important than a well-stocked tool box that positions them to puzzle through with their children changing gender practices, work expectations, media culture and consumer pressures. Above all, the culture of parenting is one that is shaped by the challenges of an emergent future rather than a settled past. (Daly, 2004: 7)

Children and Their Families

The view of parents 'puzzling through *with their children*' the dilemmas and challenges of a rapidly changing world positions children as active participants in the process. In some ways, as sociologist Barrie Thorne points out, it's the difference between 'bringing up' and 'growing up'. Thorne says she finds it helpful to deal with this difference by thinking of child-rearing as a 'shared *caring project*', which brings together and makes visible the work of many actors. In a series of vivid metaphors, she likens child-rearing to 'the producing of a movie, the building of a house, or the moment-by-moment improvisation . . . of a dance'. And children, she notes, 'often prefer to dance or to build, at least in part, according to their own designs' (Thorne, 2001: 365–6).

The current 'culture of parenting', as described above by Daly, places stress on children as well as parents. The hurried, time-stretched, hyper-organized environment of many middle-class families may produce children whose access to piano lessons and soccer camps and math tutors gives them considerable cultural capital, which will probably parlay into privilege in the competitive adult world they will shortly enter. As part of the practices of intensive mothering described by Hays (1996), this environment also produces children accustomed to having their needs met and feeling entitled to being heard (Lareau, 2002). But if many children's needs are indulged in middle-class households like these, other needs may not be met so well. Daly notes that, contrary to popular belief, parents may not be spending less time with their children. Rather, the time parents and children spend together has become more 'goal-oriented, structured, and saturated with activity' (Daly, 2004: 3). This is vividly illustrated in the comment of one of Hochschild's interviewees, a mother in full-time paid employment:

> **Quality time** is seven-thirty to eight-thirty at night, and then it's time for bed. I'm ready at seven-thirty, but Melinda has other ideas. As soon as quality time comes she wants to have her bath or watch TV; *no way* is she going to play with Mommy. Later, when I'm ready to drop, *then* she's ready for quality time. (Hochschild, 1997: 216)

Children, especially very young ones, have their own ideas about how to spend time. Hochschild points out what all parents know: when left to their own devices, children's pace of life is different. They dawdle, then they run, in what she calls the 'stop and go of childhood itself' (ibid.). Ehrensaft, who described the competing images of children as either 'miniature adults' or 'innocent cherubs', would see the dawdling, playful child as the innocent cherub. But increasingly, children are expected to be 'miniature adults', fitting in with all the time demands and absences from home required by adult work schedules. The paradox is that when they *are* home, they may be indulged and often materially overcompensated by parents who feel guilty about the needs they may not be meeting. Ehrensaft calls such children 'kinderdults' (half children—'Kinder' is the German word for children—and half adults). They live in a world where in one sense childhood has disappeared and in another sense, because of children's prolonged dependence on their parents while completing their education, it goes on longer than it has in the past (Ehrensaft, 2001: 305–6).

Parents differ in their ability to provide for their children financially. But this is only one way differences among parents set up differences among children. In the same way that children who are ill or who have other special needs can transform the lives of their parents, so there are many children whose lives are shaped by the needs or limitations of parents. Some parents may not be able to provide much guidance to children navigating their way to adulthood in Canadian society. These children must become 'kinderdults' of a different kind. For example, 11-year-old Sanela, whose father was killed in the war in the Balkans, came to Canada as a refugee with her seriously ill mother and two younger siblings. With a mother preoccupied with her illness and grieving her many losses, and with siblings she needed to care for, Sanela had responsibilities and worries most would agree were far beyond those an 11-year-old should bear. Fortunately, some external help was available. She was part of a national play program for at-risk refugee children, designed to help children 'traumatized by the experiences of war and migration' (Fantino and Colak, 2001: 592). Fantino and Colak point out that 300,000 immigrant children (about 15 per cent of them refugees) came to Canada between 1995 and 1999. These are children who must bridge significant cultural and generational differences. At school, they want to fit in and be accepted by their peers. At home, they may experience a 'dependency and role reversal' by becoming 'interpreters and "**cultural brokers**"' for their parents (ibid., 589).

Children like Sanela clearly need help from outside the family to get their special needs met. But Daly's analysis of the culture of parenting, described above, suggests that it is not easy for most parents to meet the increasingly high social expectations put upon them. Making parents alone responsible for children's needs that are framed by experts as ever more pressing puts parents in a very difficult position. Negotiation and compromise seem to be the best strategies at present.

Conclusion

The challenges and difficulties of raising children will not put people off. The vast majority of young Canadians intend to raise families, no doubt because they are aware of the rich rewards of a relationship, and an endeavour, like no other. As this chapter has shown, however, people do not go about the job of parenting as free agents, able to make up the rules as they go along. In any culture, parenting practices are shaped by powerful ideologies about mothering and fathering. Mothering and fathering are constructed in response to prevailing understandings about the nature and needs of children; these needs change as expert opinion changes. But mothers and fathers also face economic pressures, shaped in part by their understandings of their children's material needs. Working to meet these needs obligates them to employers who see them as workers, not parents. Both mothers and fathers experience 'cultural contradictions' (Hays, 1996).

One way out of the dilemma is to provide parents with more public support. Jenson (2004) has noticed a move in this direction from Canada's public policy-makers. She points to a shift in the 1990s from a policy framework or paradigm based on the assumption that parents have full responsibility for children, to one she labels an 'investing-in-children' paradigm. The assumption of this second paradigm is that parents are also workers, that families are changing, and that the care of children must be shared by the broader community. Jenson argues that this shift in thinking has come partly as governments become more aware of the economic and social risks many children confront, but also because they have become more willing to listen to experts and advocates for children. One example of this is the federal government's investment, through Statistics Canada, in the National Longitudinal Study of Children and Youth, intended to provide detailed ongoing information about Canada's 'vulnerable children' (Willms, 2002). When child-centred policies lead to child-centred programs—like quality daycare, as one example—the lives of many parents will be made easier, and the lives of children will be enriched.

Study Questions

1. How are terms like 'single-parent family' and 'same-sex couple' connected to the discussion about SNAF as an ideological code?
2. A small but slowly growing minority of couples are challenging ideologies of mothering and fathering by trading places, so that the father is the main care provider for children and the mother is the main breadwinner. How hard would that be to do in the community in which you live?
3. Why might men be reluctant to take advantage of 'family-friendly' workplace policies?
4. Why is parenting advice based on the new brain research framed as particularly challenging for mothers?

Glossary

Baby boom The sharp increase in birth rates in industrialized countries in the 1950s and 1960s.

'Cultural broker' Individual in a position to explain the workings of a new culture to another person.

Enlightenment The eighteenth-century philosophy emphasizing reason, science, and individualism rather than tradition and religious beliefs.

Ethnography Detailed field study based on extensive observation and interviews.

Gender-neutral Equally applicable to women and men.

Ideology A system of connected ideas and beliefs about a subject.

Neo-liberalism A political philosophy geared to restructuring society (partly by reducing social programs and placing responsibility on individuals to solve social problems) to better meet the demands of the global marketplace.

Quality time The term popularly used to describe the special time some working parents schedule to devote exclusively to their children.

Social parenthood The practice and experience of parenthood by adults who have no biological connection to the children they are parenting.

Work–family balance The term used in organizational contexts to describe the family and workplace responsibilities of working parents.

Websites

www.cfc-efc.ca
This public education website of Child and Family Canada includes resources on children and families from 50 non-profit organizations.

www.cprn.org.en/kids.cfm
Canadian Policy Research Networks is a non-profit 'think-tank' focusing on several key social issues. As part of its family network, CPRN has recently started the Kids Canada Policy Digest, an extensive on-line inventory of policies, programs, and research reports relating to children and families across Canada.

www.investinkids.ca
Invest In Kids website has as its main focus the first five years of the child's life. Parenting resources (based on the 'new brain research') to encourage optimal early years development can found here.

www.worklifecanada.ca
The Centre for Work, Families and Well-Being at the University of Guelph offers a compendium of Canadian statistics about work and family. It also has information about recent research projects, including the Father Involvement Research Alliance administered by the University of Guelph.

Further Readings

Arnup, Katherine. 1994. *Education for Motherhood: Advice for Mothers in Twentieth-Century Canada.* Toronto: University of Toronto Press. This is an interesting and accessible history of professional advice to Canadian mothers, documenting changing trends and mothers' responses.

Cook, Daniel Thomas. 2004. *The Commodification of Childhood: The Children's Clothing Industry and the Rise of the Child Consumer.* Durham, NC: Duke University Press. This short book is a fascinating history of the marketing of children's clothing, showing how over the first half of the twentieth century children's clothing retailers used highly differentiated age-based clothing to 'produce' correspondingly differentiated stages of childhood.

Fox, Bonnie. 2001. 'The formative years: How parenthood creates gender', *Canadian Review of Sociology and Anthropology* 38, 4: 373–90. Based on the author's study of a group of heterosexual couples as they made the transition to parenthood, this article illustrates how particular versions of mothering and fathering are negotiated.

Townsend, Nicholas. 2002. *The Package Deal: Marriage, Work and Fatherhood in Men's Lives.* Philadelphia: Temple University Press. This book is a study of the life stories of a group of men in a northern California town. The author explores their understandings of work, family life, and particularly fatherhood.

References

Ambert, Anne-Marie. 1994. 'An international perspective on parenting: Social change and social constructs', *Journal of Marriage and the Family* 56: 529–43.

Ariès, Philippe. 1962. *Centuries of Childhood*. New York: Alfred A. Knopf.

Arnup, Katherine. 1994. *Education for Motherhood*. Toronto: University of Toronto Press.

Beaujot, Roderic. 2000. *Earning and Caring*. Peterborough, Ont.: Broadview Press.

———. 2004. 'Delayed life transitions: Trends and implications'. Ottawa: Vanier Institute of the Family.

Brotherson, Sean, David Dollahite, and Alan Hawkins. 2005. 'Generative fathering and the dynamics of connection between fathers and their children', *Fathering* 3: 1–28.

Cherlin, Andrew J., and Frank F. Furstenberg. 1994. 'Stepfamilies in the United States: A reconsideration', *Annual Review of Sociology* 20: 359–81.

Christiansen, Shawn, and Rob Palkovitz. 2001. 'Why the "good provider" role still matters: Providing as a form of paternal involvement', *Journal of Family Issues* 22: 84–106.

Chunn, Dorothy. 2003. 'Boys will be men, girls will be mothers: The legal regulation of childhood in Toronto and Vancouver', in Nancy Janovicek and Joy Parr, eds, *Histories of Canadian Children and Youth*. Toronto: Oxford University Press.

Collins, Patricia Hill. 1999. 'The meaning of motherhood in black culture and black mother–daughter relationships', in Maxine Baca Zinn, Pierrette Hondagneu-Sotelo, and Michael A. Messner, eds, *Through the Prism of Difference*. Boston: Allyn and Bacon.

Cook, Daniel Thomas. 2004. *The Commodification of Childhood*. Durham, NC: Duke University Press.

Daly, Kerry. 2004. 'The changing culture of parenting'. Ottawa: Vanier Institute of the Family.

——— and Rob Palkovitz. 2004. 'Guest editorial: Reworking work and family issues for fathers', *Fathering* 2: 211–13.

Deutsch, F., and S. Saxon. 1998. 'Traditional ideologies, non-traditional lives', *Sex Roles* 38: 331–62.

Doherty, William, Edward Kouneski, and Martha Erickson. 1998. 'Responsible fathering: An overview and conceptual framework', *Journal of Marriage and the Family* 60: 277–92.

Doucet, Andrea. 2004. '"It's almost like I have a job, but I don't get paid": Fathers at home reconfiguring work, care and masculinity', *Fathering* 2: 277–303.

Dunne, Gillian. 2000. 'Opting into motherhood: Lesbians blurring the boundaries and transforming the meaning of parenthood and kinship', *Gender & Society* 14, 1: 11–35.

Duxbury, Linda, and Chris Higgins. 2002. *2001 National Work-Life Conflict Study: Report One*. Ottawa: Health Canada.

Ehrensaft, Diane. 2001. 'The kinderdult: The new child born to conflict between work and family', in Rosanna Hertz and Nancy L. Marshall, eds, *Working Families: The Transformation of the American Home*. Berkeley: University of California Press, 304–22.

Fantino, Ana Marie, and Alice Colak. 2001. 'Refugee children in Canada: Searching for identity', *Child Welfare* 80: 587–96.

Fox, Bonnie. 2001. 'The formative years: How parenthood creates gender', *Canadian Review of Sociology and Anthropology* 38: 373–90.

Glenn, Evelyn Nakano. 1994. 'Social constructions of mothering: A thematic overview', in Evelyn Nakano Glenn, Grace Chang, and Linda Rennie Forcie, eds, *Mothering: Ideology, Experience and Agency*. New York: Routledge.

Hays, Sharon. 1996. *The Cultural Contradictions of Motherhood*. New Haven: Yale University Press.

Hochschild, Arlie. 1989. *The Second Shift*. New York: Avon.

———. 1997. *The Time Bind*. New York: Metropolitan Books.

James, Allison, and Adrian L. James. 2001. 'Childhood: Toward a theory of continuity and change', *Annals of the American Association of Political and Social Sciences* 575: 25–37.

Jenson, Jane. 2004. 'Changing the paradigm: Family responsibility or investing in children', *Canadian Journal of Sociology* 29, 2: 169–92.

Juby, Heather. 2003. 'Yours, mine and ours: New boundaries for the modern stepfamily', *Transitions* 33, 4: 3–6.

———, N. Marcil-Gratton, and C. LeBourdais. 2005. *Moving On: The Expansion of the Family Network after Parents Separate*. Ottawa: Department of Justice. Catalogue no. 2004–FCY–9E.

Lareau, Annette. 2002. 'Invisible inequality: Social class and childrearing in black families and white families', *American Sociological Review* 67: 747–76.

LaRossa, Ralph. 1988. 'Fatherhood and social change', *Family Relations* 37: 451–8.

———. 1997. *The Modernization of Fatherhood*. Chicago: University of Chicago Press.

Luxton, Meg, and June Corman. 2001. *Getting By in Hard Times: Gendered Labour at Home and On the Job*. Toronto: University of Toronto Press.

Marks, Loren, and Rob Palkovitz. 2004. 'American fatherhood types: The good, the bad and the uninterested', *Fathering* 2: 113–29.

Mason, M., S. Harrison-Jay, G.M. Svare, and N.H. Wolfinger. 2002. 'Stepparents: De facto parents or legal strangers?', *Journal of Family Issues* 23, 4: 507–22.

Miall, Charlene, and Karen March. 2003. 'A comparison of biological and adoptive mothers and fathers: The relevance of biological kinship and gendered constructs of parenthood', *Adoption Quarterly* 6: 7–39.

Nelson, Fiona. 1996. *Lesbian Motherhood: An Exploration of Canadian Lesbian Families*. Toronto: University of Toronto Press.

Palameta, B. 2003. 'Who pays for domestic help?', *Perspectives*: 39–42 (Statistics Canada Catalogue no. 75–001–XPE).

Parsons, Talcott. 1955. 'The American family: Its relations to personality and to the social structure', in Talcott Parsons and Robert F. Bales, eds, *Family Socialization and Interaction Process*. Glencoe, Ill.: Free Press.

Pleck, Joseph. 1987. 'American fathering in historical perspective', in Michael Kimmel, ed., *Changing Men: New Directions in Research on Men and Masculinity*. Newbury Park, Calif.: Sage.

Pollock, Linda. 1983. *Forgotten Children*. Cambridge: Cambridge University Press.

Ranson, Gillian. 2004. 'Paid work, family work and the discourse of the full-time mother', in Andrea O'Reilly, ed., *Mother Matters: Motherhood as Discourse and Practice*. Toronto: Association for Research on Mothering.

Rapoport, R., and L. Bailyn. 1996. *Relinking Life and Work: Toward a Better Future*. New York: Ford Foundation.

Reimann, R. 1997. 'Does biology matter? Lesbian couples' transition to parenthood and their division of labor', *Qualitative Sociology* 20, 2: 153–85.

Roy, Kevin M. 2004. 'You can't eat love: Constructing provider role expectations for low-income and working-class fathers', *Fathering* 2: 253–76.

Scheper-Hughes, Nancy. 1999. '(M)Other love: Culture, scarcity and maternal thinking', in Maxine Baca Zinn, Pierrette Hondagneu-Sotelo, and Michael A. Messner, eds, *Through the Prism of Difference*. Boston: Allyn and Bacon.

Shorter, Edward. 1977. *The Making of the Modern Family*. New York: Basic Books.

Silver, Cynthia. 2000. 'Being there: The time dual-earner couples spend with their children', *Canadian Social Trends* 57: 26–9.

Smith, Dorothy. 1993. 'The Standard North American Family: SNAF as an ideological code', *Journal of Family Issues* 14: 50–65.

Statistics Canada. 2002a. *Profile of Canadian Families and Households: Diversification Continues*. Catalogue no. 96F0030XIE2001003. Ottawa: Ministry of Industry.

———. 2002b. *The Daily*, 11 July. At: <www.statcan.ca/ Daily/English/020711/d020711a.htm>.

———. 2003. *Women in Canada: Work Chapter Updates*. Catalogue no. 89FO133XIE. Ottawa: Ministry of Industry.

Thorne, Barrie. 2001. 'Pick-up time at Oakdale elementary school: Work and family from the vantage points of children', in Rosanna Hertz and Nancy L. Marshall, eds, *Working Families: The Transformation of the American Home*. Berkeley: University of California Press.

Townsend, Nicholas. 2002. *The Package Deal: Marriage, Work and Fatherhood in Men's Lives*. Philadelphia: Temple University Press.

Walker, Alexis, and Lori McGraw. 2000. 'Who is responsible for responsible fathering?', *Journal of Marriage and the Family* 62: 563–9.

Wall, Glenda. 2004. 'Is your child's brain potential maximized? Mothering in an age of new brain research', *Atlantis* 8: 41–50.

Walzer, Susan. 1996. 'Thinking about the baby: Gender and divisions of infant care', *Social Problems* 43: 219–34.

Wearing, Betsy. 1984. *The Ideology of Motherhood*. Sydney: George Allen and Unwin.

Wilkie, Jane. 1993. 'Changes in U.S. men's attitudes toward the family provider role, 1972–1989', *Gender & Society* 7: 261–79.

Willms, J. Douglas. 2002. *Vulnerable Children: Findings from Canada's National Longitudinal Survey of Children and Youth*. Edmonton: University of Alberta Press.

CHAPTER 5

Separation and Divorce: Fragmentation and Renewal of Families

Craig McKie

Learning Objectives

- To understand that family breakdown and divorce are separate processes.
- To appreciate that Canadians may choose the family context in which they live with few restrictions, and that many are choosing not to marry and thus do not require divorce if their relationships dissolve.
- To learn that divorce has become increasingly easily available since 1968.
- To discover that family breakdown has unfavourable consequences for the previous partners and any children they may have, and that these consequences may be made more difficult by a bitter divorce.
- To recognize that families that break down often experience a substantial and persistent decline in their standard of living.
- To understand that members of some religious communities may require additional religious divorce processes in addition to civil divorce in order for a person to remarry within those religious communities.
- To recognize that forming new families from remnants of old families brings a new range of adjustment problems for parents and children.

Introduction

It is remarkable how rapidly the personal rights and freedoms of individual Canadians emerged in family matters and became established in law in the second half of the twentieth century. Canadians are now free in the main to live, love, and cohabit as they wish, and comparatively easily freed of previous spousal relationships should they so choose. In less than 60 years, for instance, we have gone from a rigid and uncongenial divorce regime, which denied divorce with dignity to most Canadians, to the present era in which childless couples can jointly apply for an uncontested divorce by simple written assertion of marriage breakdown and can be certain of receiving one in short order without further complications.

Also in this period, provincial family legislation, which covers most separating couples whether married or not, was completely overhauled, and Canadians acquired a Charter of Rights and Freedoms that explicitly guaranteed freedoms of association, religious belief, and other fundamental freedoms, which pertain indirectly to the right to live in almost any family context one desires and which cannot be easily overridden by legislation. But divorce, and the allied provincial family law processes, nevertheless remains potentially litigious and adversarial in nature to this day. In operation, divorce is not often about reaching a civil and peaceful redefinition of future interests. The objective is still a binding, written, and enforceable contract between former marital partners that redefines their obligations to each other in perpetuity.

The fundamental changes in Canadian divorce and provincial family law in the twentieth century have gone hand in hand with the rapid secularization of Canadian society and diminution both of religious ideologies of all types and of theocratic social control of much mating behaviour that used to attract religious admonition. The arrival of same-sex marriage (and divorce) in the early twenty-first century is but one more step in the same direction. Few impediments now exist for any Canadian to cohabit however and wherever and with whomever he or she wishes, and to subsequently dissolve any such household without fear of legal prosecution. Residual restrictions are confined to bigamy and polygamy where multiple formal marriages are involved, and situations involving the sexual exploitation of minor children and close relatives, always provided these come to the attention of law enforcement authorities.

The social imperative to clarify and relabel a broken family arrangement (whether based on a marriage or more commonly, as time goes by, not so based) remains strong. Clarity is required in sexual access issues, in support obligations, and in the child access rights that inevitably arise when families fragment, through separation or death, to become lone-parent families, then often reformulate themselves within the context of a new marital union. While the English language lacks complex naming conventions for ex-kin and for step-kin, the law helps to clarify the obligations if not the exact nature of complex multiple-family arrangements that have become very common in the recombined families of the present era. They are more common in large part because we typically live much longer lives and, as a result, relationships have much more time at risk than was the case just a few generations ago. This felt necessity to rectify relationships and renew the nature of obligations seems very widespread, though the substance of the rules-making systems differs widely around the world.

The nature of those codes of practice, some being rules of practical application and some based in theological beliefs, is still in flux. Theological conflict concerning separation and divorce still often derives from the medieval dispute within Christianity over whether marriage is a sacrament (and thus permanent) or not a sacrament and thus dissolvable by the judicial organs of the state alone. There is much nuance in this argument as it has developed over the last 500 years, but contemporary Canadian practice clearly is informed by the latter, more liberal and permissive interpretation. The influence of religious views may still be seen, though, in the prohibition of multiple concurrent marriages (which are permitted under certain cir-

cumstances in the Islamic tradition—bigamy is criminalized in Canada by Section 290 and polygamy by Section 293 of the Criminal Code), and in the requirement for an authoritative legal process to divorce (in contrast to the much more informal Islamic divorce process or the requirement for a religious divorce process in some other cultures and religious traditions).

While the force of religious injunctions on mating behaviour in Canadian society has now considerably abated, its residue can still be seen in the laws of the land and, of course, in the culture-based behaviour of members of other cultures who have made a new life for themselves in Canada. Customs such as arranged marriages persist in this country though seldom seen or discussed openly. In the end, the personal freedoms conferred by the Charter of Rights and Freedoms and the accumulated jurisprudence of the common-law system have allowed Canadians to be innovative in forming and dissolving their social relationships with little or no fear of ecclesiastical retribution for their departures from expectations.

No better example of incremental liberalization of family law can be cited than the contemporary extension of marriage rights and obligations, and the inevitable extension of divorce rights, to same-sex couples. The first divorce of a former same-sex married couple was awarded in Ontario in September 2004. The unhappy couple, whose marriage lasted only five days, wished to remain anonymous.

The Legal Environment for Divorce in Canada

The terms and conditions for granting a divorce or a family law settlement in any given era are a direct reflection of the positive values attributed to an intact marriage (the contract being ended by divorce) or a non-marriage-based family (which is being dissolved and its assets distributed under provincial family law). Dissolution of either cannot seem to be too easy or costless lest offence be given to the ideals of the institution of the **family**. The way in which these values are expressed, however, is very much bound up in the conventional rhetoric of a particular era.

Until comparatively recently, roughly to the end of the nineteenth century, a marriage in essence was the transfer of chattel (a woman) from one owner (the father) to a new owner (the father of the prospective husband) in return for or together with tangible and intangible valuables such as a dowry, mutual enjoyment and protection, and the production of heirs to the family fortunes. Assent by the actual marrying couple was most often a formal requirement for marriage but coercion was by no means unknown. Indeed, some aspects of the traditional wedding in Canada still mirror this practice in ritual, as in the giving away of the bride by the father or a stand-in for the father. If, for the moment, one sees a marriage in this historical context as a commercial transaction between one male as a seller and another male as purchaser, then it stands to reason that the premature end of a marriage was the occasion for the reassessment of the terms of the initial transaction. If, after a marriage, adultery took place, a male (but not a female) third party could be sued for money damages for what was termed 'criminal conversation'. This arrangement gave rise to the still common expression 'a double standard' since husbands and wives were bound by different standards of behaviour.

A marriage was thus not only a relationship between partners but also a contractual building block of society, somewhat akin to a diplomatic agreement between clans, in which the state had a continuing and vital interest. A married couple had in some sense a capital value, which could be damaged through misbehaviour, and sanctions against offenders were called for.

But in the early twentieth century this view began to change. Looked at in this new fashion, the interests of the state and of the parties to a failed marriage came to lie in the peaceful simplification of the contractual tangle. Resolution lay in affixing new and continuing financial obligations, assessing damages, and apportioning the assets of the dissolving union in an orderly and predictable fashion. Once

these matters had been resolved, then the marriage contract itself could be dissolved (though the process was costly, tedious, and often involved perjury), in much the same way a business corporation is wound up and its charter surrendered.

Prior to 1968 in Canada, the availability of divorce was a provincial patchwork. Some provinces (for example, Nova Scotia) had their own divorce legislation and others (such as Quebec and Ontario) did not. This situation arose because divorce is a federal power under the Constitution, but successive Canadian governments failed to legislate in this area, leaving pre-Confederation statutes and practices still in place in some provinces. Persons living in provinces without divorce legislation who wished to obtain a divorce had to file a petition with the Senate of Canada alleging and providing proof of a marital offence (adultery, desertion, etc.) as grounds. A special committee of the Senate reviewed these petitions and if it found that the evidence provided was sufficient, the marriage would be ended by an Act of Parliament. This system was unfair on its face since it required the financial means to secure evidence and to file the petition, and also because it led to the falsification of grounds (such as trumped up adultery with confirming photos). Almost all of this unseemly and duplicitous political theatre, a legacy of centuries of British legal practice that Canada had inherited, ended in 1968, though adultery remains a ground for divorce to this day.

Modern divorce legislation, which dates from the Divorce Act in 1968, has removed from the mix all vestiges of the financial interests of parents as injured parties and changed the conflict to one strictly between the divorcing partners themselves. It also lessens the importance of the notion of marital offences (though many, such as bestiality, remained listed as causes for a divorce action from 1968 to 1985) and moved to a predominantly 'no fault' basis of settlement that abandons the notion of assessment of damages. But the core of the process remains the same. The parties are obliged to demonstrate marriage breakdown, settle their financial obligations in some fashion, settle custody and residency arrangements for any minor children of the marriage, and divide the assets and future income according to guidelines set out by the state. If the partners are unable to reach a settlement on these issues, a court will do it for them in a judgement. In other words, and in spite of extensive reform, divorce is still treated in many respects as the dissolution of a failed corporation.

The Ebb and Flow of Marital Unions

Most, but not all, Canadians find themselves in a marriage-like relationship at one time or another in their lives. A small proportion of people remain single and apart for their entire lives but this is surely atypical in present times. Figure 5.1 shows in rough detail some of the more prominent pathways. A newly formed couple has a number of choices. The partners may choose to cohabit on a short-term trial basis (the dissolution of which does not typically give rise to any legal process at all); they may form a durable common-law union (perhaps out of a

preference or perhaps out of necessity if there is an impediment such as a previous undissolved marriage) so as to present themselves to the world as the equivalent of married. This latter status does give rise to legal consequences under provincial family law if the union dissolves and was of considerable duration. And, of course, the couple can marry, in which case both family law and divorce law apply if the marriage ends in a separation. Finally, members of any of these three types of unions can, if they are agreeable, ignore the law altogether and proceed to the formation of new unions (always provided that, if married, they cannot legally remarry with impunity). It goes without saying that many couples remain in one stage or another, perhaps for the life of one of the married couple, then perhaps to enter the cycle again as a widow or widower with a remarriage late in her or his own personal life cycle. The death of a mate in a sense is similar to separation since it demands another kind of family law action, namely the distribution of the assets of the

Figure 5.1 The Life Cycle of Marital Union Formation and Dissolution

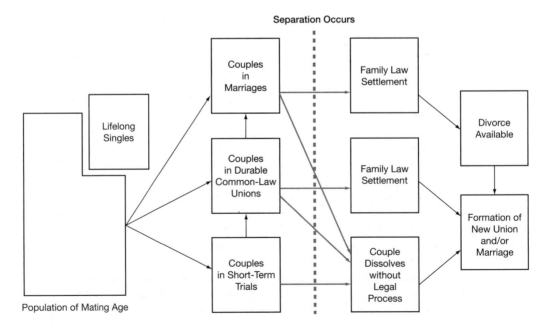

departed spouse, sometimes with probate. When a separated spouse dies, the two types of legal action can become intertwined.

In the present era of divorce in Canada, which dates from the passage of the Divorce Act (1968), the number of divorces granted in Canada increased dramatically as an initial wave of people who could not obtain divorces easily under the previous divorce regime took advantage of the new liberalized legislation to obtain divorces. Between 1971 and 1982, the annual total number of final decrees awarded rose from 29,684 to 70,430. A further revision of the Act in 1985 made marriage breakdown the sole grounds for divorce and eased the evidentiary standard to the demonstration of breakdown. Marriage breakdown is now indicated either by (1) separation of one year's duration; (2) adultery that can be proven; or (3) demonstration of intolerable mental or physical cruelty. Once again, after this revision the number of divorces increased, reaching a peak in 1987 at 96,200. Thereafter, total numbers levelled off and then declined as the backlog was cleared.

From the summary of divorces granted for the years 1998–2002 (Table 5.1) we can see that the number awarded in Canada in recent years has held steady at approximately 70,000 (down from the all-time peak of 96,000 in 1987). This represents a rate of 223.7 divorces for every 100,000 persons in Canada in 2002. The risk of married couples in Canada divorcing now reaches a peak after the fourth anniversary and thereafter declines rapidly. In about two-thirds of cases, child custody decisions were privately settled without judicial intervention. Of the minority of cases that were decided by a court, about half the decisions in 2002 were in favour of mothers. A further 42 per cent of the decisions involved joint custody, leaving a small minority of cases in which a father was awarded sole custody (about 9 per cent). Paternal sole custody remains unusual, as it always has been. Typically, paternal sole custody is awarded where older children close to the age of majority have expressed a preference (Statistics Canada, 2004a).

As to the probability of the marriages of Canadians ending in divorce, Statistics Canada has

Table 5.1 Divorces Granted in Canada, 1998–2002

	1998	1999	2000	2001	2002
Canada	69,088	70,910	71,144	71,110	70,155
Newfoundland and Labrador	944	892	913	755	842
Prince Edward Island	279	291	272	246	258
Nova Scotia	1,933	1,954	2,054	1,945	1,990
New Brunswick	1,473	1,671	1,717	1,570	1,461
Quebec	16,916	17,144	17,054	17,094	16,499
Ontario	25,149	26,088	26,148	26,516	26,170
Manitoba	2,443	2,572	2,430	2,480	2,396
Saskatchewan	2,246	2,237	2,194	1,955	1,959
Alberta	7,668	7,931	8,176	8,252	8,291
British Columbia	9,827	9,935	10,017	10,115	10,125
Northwest Territories*	93	83	94	83	68
Nunavut*			7	8	6

*Nunavut totals are included under NWT for 1998 and 1999.

SOURCE: Adapted from the Statistics Canada CANSIM database, Table 053–0002, at <www.statcan.ca/english/Pgdb/fail02.htm>; accessed 3 Jan. 2005.

reported that 'the proportion of marriages expected to end in divorce by the 30th wedding anniversary was 37.9 per cent in 2001 and 37.6 per cent in 2002' (ibid.). These rates are lower than a recent high of 40 per cent in 1995 and much below the all-time high of 50.6 per cent established in 1987, but above a recent low of 34.8 per cent in 1997 (Statistics Canada, 2002b). The variability of these proportions reflects many factors, such as the extrapolation of the then-current annual divorce totals—but to be clear, the calculation does *not* predict the probability of divorce for any particular married couple.

The average age of those divorcing has gradually increased. By 2002, the average age at divorce was 43.1 years for men and 40.5 years for women (Statistics Canada, 2004a), reflecting both later age at marriage and the increasing number of younger Canadians whose unions are not based on a marriage. For instance, Statistics Canada (2002a) reported that in 2001, a clear majority of young Canadians aged 20 to 29 years chose *not* to base their first union on a marriage. There is no current statistical basis for estimating the proportion of all unions (including both those based on a marriage and those that are not) that have ended or will end in a separation.

Within the total of about 70,000 divorces annually, the proportions in each province and territory are roughly the same year after year even though some provincial populations are growing rapidly as a result of immigration (for example, Ontario) and some are losing population as a result of out-migration (such as Newfoundland and Labrador). Since the overall number of Canadians has increased during the period (and more importantly, since the number of Canadians in the marriageable years has increased even more as a result of the general aging of the population), the rate of occurrence might seem to be going down. However, as we have seen, a rapidly increasing number of Canadians do not marry when they form their unions and are thus never in need of a divorce. In 2001, for instance, the crude marriage rate in Canada (4.7 marriages for every 1,000 people) was the lowest ever

recorded.[1] Part of the reason for this decline is to be found in the marked decrease in a type of marriage that was entered into in previous eras as a direct result of extramarital pregnancy. More than a few of our parents and grandparents married at an early age and in a great hurry because of just such a predicament. Today, the ready availability of medical abortions (in 2001, there were about 107,000 performed in Canada, terminating about 24 per cent of all pregnancies: Statistics Canada, 2004b) and the generally liberal access to contraceptives of all sorts help limit the number of such panic marriages. Such hasty marriages would have been at great risk of a subsequent separation and divorce because of the youthfulness of the new partners, the tensions of having a young baby in the new household, and the improbability of such partners spending the next 65 years together, as life expectancy figures suggest they might. On the other side of the ledger, Statistics Canada reports that in 2001 almost 1.2 million Canadian couples were living in a common-law relationship, up sharply by 20 per cent since 1995 (Statistics Canada, 2002a).

The possible inference that fewer relationships are being dissolved today is not called for.[2] Indeed, the opposite is probably the case; however, many separations today have no statistical or legal consequences. Further, the current divorce totals for a given year do not reflect the separation reality for that year. This is because of a considerable delay in obtaining a divorce from first filing—and first filing on separation grounds alone can only occur when a year has elapsed following the separation. Part of this delay is the result of satisfying the requirements of the legal process, part is a function of court capacity, and part is the general economic condition that affects the ability of the parties to pay the not inconsiderable costs for the process to proceed to conclusion. And it is certain that many of the persons in Canada who will be awarded divorces in Canada this year are already firmly locked into new relationships when the final decree is granted. For instance, for a decade, approximately 35 per cent of new marriages have

Box 5.1 Rules of Marital Dissolution

The rules pertaining to ending marriages can take two major forms: those embodied in religious assertions and those embedded in law. The two sets of imperatives can exist, as they often do in Canadian society, in fundamental conflict. In Canadian society, individuals are free to ignore both sets of rules in their own private lives, providing they are willing to live with the consequences of their failure to act, as in declining to file for a divorce, for instance. Today, the individual Canadian is free to form and to dissolve whatever alternative mating arrangements he or she might choose to adopt (with perhaps the sole exceptions that actual polygamy is forbidden by law when a person enters into multiple formalized marriages, though prosecutions are rare in the extreme, and where sex with minors is involved and prosecutions are common).

Rules of marital union dissolution do several things:

- They define the circumstances under which marital pair bonds can be formally dissolved.
- They make adjudication of disputes systematic.
- They define which public figures are entitled to adjudicate marital disputes.
- They attach the obligations for familial support systematically and if necessary unilaterally, and they provide for enforcement of support orders.
- They define the obligations of ex-partners to each other.
- They redivide social space into realms of those eligible for permissible new pair bonds, define those who are disallowed candidates, and criminalize violations of these boundaries, such as occurs, for example, with incest.
- They create permissive space for future intimate behaviour and also define its limits.

included at least one previously married spouse.[3] These provisos and qualifications all highlight the importance of considering relationship formation and dissolution (a process in social behaviour) separately from the divorce process (a process in law).

The Emergence of Shariah Law in Canadian Legal Institutions

Because Canadian society now consists of individuals from many places and cultures, it is not possible to generalize about how Canadians actually live out their pair bonding and dissolution experiences. What we all experience in common is the

law. Whether or not religious rules apply is now strictly a matter of individual choice, in striking contrast to earlier periods when the demands of religious edicts were sometimes harsh and imposed with considerable force. Some cultural practices that newcomers to Canada might otherwise be inclined to follow are ruled out by law, as is multiple marriage, or are granted no standing in law, as is religious divorce. One striking departure from this pattern has begun to emerge, however.

The gradual and subtle introduction of Islamic law (shariah) in Canada has raised some difficult and troubling questions. In the normal course of events, countries have one universal system of civil and criminal codes. Indeed, it is one of the elemental aspects of democracy that all citizens be accorded the same rights and privileges under law. Canada has always been an exception to this rule by the acceptance of the Civil Code system in Quebec, an integral part of the historic bargain that brought Quebec into Confederation. Other slight departures of a purely optional nature have existed for some time. Among these are the orthodox Jewish requirement for a religious *get*[4] or divorce before remarriage can occur, and a similar Roman Catholic requirement for a religious **annulment**. The *get* has been an especially vexing problem for some divorcing wives because it is granted (or not) exclusively by the husband of the failed marriage. Lawsuits of the common civil variety to compel the delivery of a *get* are not unknown.

But the introduction of shariah principles in recent years is a qualitatively different initiative. In reflection of the growing diversity of cultural origins present in Canadian society, disputes involving Muslim women's dowries, divorce, inheritance, and property ownership have actually been arriving in civil court.

In Ontario until very recently, judges might choose to refer such cases to an Islamic tribunal for binding arbitration, provided the parties were willing.[5] However, the matter of parallel justice systems in Ontario came to a head in early 2006 when the government of Ontario ultimately decided against continuing this practice. The Family Statute Law Amendment Act, passed 14 February 2006, ensures that only Ontario family law can be used in binding arbitrations in Ontario. According to Attorney General Michael Bryant, 'the bill reaffirms the principle that there ought to be one law for all Ontarians' (Gillespie, 2006).

In British Columbia, a judge recently upheld a Muslim woman's *maher*, a form of prenuptial agreement that defines in advance the amount of payment to be made upon subsequent marriage termination. Acknowledging that a *maher* has force and effect in Canadian courts as a contract (even though it has purely religious legitimacy) is a step in the direction of parallel legal systems, which is completely alien to the Canadian legal context. Although it does have some resonance with sentencing circles and restorative justice initiatives carried out in Aboriginal communities across Canada with the blessing of the courts, the fact remains that some few separation and divorce proceedings in Canada are now taking place in a purely religious context, with judgements only subsequently confirmed (as in 'rubber-stamped') in a conventional civil court document. Actions such as that of the province of Ontario in disallowing the use of religion-based tribunals in the settlement of civil disputes may simply drive these activities underground.

The Emotional, Social, and Economic Fallout of Marital Discord, Separation, and Divorce

The effects of separation of a previous couple occur independent of any subsequent divorce process. Separation is a social fact, as are the factors that most often give rise to it. Divorce remains an *ex post facto* legal recognition of that social fact; it merely confirms the obvious, though it may have incidental stigmatizing effects on self-identity for those affected.

In no sense, then, does the legal act of divorce cause suffering and hardship. There is no denying that these often arise in the process of ending marital households, and, in particular, economic stress and emotional trauma impinge on the lives of any children of the household. Nevertheless, it would be mistaken to see these as arising from actions in the civil legal system, though that suffering and hardship can undoubtedly become more bitter there. Rather, the operations of provincial family law and the federal Divorce Act seek to bring both accountability and renewal of social futures to the separated couple, together with counsel and advice on reducing disharmony and fostering a positive environment for the fragments of any previously united family. Admittedly, the extent of the success of those efforts is mixed.

Recent literature tends to combine the effects of separation and divorce as if they were a single

Box 5.2 Divorce Canadian Style

- To be divorced, you must first be married—but to be separated and/or have support orders and custodial judgements entered against you, you need not first be married. **Separation** is a social process of relationship dissolution; divorce is a legal process of marriage dissolution. One can be separated from more than one other person at a time. Some separated Canadians never divorce and simply cohabit with a new partner, as is their right.

- A couple in Canada may live together without legal marriage. In the fullness of time (a period that differs from province to province) they will be considered to be a social unit and thus exposed upon separation to family law in respect of property divisions, and to support obligations and custody arrangements for any minor children. Likewise, they are considered as an economic unit under the Income Tax Act after the passage of a certain amount of time. Consensual unconventional couple arrangements not based on a marriage are seldom if ever the subject of legal censure; their subsequent dissolution does not result in a divorce or come to public attention at all (except possibly in regard to how they have declared their income for tax purposes).

- If you marry in violation of the legal consanguinity ('shared blood') provisions or bigamously, the marriage is invalid. It can be annulled and if you committed bigamy you can be charged. But, if your marriage was invalid at the outset, you cannot obtain a divorce. Where this leaves children of such a non-marriage is anybody's guess, but in general the marital status of one's parents is now irrelevant for most if not all legal purposes.

- Children of dissolved marriages or marriage-like unions most often reside with a female parent by well-entrenched habit. This is the result of decades of court decisions and custom both in Canada and elsewhere, which have held custody of and residence with the mother to be preferable. Joint custody now figures prominently in the Canadian picture, though not necessarily joint residence. Access and residential arrangements for dependent children are different from custody. Joint parenting arrangements may exist in the presence of a custody award to one parent.

- Foreign divorces may or may not be recognized in a Canadian province for the purposes of remarrying. As with the status of foreign marriages, out-of-country divorces are honoured out of courtesy most of the time, but an application for recognition in a Canadian province is required. The principle involved is referred to as judicial **comity** or the accommodation of foreign legal decisions. It might not extend to arranged marriages of minor children or to sham divorces obtained in a foreign country, however.

- In Canada, contact with religious authority is not at all necessary for divorce or for the definition of support obligations that arise from dissolved relationships. Nevertheless, some religious communities maintain tradition-based non-legal parallel processes for divorce and for the adjudication of private domestic disputes. Religious divorces and annulments have, in general, no applicability or standing in the civil courts.

package—inappropriately, if only for the reason that many separations cannot give rise to a divorce because no marriage has been contracted. For instance, a recent study based on results from the 2001 British census asserts that about three-quarters of current British family separations involving children in the United Kingdom today involve unmarried partners (Frean, 2005). In conceptually consolidating the consequences of separation and divorce, much literature tends to attribute to divorce effects that might more appropriately be seen as the effects of relationship breakdown, or even results of the prior dysfunctionality of families that ultimately dissolve. In this admittedly complex situation, it cannot be easily established that many observed effects might not have occurred even if the couples in conflict had stayed together.

Keeping in mind this important caveat, what are the observed effects of family separations? Reginald Bibby has recently addressed this question with published results from a large survey in 2003 of Canadians (Bibby, 2005: 65–70). Bibby finds a large number of impacts, among them (1) social strain with relatives who often disapprove; (2) decreased quality of school and workplace performance of the former spouses and of their children; (3) negative emotional impacts; and (4) financial hardship. But close to nine in 10 of Bibby's separated/divorced respondents reported being happier on balance after the separation than before it, though many are hesitant to cohabit again in light of their experiences. For the children of separation/divorce, Bibby reports a number of negative effects. For instance, he reports that two-thirds of such children later in life report that family dissolution made life 'harder for us', more than 50 per cent said they 'didn't have enough money', and significant proportions reported feelings of inferiority, embarrassment, and weaker school performance, particularly for male children. Again, it is necessary to restate that implicit comparisons to intact families rather than to a hypothetical situation had their own conflicted families persisted are shaky.

In an earlier review of the literature, Anne-Marie Ambert noted the following measurable consequences of divorce: poverty (especially for women); higher incidence of depression, anxiety, and other emotional disorders; and increased risk of problems for children of divorced parents including such behaviour problems as fighting and hostility, lower educational attainment, adolescent pregnancies, and long-term risk for further marital problems (Ambert, 2002: 17–19).

What is the cause and what is effect? Looking at the precursors of family dissolution, for instance, one obvious dimension of family breakdown involves a tense and potentially violent style of relating between spouses in chronic conflict, a situation that might be one of the more important reasons why one spouse leaves the other. The tension and violence do not arise in isolation. Each might stem from well-founded anger at the behaviour of the other, or for oft-cited reasons of financial stress, medical condition, misuse of drugs and alcohol, or infidelity—the list of possible triggering behaviours would be very long indeed. If nothing else, domestic assault figures indicate that the marital household in conflict is one of the primary locations in which Canadian crimes of violence occur. In light of this fact, accounts of post-separation hardships must be weighed against the real risks of physical and emotional trauma, which are greatly diminished by separation.

For the balance of family breakdowns, including those unions that never involved a marriage or overt violence, there are as many reasons for discord as there are partners. Unhappiness, frustration, and the 'gradual growing apart' prominently mentioned by Bibby as a pre-eminent 'cause' are persistent features of the human pair-bonding condition, as is perhaps the resolve to do better the next time. Though there could be no accounting of these causes and effects (and many are both causes and effects), it is certain that all spousal unions of whatever form are subject to such pressures from time to time.

Many children experience at least one episode of living in a lone-parent family at some time during their early years and they tend to experience such interludes as negative. While such periods of time may relieve them of the burden of living in the harsh environment of marital discord, the long-term consequences of the insecurities such episodes may produce cannot but have an effect later in their adult years. Myles Corak has shown that 'parental divorce seems to influence the marital and fertility decisions of children. . . . Adolescents whose parents divorced tend to put off marriage, and once married suffer a greater likelihood of marital instability' (Corak, 1999: 5). Again, though, it is better to read 'divorce' as 'permanent separation' in these conclusions. Typically, separation brings with it a decline in standard of living as the expenses of maintaining two households instead of one are absorbed. This must also have effects in constraining what is financially feasible for the children of a dissolved union, and, of course, for the separated partners as well.[6]

The Lone-Parent Family and the Recombined Family

According to the present census classification, families in Canada may be divided into families of now-married couples with or without children, common-law (unmarried) couples with or without children, and lone-parent families. Married couples form the largest of the three categories, although they represent a gradually declining proportion of the total. However, the statistical snapshot of Canada's families taken every five years disguises the fact that many of today's families (or fragments therefrom) were once to be found in one of the other categories. For many, family structure is episodic over the long life course typical of today's Canadians: spells of coupledom are interspersed with periods of lone parenthood or being single.

Data from Statistics Canada's Family History Survey showed that by 1984 about 18 per cent of Canadian women aged 18 years and over had been at one time lone parents. In that survey, the typical duration of lone-parenthood for Canadian women was just over five years on average (Moore, 1989: 342). For many years, and continuously since 1991, there have been at least one million lone-parent families in Canada at any given time, more than 80 per cent headed by a woman. At the time of each five-year census, however, this group is not composed of all or even of predominantly the same people as in the previous census. By any standard single mothers with dependent children are among the poorest of Canadians (by either asset or income measures).

The major difficulties for lone parents relate to child care (expenses, availability, hours of operation, and transport to and from), lack of skills and training (as a result of time spent out of school and/or the labour force), the employment practices of Canadian employers (inflexibility and lack of concern), adequacy and affordability of housing, the continuing effects of elevated stress, and, perhaps most importantly, the unfulfilled need for social and emotional support. Over the long run, low incomes produce low pension entitlements, fewer household and personal assets, and sparse interpersonal networks, all giving rise to the prospect of a potentially troublesome old age.

Many millions of Canadians have experienced episodes of living as children in a lone-parent family. In earlier decades, this was most likely the result of the premature death of a parent, especially during wartime when in addition to mortality there may have been very prolonged absences of a parent without any certainty that he might someday return. Today, life as a child in a lone-parent family is most likely the result of the separation of parents, whether or not they were ever married. With the passage of time, many lone parents establish new relationships—indeed, that may be the only way out of the lone-parenthood wilderness for many. A relatively small proportion of Canadian two-parent families with children now contain a step-parent, most often a stepfather who occupies the position by virtue of establishing a residential marital relationship with a separated mother and her child or children.[7] Sometimes, newly arrived biological or adoptive children of the current union partners are blended into the family. In addition, one or both partners may have other children who are not living with them. Some may reside with the new couple sporadically and some may live elsewhere but visit the household. These combinations take so many forms, all arising out of the need to satisfy the many conflicting demands on time and money of parents, that neat summation is difficult. In contemporary Canadian family life, innovation is a keyword.

Stepfamilies and Blended Families

When remnants of previously dissolved families combine in a new relationship they tend to become unremarkable in their communities because, for most purposes, they are indistinguishable from their always-intact family counterparts. Their household income levels are on average much closer to those of **intact families** than they are to those of lone-parent families headed either by a man or by a woman (Juby et al., 2003: 6, Figure 1). This parity is attributable almost entirely to having two adult earners in the labour force, a pivotal marker for potential prosperity in Canadian society today.

While immediate friends and family members may know of previous marital dissolutions the newly combining family members may have experienced, for outsiders the cues are subtle. Perhaps there are differing surnames, physical dissimilarities among children of the family, patterns of periodic visits by other adults, or other distinguishing signals. These might give vague clues to outsiders of a non-traditional family history. But even these aspects cannot be taken as decisive for identification purposes. Enough variation exists in the population of Canadian families now that most outsiders have learned not to press questions in the forward manner their grandparents might once have followed. Today's typically high levels of residential mobility—in a society where 80 per cent of the population reside in urban areas—have disrupted the dense web of community knowledge about family genealogy that characterized nineteenth- and early twentieth-century Canadian agrarian society.

Combined families' unremarkable social status also is aided by treatment under the law in much the same manner as their more traditional counterparts and significantly also by the census of Canada, in that no questioning is directed to family history, only to the family present. This means that the considerable data resources generated by the census remain mute on the question of **stepfamilies** in general and **blended families** in particular. It is only when surveys specifically ask about the family history of current household members that information may emerge. In Canada, the General Social Survey, conducted annually by Statistics Canada, gathers information on such families, and then not on every cycle or in exhaustive detail. Likewise, commercial survey firms seldom venture onto this ground. In the future, the relatively new National Longitudinal Survey of Children and Youth from Statistics Canada promises to provide much of the missing detail.[8] For now we lack data about the long-term dynamics of combined families. One suspects that many combined families appreciate this anonymity and welcome their integration into society as conventional families that appear stable, traditional, and unproblematic for their surrounding communities. If for no other reason, publicly accepted integration means that they can leave behind the derogatory cultural stereotyping that step-parents have attracted over the millennia.

As one would expect in a society in which minor children of a dissolved family overwhelmingly reside with the mother, one large category of stepfamilies contains a mother with her biological child or children, joined in the new domestic relationship with a man who has assumed the role of stepfather to her children. For instance, in the General Social Survey conducted by Statistics Canada in 2001, about 50 per cent of current stepfamilies (estimated to total 503,000 in 2001, in contrast to 3,768,000 'intact' families reported) contained only the mother's children, only 10 per cent had solely the father's children, and the remaining 40 per cent contained a blend of the new couple's children (either from two or more previous relationships or jointly in the current one). In about 80 per cent of the blended cases, the new couple had children by birth or adoption (Statistics Canada, 2002a). Note that because of the present orientation of the question asked, today's 'combined families' will cease to be 'combined' as soon as older children leave the household. When all the adult children born of only one current parent have left, what remains is simply a childless couple unless all of the children were born of the couple or unless all children born of either parent were adopted by the complementary partner. The question not asked is whether or not the respondent has *ever* lived in a combined and/or blended family setting. We simply do not know how many Canadians have experienced a combined family episode at some time in their lives or much about what happened in it.

When questioned in the Reginald Bibby survey mentioned previously, respondents who had entered a new marital relationship that involved step-parenting reported very positively on their experience. About 80 per cent characterized their new relationships as being much happier than their earlier ones. About the same proportion said that they had adjusted very or fairly well to their new partner's children and that the children had adjusted well to them. Men were slightly more positive than women, and those who had been previously married were more positive than those who had never previously married before entering a new combined family with a previously attached spouse and children. However, only about 56 per cent of stepchildren, when asked to look back on their childhoods, reported they got on well with step-parents while 65 per cent reported similarly about relations with step-siblings. Significant numbers of grown stepchildren are thus indicating strain in the combined family, though it is not clear that this strain is inherently worse than in intact families (Bibby, 2005: Tables 6.9–6.11).

A combined family may change the surnames of some members in favour of a single last name, a legal process that is quite easily and inexpensively done. A cost in lost identity may ensue, however, as surnames continue to convey origins and expectations, albeit to a much lesser extent than in the past when surname often conveyed membership in a mythic kinship collective centred on a particular place on earth.

One may speculate as to the nature of the special strains of the combined family setting, all the more so if the separation and combination cycle happens more than once. There may be non-custodial parental visits, conflicts among parental practices and expectations, awkwardness in formal introductions, and some degree of financial 'fallout' from previous failed relationships. Often there also will be new 'kin' and kinship relations to be learned for a larger-than-normal number of extended families, titles for which the language often fails. These exceptional relationships form a more complex kinship puzzle than usual for the children of a combined family, one that does not fade with maturity but becomes more complex as time goes by. For the mature children of some families this ultimately adds extensive obligations to a multiplicity of aging parents along with their other responsibilities as adults. Children of combined families may well find themselves in late middle age with four or more parents to assist in their declining years, parents who may have experienced financial reversals in their lives due to family dissolution and who may have remained the poorer for it.

Recent Developments in Divorce and Family Law

A recent series of court decisions made same-sex marriages not only legal but also easily available in most parts of Canada. These judgements had a series of quite predictable consequences outside of the obvious one that same-sex marriages might now be conducted. It was immediately evident that married same-sex couples would require access to divorce and family law financial settlements, access that necessitated the rewriting of much of the existing family legislation. Since some same-sex couples facing divorce in the future will have minor children—whether from a previous relationship, conceived through some technical means, or adopted—new paradigms of child custody and shared parenting will also be required since traditional preference for custody to the mother is still overwhelmingly followed in social practice (it is probably declining very slowly with time) but is not particularly relevant in the same-sex context.[9]

In addition, a slight but significant movement has appeared in the direction of rehabilitating 'fault' or marital misconduct as a factor in financial settlements attendant to divorce. For instance, the British Columbia Appeals Court held in a judgement in 2004 that a Vancouver woman, Sherry Leskun, whose husband Gary left her for a remarriage to another woman, should continue to receive support payments (Schmitz, 2004: A2). In the normal course of events this woman might reasonably have expected that her $2,250 monthly support payment would be terminated with the passage of some few years after divorce as the Act intends. There is in Canada a general expectation under the legislation that former spouses must begin to support themselves after a transitional period normally limited to just a few years and without regard to marital offences committed by the other party. But in this case, the Court ruled that 'emotional devastation' caused by adultery had undermined her ability to work. This judgement was subsequently upheld by the Supreme Court of Canada on the narrow grounds that while spousal misconduct cannot be considered, its emotional consequences can be. But the BC Appeals Court ruling does raise an important question outside the bounds of law. Why should serious misconduct be subject to sanction in virtually all arenas of social life *except* in marriages?

Other evidence of a slight hardening of attitude towards former spouses in the throes of a marital dissolution can be found. For instance, Ontario recently announced new legislation to increase the maximum prison sentence from three to six months for failure to pay child support established under court orders. Each year in Ontario, a few hundred non-compliant parents spend time behind bars and may also lose their drivers' licences as well as hunting and fishing licences.

But for whatever reason, defaulting spouses in Ontario still owed at least $1.2 billion in early 2005. Much of this debt is not recoverable, either because the defaulter's whereabouts are unknown or because the defaulter has no funds to attach (as in the old lawyer's adage, 'you can't get blood out of a stone'), or even because the defaulter is in jail and is therefore unable to be employed.

In another decision, the Supreme Court of Ontario has ruled that a woman who left her common-law husband of more than 20 years some few months before he died is not entitled to the survivor pension she would have received were she to have been married to or still living with the deceased at the time of his death. This ruling has the effect of asserting that *a common-law relationship is over in law at the time of separation*. Continued cohabitation (as signified by the intent of both parties to be together) is required to establish a claim to survivor benefits. Thus, a common-law partner who leaves a relationship immediately acquires the status of divorced spouse no matter the conditions under which he or she left the household. This judgement effectively diminishes the emergent parity between married and common-law couples and holds that married couples have a higher degree of obligation to each other than their unmarried counterparts (Paraskevas, 2004: A2).

In a few cases divorce settlements have been reopened well after the fact to take into account new realities, such as a big lottery win that was hidden and then cashed in only after the family law settlement was signed, or the permanent incapacitation of an ex-spouse occurring after an agreement was reached. These reopenings are very uncommon, as are support awards made against former wives in favour of former husbands. In practice, support payments and the post-separation splitting of assets seem intended to work as parts of a capital redistribution system meant to enhance the economic status of ex-wives and their minor children. In creating such a system, governments hoped that the necessity for large state transfer payments to otherwise bereft ex-spouses would decline. Ex-spouses are additionally instructed (if not already employed) to get a job as soon as possible. Overall, this system, in place for more than 30 years, has been remarkably unsuccessful in addressing the continuing problem of lone-parent poverty, defined either in terms of asset ownership or of income levels. Inadequate enforcement of support payment orders remains a largely unresolved issue, as is the meagre supply of assets and income to attach or divide in very many cases. Poor couples who divide their incomes and assets simply get poorer separately.

Conclusion

Major changes in social practice and in the legal environment have gone hand in hand with demographic changes to greatly enhance the episodic nature of spousal unions in Canada in the last half-century. On the demographic side, the rapid extension of life expectancies and widespread immigration/migration, with consequent dispersal and mixing of previously static populations, have produced a greater awareness of alternatives among people who are experiencing unsatisfactory domestic arrangements. The effect of perceived alternatives has raised the importance accorded to choice in marital matters, or more broadly, to an entitlement to happiness. These and other related factors have in turn contributed to the loosening of once-strict legal regimes for social control in family matters as they applied historically both to cohabitation and to its termination in separation. Likewise, newcomers to Canadian society, who often have become adherents to somewhat unfamiliar religious credos

and modes of family life, are free to continue in their beliefs and practices when they are not in fundamental conflict with Canadian law.

There are few indications that Canadians are now less likely to cohabit in a marriage or marriage-like union at some point in their lives than they were in the past. Likewise, there is little indication that present unions are now more durable or less conflict-prone than they were in the past. Certainly, the emotional and economic consequences of separation on cohabiting partners and on their children are no easier to endure now than formerly. Often, the result of separation continues to be a descent into a period of intense poverty and personal turmoil.

Looked at in a purely legal context, however, proportionately fewer separating partners are in need of a divorce because fewer cohabiting couples are married. Thus, both marriage and divorce have been to some extent pushed towards the margins of social life in the years since the federal Divorce Act was enacted in 1968. On the other hand, provincial family law settlements have become much more central as separating couples unwind their financial entanglements and define the overhang of future support obligations, particularly where minor children are involved. In view of the substantial number of combined families in Canadian society, there seems no slackening in the willingness to try cohabitation again for a second or subsequent time. Each recombinant union contributes in its own unique way to the dense thicket of contemporary kinship charts and support obligations defined with the assistance of the ever present legal profession

Notes

1. Provisional data for 2002 and 2003 show further declines in the number of marriages to 147,634 and 138,247 respectively (CANSIM, table 053–0001).
2. The data from the 2001 General Social Survey conducted by Statistics Canada clearly show a 'growing instability in the unions of today's women. The prob-

ability of seeing their first unions dissolve is increasing: women ranging in age from 30–39 are expected to be twice as likely to see their unions end in separation or divorce as women ranging in age from 60 to 69.' Statistics Canada, *Changing Conjugal Life in Canada*, July 2002, Catalogue no. 89–576–XIE, 5.

3. Vanier Institute of the Family, Chart 21, 'Proportion of marriages in which at least one spouse has been previously married (1970–1996)'. At: <www.vifamily.ca/ library/profiling2/chart21.html>.

4. A *get* is a Jewish religious document purported to be necessary to separate the combined soul of a married man and woman. Without a proper *get*, even though the man and woman have physically separated, they are still bound together in some mystical fashion—and considered to be still fully married. The great difficulty for contemporary life is that the wife *cannot* initiate the process.

5. The Arbitration Act (1991) in Ontario allowed faith-based arbitration (for Muslims, Jews, and members of other established faiths) in matters of divorce, custody, and property disputes such as inheritance outside the formal court system. Participation was supposed to be voluntary but as sociologists know well, informal social pressure to comply can be intensely coercive. That part of shariah law that pertains to criminal events is clearly contrary to the Charter of Rights and Freedoms, but this does not mean that Canadian Muslims might not some day challenge this aspect as well. The orthodox Jewish arbitration system (*Beth Din*) provides rabbinical decisions, the substance of which are then embodied in a conventional court document of settlement. Rabbinical decisions now deal with separation, division of assets, and other civil matters involving business disputes. This avenue is available in large Canadian cities only where community numbers warrant it.

6. For a graphic view of the economic impacts of being in a lone-parent family, see Chart 4, 'Real Median Disposable Income', in Garnet Picot and John Myles, *Social Transfers, Changing Family Structure and Low Income among Children*, Statistics Canada Research Paper Series, no. 82, 1995, Catalogue no. 11F0019MIE, 10.

7. Vanier Institute of the Family, *Profiling Canada's Families II*, Section 28, 'Mine, yours and ours—Canada's "blended" families'. At: <www.vifamily.ca/ library/profiling2/parti28.html>.

8. Data from the 1994–5 cycle of the NLSCY suggest that Canadian families by type are as follows: 75.7 per cent intact, 14.5 per cent lone mother, 1.1 per cent lone father, 0.1 per cent lone stepparent, 6.1 per cent blended stepfamily, and 2.5 per cent non-blended stepfamily (where 'blended' means a family in which at least one of the children does not have the same biological or adoptive parent as the others). Nicole Marcil-Gratton, 'Lone parents and their children', *Transition Magazine* (Spring 1999): 29, 1.

9. Custody disputes between former same-sex spouses are not unknown. For instance, in September 2004 a Vermont court found Lisa Miller-Jenkins in contempt for failure to allow the non-biological parent, Janet Miller-Jenkins, visitation with their two-year-old daughter. Jonathon Finer, 'Vermont judge cites domain over same-sex custody fight', *Washington Post*, 9 Sept. 2004, A11.

Study Questions

1. Is lessening the incidence of separation and divorce in Canada a desirable social goal? In your view, what mechanisms might be useful to decrease the incidence of separation and divorce in Canada? Which would be most likely to succeed?

2. How do Canadian rates of separation and divorce compare to those in other countries? Is there anything Canadians can learn from the experience in other countries?

3. What proportion of Canadian children will experience an episode of living in a lone-parent family in the years to come? Is that proportion likely to rise or fall in the future?

4. Why has the role of step-parent been portrayed so negatively in the past?

5. How many same-sex divorces can Canadians expect to see in the years to come?

6. What public policies might be enacted to address and remedy the poverty of post-separation lone-parent families in Canada?

Glossary

Annulment The retroactive finding that an attempted marriage union violated the terms of marriage from the outset.

Blended family The marital union of two people, at least one of whom was previously in a marriage or marriage-like union and is also a parent. A blended family is created when one parent of an established family marries or cohabits with another such partner, and all their children are considered members of the new family.

Comity The recognition extended by states in their own territory, courts, and institutions to the legal status and rights of citizens of other countries. Thus, country A would typically recognize marriages and divorces conducted in country B and vice versa. Comity would normally apply between provinces in Canada as well. The word originally meant 'courtesy'.

Divorce The legal dissolution of a valid marriage.

Family A married couple or common-law couple, with or without children of either or both spouses, or a lone parent, regardless of that parent's marital status, having at least one child living under the same roof.

Intact families Families in which all children in the household are the biological and/or adopted offspring of both members of the couple.

Separation The end of a marriage or marriage-like relationship resulting from causes other than death.

Stepfamilies Families in which at least one of the children in the household is from a previous relationship of one of the parents.

Further Readings

Gentleman, Jane F., and Evelyn Park. 1997. 'Divorce in the 1990s', *Health Reports* 9, 2 (Statistics Canada Catalogue no. 82–003–XPB). A numerical review of trends in Canadian divorce in the 1990s.

Hudson, Joe, and Burt Galaway, eds. 1993. *Single Parent Families: Perspectives on Research and Policy*. Toronto: Thompson Educational Publishing. A book of readings on lone-parent families in Canada.

Lochhead, Clarence, and David Hubka. 1994. *The Extent, Composition and Economic Characteristics of Blended, Common-Law and Single-Parent Families in Canada, and Family Expenditure on Child Care*. Ottawa: Department of Justice Canada, Working Document 1994–12e. A comprehensive account of the characteristics of such families in Canada.

McKie, D.C., B. Prentice, and P. Reed. 1983. *Divorce: Law and the Family in Canada*. Ottawa: Statistics Canada, 1983. An overall view of marriage, divorce, and family law in Canada from early settlement times to approximately 1982. It contains tabular data from the Central Divorce Registry at the Department of Justice and from the Office of the Official Guardian in Ontario, and a life table indicating the probability of divorce in each single year of marriage based on then available data.

Statistics Canada. 2002. *Changing Conjugal Life in Canada*. General Social Survey—Cycle 15, Catalogue no. 89–576–XIE, July. A recent account of the emergent types of cohabitation in Canadian society, including an overview of how separation and divorce have changed the nature of Canadian family life.

Websites

www.vifamily.ca/about/about.html
The Vanier Institute of the Family provides a great deal of information on all aspects of contemporary family life, including separation and divorce and their consequences. Many of the publications are free to download from the site, most often in Acrobat format.

http://laws.justice.gc.ca/en/D-3.4/text.html)
Various essential documents can found at this government of Canada site, including the current Divorce Act and the current provincial family law for Ontario.

www.e-laws.gov.on.ca/DBLaws/Statutes/English/90f03_e.htm

This site features a legislative history overview for Ontario.

www.cfcs.gov.on.ca/CFCS/en/programs/SCS/FamilyResponsibilityOffice/default.htm

The Family Responsibility Office for Ontario has many free publications to download. Each of the provinces and territories has its own legislation and usually a copy is available on-line.

http://canada.justice.gc.ca/en/ps/pad/resources/divorce/index.html

Information on a number of topics related to divorce and separation can be found at this federal Justice Department site.

www.duhaime.org/family/default.aspx

Duhaime's Canadian Family Law Centre provides a wealth of information on separations and divorce in Canada and has even more information specific to British Columbia, including links to BC family legislation. It has an excellent section on the treatment of matrimonial property and spousal support in Canada.

www.international-divorce.com/d-canada.htm

This page contains a brief summary of the Canadian family law regime, as well as links to the comparable family legislation in dozens of other countries around the world.

http://canada.justice.gc.ca/en/ps/sup/pub/2003-FCY-2/2003-FCY-2.html

This site presents a study (also available as a downloadable pdf file) that, for the first time in Canada, analyzes data based on the situation 'before' and 'after' certain family transitions, such as parents' separation or family recomposition, thereby providing new insight into the relationship among family change, income, and labour force participation.

References

Ambert, Anne-Marie. 2002. *Divorce: Facts, Causes and Consequences*, rev. edn. Ottawa: Vanier Institute of the Family.

Bibby, Reginald A. 2005. *Future Families Project: A Survey of Canadian Hopes and Dreams*. Ottawa: Vanier Institute of the Family.

Corak, Myles. 1999. *Death and Divorce: The Long-term Consequences of Parental Loss on Adolescents*. Research Paper Series, No. 135. Catalogue no. 11F0019MIE. Ottawa: Statistics Canada.

Frean, Alexandra. 2005. 'Unmarried families are more likely to fall apart', *The Times* (London, Ont.), 5 Feb.

Gillespie, Kerry. 2006. 'Ontario bans binding religious arbitration', *Toronto Star*, 15 Feb.

Juby, Heather, Céline Le Bourdais, and Nicole Marcil-Gratton. 2003. *Linking Family Change, Parents' Employment and Income and Children's Economic Well-Being: A Longitudinal Perspective*. Research Report 2003–FCY–2E. Ottawa: Department of Justice Canada.

Moore, Maureen. 1989. 'Female lone parenting over the life course', *Canadian Journal of Sociology* 14, 3: 335–52.

Paraskevas, Joe. 2004. 'Survivor pension denial upheld', *Vancouver Sun*, 29 Oct.

Schmitz, Cristin. 2004. 'B.C. ruling puts fault into no-fault divorce', *National Post*, 27 Sept.

Statistics Canada. 2002a. 'Changing conjugal life in Canada', *The Daily*, 11 July.

———. 2002b. 'Divorces', *The Daily*, 2 Dec.

———. 2003. 'Marriages', *The Daily*, 20 Nov.

———. 2004a. 'Divorces', *The Daily*, 4 May.

———. 2004b. 'Pregnancies', *The Daily*, 27 Oct.

CHAPTER 6

'Mid-Life Crises': Understanding the Changing Nature of Relationships in Middle-Age Canadian Families

Karen M. Kobayashi

Learning Objectives

- To understand the nature of intergenerational co-residence in mid-life families.
- To appreciate the nature of support/care given to older parents by mid-life adults, usually daughters.
- To learn about the nature of intergenerational ambivalence in mid-life families.
- To discover emergent research about diversity in mid-life families.
- To be able to discuss the relationship between mid-life families and social policy.

Introduction

The application of a **life-course perspective** to the study of families has resulted in a partitioning of family time into stages, allowing researchers to isolate and examine the changing nature of relationships at different periods of the family life course. Given this life-course focus on the interplay between 'aging, social change, and family dynamics' (Moen, 1991: 135), researchers have applied a synchronous theoretical framework to examinations of family change over time at both the micro and macro levels.

This chapter focuses on the mid-life stage in families, often referred to in the literature as the 'sandwich stage' because of its chronological placement between young adulthood and later life along the family life-course trajectory. Recently, however, with the increasing demographic complexity of North American families, it has become even more difficult to assign distinct structural markers, such as age, to entrance and exit from life-course stages. The age range of 45–64 years,

previously used to define middle age, is no longer seen as valid or appropriate. As Allen et al. (2000: 913) point out in their review of the literature on families in the middle and later years, 'there is no agreed upon chronological or processual definition of middle age.' Indeed, it is the transitions to various stages (e.g., the return to work, the 'empty nest', caregiving) triggered by the occurrence of life events in the domains of work and the family (e.g., re-entry into the paid labour force, adult children leaving home, care for aging parents), and not age markers per se, that seem to define the parameters of mid-life in the family literature.

In the family domain, 'demographic changes highlight the evolving nature of mid-life' (Antonucci and Akiyama, 1997: 147). For example, with the increasing age at first marriage for both men and women in Canada over the past few decades, the transition to parenthood has inevitably been delayed into the thirties for many couples.[1] With the mean age at first birth for women at just under 30 years of age (29.5 years) in 2002 (Statistics Canada, 2004) and average life expectancy at almost 80 years (79.7 years) (Statistics Canada, 2005), Canadians are more likely to be well into their forties and fifties—at one time the definition of a middle-age family—while being 'sandwiched' between the needs of growing children and aging parents (Allen et al., 2000). This trend is likely to continue well into the future as the pursuit of career trajectories (i.e., post-secondary education and full-time employment) and of family interests and responsibilities becomes increasingly 'normative' for Canadian women.

What are the implications of these changing demographic trends for middle-age families? This chapter explores the impact of such changes in the broad contexts of living arrangements and inter-generational relationships, two of the main areas of sociological research on mid-life families in Canada and the United States.

Co-residence and Home-Leaving

Recent statistics from the 2001 census indicate that over one-half (58 per cent) of young adults aged 20–4 years and almost one-quarter (24 per cent) aged 25–9 years still co-reside with their parents, supporting the contention that 'mid-life parent-hood often comprises prolonged periods of co-residence with grown adults' (Mitchell, 1998a:2). The provinces with the highest proportion of **intergenerational co-residence** (young adults 20–9 years with their parents) are Newfoundland and Labrador and Ontario at 50.9 per cent and 47.1 per cent, respectively, but all provinces have seen substantial increases in co-residence over the past 20 years (see Figure 6.1 and Table 6.1). This

new family arrangement coupled with an increase in the average age at first birth means that mid-life parents may be well into their fifties before expe-riencing an '**empty nest**', if ever. Such a delay in the transition to a one-generation household has implications for parent-child relationships in the latter years of middle age as it is likely to coincide with the timing of parents' retirement planning or, in cases of prolonged co-residence, the passage into retirement. This intersection of key transition points along family and work trajectories in mid-life reflects the multiple linkages of roles in these two domains over the adult life course.

Why is it taking longer for recent cohorts of young adult children to leave the parental home to establish residential independence? There are a number of reasons for the postponement of this life course transition. Research indicates that chil-dren's economic/financial needs are a key factor influencing the home-leaving behaviour of young adult children (Carr, 2005; Cohen and Kaspar,

Figure 6.1 Percentage of Young Adults Living in the Parental Home, Canada

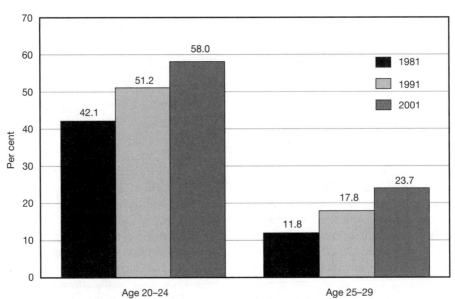

SOURCE: Adapted from Statistics Canada (2002).

Table 6.1 Proportion of Young Adults Ages 20 to 29 Living with Their Parent(s), Canada, Provinces, and Territories, 1981 and 2001

	1981 (%)	2001 (%)
Canada	27.5	41.1
Newfoundland and Labrador	35.9	50.9
Prince Edward Island	33.5	42.1
Nova Scotia	30.8	38.0
New Brunswick	31.3	38.5
Quebec	31.9	39.2
Ontario	29.8	47.1
Manitoba	24.4	36.1
Saskatchewan	18.9	29.8
Alberta	15.6	30.6
British Columbia	21.8	40.2
Yukon	12.9	30.9
Northwest Territories	22.1	30.8
Nunavut	—	32.2

SOURCE: Adapted from Statistics Canada (2002).

2002; Mitchell and Gee, 1996; Shehan and Dwyer, 1989; White, 1994). Mid-life parents, who presumably are in their peak earning years, provide a significant amount of financial and instrumental support to co-resident children at this stage in the family life course. Assistance takes multiple forms, including the payment of tuition and other fees for post-secondary education and/or vocational training, and, most importantly, the continued provision of housing, utilities, meals, and transportation. Given increases in unemployment and underemployment rates, declines in affordable housing, and the trend towards extensions in schooling for young adults over the past few decades, parents may continue to be, as noted earlier, the primary resource for adult children well into later life (Mitchell, 1998b; Settersten, 1999).

The shift in the timing of home-leaving among young adults can also be attributed to the continuation of a long-term trend towards postponement of marriage. Census data for 2001 indicate that the average age at first marriage is currently 28.2 years for women and 30.2 years for men, up from 22.0 and 24.4 years, respectively, in 1975 (Statistics Canada, 2003a; Vanier Institute of the Family, 2004). The increasing age at first marriage coupled with the propensity of young adults for leaving home just prior to marriage, for a number of different reasons ranging from economic to cultural, has resulted in prolonged periods of intergenerational co-residence in mid-life Canadian families (Mitchell and Gee, 1996). The timing of parents' transition to an 'empty nest', then, can be seen as directly linked to the inter-relationship between economic and marital status characteristics of adult children.

In addition to the economic and marital characteristics of adult children, family structure plays an important role in determining home-leaving behaviour. Young adults living in blended or stepfamilies are more likely to leave home early than those who reside in either single- or two-parent biological families (Eshleman and Wilson, 2001; Mitchell, 1994). Premature home-leaving by adult stepchildren is related to a weakened sense of mutual obligation as family members in step-parent–stepchild relationships and related conflict over power relations within these families (Aquilino, 2005; Eshleman and Wilson, 2001). Divorce and widowhood also influence co-residence patterns in mid-life Canadian families: there is a decreased likelihood that adult children will live at home if parents are divorced or a parent is widowed (Boyd and Norris, 1995). This may be due to the custodial or widowed parent's decreased ability to provide financial support to adult children in co-resident families, an impetus for the child to seek residential independence (Aquilino, 2005).

Although intergenerational co-residence is regarded in the literature primarily as a reflection of adult children's needs, Ward and Spitze (1996: 537) note that children do not always express satisfaction with this living arrangement. In fact, they maintain that 'coresidence [actually] violates the child's norms and expectations about adulthood and independence, and [that] children may experience greater strain over exchanges in shared households.' The recognition of a tension between co-resident parents and adult children and its relationship to living arrangements has been a focus of research on the quality of intergenerational relationships in mid-life families (Mitchell and Gee, 2003; Shehan and Dwyer, 1989; Ward and Spitze, 1996). In many cases, incongruence between parents and young adult children over expectations for support may lead to intergenerational disputes within the family (see Box 6.1). Within more traditional immigrant cultures, parent–child incongruence on adherence to core family and religious values (e.g., filial obligation, family shame) can be the source of extreme conflict leading to the eventual breakdown of the nuclear family unit.

The intersection of ethnicity and immigrant status has implications for continuing co-residence in mid-life families. North American research indicates a stronger sense of obligation to support young adult children in Asian immigrant families (Kamo, 2000; Mitchell and Gee, 2003). Mitchell and Gee (2003), in a study of multi-generational households, include an exploration of the co-residential experiences of Chinese and South Asian immigrant families, currently the two largest visible minority populations in Canada (Statistics Canada, 2003b). Their findings, although limited by a small sample size, highlight the salience of cultural preferences (for example, mid-life parents' complete assumption of all financial responsibilities for their young adult children as an expression of their parental obligation to take responsibility for their children) and not economic needs as the key determinants of living arrangements over the family life course. Results from Pacey's (2002) comparative study between Canadian and Chinese-Canadian immigrants support these findings in a sample of older adults.

The importance of cultural exigencies can be seen even in the context of post-immigrant visible minority families. In a study on parent–child relationships in Japanese-Canadian families, third-generation mid-life children recalled that both cultural and socio-economic factors shaped their preferences to co-reside with parents as young adults (Kobayashi, 1999). Despite the Canadian-born status of the mid-life parents, there was an enduring expectation that the nuclear family would stay intact until children, particularly daughters, made the transition to marriage. This cultural 'pull factor', combined with the economic necessity, in many cases, on the part of adult children to remain at home, formed the basis for intergenerational co-residence in mid-life families.

Box 6.1 Intergenerational Conflict in a Cluttered Nest: The Voice of a Young Male, Indo-Canadian Adult Child

I personally feel my father is not living up to that obligation of taking care, of being supportive, and fulfilling his roles, for example, tuition fees. Every time I have asked for money, he's refused. [This son does not contribute to the household finances.] Me and my father don't speak to each other, so that is kind of rough. I've laid down the foundation of the dynamic in my family. Now, there's problems. There's that implicit assumption that the younger, the kids will take care of the parents, right? Now my grandparents are also feeling like my parents are not living up to their obligations.

SOURCE: Mitchell and Gee (2003). Reprinted with permission of authors.

Returning Home

The return of adult children to the parental home in young adulthood is becoming an increasingly common experience in contemporary middle-age families. These young adults, referred to in the literature as 'boomerang kids' (Mitchell and Gee, 1996; Mitchell, 1998b) due to their pattern of leaving the family 'nest' and returning again at some point(s) over the family life course, have been the focus of a number of recent studies on parent–adult child co-residence (Mitchell, 1998b; Mitchell et al., 2002; Ward and Spitze, 1996; White, 1994). This literature has examined the antecedents and consequences of a 'cluttered nest' both for home-returning children and for their parents.

The experience of home-returning is shaped mainly by adult children's needs and social situations, particularly economic necessity and/or marital status transitions. The antecedents of return co-residence are, in fact, remarkably similar to those for continuing co-residence. Ward and Spitze (1996: 537), in a comparative study on living arrangements in the United States, find that co-residence by parents and adult children, whether continuing or return, is largely a 'response to the circumstances of children'. Indeed, the return of adult children to the parental home is often precipitated by marital disruption (i.e., separation, divorce, or the breakup of a common-law relationship) and/or economic difficulties (i.e., transition from full-time employment to unemployment or underemployment, single parenthood). This finding is supported by the results of studies undertaken by Mitchell and Gee (1996) and Mitchell (1998b) in the Canadian context.

How does the return of children to the 'empty nest' affect mid-life family relationships? Although much has been written on the consequences of the 'cluttered nest' in mid-life, research findings in this area have often been contradictory. The effects of **boomerang children** on family relationships have ranged from positive to negative. On the positive side, the overall marital satisfaction of mid-life parents has been found to be quite high among those who are living with returning children as parents may receive additional support (emotional, instrumental, financial) from pooled resources (Mitchell and Gee, 1996; Ward and Spitze, 1998). Thus, returning children may actually act as the antidote to 'empty nest syndrome' for parents. Of negative consequence, however, is the decrease in self-reported relationship satisfaction between parents and adult children in the post-return home period due to conflicts over power relations in the home (Kobayashi, 1999). Returning adult children may not adapt well to the reassertion of authority by parents within the household, particularly if the 'ground rules' are not open for negotiation. The negative effects of home-returning are multiplied even further in families of children who are 'serial home leavers', those who leave and return multiple times (i.e., three or more) over the family life course (Mitchell and Gee, 1996).

Support for Older Parents

Cutbacks to health care and social services over the past decade in Canada have precipitated an increased reliance on the family by governments at all levels for the care of older adults. This issue is particularly salient for mid-life families—Michelson and Tepperman (2003: 56) point out that almost one-half of caregivers are between the ages of 35 and 54 years, with an average age of 51. What will be the consequences of changes to public policy and programs for mid-life families? This is an important and timely question as Canada faces the challenges of aging in an unusually high proportion of the population early this century.

For the first time in our history, it is estimated that Canadian adults will spend a longer time caring for their aging parents than they spent in raising their children (McDaniel, 2005). Given the gendered nature of caregiving in our society, this means that the burden of care will continue to fall on women in mid-life (Dentinger and Clarkberg, 2002; McDaniel, 2005). Although the compression of morbidity to the latter years of old age

(80 +) has resulted in a greater number of disability-free years for older parents, the need for social support from middle-aged children (daughters, in particular) remains fairly constant over time. This is because **social support** is comprised of three main domains—financial, instrumental, and emotional—and need for assistance in each of these areas is influenced by the timing of a number of later life-course transitions, namely widowhood, retirement, and the onset of chronic illness. As older parents experience these transitions in later life, their reliance on middle-aged adult children increases either temporarily or long term. The extent to which support is provided (the adult child's response) is dictated both by parents' assistance needs and by the quality of the parent–child relationship. For some mid-life adult children, being 'sandwiched' between the competing demands of caregiving for young adult children and older parents can be extremely stressful, leading to negative financial and health outcomes (Gee and Mitchell, 2003).

An older parent's experience of widowhood, an often unexpected transition, has consequences for support ranging from temporary assistance with some activities of daily living like bill payments or grocery shopping (instrumental support) to permanent reliance on children for financial help and/or companionship to combat depression (emotional support). Of course, in the latter situation, the long-term need for assistance may require a complete restructuring of children's lives as they try to negotiate caregiving with full-time work and parenting roles and responsibilities. Although multi-generational co-residence may be the best solution, it may cause considerable strain on the relationship between parent and child.

It is less likely that retirement, a transition that older parents are expected to have planned for during their working lives, will have such an onerous effect on middle-aged children's lives. In fact, if healthy, financially secure, and married, retired parents may end up providing financial or instrumental assistance to children in the form of child care and domestic and yard work. Nevertheless, there is great diversity in the older adult population, and a large proportion of Canadians have a difficult time adjusting financially and emotionally to retirement. Older parents in this group require the most support from children to help them adjust to the truncation of their work trajectory.

Perhaps the transition that gives rise to the most significant alteration in the family trajectory of middle-aged children is the onset of chronic disease or disability in an older parent(s). Support is transformed into caregiving when a parent becomes ill; this transformation is salient in that it requires a great deal of sacrifice (temporal, emotional, financial) on the part of middle-aged children, mainly daughters, who often are forced to make life-altering decisions regarding work and family in a very short period of time.

Intergenerational Ambivalence

Despite increases in continued and return co-residence of adult children in mid-life families over the past few decades, these experiences are still considered non-normative by Canadian society. An expectation persists that adult children will leave the parental home, which also is regarded as an indicator of the success of parents' child-raising skills or abilities. The launch of children from the nest is perceived as parents' 'raison d'être', a key transition point along the family life course trajectory. Given the salience of this event, it is not surprising that incompatibility between parents' expectations and children's behaviour in this regard may often lead to ambivalence in intergenerational relationships (Fingerman et al., 2004).

A recent concept in the sociological literature on the family, **intergenerational ambivalence** has been used to describe mid-life parent–child relationships. To date, it has been used to examine relationships between adult children and their aging parents and in-laws (Pillemer and Suitor, 2002; Willson et al., 2003), and to explore the nature of social ties—with both family and friends—in a diverse age sample of adolescents and adults (Fingerman et al., 2004). Findings from Willson et al.'s study point to the significance of gender in ambivalent social relationships. Mid-life women are more likely to experience ambivalence in their relationships with each other and in their roles as caregivers to older parents and in-laws, suggesting that 'structural arrangements give rise to ambivalence and the relationship experience is shaped by gender within the context of socially defined demands and obligations' (Willson et al., 2003: 1068). The exception, it seems, is in mid- to later-life sibling relationships, where women (positively) report close ties and the most social contact with their sisters (Connidis, 2001; Connidis and Campbell, 1995).

Diversity in Mid-life Families

Studies of satisfaction in marital and parent–child relationships in mid-life have tended to examine relationship quality as it is impacted by intergenerational living and/or social support arrangements with children (e.g., Carr, 2005; Marks, 1995; Mitchell and Gee, 1996), only occasionally highlighting the actual relationship between or well-being of members of the dyad. This myopic view of mid-life families is problematic in that it fails to recognize the experiences of separated/divorced, remarried, childless, parentless, gay and lesbian, and long-term or permanent 'empty nest' families, groups of emerging importance in the mid-life Canadian population. We will focus on a few of these groups in this chapter.

SEPARATED/DIVORCED

The topic of divorce has recently been the focus of research examining the impact of marital status transitions on spousal and children's well-being over the life course (Montenegro, 2004; Williams and Umberson, 2004). In an American Association of Retired Persons (AARP)-funded study based on 1,147 interviews with men and women who had been divorced at least once during their forties,

fifties, or sixties, the effects of divorce are profound; that is, the findings indicate that the divorce experience is 'more emotionally devastating than losing a job, about equal to experiencing a major illness, and somewhat less devastating than a spouse's death' (Montenegro, 2004: 7) (see Box 6.2). Clearly, divorce is perceived as a disruptive and stressful event when it occurs in mid-life, potentially leading to a number of negative life-course consequences.

Perhaps the most significant consequences of divorce in mid-life are its effects on parent–child relationships and the well-being of children. Indeed, the primary reason for partners remaining in an unhappy marital union and delaying separation is concern over the welfare of their children (McDaniel and Tepperman, 2004; Montenegro, 2004). With the experience of divorce increasingly becoming a mid-life phenomenon,[2] children who are most likely to be affected by parental divorce are in their late adolescent to young adult years. At this stage in the life course, children are in the process of forming attitudes about marriage and family themselves and may be more vulnerable to the negative impact of parental disagreement or conflict (Kozuch and Cooney, 1995). Despite concerns over the long-term effects of divorce on children's attitudes and behaviours, there is little evidence to suggest that exposure to the marital disruption of mid-life parents negatively affects the quality of parent–child relationships, children's ability to cope with challenging life events such as moving, or their overall optimism about marriage (Dunlop and Burns, 1995; Landis-Kleine et al., 1995; Taylor et al., 1995).

How do mid-life parents themselves fare in the aftermath of divorce? The ability to cope varies greatly according to gender. In the financial domain, middle-aged women, particularly those with sole or majority custody of adolescent or young adult children, are more likely than their male counterparts to fear (and to actually experience) economic instability (Finnie, 1993; Montenegro, 2004). Emotionally, although both

Box 6.2 After 40, It's Wives Who Divorce the Husbands

Two-thirds of divorces after age 40 are initiated by wives, debunking the myth of an older man divorcing his wife for a younger woman, a new survey shows.

'That obviously happens, but mostly it's women who are asking for the divorce', said Steve Slon, editor of *AARP the Magazine* . . . . The magazine will publish the results Thursday in its July–August issue.

'The Divorce Experience: A Study of Divorce at Mid-life and Beyond' surveyed 1,147 people ages 40 to 79 who had divorced in their forties, fifties or sixties. The questionnaire survey, completed in December, had a margin of sampling error of plus or minus 3 percentage points.

The survey found that women over age 40 seemed more aware of problems in their marriages, while men were more likely to be caught off-guard by their divorces. Twenty-six per cent of men said they 'never saw it coming', compared with 14 per cent of women.

'The increase in women initiating a divorce reflects the empowerment of women to leave bad marriages', said Linda Fisher, AARP's director of national member research. 'Thirty years ago, many of these women might not have been able to (divorce) because of lack of self-confidence and financial means', she said. 'Women are more likely to have more self-confidence and the means to leave a marriage when the circumstances are untenable.'

The AARP study found that most women said they filed for divorces because of physical or emotional abuse, infidelity, or drug and alcohol abuse. Men said they sought divorces because they fell out love, they had different values or lifestyles, or infidelity.

The report also found that most older divorced people move on to other serious relationships.

Seventy-five per cent of women in their fifties reported enjoying serious, exclusive relationships after their divorces, often within two years. Eighty-one per cent of men in their fifties did the same.

SOURCE: Chaka Ferguson, Associated Press Writer, Yahoo! News, 26 May 2004.

men and women experience loneliness and depression following marital dissolution, women have greater rates of depression and distress than do men in the post-divorce period (Wu and Hart, 2002). This is not surprising in view of women's distress being largely tied to their feelings of anxiety over their children's well-being as well as the uncertainty surrounding their financial status (Montenegro, 2004). Loss of spousal support, however, appears to have a significant impact on men's overall health; that is, separation/divorce results in both poorer physical and mental health for men (Wu and Hart, 2002), suggesting that the instrumental and emotional support wives provide in marital unions is an important determinant of health for husbands. This is not the case for women, who tend to have stronger informal support networks (friends and family) outside of marriage and, thus, do not suffer such notable declines in their physical well-being.

REMARRIED

According to statistics on marriage in Canada, remarriage, like divorce, is a mid-life transition, with the average age of remarriage for previously divorced women being 41.4 years and the average age for men, 45.0 years (Statistics Canada, 2003a). Remarriage in mid-life is also a gendered transition: men are more likely than women to remarry, a pattern that holds well into later life (Ambert, 2002). There may be a number of reasons for this, including the idea that divorced or widowed women in middle to older age groups greatly value their new-found independence and thus prefer to remain single (Baker, 2001). For men, it may be the case that they find it difficult to make the transition to being 'on their own' without the emotional and instrumental support of a partner and subsequently seek out companionship soon after a divorce to fill that void. Although research on remarriages in general indicates that these couples are at an increased risk of divorce compared to first marriages, it has been suggested that remarriages in mid- to later life may actually have a lower likelihood of marital disruption. This is especially the case when both partners have previously been married (Wu and Penning, 1997).

The remarriage of two previously married individuals in mid-life often involves the 'blending' of two families, referred to in the literature as a 'complex stepfamily'. This reconstitution, that is, the integration of adolescent and/or young adult stepchildren into a new family form, brings with it a number of challenges at this stage of the life course. In mid-life families, the adaptation process for stepchildren is influenced by a number of factors, including children's age at their parent's remarriage, their residential status (co-resident or not), and the quality of the parent–child relationship prior to the remarriage. For example, the difficult period of adjustment that many co-resident children undergo soon after a parent's remarriage may be attributed, in part, to their resentment at the introduction of another authority figure into the home. Depending on the child's age, this may coincide directly with the development of his/her desire to establish a sense of independence from the family, with the step-parent perceived as yet another barrier to the achievement of this goal (Hetherington and Kelly, 2002). Of course, the degree of closeness between parents and their children prior to remarriage has a significant impact on the adaptation of children to their new family structure. Children who have close relationships with their custodial parent in the pre-remarriage period are likely to adjust better to a stepfamily arrangement than those who have a history of conflicted or strained relations (Ahrons and Tanner, 2003).

GAYS AND LESBIANS

Gay and lesbian families in mid-life are becoming increasingly diverse as more and more same-sex partners in middle age are making efforts to 'blend' existing families or to have children together either via medical technology or through adoption (Epstein, 1996; Miller, 1996). Such emergent family forms may be referred to as 'new nuclear' or 'new blended', with same-sex dyads forming the nucleus of the family unit. Often the result of the end of a heterosexual union(s), the 'new blended' family is part of a mid-life phenomenon in Canadian families. As once-married partners 'come out' after years of marriage and child-rearing, they find themselves trying to negotiate both a divorced and a new sexual identity in middle age. For custodial parents, in particular, this may be a difficult period of adjustment for themselves and their adolescent and/or young adult children. Bringing together families who have not yet made their own transitions to a gay- or lesbian-headed single-parent unit may result in conflicted relations early on in the 'new blended' family (Epstein, 1996).

Recently, the caregiving relationships of mid-life gays and lesbians have been recognized as important topics in the literature on social support in families. One of the key exploratory studies to emerge in this area focuses on the experiences of mid-life and older gays caring for chronically ill partners (Hash, 2001). The findings highlight a number of important similarities and differences between the experiences of gays and lesbians and heterosexual caregivers. Not surprisingly, homophobic attitudes of informal (family and friends) and formal (health-care and human services professionals) resources are a major barrier to providing care for chronically ill loved ones. Beyond that, on a structural level, unsupportive policies and practices serve to exacerbate the problem of discrimination and/or non-recognition of same-sex partnerships in the context of caregiving.

CHILDLESSNESS

Childlessness in mid-life can be either by choice or due to **involuntary infertility**, the inability to conceive despite the wish to conceive (Ambert, 2005). As the average age at marriage continues to increase in Canadian society, one of the principal reasons for involuntary childlessness has become delayed child-bearing. A woman's decision to put off starting a family until her mid- to late thirties and forties may have profound implications for her ability to conceive, given that significant fertility declines take place from the age of 35 years onward (Heaton et al., 1999). For mid-life women with fertility issues, one of the most often sought options for child-bearing is assisted reproductive technology (i.e., in vitro fertilization).

Despite their higher propensity for divorce (controlling for number of years married), childless couples report greater marital satisfaction on a number of relationship dimensions than those who are parenting (Twenge et al., 2003). In another study comparing parents and childless couples, Koropeckyj-Cox (2002) tests a typology of parental status from Connidis and McMullin (1993) in her exploration of the factors influencing subjective well-being among mid- to later-life individuals in these two groups. The findings indicate that parental status in mid-life is linked to psychosocial well-being; good-quality relationships between parents and adult children are associated with a sense of positive well-being among parents in mid- to later life. Further, the relationship between child-

lessness and well-being is gendered: women who are childless report higher levels of distress than their male counterparts and have, overall, lower subjective well-being than mothers in close parent–child relationships.

Conclusion

This chapter has provided an overview of the key research areas in the study of mid-life families in North America. Wherever possible, connections to the Canadian literature have been made. It is important to note that Statistics Canada, through the collection of detailed family data in the census and General Social Surveys (i.e., Cycles 5.0, 10.0, 15.0), is a valuable resource for information on changing patterns of family life over time. Co-residence, social support, caregiving, and marital transitions are but a few of the broad topic areas relevant to mid-life families that can be explored using national data sets. The door is also now wide open to pursuing new research projects on such emergent topics as intergenerational ambivalence in mid-life parent–young adult relationships, the ethnocultural dimensions of parent–child co-residence in mid-life, and partnership satisfaction in mid-life gay and lesbian unions.

As contemporary family researchers, we need to expand our definitions of family life-course stages and recognize the linkages between lives at individual and structural levels. In addition, in a field that has long been dominated by quantitative research, greater acknowledgement and appreciation are needed of the contributions that qualitative and mixed-method studies have made and have yet to make to the growing body of literature on the family life course. Although this has been an uphill battle for many years, recent published exploratory work by Mitchell and Gee (2003), Carr (2005), and Hash (2001) on mid-life families have fuelled our optimism for change. Mid-life family researchers can learn much from family gerontologists, who have for some time recognized the value and importance of narrative research (see the work of Bill Randall, Gary Kenyon, Phillip

Clark, Brian DeVries, and Jay Gubrium, for examples) in understanding the lived experiences of older adults and their family members.

Finally, this chapter would not be complete without a discussion of the relationship between mid-life families and social policy. Three central issues need to be highlighted in this regard: (1) mid-life parent–young adult co-residence; (2) social support in mid-life child–older parent relationships; and (3) diversity in mid-life families.

With young adults finding it increasingly difficult to leave the parental nest (and increasingly necessary to return) for financial reasons, parents have become the social safety net for their children regardless of their own socio-economic position (Mitchell and Gee, 1996). Since research in this area has, for the most part, focused on middle- to upper-class parents (those with the financial means to assist adult children through co-resident living arrangements), the experiences of low-income families have been all but ignored. In Canada, the consequences for young adult children are most dire for those whose parents lack the financial means to provide assistance by allowing them to stay at (or return) home. Cuts to social welfare programs over time have weakened the 'knots of the net' in low-income families, increasing the likelihood of earlier than expected launches and the posting of 'no re-entry' signs for children wanting to return home. As a result, young adult children may be forced into a cycle of poverty, living out on the streets, suffering from chronic unemployment or underemployment, and subsequently engaging in high-risk behaviours like drug and alcohol abuse.

The issue of social support to older parents has been of primary interest to governments in light of reductions to health-care spending in this country. At one time, a shared responsibility existed between government and family; now, the provision of social support and **caregiving** to older adults has been pushed further and further away from the public into the family domain. Responsibility for support has become more 'informalized' as hospital and community support service budgets have been cut. Who bears the brunt of this excess burden for care? The onus falls squarely on the shoulders of mid-life women—the **sandwich generation**—who are the primary caregivers to older parents and parents-in-law in addition to co-resident adolescent and/or young adult children. As a result of this 'caregiving squeeze', middle-aged women have a higher likelihood of transitioning from full-time to part-time employment or of leaving the paid workforce altogether. To date, despite the findings from numerous research studies and reports (e.g., Fast et al., 1997; Keating et al., 1999), neither government nor employer-supported policy has adequately addressed the issue of paid leave for **elder care** for mid-life women.

Recognition of the diversity in mid-life Canadian families in the policy domain has been limited for the most part to issues of class, gender, and family structure. For example, governments have focused their efforts on the development of social welfare policy and programs for young to middle-age single mothers (female-headed lone-parent families) living at or below the low-income cut-off line (LICO), a group characterized by intersecting identity markers of diversity. With the continuing emergence of diverse family forms in mid-life, such as gay and lesbian-headed families and childless (by choice or not) couples, it is imperative that governments develop and institute policies that address and attempt to break down systemic barriers (e.g., definitions of 'parent' in maternity/paternity leave policy, definitions of 'family' for caregiving leave) that have, to date, served to marginalize these groups in Canadian society.

Research and policy must inform one another. Given the increasing diversity of the Canadian population in terms of age, class, ethnicity, immigrant status, sexual orientation, and family structure, it is clear that a broader mandate for family research in this country must be developed. Such an initiative is needed to address some of the critical policy issues for mid-life families and the implications for their aging in the coming decades.

Notes

1. It should also be noted here that a growing number of Canadian adults are opting not to have children, thereby increasing the number of childless couples in mid-life.

2. According to Statistics Canada (2004), the age profile of separated and divorced Canadians is changing: from 1986 to 2002, the average age at divorce increased by just over four years, to 43.1 for men and 40.5 for women.

Study Questions

1. Explain the term 'boomerang children'. What factors have contributed to the emergence of this phenomenon in mid-life Canadian families?
2. Identify some of the key policy issues related to social support in mid-life families.
3. What are some of the consequences of divorce in mid-life? Of remarriage?
4. How would you design a study to explore the intersections of identity markers of diversity (e.g., age, ethnicity, sexual orientation) in mid-life families?

Glossary

Boomerang children The term given to adult children who return to the 'empty nest', alone or with a family, subsequently 'cluttering' it again. Recent research indicates that young adults, particularly men, are more likely to return for financial reasons and/or instrumental support (i.e., assistance with meals, cleaning, child care).

Caregiving The social support provided to older adults when they can no longer function independently as a result of deteriorating physical and/or mental health status—i.e., social support that is *required* by the older adult. Sources can be either informal (i.e., family and friends) or formal (i.e., professional caregivers: doctors, nurses, social workers, rehabilitation therapists, paid home-care workers).

Elder care The care provided to older/later life (i.e., 65+ years) family members and/or friends. The care can range from occasional support with grocery shopping to full-time (24/7) nursing-type assistance requiring caregiver–care recipient co-residence.

Empty nest A family life-course stage when all of the children have transitioned to adulthood and left home to begin their own lives ('flown the nest').

Intergenerational ambivalence In mid-life families, the ambivalent or conflicted feelings that result from the incompatibility between parental expectations and children's behaviour.

Intergenerational co-residence A residential arrangement in mid-life in which at least two generations, most often parents and young adult children, live together.

Involuntary infertility The inability to conceive a child despite the desire to have a child.

Life-course perspective A paradigm for understanding both continuity and change across time and generations; combines the study of social structure with the experience of individuals over the life course (i.e., history, society, and biography). The key concepts in the study of the life course are life events, transitions, and trajectories (pathways).

Sandwich generation Middle-generation cohorts sandwiched between older and younger cohorts in a population; more specifically, adults in mid-life (40–64 years) who have at least one child in the household and at least one living parent for whom they are the primary caregivers and who often resides in the household.

Social support The assistance (i.e., instrumental, emotional, and financial) that people give to one another. Sources can be either informal (i.e., family and friends) or formal (i.e., paid home-support service workers such as homemakers, companions).

Further Readings

Connidis, Ingrid Arnet. 2001. *Family Ties and Aging.* Thousand Oaks, Calif.: Sage. A Canadian book that effectively integrates theory and current research about contemporary mid- to later-life family relationships. Connidis's inclusion of discussions on the relationships of emergent family types (e.g., childless older adults, common-law partnerships, gay and lesbian partnerships) that have often been neglected or ignored in the social policy and research domains makes this a timely and important contribution to the literature on aging and families.

Fast, Janet E., and Norah C. Keating. 2000. *Family Caregiving and Consequences for Carers: Toward a Policy Research Agenda.* Ottawa: Canadian Policy Research Network. Commissioned by the CPRN, one of the first reports to outline a research agenda to examine the social policy implications of family caregiving work. Focusing on the consequences in a number of domains (e.g., work, family) for the care provider, the report highlights the need for government and employer-initiated policies and programs that are sensitive to the diverse challenges facing caregivers.

Settersten, Richard A., Jr. 1999. *Lives in Time and Place: The Problems and Promises of Developmental Science.* Amityville, NY: Baywood. Integrating life-course concepts, theory, and research from sociology, psychology, and anthropology, this book breaks new ground in the aging and life-course literature. It successfully argues for the adoption of a more integrated, interdisciplinary approach to the study of human lives over time that more fully explores the relationship between social structure and agency in such domains as work, education, and the family. Policy-relevant discussions are highlighted throughout.

Donaldson, Christa. 2000. *Midlife Lesbian Parenting.* Binghamton, NY: Haworth Press. This innovative and important book focuses on the experiences of nine mid-life lesbian mothers parenting young children. The findings highlight the structural and individual (personal) challenges that face these middle-aged mothers on a day-to-day basis.

Websites

www.olderwomensnetwork.org/publications/research/ economicsecurityofmidlifewomen.htm
A presentation of the executive summary and recommendations of the Older Women's Network (Ontario Inc.) report on the economic security of mid-life women.

www.swc-cfc.gc.ca/pubs/index_e.html
A comprehensive listing of Status of Women Canada's policy research publications. The list includes publications on the integration into policy research, development, and analysis of identity markers of diversity for women.

www.aarp.org/research/reference/publicopinions/ aresearch-import-867.html
A discussion of the key findings from a groundbreaking American Association of Retired Persons (AARP) study

(2004) on divorce in mid- and later life. Also featured are links to the study's executive summary and full report.

www.vifamily.ca/library/cft/strengths.html
A comprehensive discussion of families over the life course in Canada, including a presentation of research findings on identity markers of diversity.

www.asaging.org/networks/index.cfm?cg=LGAIN
The Lesbian and Gay Aging Issues Network (LGAIN), a constituent unit of the American Society on Aging, brings together professionals and academics from all disciplines in the field of aging to address the unique concerns of older lesbians and gay men (also relevant to mid-life lesbians and gays). The organization's home pages include a selection of useful articles from the group's quarterly newsletter, *OutWord.*

References

Ahrons, Constance R., and Jennifer L. Tanner. 2003. 'Adult children and their fathers: Relationship changes 20 years after parental divorce', *Family Relations* 52: 340–51.

Allen, Katherine R., Rosemary Blieszner, and Karen A. Roberto. 2000. 'Families in the middle and later years: A review and critique of research in the 1990s', *Journal of Marriage and the Family* 62: 911–26.

Ambert, Anne-Marie. 2002. *Divorce: Facts, Causes, and Consequences*. Ottawa: Vanier Institute of the Family.

———. 2005. *Changing Families: Relationships in Context*, Canadian edn. Toronto: Pearson Education Canada.

Antonucci, Toni, and Hiroko Akiyama. 1997. 'Concern with others at mid-life: Care, comfort, or compromise?', in M.E. Lachman and J.B. James, eds, *Multiple Paths of Mid-life Development*. Chicago: University of Chicago Press, 147–69.

Aquilino, William S. 2005. 'Impact of family structure on parental attitudes toward the economic support of adult children over the transition to adulthood', *Journal of Family Issues* 26: 143–67.

Baker, Maureen. 2001. *Families, Labour and Love*. Vancouver: University of British Columbia Press.

Boyd, Monica, and Doug Norris. 1995. 'Leaving the nest? The impact of family structure', *Canadian Social Trends* (Autumn 1995): 14–17.

Carr, Deborah. 2005. 'The psychological consequences of mid-life men's social comparisons with their young adult sons', *Journal of Marriage and Family* 67: 240–50.

Cohen, Phillip N., and Lynne M. Caspar. 2002. 'In whose home? Multigenerational families in the United States', *Sociological Perspectives* 45: 1–20.

Connidis, Ingrid A. 2001. *Family Ties and Aging*. Thousand Oaks, Calif.: Sage.

——— and Lori D. Campbell. 1995. 'Closeness, confiding, and contact among siblings in middle and late adulthood', *Journal of Family Issues* 16: 722–45.

——— and Julie A. McMullin. 1993. 'To have or have not: Parent status and the subjective well-being of older men and women', *Gerontologist* 33: 630–6.

Dentinger, Emma, and Marin Clarkberg. 2002. 'Informal caregiving and retirement timing among men and women: Gender and caregiving relationships in later mid-life', *Journal of Family Issues* 23: 857–79.

Dunlop, Rosemary, and Ailsa Burns. 1995. 'The sleeper effect—Myth or reality?', *Journal of Marriage and Family*, 57: 375–86.

Epstein, Rachel. 1996. 'Lesbian families', in Lynn (1996: 107–30).

Eshleman, J. Ross, and Susannah J. Wilson. 2001. *The Family*, 3rd Canadian edn. Toronto: Pearson Education.

Fast, Janet E., Norah C. Keating, Leslie Oakes, and Deanna L. Williamson. 1997. *Conceptualizing and Operationalizing the Costs of Informal Elder Care*. NHRDP Project No. 6609–1963–55. Ottawa: National Health Research and Development Program, Health Canada.

Fingerman, Karen L., Elizabeth L. Hay, and Kira S. Birdett. 2004. 'The best of ties, the worst of ties: Close, problematic, and ambivalent social relationships', *Journal of Marriage and Family* 66: 792–808.

Finnie, Ross. 1993. 'Women, men, and the economic consequences of divorce: Evidence from Canadian longitudinal data', *Canadian Review of Sociology and Anthropology* 30: 205–41.

Gee, Ellen M., and Barbara A. Mitchell. 2003. 'One roof: Exploring multi-generational households in Canada', in M. Lynn, ed., *Voices: Essays on Canadian Families*, 2nd edn. Scarborough, Ont.: Nelson Thomson Learning, 291–311.

Goldscheider, Frances K., and Julie DaVanzo. 1989. 'Pathways to independent living in early adulthood: Marriage, semiautonomy, and premarital residential independence', *Demography* 26: 597–614.

Hash, Kristina. 2001. 'Caregiving and post-caregiving experiences of mid-life and older gay men and lesbians', Ph.D. thesis, Virginia Commonwealth University.

Heaton, Tim B., Cardell K. Jacobson, and Kimberlee Holland. 1999. 'Persistence and chance in decisions to remain childless', *Journal of Marriage and the Family* 61: 531–9.

Hetherington, Mavis, and Joan Kelly. 2002. *For Better or For Worse: Divorce Reconsidered*. New York: Norton.

Hiedemann, Bridget, Olga Suhomlinova, and Angela M. O'Rand. 1998. 'Economic independence, economic status, and empty nest in mid-life marital disruption', *Journal of Marriage and the Family* 60: 219–31.

Kamo, Yoshinori. 2000. 'Racial and ethnic differences in extended family households', *Sociological Perspectives* 43: 211–29.

Keating, Norah C., Janet E. Fast, Judith Frederick, Kelly Cranswick, and Cathryn Perrier. 1999. *Eldercare in Canada: Context, Content, and Consequences.* Ottawa: Statistics Canada, Housing, Family and Social Statistics Division.

Kobayashi, Karen M. 1999. '*Bunka no Tanjyo* (Emergent Culture): Continuity and Change in Older *Nisei* (Second Generation) Parent–Adult *Sansei* (Third Generation) Child Relationships in Japanese Canadian Families', Ph.D. thesis, Simon Fraser University.

Koropeckyj-Cox, Tanya. 2002. 'Beyond parental status: Psychological well-being in middle and old age', *Journal of Marriage and Family* 64: 957–71.

Kozuch, Patricia, and Teresa M. Cooney. 1995. 'Young adults' marital and family attitudes: The role of recent parental divorce, and family and parental conflict', *Journal of Divorce and Remarriage* 23: 45–62.

Landis-Kleine, C., Linda Foley, Loretta Nall, P. Padgett, and L. Walters-Palmer. 1995. 'Attitudes toward marriage and family held by young adults', *Journal of Divorce and Remarriage* 23: 63–73.

Lynn, Marion, ed. 1996. *Voices: Essays on Canadian Families.* Toronto: Nelson Canada.

McDaniel, Susan. 2005. 'The Family Lives of the Middle-Aged and Elderly in Canada', in Maureen Baker, ed., *Families: Changing Trends in Canada.* Toronto: McGraw-Hill Ryerson, 181–99.

——— and Lorne Tepperman. 2004. *Close Relations: An Introduction to the Sociology of Families.* Toronto: Pearson Education.

Marks, Nadine F. 1995. 'Mid-life marital status differences in social support relationships with adult children and psychological well-being', *Journal of Family Issues* 16: 5–28.

——— and James David Lambert. 1998. 'Marital status continuity and change among young and mid-life adults: Longitudinal effects on psychological well being', *Journal of Family Issues* 19: 652–86.

Michelson, William, and Lorne Tepperman. 2003. 'Focus on home: What time-use data can tell about caregiving to adults', *Journal of Social Issues* 59: 591–610.

Miller, James. 1996. 'Out family values', in Lynn (1996: 131–60).

Mitchell, Barbara A. 1998a. 'The refilled nest: Debunking the myth of family in crisis', paper presented at the ninth annual John K. Friesen Conference, 'The Overselling of Population Aging', Simon Fraser University, 14–15 May.

———. 1998b. 'Too close for comfort? Parental assessments of "boomerang kid" living arrangements', *Canadian Journal of Sociology* 23: 21–46.

——— and Ellen M. Gee. 1996. '"Boomerang kids" and midlife parental marital satisfaction', *Family Relations* 45: 442–8.

———, Andrew V. Wister, and Ellen M. Gee. 2002. 'There's no place like home: An analysis of young adults' mature coresidency in Canada', *International Journal of Aging and Human Development* 54: 57–84.

Moen, Phyllis. 1991. 'Transitions in mid-life: Women's work and family roles in the 1970s', *Journal of Marriage and the Family* 53: 135–50.

Montenegro, Xenia P. 2004. 'The divorce experience: A study of divorce at mid-life and beyond', Report published by the AARP, May.

Pacey, Michael. 2002. 'Living alone and living with children: The living arrangements of Canadian and Chinese-Canadian seniors'. SEDAP Research Paper #74. Hamilton, Ont.: McMaster University.

Pillemer, Karl, and Jill J. Suitor. 2002. 'Explaining mothers' ambivalence toward their adult children', *Journal of Marriage and Family* 64: 602–13.

Settersten, Richard A. 1999. *Lives in Time and Place: The Problems and Promises of Developmental Science.* Amityville, NY: Baywood.

Shehan, Constance L., and Jeffrey W. Dwyer. 1989. 'Parent–child exchanges in the middle years: Attachment and autonomy in the transition to adulthood', in J.A. Mancini, ed., *Aging Parents and Adult Children.* Lexington, Mass.: Lexington Books, 99–116.

Statistics Canada. 2002. *2001 Census of Canada: Profile of Canadian Families and Households: Diversification Continues.* Ottawa: Statistics Canada, Catalogue no. 96F0030XIF2001003. At: <www.statcan.ca>; accessed 20 Feb. 2005.

———. 2003a. 'Marriages, 2001', *The Daily*, 20 Nov.

———. 2003b. 'Census of population: Immigration, birthplace and birthplace of parents, citizenship, ethnic origin, visible minorities and Aboriginal peoples', *The Daily*, 21 Jan.

———. 2004. 'Births, 2002', *The Daily*, 19 Apr.

———. 2005. 'Health indicators', *The Daily*, 1 Feb.

Steinberg, Laurence, and Susan B. Silverberg. 1987. 'Influences on marital satisfaction during the middle stages of the family life cycle', *Journal of Marriage and the Family* 49: 751–60.

Strong, Bryan, Christine DeVault, and Theodore F. Cohen. 2005. *The Marriage and Family Experience: Intimate Relationships in a Changing Society*, 9th edn. Belmont, Calif.: Thomson Wadsworth.

Treas, Judith, and Leora Lawton. 1999. 'Family relations in adulthood', in M. Sussman, S.K. Steinmetz, and G. Peterson, eds, *Handbook of Marriage and the Family*. New York: Plenum Press, 425–38.

Twenge, Jean M., W. Keith Campbell, and Craig A. Foster. 2003. 'Parenthood and marital satisfaction: A meta-analytic review', *Journal of Marriage and the Family* 65: 574–83.

Vanier Institute of the Family. 2004. *The Future Families Project: A Survey of Canadian Hopes and Dreams*. Ottawa: Vanier Institute of the Family. At: <www.vifamily.ca/library/future/notes.html>.

Ward, Russell, and Glenna Spitze. 1996. 'Will the children ever leave? Parent–child coresidence history and plans', *Journal of Family Issues* 17: 514–39.

——— and ———. 1998. 'Sandwiched marriages: The implications of child and parent relations for marital quality in midlife', *Social Forces* 77: 647–66.

White, Lynn. 1994. 'Coresidence and leaving home: Young adults and their parents', *Annual Review of Sociology* 20: 81–102.

Williams, Kristi, and Debra Umberson. 2004. 'Marital status, marital transitions, and health: A gendered life course perspective', *Journal of Health and Social Behavior* 45: 81–98.

Willson, Andrea E., Kim M. Shuey, and Glen H. Elder, Jr. 2003. 'Ambivalence in the relationship of adult children to aging parents and in-laws', *Journal of Marriage and Family* 65: 1055–72.

Wu, Zheng, and Randy Hart. 2002. 'The effects of marital and non-marital union transition on health', *Journal of Marriage and the Family* 64: 420–32.

——— and Margaret Penning. 1997. 'Marital instability after midlife', *Journal of Family Issues* 18: 459–78.

CHAPTER 7

Aging in Canadian Families Today

Lori D. Campbell and Michael Carroll

Learning Objectives

- To better understand the diversity and complexity in older people's lives and family relationships.
- To gain knowledge about different marital statuses in later life.
- To understand the historical development of retirement in Canada and factors that influence people to retire.
- To gain information on older people's recreation and leisure activities.
- To understand the support that older people provide to younger family members, as grandparents, through financial assistance, and by inheritance.
- To better appreciate the support that family members provide to older people, particularly related to filial and spousal care.

Older Canadians have rich and varied relationships with their kin and are often very involved in the lives of other family members, exchanging time and support with spouses, children, grandchildren, and others. And with the changes that have been occurring in the form and structure of families as a result of greater longevity, increased divorce, remarriage, and other socio-demographic factors, aging within a family context has become more complex and diverse than ever before. How best to think about all this? The metaphor suggested some time ago by Kahn and Antonucci (1980) is that we travel through life as part of a **social convoy** with other family members. What can we expect as we travel along as members of this convoy? Providing some answers to this question is the primary goal of this chapter.

The chapter starts by looking at various marital statuses that older adults occupy, including marriage, widowhood, divorce, and lifelong singlehood. We then look at two subjects that loom large in all discussions of older people—retirement and recreation/leisure—and here a special concern will be how these things are affected by family relationships. Next we will consider **intergenerational exchange**—the exchange of support between older and younger generations. First, we will look at what often is ignored: the tremendous amount of support that flows from older family members to younger family members, including grandparenting, financial assistance, and, ultimately, inheritance. Next we consider the support that families provide to older family members in the form of caregiving. The chapter closes by considering a dark side that exists in some families: abuse against older people.

Marital Statuses of Older People

BEING MARRIED IN LATER LIFE

Most Canadians marry, and almost one-half of those who do marry remain so until the death of their spouse. In 2001, 90 per cent of men and women aged 50 to 69 had been married at least once (Statistics Canada, 2001). Further, 57 per cent of people 65 years of age or older live with their spouse (Lindsay, 1999). There is, however, a gendered pattern here: at all older ages, men are more likely to be married than are women. At age 85 and older, for example, about 50 per cent of men are married as compared to about 10 per cent of women (ibid.). The greater likelihood that men who marry will still be married in later life results from two interrelated demographic processes:

women tend to live longer than men and men are more likely to remarry.

There are advantages to being married in later life. Older married couples, for example, tend to have more financial resources than unmarried older people. They also report greater happiness and life satisfaction than those who are separated, divorced, or widowed (Cotton, 1999). Many 'empty nest' older couples (couples whose children have grown and moved away from home) find this a particularly enjoyable period of their marriage with more time for themselves and each other (Heidemann et al., 1998). On the other hand, it is also true that the advantages in late-life marriage tend to be associated with 'good' marriages. A poor-quality marriage that involves constant bickering and where one or both people feel unhappy or dissatisfied tends to be linked to depression, lower life satisfaction, and poor health. It is the quality of the committed relationship between a couple, and not marriage per se, that is important for positive well-being and life satisfaction (Peters and Liefbroer, 1997).

Although the majority of older couples are married (in a legal sense), about 5 per cent of Canadians aged 55 or older live in common-law relationships (Statistics Canada, 2003a). Many of these older people have been previously married and choose this relationship in place of a remarriage. Chevan (1996) finds that common-law relationships in later life are more likely among older men than older women (i.e., there are fewer older men to begin with, and men tend to mate with women who are younger), among those who are poorer, and among the separated and divorced.

WIDOWHOOD

For most older couples in Canada today, marriage will end with the death of a spouse rather than through divorce—although there is a gendered pattern here (Novak and Campbell, 2005). Among women aged 75–84, for example, 59 per cent are widowed; the comparable figure for men in the same age group is only 18 per cent. Even at age 85 and older, widowed women outnumber widowed men by about two to one (39 per cent of men com-

pared to 80 per cent of women). Overall, approximately 80 per cent of those who are widowed in Canada are older women. For women, in other words, widowhood has become an expected life event in old age (Martin-Matthews, 1999).

The death of a spouse is one of the most stressful events that older people experience. Widowhood brings not only the loss of companionship, intimacy, and emotional closeness, but also the loss of the married role or status. This role loss can affect one's self-identity in a significant way. Widowed women report feeling stripped of their long-term, deep-rooted identity as a 'wife' (van den Hoonaard, 1997) and forced to take on a strange 'uncoupled identity' (Cicirelli, 2002).

The loneliness that can result from widowhood can be difficult for both men and women. Feelings of loneliness, however, may be more profound for widowed men. Widowed women tend to have larger social networks and more social supports in later life than widowed men (Campbell et al., 1999). In fact, men's greatest source of companionship and support is most often their spouse and men tend to be connected to larger social networks through their wives. The result is that the loss of a spouse can result in greater social isolation for a husband than for a wife. Indeed, while life satisfaction declines for both women and men after the death of a spouse, this decline tends to be greater for men (Chipperfield and Havens, 2001).

Financial stress can be another result of widowhood, particularly for women. The death of a spouse leaves many older women economically disadvantaged in their later years. Burkhauser and his colleagues (2005), for example, found that in the United States, Germany, Great Britain, and Canada the average household income for women falls following the death of her husband. In all countries, the main source of income decline for older widowed women is the loss of their husbands' social security or pension income.

DIVORCE

Among Canadians between the ages of 65 and 74, about 5 per cent of men and 6 per cent of women are divorced (Lindsay, 1999). Canadian divorce rates, though, have increased significantly since the early 1970s. As a result, researchers today suggest that 38 per cent of Canadians will divorce before their thirtieth anniversary (Statistics Canada, 2003b) and more people are in fact divorcing later in life (Statistics Canada, 2004). Partly, this increase in the divorce rate followed the liberalization of Canadian divorce law in 1968 and then again in 1986, but it may also reflect a greater acceptance of divorce among the older population. The percentage of older divorced people who remarry is small (Cohen, 1999), although older divorced men are much more likely to remarry than are older women.

Although divorce in later life can result in economic difficulties for both men and women (Davies and Denton, 2002), this is particularly true for older women (McDonald, 1997; McDonald et al., 2000). In fact, divorced and separated older women tend to be the *most* economically disadvantaged of all unmarried older women in Canada. As McDonald and Robb (2004: S95) state: 'separated and divorced women are the poorest of all older unattached women in Canada and the group that should be the focus of public concern.'

With increasing divorce rates, gains in life expectancy, the aging of the younger divorced population, and low rates of remarriage in later life, researchers predict that the number of divorced older people will increase in the future. This calls for an increase in research that examines the lives of older divorced men and women with regard to the nature and quality of their family relationships and their social, psychological, and economic well-being.

LIFELONG SINGLEHOOD

A small percentage of older Canadians have never married. About 7 per cent of older people in Canada are lifelong singles (Lindsay, 1999). Many people believe that older lifelong singles are lonely, socially isolated people who have 'failed to marry'. Some even question whether never-married, childless older adults (the majority of older never-married people today) are part of a 'family unit'. In fact, however, research finds that most lifelong singles are socially connected to both family and friends (Connidis, 2001). Older single women in particular form close bonds with friends and family, often playing important supportive roles in the lives of their parents, siblings, and nieces and nephews (Campbell et al., 1999).

In some of the earliest work on the never-married, Stein (1981) developed a typology of singlehood based on whether people perceived their single status as temporary or permanent and as voluntary or involuntary. Stein and others (e.g., Dykstra, 1995) found that those who view their singlehood as voluntary (that is, as a conscious choice) tend to report less loneliness, greater life satisfaction, and more contentment with their circumstances than those who are single by circumstance. Many never-married older people lead happy, fulfilling lives, and many, particularly older women, tend to feel they have greater freedom and autonomy than if they had married. On the other hand, the never-married who need care in later life are more likely to require institutional care because they are without a spouse and/or children who might provide care outside of an institution.

Retirement, Recreation, and Leisure

Today in Canada, fewer people work beyond the age of 65 than at any other point in our history. In 2002, only about 11 per cent of men and about 4 per cent of women over the age of 64 were still working (Statistics Canada, 2003c). Moreover, it seems clear that many Canadians want to retire early. About 60 per cent of workers between the ages of 16 and 44, for example, report that they plan to retire at or before age 60 and, in fact, about 40 per cent plan to retire at or before the age of 55 (Novak and Campbell, 2005).

We know that the decision to retire is influenced by a number of factors. Two of the more significant factors for both men and women are health (or more precisely, declining health) and the amount of retirement income the individual can expect to receive. But as an increasing number of investigators are pointing out (van Solinge and Henkens, 2005), the decision to retire is also often influenced by family considerations, particularly for women. There is, for example, some tendency for married couples to retire at the same time. One reason for this may be that retiring at the same time permits them to participate in leisure activities as a couple. In other cases, however, something else seems to be at play. There is evidence, for example, that wives feel pressure to retire when their husbands retire, although the reverse is not true (Chappell et al., 2003). Likely what this gendered pattern reflects is a continuing cultural emphasis on the 'husband as breadwinner' model, or at least a continuing emphasis on the husband—not the wife—being the one who contributes most of the family income (Szinovacz and Davey, 2004). In other words, because a wife continuing to work when her husband has retired would violate the 'husband as breadwinner' model, wives feel pressured to retire when their husbands retire. Something else that can often affect a woman's decision to retire is the need to provide care to an aging relative because (as we will discuss later) it is still the case in our society that women are far more likely than men to be the ones who provide care to aging relatives.

A relatively large literature now looks at what older people do with their leisure and recreation time. One recent review of this literature (Novak and Campbell, 2005) suggests that older Canadians spend a lot of their time alone (and certainly spend more time alone than younger adults); spend most of their leisure time on passive, media-related activities (reading; watching TV); and spend some time travelling (and indeed are travelling more now than was the case among older people in the past). But this same review also makes it clear that, with recreation and leisure among older people, some patterns vary by gender and geographic location. Older women, for example, are more likely than older men to spend time visiting friends and family, playing bingo, attending religious services, and shopping; men are more likely to participate in sports, gardening, and other outdoor activities and to visit a pub.

A common concern of investigators studying leisure and recreational activities among the older population is to assess the effect that particular leisure time/recreational activities have on mental and physical well-being. Several studies, for example, suggest that physical exercise is associated with greater feelings of well-being and less depression, and leads to improved cognitive functioning, improvements in muscle flexibility, and reduced incidence of diabetes (Novak and Campbell, 2005). Other studies have found a strong positive correlation between engaging in social activities (visiting family and friends, being involved with a church or service organization, volunteering, etc.) and measures of health and psychological well-being among older people (Menec, 2003). While the question of causality in these correlational studies is always somewhat uncertain—for example, does being involved with a church group promote physical health or are those people who are physical healthy more likely to join a church group?—the consensus is that staying active in later life is beneficial.

Increasingly, investigators have recognized that 'family context' can affect the choices that older people make about their leisure time and recreational activities. For example, how does the death of a spouse affect how much time someone spends on leisure time and recreational activities? Certainly, we might expect that the death of a spouse would lead to less participation in those activities where the couple had done things together—and this *is* a common finding. But it also appears that losing a spouse has a more generalized effect. A study of leisure activities among older adults in Winnipeg over an eight-year period (Strain et al., 2002) found that someone who lost her/his spouse was more likely to show an across-the-board reduction in leisure activities (that is, to participate less in all leisure activities, even those that had not involved the spouse) as compared to people who have not lost a spouse. Exactly why losing a spouse seems to produce such generalized reduction in leisure activities is still an open question. Still, it is not hard to imagine that such loss might lead to a generalized decline in leisure activities because it deprives people of the support and encouragement that make participation even in 'solitary' activities (such as gardening) more likely and/or because it deprives them of someone with whom they can share their successes in whatever it is they are doing.

Caregiving, in particular the need to provide care to an aging spouse or elderly parent, can also affect patterns of leisure and recreation among older adults. Certainly the need to provide care, especially care to a spouse or parent with a severe disability such as Alzheimer's disease, often limits a person's ability to do other things if only because it is so time-consuming and because it is difficult to schedule 'away time'. Indeed, caregivers themselves report that loss of leisure—in particular, loss of the ability to travel (that is, to take extended trips)—is one of the most negative consequences of the caregiving experience (Gladwell and Bedini, 2003).

On the other hand, providing care can sometimes open up opportunities that might not otherwise be available. Burr et al. (2005), for example, found that older adults providing care to someone were *more likely* than non-caregivers to engage in volunteer work outside the context of their own caregiving. The authors suggest that one of the things operative here is that caregivers are especially likely to be in contact with organizations and social networks that promote volunteering and so are more likely to be aware of volunteering opportunities and to be asked to volunteer. Someone caring for a spouse with Alzheimer's disease, for example, might be in contact with the local Alzheimer's Society and so might become involved with the fundraising and educational activities that such a society sponsors.

The Support That Older People Provide to Their Families

Although much of the social support literature tends to focus on the support and assistance that older people receive from family, the fact is that over the life course older people provide significantly more support to their children and grandchildren than they receive (Robb et al., 1999). Older family members give support in a number of ways: caregiving assistance to a spouse (something that will be discussed later in this chapter); help to their children in caring for their grandchildren; financial assistance to their children during their lifetime; and estate wealth and cherished family possessions to adult children and other family members upon their death. In a very real sense, in other words, older family members are especially important in maintaining the social convoy in which we travel through life.

Grandparenting

Being a grandparent is now something that most people will experience. In Canada, 80 per cent of those who are 65 or older are grandparents. If we restrict our attention to people 65 or older who are parents (putting aside, in other words, older people who have never had children), that percentage jumps to 86 per cent for men and 94 per cent for women (Kemp, 2003). Looking at things from the perspective of grandchildren, the vast majority (more than 90 per cent) of Canadians aged 15–19 have at least one living grandparent and a majority have two or more living grandparents (ibid.).

In thinking about the relationship between grandparents and grandchildren, we need to take into account two interrelated demographic trends that have changed the social significance of grandparenthood over the past several decades. First, people are living longer, which means that the lives of grandchildren and grandparents now overlap for much longer periods than in the past. In Canada, for example, people usually become grandparents in their mid- to late fifties (ibid.) and thus, with increased lifespans, it is common for grandchildren and grandparents to know each other for periods of 20–40 years (Kemp, 2004).

The second demographic trend that has affected grandparenthood is the general decrease in fertility. On the one hand, declining fertility has meant less of an overlap between 'active parenting' and grandparenting, that is, people now are less likely to be raising their own children when they become grandparents (Kemp, 2003). On the other hand, declining fertility has also meant that grandparents now have fewer grandchildren than in the past and so have more of an opportunity to be 'present' in the life of any one grandchild than was previously the case (Gauthier, 2002). The net result is that grandparents today are in a better position than grandparents in the past to develop relationships, and often long-term relationships, with their individual grandchildren.

Still, the fact that the opportunity for developing a relationship with grandchildren exists does not mean that everyone takes advantage of that opportunity in the same way. The one conclusion that comes through most consistently in all studies of grandparenthood is that there is no one 'grandparent role' in our society and that the relationship that grandparents establish with their grandchildren can vary greatly (Kemp, 2004). Some grandparents see their grandchildren quite often, some hardly ever; some grandparents quite willingly help out by caring for their children's children, but many do not; some grandparents actively take on a 'storyteller' role that connects their grandchildren to the past, while many others do not (Gautier, 2002).

There appears to be a slight tendency for a person's 'favourite grandparent' to be a grandmother rather than a grandfather (Dubas, 2001). It also appears that **maternal grandparents**, that is, the mother's parents, are more likely than **paternal grandparents** (the father's parents) to help out their married children by providing care to preschool grandchildren (Gautier, 2002). What seems to be happening is that the traditional emphasis on mothers having primary responsibility for child care is to some extent being shifted to the wife's parents when a wife/mother herself needs help caring for her children. In turn, the fact that maternal grandparents are more likely to care for grandchildren when they are young might help to explain why in later life grandchildren are more likely to report feeling emotionally close to their maternal

grandparents than to their paternal grandparents (Chappell et al., 2003).

When interviewed, most grandchildren will say that they respect their grandparents. This does not mean, however, that grandchildren necessarily consider grandparents to be wise or especially knowledgeable or that they follow the advice grandparents offer. Quite the contrary, Kemp's (2004) study of adult grandchild/grandparent relationships in southwestern Ontario suggests that these relationships work best when both parties adopt a policy of 'non-interference'. For grandparents this means recognizing that it would be inappropriate for them to criticize the behaviour of their adult grandchildren, and for grandchildren it means recognizing that their grandparents are 'set in their ways' and so there is little point in trying to get them to change on any particular issue. In Kemp's study, 'respect' meant that grandchildren showed appreciation for the sacrifices their grandparents had made, and they made a concerted effort not to say anything to their grandparents that would call attention to physical or mental disabilities that are stereotypically associated with aging.

A growing segment of 'grandparenting' literature looks at **skip-generation households**, that is, households where grandparents are raising grandchildren without parents being present in the home. Such households are especially likely to be found in communities characterized by high rates of poverty and unemployment. In the United States, for example, although most skip-generation households are headed by white grandparents, a disproportionate number of such households are headed by black American and Hispanic-American grandparents (Hooyman and Kiyak, 2005). In Canada, First Nations communities—where the problems caused by poverty, unemployment, and governmental neglect have been long-standing—similarly account for a disproportionate share of such households. Thus, although First Nations individuals account for only about 3 per cent of the total population in Canada and only 1.4 per cent of the population over the age of 45, more than 17 per cent of the grandparents raising a grandchild without a parent present are of First Nations descent (Fuller-Thomson, 2005). Nunavut has the highest proportion of skip-generation households (2.3 per cent of all children aged 0–14 live in such a household) and Quebec has the lowest (0.2 per cent) (Milan and Hamm, 2003).

Parental divorce can also affect the grandparent–grandchild relationship. In Canada today, more than one-third of marriages are likely to end in divorce, and in the United States that figure is close to one-half (Connidis, 2001; Beaujot, 2005). Connidis (2001) found that the single most important factor shaping the grandparent–grandchild relationship in the wake of divorce is child custody: since mothers are far more likely to retain custody than fathers, maternal grandparents are more likely to be involved with their grandchildren than paternal grandparents in the post-divorce period. Even so, paternal grandparents do make an effort to stay in contact with their grandchildren. For Connidis this is most of all evident in the finding that contact between fathers and their children falls off more sharply than contact between paternal grandparents and their grandchildren. Finally, and perhaps surprisingly, the available literature (reviewed ibid.) suggests that grandchildren can form close ties with their grandparents even if the middle generation has divorced and that divorce may sometimes have positive benefits, as when a parent remarries and a child's family network—including ties to step-grandparents—is expanded.

In many cases, the custodial parent, which usually means the mother, has acted to block her ex-husband's parents from having access to her children. Situations of this sort have given rise to a number of legal initiatives, in both Canada and the United States, to secure visitation rights on behalf of grandparents. Four provinces—Alberta, British Columbia, New Brunswick, and Quebec—and Yukon have enacted laws that provide for grandparent access, and the federal Divorce Act (though not singling out grandparents) allows people other than a parent to apply for access to a child (Goldberg, 2003). Article 611 of the Civil Code of Quebec, for example, says that 'In no case may the father or the mother, without grave reason, interfere with personal relations between the children and his grandparents' (cited ibid.). Most Canadian provinces, however, do not have legislation protecting grandparent visitation rights and an increasing number of judicial precedents, in both Canada and the United States, have strengthened the right of parents—and parents alone—to decide who should have access to their children so long as there is no evidence that the parent is putting the well-being of her/his children at risk (ibid.). The net effect of recent court decisions, in other words, is to make grandparent access to grandchildren less of a 'right' and to shift the burden of proof to grandparents to show that their grandchildren would be harmed if they did not have contact with them. In the United States, where the subject of grandparent visitation has been more extensively researched, this likely explains why only a small proportion (about a third) of grandparents who petition for access are successful (Henderson, 2005).

OLDER PARENTS' FINANCIAL ASSISTANCE TO YOUNGER GENERATIONS

Older people provide more financial assistance to family members than they receive (Stone et al., 1998). In providing this assistance, however, parents tend not to provide financial assistance to their adult children equally. Generally, they give more financial support to those children who have greater financial needs. McGarry and Schoeni (1997), for example, found that adult children with lower incomes were far more likely to receive financial assistance from their parents than adult children with higher incomes. McGarry and Schoeni also found no evidence that the amount of care that adult children had provided to their parents increased the likelihood of receiving more financial assistance.

Something that does affect the amount of financial assistance parents provide to their adult children is the nature of the relationship they had with their children in the past. Silverstein et al. (2002), in a longitudinal study of American parents and their children from 1971 to 1997, found that the more parents had engaged in common activities with their young children—including things like attending family gatherings together, talking together about important matters, having dinner together—the more likely were these parents to provide those children with financial assistance in later life.

Ploeg and her colleagues (2003) have identified some of the reasons why older parents provided financial assistance to their adult children and grandchildren. One important finding was that these older parents very much wanted to help younger family members 'build' or 'rebuild' their lives and futures. For example, parents gave financial assistance to adult children to help them start their families and careers (for wedding expenses, to buy a home or car, or to start a business). Parents also gave assistance to children who had experienced difficult life transitions, such as divorce, the loss of a job, or illness, to help them get back on their feet. As well, older parents often gave money to their grandchildren for educational needs, both in the present and for the future. While this is to help the grandchildren themselves, it is also often seen as a way of relieving the middle generation of a financial burden.

Finally, Ploeg and her colleagues also found that older parents often referred to their own experiences in the past when explaining why they were willing to provide financial assistance to younger family members. Some said that they themselves had received financial assistance from their own parents and wanted to help their own children in the way they had been helped. Others said that they had needed financial assistance earlier in life but had *not* received it from their own parents, and so wanted to help their children so that their children would be spared the suffering they themselves had experienced. Still other parents saw giving financial assistance to their children as a kind of 'early inheritance', and talked about their pleasure in having the financial resources to provide such assistance when it was needed and while they were still alive and able to enjoy the experience of giving.

Box 7.1 Financial Assistance to Adult Children

In the study by Ploeg and her colleagues (2003), older parents talked about their reasons for providing financial assistance to adult children. As the comments below reflect, parents provided assistance out of feelings of love and commitment to their family, and to help their children as they were building their own families and careers or rebuilding their lives after difficult life transitions.

The time when people need assistance is when they are young, starting their lives, starting their jobs, starting their families, saving for their children's future, not when they have finally established themselves comfortably.

Both [our] daughters had unhappy marriages and are now divorced. They needed financial assistance to rebuild their lives. We feel that assisting our children has been our best investment.

I cannot describe the joy of sharing assets with my children, helping them to advance in life.

FAMILY INHERITANCE

Although older people provide a range of assistance to family members during their lifetime, inheritance remains an important mechanism for passing on family wealth and property, particularly from older to younger generations. Inheritance decisions made by older family members, however, can affect individual family members, family relationships, and the entire family network. Decisions made about how estates will be bequeathed can create conflict within families and feelings of anger between and among potential heirs.

Although will-making has become more common over the past century or so, as wealth accumulation and home ownership has increased, a substantial number of older people still do not have a legal will. Those who are older (60 or older) are more likely to have a will compared to adults at mid-life. Wills are also more common among those with higher incomes, greater assets, and more education. Older married or widowed people, particularly those with children, are also more likely to have made a will (O'Connor, 1996). Spouses and children are most likely to be named as beneficiaries by both men and women (Finch et al., 1996). And while most parents provide equally for all their children in their wills (McGarry, 1999), some parents feel that a more equitable division of wealth is to bequeath more to children who are at a greater financial risk or those with disabilities (Rossi and Rossi, 1990). Further, the decisions that older family members make about the passing on of their property and possessions seem to reflect the cumulative nature of their family relationships over the life course rather than the quality of those ties nearer the end of their life (Finch et al., 1996).

When family members, particularly adult children, do not share a parent's perception of what is 'fair' in regard to the division of wealth, this can create conflict or tension within the family. Disagreement about what is fair is often especially intense in connection with cherished family possessions (Stum, 2000). Even if family members agree that these objects and mementos should be divided equally, it is often difficult to agree on the 'value' of such possessions, as value can be financial, emotional, or an interweave of both (Lustbader, 1996). Stum (2000) found that one major source of potential conflict in families centred on a lack of communication or miscommunication around the meaning that particular objects had for individuals. As one respondent in Stum's (2000: 194) study said: 'I have seen jealousy, hate, and non-speaking sisters and brothers because they think they were cheated out of something.' As families become increasingly diverse and complex as the result of divorce and remarriage—as, for example, the number of stepchildren and step-grandchildren within a family network increases—it seems likely that the potential for conflict over 'fairness' issues might also increase.

Support Provided to Older Family Members

In thinking about older adults and their need for care, we must be careful not to exaggerate. We certainly shouldn't think of older people who have physical or cognitive disabilities as being cared for within an institutional setting. On the contrary, in 2001 only 9 per cent of women over the age 65 and only 5 per cent of men over 65 were living in long-term care facilities, and in both cases these percentages are a bit *lower* than what they had been in 1981 (Statistics Canada, 2003d). Most older people live with a spouse or live alone, though the exact pattern varies by gender (Statistics Canada, 2003d). Most older men (61 per cent), for example, live with a spouse/partner and no children while only 16 per cent live alone; by contrast, older women are equally likely to be living with a spouse/partner and no children (35 per cent) as to be living alone (35 per cent). On the other hand, there is no denying that many older Canadians—especially when they advance into their eighties and nineties—do require assistance from others and most often that assistance is provided by other family members.

Caregiving by Adult Children

In the vast literature on caregiving in later life, one of the most consistent findings is that women provide more care to older family members than men (Laditka and Laditka, 2000). Stoller (1994) estimates that among adult children providing care to elderly parents, daughters outnumber sons three to one. Furthermore, this greater likelihood that daughters will provide care persists after controlling for other caregiver and care receiver characteristics known to affect the likelihood of providing care (Dwyer and Coward, 1991). In the end, in other words, women—daughters or daughters-in-law—are most likely to provide care to aging parents or parents-in-law. Daughters are more likely to assist parents with care tasks that are consistent with traditional female roles in families, such as domestic and household chores and personal care, while sons who provide care tend to assist with tasks consistent with normative roles for men in families, such as outside household maintenance and yard work or financial matters (Chang and White-Means, 1991; Stoller, 1990).

Cultural beliefs that women are the 'nurturers' within families may place greater expectations on adult daughters to provide care to parents than is true for sons. This may be particularly salient for personal care tasks because of the cross-gender taboos related to care of an intimate and personal nature, in that it is less acceptable and less expected for sons to provide this kind of care, particularly if that care is needed by mothers (Arber and Ginn, 1995; Davidson et al., 2000).

Spousal Care

Married people not only have a live-in companion in later life, but they also have a live-in caregiver as well. In fact, most older spouses name their husband or wife as their primary provider of support and care, and couples tend to rely on each other more than on other social ties (Barrett and Lynch, 1999). Married people are also much less likely than those who are unmarried to require institutional care because of their live-in support system (Connidis, 2001).

Wives take on the role of spousal caregiver more often than do husbands. As married women

---

Box 7.2 Sons' Experiences in Filial Caregiving

Campbell and Carroll (2006) have examined adult sons' experiences of providing care to older parents in the context of gender and masculinity. The following comments capture their emotionality within **filial caregiving**, their strong commitment to care, and their emphasis on fairness and reciprocity.

I love my mum [but] sometimes it is frustrating and sometimes it's overwhelming. . . . [There's] a sense of feeling very spread out.

You wouldn't want to be around me sometimes . . . I would cry my eyes out in some cases because it was so frustrating.

I feel good that he spent that many years raising me and then that I was able to give some back.

She cared for me when I was a baby. . . . [T]hey [parents] are part of why you are successful or why you are where you are, and, you know, it's only fair to pay it back to them.

tend to outlive their mates, they often assume the role of caregiver during their husbands' illness. Spousal caregivers feel a strong commitment to care—out of feelings of both duty and love (Ross et al., 1997a). Many also express feelings of satisfaction about their role in care (Chappell and Kuehne, 1998). However, providing care to an older family member with physical or cognitive impairment can lead to stress and distress, which researchers call **caregiver burden** (Levesque et al., 1998). Spouses tend to report greater feelings of distress and burden than do children who provide care to older parents. Spousal caregivers can experience significant burden when they have their own health problems to deal with and have few financial or social resources to assist them with their care. Yet, despite these challenges, spousal caregivers often resist the help of formal services, wanting to provide the best care they can themselves for their partner (O'Connor, 1999).

In a study of **spousal caregiving** conducted in the UK (Davidson et al., 2000), chronically ill husbands were more difficult and demanding than were wives receiving care from their husbands. Davidson and her colleagues suggest that this was due, in part, to husbands' unfamiliarity or lack of experience with the care and household tasks that were required. Chronically ill wives, by comparison, knew the work that was involved (having performed household and care work throughout their adult lives) and, therefore, were less likely to make demands and more grateful for the care that they received. However, the researchers also found that even if the husband was receiving care, he still sought to hold his position as 'family head' and to maintain as much control as possible in the home. Calasanti (2004) suggests that chronic illness presents a significant threat to men's sense of self and their masculine identity. Illness can create a barrier for men in areas where they had previously felt power or control, such as in their work and their sexuality. Chronic illness can leave a man feeling vulnerable and powerless, 'and raise his self-doubts about masculinity' (Charmaz, 1995: 268). Charmaz and

Calasanti both contend that for chronically ill men receiving care from a spouse, their inability to 'control' their health may lead them to find other ways to affirm their masculinity. This can mean exerting control over their wife and household—the one area they still have left to them.

When a spouse moves into a long-term care facility, the stress of caregiving tends to continue, as caregivers experience feelings of loneliness and guilt after institutionalization (Loos and Bowd, 1997). Many women feel unable to get on with their lives: they feel a strong commitment to their institutionalized husband but also the loneliness of widowhood. Rosenthal and Dawson (1991) used the concept of **quasi-widowhood** to capture these feelings. In their study, women experienced a range of emotions after the husband was institutionalized, including feelings of grief, anger, sadness, and guilt (Rosenthal and Dawson, 1994). Yet, these women continue to maintain close ties to their husbands and the institutions. In one study, more than 80 per cent of wives visited their husbands several times each week, with 20 per cent visiting daily (Ross et al., 1997a, 1997b). These frequent visitors were involved with various care tasks, such as decorating the room and bringing in favourite foods, as a way to maintain a close bond to the husband and to keep their role as wife and supporter active. However, research finds that wives who are able to detach themselves from their caregiver role, by visiting less often and allowing nursing home staff to perform more of the caring functions, tend to cope better with their husbands' situations. These women report feeling less depressed and 'sort of like a widow' (Ross et al., 1994: 29) as they go through the process of moving on with their lives.

The Darker Side of Family: Abuse against Older Persons

Some time ago, using data from a random sample of older people (aged 65 or older) living in private dwellings, Podnieks et al. (1990) found that about 4 per cent of these people had experienced abuse since turning 65. A more recent Canadian survey (Dauverne, 2003) suggests that this figure is 7 per cent. Whether rates of abuse against older people have truly increased, however, or whether Canadian investigators are now using a more expansive definition of abuse, is a matter of debate (Novak and Campbell, 2005).

Is elder abuse a distinctively 'family' problem? At one level, no. If we look specifically at violent crimes in which the victim is an older person, then data provided by police departments suggest that in about two-thirds of these cases the perpetrator is a non-family member, most often a stranger (Davergne, 2003; AuCoin, 2005). Older people, in other words, are often assaulted by non-family members just as people at other ages are often assaulted by non-family members. Still, although older adults might seem to be 'easy targets', the fact is that they are significantly *less* likely to be the victims of violent crime than people in every other age category (AuCoin, 2005).

A different picture emerges, however, when we look at victims of domestic abuse, that is, at cases where the person who abuses an elderly person *is* a family member. In these cases, abuse most often takes the form of emotional abuse and—less frequently—financial abuse and sexual or physical violence (Dauvergne, 2003). And in the vast majority of cases—especially when they involve violence—the person responsible for the abuse of an older person is usually either a spouse or an adult child. Many older people, in other words, are being abused by very close family members. Why?

Investigators have explained the abuse of older people in a variety of ways, but most reviews (see AuCoin, 2005; Novak and Campbell, 2005; McDonald and Collins, 2000) suggest that explanations fall into three categories. (1) The disabilities associated with the elderly put them at risk of abuse either because they are less able to fend off abuse than people who are not disabled and/or because their disability causes people around them to become frustrated. (2) The abuse of elderly persons is a continuation of pre-existing patterns.

This sometimes means that a child abused by a parent has learned abusive behaviour and so is predisposed to abuse the parent as the parent ages. But it also means that a person who abuses her/his spouse in old age is often someone with a long history of abusing the spouse. (3) Abuse against older people is sometimes explained by caregiver stress, such as that experienced by someone caring for a spouse with Alzheimer's disease. Each of these explanations has its proponents and each has some degree of empirical support. Moreover, they are not mutually exclusive.

What is easy to overlook in thinking about the abuse of older people is the matter of gender. Although studies vary somewhat, the general finding is that at least with regard to abuse that involves *violence* directed against an elderly person by a family member, the perpetrators are overwhelmingly (in 80 per cent or more of the cases) male (Dauvergne, 2003, AuCoin, 2005). This usually means that when older people are abused by a family member, they are abused by an adult son or by a husband. Thus, the abuse of older family members must be considered part of a larger cultural pattern, since males in our society account for *most* instances of violence. Males, for example, account for the vast majority of murders, almost all rapes, most instances of road rage, etc. As a number of feminist authors (e.g., Kimmel, 2000) have pointed out, to ignore the fact that perpetrators of violence are male is to ignore one of the most important patterns that emerges from the study of violence (in this case, from the study of domestic violence directed against elderly people).

The question we need to ask, in other words, is not why some *people* direct violence against older people but why so many *males* direct violence against older people. While some people have attributed this to biology (raging testosterone, for example), a careful examination of the evidence reveals a number of patterns inconsistent with a purely biological explanation (Kimmel, 2000). Nor can male violence be reduced to a matter of patriarchy (male dominance over females) because in many cases—in the case of murder, for example—male violence is directed more against other males than against females. Most likely, feminist researchers suggest, male violence derives from the way in which masculinity is defined in our culture, i.e, ours is a culture in which being aggressive in interpersonal relationships is a way of validating a masculine identity (Kimmel, 2000). Although feminist arguments of this sort have begun to make their way into the general literature on domestic violence, they have not as yet had much impact on the way we think about the abuse of older people.

Conclusion

We started this chapter by suggesting that the idea of a 'social convoy' is a useful metaphor for thinking about the relationship between family and aging over the life course. What should now be clear is that the precise nature of our particular convoy will depend on the family members who are part of it, the people we lose along the way, what we chose to do with our time, and whether and how the relationships in which we are enmeshed—between husband and wife, parents and children, grandparents and grandchildren—are or are not strengthened by acts of mutual generosity and care. What should also be apparent is that our experience of these social convoys—even now—will typically be quite different for men and women. Although many of the patterns we have described and discussed result from structural or cultural conditions that will be little affected by the decisions we make as individuals, the first step in effecting change—always—is becoming aware of the problem and the possibilities for change. And finally, what should be clear from this discussion is that older people are an integral part of family, as spouses, parents, and grandparents, and in the care, support, and affection they share with other family members in their social convoy.

Study Questions

1. Discuss similarities and differences in the experience of widowhood for men and women in later life.
2. Explain factors that influence people's decisions to retire.
3. Identify the two interrelated demographic trends that have changed the social significance of grandparenthood over the last few decades, and explain how these trends have influenced this family role.
4. Explain how parental divorce can affect the grandparent–grandchild relationship.
5. Discuss the roles that sons and daughters play in filial caregiving.

Glossary

Caregiver burden Feelings of physical and emotional stress and depression that caregivers often experience.

Filial caregiving Care provided by adult children to older parents.

Intergenerational exchange The exchange of support and assistance between generations, very often between adult children and their parents.

Maternal grandparents The mother or wife's parents.

Paternal grandparents The father or husband's parents.

Quasi-widowhood Feelings of grief, loss, and depression that women experience following their husband's placement in a long-term care facility.

Skip-generation households Grandchildren living with grandparents without the middle/parent generation being present.

Social convoy A model of support that involves a network of close family and friends who travel through life together, providing reciprocal social support.

Spousal caregiving Care provided by one's husband or wife.

Further Readings

Connidis, Ingrid A. 2001. *Family Ties and Aging.* Thousand Oaks, Calif.: Sage. A comprehensive overview of aging within a family context, including older adults' relationships with spouses, children, siblings, and grandchildren as well as the family ties of divorced, childless, and never-married older adults and older gays and lesbians.

Denton, F.T., D. Fretz, and B.G. Spencer, eds. 2000. *Independence and Economic Security in Old Age.* Vancouver: University of British Columbia Press. A collection of articles on issues and trends in retirement: the role of the economy in decisions surrounding retirement, unexpected retirement, and options to traditional retirement.

Gee, Ellen M., and Gloria M. Gutman, eds. 2002. *The Overselling of Population Aging: Apocalyptic Demography, Intergenerational Challenges, and Social Policy.* Toronto: Oxford University Press. This edited volume of Canadian research challenges the 'alarmist' perspective of population aging. It focuses on such topics as aging families, intergenerational caregiving, and retirement income.

Kramer, B.J., and E.H. Thompson, eds. 2002. *Men as Caregivers.* New York: Springer. A comprehensive overview of men as caregivers, including men who care for a family member with dementia, gay men who provide care to their partners with AIDS, and sons who care for older parents.

Novak, Mark, and Lori Campbell. 2005. *Aging and Society: A Canadian Perspective*, 5th edn. Scarborough, Ont.: Nelson Publishing. A current and comprehensive overview of aging in Canada that includes topics such as demographics of the aging population, personal health and illness, work and retirement, and family life and social support.

Van den Hoonaard, D.K. 2001. *The Widowed Self: Older Women's Journey through Widowhood.* Waterloo, Ont.: Wilfrid Laurier University Press. Research that uses autobiographical accounts from a group of Canadian widowed women.

Websites

www.seniors.gc.ca
Seniors Canada On-Line is a government of Canada website that provides information on a range of subjects such as care for seniors, resources for caregivers, and end-of-life issues that will be of interest to older Canadians, their families, caregivers, and others.

www.fifty-plus.net
CARP (Canada's Association for the Fifty-Plus) is a non-profit organization for Canadians 50 years of age and older that promotes the rights and quality of life of older Canadians. The magazine, *50 Plus*, is published by this organization.

www.paguide.com
'Canada's Physical Activity Guide to Healthy Active Living for Older Adults' (2000), directed at older adults on the importance of physical activity for good health and improved quality of life, includes ways to increase physical activity in later life.

www.ccc-ccan.ca
The Canadian Caregiver Coalition brings together researchers, professionals, caregivers, organizations, and other groups to give voice to caregivers and to promote societal awareness of the needs of Canadian caregivers.

www.phac-aspc.gc.ca/ncfv-cnivf/familyviolence
The National Clearing House on Family Violence, a resource centre operated by Health Canada, provides information on family violence and abuse for Canadians.

www.phac-aspc.gc.ca/seniors-aines
The Division of Aging and Seniors within Health Canada provides information for older Canadians and others interested in aging issues.

References

Arber, Sara, and Jay Ginn. 1995. 'Gender differences in informal caring', *Health & Social Care in the Community* 3: 19–31.

AuCoin, Kathy. 2005. 'Family violence against older adults', in *Family Violence in Canada: A Statistical Profile 2005*. Statistics Canada Catalogue no. 85–224–XIE. Ottawa: Canadian Centre for Justice Statistics, 78–89.

Beaujot, Roderic. 2005. 'Families', in James J. Teevan and W.E. Hewitt, eds, *Introduction to Sociology: A Canadian Focus*, 8th edn. Toronto: Pearson, 221–49.

Barrett, A.E., and S.M. Lynch. 1999. 'Caregiving networks of elderly persons: Variations by marital status', *Gerontologist* 39, 6: 695–704.

Burkhauser, Richard V., Philip Giles, Dean R. Lillard, and Johannes Schwarze. 2005. 'Until death do us part: An analysis of the economic well-being of widows in four countries', *Journals of Gerontology*, Series B 60, 5: S238–46.

Burr, Jeffrey A., Namkee G. Choi, Jan E. Mutchler, and Francis G. Caro. 2005. 'Caregiving and volunteering: Are private and public helping behaviors linked?' *Journals of Gerontology*, Series B 60B, 5: S247–56.

Calasanti, Toni M. 2004. 'Feminist gerontology and old men', *Journals of Gerontology*, Series B 59B, 6: S305–14.

Campbell, L.D., and M. Carroll. 2006. 'The incomplete revolution: Theorizing gender when studying men who provide care to aging parents', *Journal of Men and Masculinities* 9 (forthcoming).

———, Ingrid Connidis, and Lorraine Davies. 1999. 'Sibling ties in later life: A social network analysis', *Journal of Family Issues* 20, 1: 114–48.

Chang, Cyril F., and Shelley I. White-Means. 1991. 'The men who care: An analysis of male primary caregivers who care for frail elderly at home', *Journal of Applied Gerontology* 10, 3: 343–58.

Chappell, Neena, Ellen Gee, Lynn McDonald, and Michael Stones. 2003. *Aging in Contemporary Canada*. Toronto: Prentice-Hall.

——— and V.K. Kuehne. 1998. 'Congruence among husband and wife caregivers', *Journal of Aging Studies* 12, 3: 239–54.

Charmaz, K. 1995. 'Identity dilemmas of chronically ill men', in D. Sabo and D.F. Gordon, eds, *Men's Health and Illness: Gender, Power, and the Body*. Thousand Oaks, Calif.: Sage, 266–91.

Chevan, A. 1996. 'As cheaply as one: Cohabitation in the older population', *Journal of Marriage and the Family* 58, 3: 656–67.

Chipperfield, J.G., and B. Havens. 2001. 'Gender differences in the relationship between marital status transitions and life satisfaction in later life', *Journals of Gerontology*, Series B 56, 3: 176–86.

Cicirelli, Victor G. 2002. *Older Adults' Views on Death*. New York: Springer.

Cohen, G.D. 1999. 'Marriage and divorce in later life: Editorial', *American Journal of Geriatric Psychiatry* 7, 3: 185–7.

Connidis, Ingrid Arnet. 2001. *Family Ties and Aging*. Thousand Oaks, Calif.: Sage.

——— and Lori D. Campbell. 1995. 'Closeness, confiding, and contact among siblings in middle and late adulthood', *Journal of Family Issues* 16, 6: 722–45.

Cotton, S. 1999. 'Marital status and mental health revisited: Examining the importance of risk factors and resources', *Family Relations* 48, 3: 225–33.

Dauvergne, Mia. 2003. 'Family violence against seniors', *Canadian Social Trends* (Spring): 10–14.

Davidson, Kate S., Sara Arber, and Jay Ginn. 2000. 'Gendered meanings of care work within late life marital relationships', *Canadian Journal on Aging* 19, 4: 536–53.

Davies, Sharon, and Margaret Denton. 2002. 'Economic well-being of older women who became divorced or separated in mid- or later life', *Canadian Journal on Aging* 21, 4: 477–93.

Dubas, Judith Semon. 2001. 'How gender moderates the grandparent–grandchild relationship: A comparison of kin-keeper and kin-selector theories', *Journal of Family Issues* 22: 478–92.

Dwyer, J.W., and R.T. Coward. 1991. 'A multivariate comparison of the involvement of adult sons versus daughters in the case of impaired parents', *Journals of Gerontology*, Series B 46, 5: S259–269.

Dykstra, P.A. 1995. 'Loneliness among the never and formerly married: The importance of supportive friendships and a desire for independence', *Journals of Gerontology*, Series B 50: S321–9.

Finch, Janet, L. Hayes, J. Masson, J. Mason, and L. Wallis. 1996. *Wills, Inheritance, and Families*. Oxford: Oxford University Press.

Fuller-Thomson, Esme. 2005. 'Canada First Nations grandparents raising grandchildren: A portrait in resilience', *International Journal of Aging and Human Development* 60, 4: 331–42.

Gauthier, Anne. 2002. 'The role of grandparents', *Current Sociology* 50: 295–307.

Gladwell, Nancy J., and Leandra A. Bedini. 2003. 'In search of lost leisure: The impact of caregiving on leisure travel', *Tourism Management* 25: 685–93.

Goldberg, Dan L. 2003. 'Grandparent–grandchild access: A legal analysis', Department of Justice Canada Background paper 2003–FCY–15E. At: <http://canada.justice.gc.ca/en/ps/pad/reports/2003-FCY-15E.pdf>. Accessed 20 Nov. 2005.

Heidemann, B., O. Suhomlinova, and A.M. O'Rand. 1998. 'Economic independence, economic status, and empty nest in midlife marital disruption', *Journal of Marriage and the Family* 60: 219–31.

Henderson, Tammy L. 2005. 'Grandparent visitation rights: Successful acquisition of court-ordered visitation', *Journal of Family Issues* 26, 1: 107–37.

Hooyman, Nancy R., and H. Asuman Kiyak. 2005. *Social Gerontology: A Multidisciplinary Perspective*. Boston: Pearson.

Ingersoll-Dayton, Berit, Marjorie E. Starrels, and David Dowler. 1996. 'Caregiving for parents and parents-in-law: Is gender important?', *Gerontologist* 36, 4: 483–91.

Kahn, R.I., and Toni C. Antonucci. 1980. 'Convoys over the life course: Attachments, roles, and social support', *Life-Span Development and Behavior* 3: 253–86.

Kemp, Candace. 2003. 'The social and demographic contours of contemporary grandparenthood: Mapping the patterns in Canada and the United States', *Journal of Comparative Family Studies* 34, 2: 187–212.

———. 2004. 'Grand expectations: The experiences of grandparents and adult grandchildren', *Canadian Journal of Sociology* 29, 4: 499–526.

——— and Margaret Denton. 2003. 'Canadian reflections on the allocation of responsibility for later life: Individuals, state, employer, and families', *Ageing & Society* 23, 6: 737–60.

Kimmell, Michael S. 2000. *The Gendered Society*. New York: Oxford University Press.

Laditka, James N., and Sarah B. Laditka. 2000. 'Aging children and their older parents: The coming generation of caregiving', *Journal of Women and Aging* 12, 1 and 2: 189–204.

Levesque, L., S. Cossette, and L. Lachance. 1998. 'Predictors of the psychological well-being of primary caregivers living with a demented relative: A 1-year follow-up study', *Journal of Applied Gerontology* 17, 2: 240–58.

Lindsay, C. 1999. *A Portrait of Seniors in Canada*, 3rd edn. Catalogue no. 89–519–XPE. Ottawa: Statistics Canada.

Loos, C., and A. Bowd. 1997. 'Caregivers of persons with Alzheimer's disease: Some neglected implications of the experience of personal loss and grief', *Death Studies* 21, 5: 501–14.

Lustbader, W. 1996. 'Conflict, emotion, and power surrounding legacy', *Generations* 20, 3: 54–7.

McDonald, Lynn. 1997. 'The invisible poor: Canada's retired widows', *Canadian Journal on Aging* 16, 3: 553–83.

——— and A. Collins. 2000. *Abuse and Neglect of Older Adults: A Discussion Paper*. Ottawa: Health Canada.

———, P. Donahue, and B. Moore. 1997. *Widowhood and Retirement: Women on the Margin*. Toronto: Centre for Applied Social Research.

——— and A.L. Robb. 2004. 'The economic legacy of divorce and separation for women in old age', *Canadian Journal on Aging* 23 (supplement): S83–97.

McGarry, K. 1999. 'Intervivos transfers and intended bequests', *Journal of Public Economics* 73: 321–51.

——— and R.F. Schoeni. 1997. 'Transfer behavior within the family: Results from the Asset and Health Dynamics Survey', *Journals of Gerontology*, Series B 52 (Special Issue): 82–92.

Martin-Matthews, Anne. 1999. 'Widowhood: Dominant renditions, changing demography, and variable meaning', in S.M. Neysmith, ed., *Critical Issues for Future Social Work Practice with Aging Persons*. New York: Columbia University Press, 27–46.

Menec, Verena H. 2003. 'The relation between everyday activities and successful aging: A 6-year longitudinal study', *Journals of Gerontology*, Series B 58: S74–82.

Milan, Anne, and Brian Hamm. 2003. 'Across the generations: Grandparents and grandchildren', *Canadian Social Trends* (Winter): 2–9. Ottawa: Statistics Canada Catalogue no. 11–008.

Novak, Mark, and Lori Campbell. 2005. *Aging and Society: A Canadian Perspective*, 5th edn. Scarborough, Ont.: Nelson.

O'Connor, C. 1996. 'Empirical research on how the elderly handle their estates', *Generations* (Fall): 13–20.

O'Connor, D. 1999. 'Living with a memory-impaired spouse: (Re)cognizing the experience', *Canadian Journal on Aging* 18, 2: 211–35.

Peters, A., and A.C. Liefbroer. 1997. 'Beyond marital status: Partner history and well-being in old age', *Journal of Marriage and the Family* 59, 3: 687–99.

Ploeg, Jenny, Lori Campbell, Margaret Denton, Anju Joshi, and Sharon Davies. 2003. 'Helping to build and rebuild secure lives and futures: Financial transfers from parents to adult children and grandchildren', *Canadian Journal on Aging* 23 (Supplement): S113–25.

Podnieks, E., K. Pillemer, J.P. Nicholson, T. Shillington, and A. Frizzell. 1989. *National Survey of Abuse of the Elderly in Canada: Preliminary Findings.* Toronto: Ryerson Office of Research and Innovation.

Robb, R., Margaret Denton, A. Gafni, Anju Joshi, J. Lian, Carolyn Rosenthal, and D. Willison. 1999. 'Valuation of unpaid help by seniors in Canada: An empirical analysis', *Canadian Journal on Aging* 18, 4: 430–46.

Rosenthal, Carolyn, and P. Dawson. 1991. 'Wives of institutionalized husbands', *Journal of Aging and Health* 3, 3: 315–34.

Ross, M.M., Carolyn Rosenthal, and P.G. Dawson. 1994. 'The continuation of caregiving following the institutionalization of elderly husbands', in *National Advisory Council on Aging, Marital Disruption in Later Life.* Catalogue no. H71–3/17–1994E. Ottawa: Minister of Supply and Services, 23–32.

———, ———, and ———. 1997a. ' Spousal caregiving in the institutional setting: Task performance', *Canadian Journal on Aging* 16, 1: 51–69.

———, ———, and ———. 1997b. 'Spousal caregiving in the institutional setting: Visiting', *Journal of Clinical Nursing* 6, 6: 473–83.

Rossi, A.S., and P.H. Rossi. 1990. *Of Human Bonding: Parent–Child Relations across the Life Course.* Hawthorne, NY: Aldine de Gruyter.

Silverstein, M., S.J. Conroy, H. Wang, R. Giarrusso, and V.L. Bengtson. 2002. 'Reciprocity in parent–child relations over the adult life course', *Journal of Gerontology*, Series B 57, 1: S3–13.

Statistics Canada. 2001. *Changing Conjugal Life in Canada.* Catalogue no. 89–576–XIE. Ottawa: Statistics Canada.

———. 2003a. 'The people: Common-law', *Canada e-Book.* Catalogue no. 11–404–XIE. Ottawa: Statistics Canada.

———. 2003b. 'The people: Break-up', *Canada e-Book.* Catalogue no. 11–404–XIE. Ottawa: Statistics Canada.

———. 2003c. 'Labour force and participation rates by sex and age group', *Canadian Statistics.* At: <www.statcan.ca/english/Pgdb/labor05.htm>; accessed 30 Nov. 2005.

———. 2003d. 'Update on families', *Canadian Social Trends* (Summer): 11–17. Statistics Canada Catalogue no. 11–008.

———. 2004. 'Divorces', *The Daily*, 4 May. At: <www.statcan.ca/Daily/English.htm>.

Stein, Peter. 1981. 'Understanding single adulthood', in P.J. Stein, ed., *Single Life: Unmarried Adults in Social Context.* New York: St Martin's, 9–21.

Stoller, Eleanor Palo. 1994. 'Teaching about gender: The experience of family care of frail elderly relatives', *Educational Gerontology* 20, 7: 679–97.

Stone, L.O., Carolyn J. Rosenthal, and Ingrid A. Connidis. 1998. *Parent–Child Exchanges of Supports and Intergenerational Equity.* Catalogue no. 89–557–XPE. Ottawa: Ministry of Industry.

Strain, Laurel, Carmen Grabusic, Mark A. Searle, and Nicole J. Dunn. 2002. 'Continuing and ceasing leisure activities in later life: A longitudinal study', *Gerontologist* 42 (2): 217–23.

Stum, M.S.. 2000. 'Families and inheritance decisions: Examining non-titled property transfers', *Journal of Family and Economic Issues* 21, 2: 177–202.

Szinovacz, Maximiliane E., and Adam Davey. 2004. 'Honeymoons and joint lunches: Effects of retirement and spouse's employment on depressive symptoms', *Journals of Gerontology*, Series B 59, 5: P233–45.

van den Hoonaard, D. 2001. *The Widowed Self: Older Women's Journey through Widowhood.* Waterloo, Ont.: Wilfrid Laurier University Press.

van Solinge, H., and K. Henkens. 2005. 'Couples' adjustment to retirement: A multi-actor panel study', *Journals of Gerontology*, Series B 60B, 1: S11–20.

Part III   Labour and Poverty

Families are not only about love and romance and caring, they also have an economic base. The material needs of family members must be met by a family economy. In order to meet the material needs of family members in a capitalist society, someone, or more than one person, must earn an income so that family members can purchase the goods and services that they need. Families do not meet all of their needs by purchasing goods and services, however. Essential work must also be performed within families. Food must be cooked, dishes must be washed, clothes must be laundered, and house-cleaning must be done. Unlike work performed in the market economy, this work is usually unpaid. The allocation of people to paid and unpaid work and the consequent division of labour in the family are crucial economic issues.

In Chapter 8, Andrea Doucet describes patterns of paid and unpaid work in families, first by looking at what has been an important topic in sociology, the relationship between gender and paid work. She considers how paid work has been dominated by a male model of employment and the changes that have occurred to that model in recent years. Historically and even today, unpaid work, like paid work, has been and is gendered. Doucet examines the gender division of labour with respect to four issues: the connections between paid and unpaid work; the relationship between paid and unpaid work and state policies; the differences and inequalities in paid and unpaid work; and, finally, the overarching question, 'What difference does difference make?'

Don Kerr and Joseph Michalski demonstrate in Chapter 9 the relevance of family and demographic changes to recent poverty trends, while also considering some of the broader structural shifts in the Canadian economy and in government policies. For example, changes in family structures alone have generated some degree of economic uncertainty, especially for women and children. After reviewing poverty trends over time, the authors consider the relationship of low income to family type and number of earners. In particular, they describe the high levels of poverty among female-headed lone-parent families. They also examine poverty among families in later life, pointing out how the rates of low income in elderly families have declined substantially in recent years and have fallen to levels below that of other age groups. In contrast, young families with children have fared less well. Finally, the authors discuss the coping strategies that poor families use to survive and consider the evidence on the consequences of poverty for poor people's lives.

CHAPTER 8

Families and Work

Andrea Doucet

Learning Objectives

- To find out about the changing forms of paid work that contest the simplicity of one single model of paid work (i.e., the standard employment model).
- To recognize the wide and diverse category of unpaid work.
- To learn about key issues in the study of paid and unpaid work, including: connections between paid and unpaid work; links between paid and unpaid work and the state; complexities involved in measuring unpaid work; and detailing the costs of care and why gender differences in paid and unpaid work do matter.
- To appreciate the strong gender divisions of labour in both paid and unpaid work, as well as the intricate links between gender, class, and ethnicity.
- To understand how paid and unpaid work are configured in our own lives as well as in those of our parents' and grandparents' generations.

Introduction

When I was growing up in a small town in northern New Brunswick in the 1960s and 1970s, my days usually began with the shrill call of the 8 a.m. whistle at the local paper mill calling the men to their work shifts. My father was one of those men. Along with hundreds of others, he would enter the mill through a front gate that was usually staffed by the mill's only female employee, have his work card punched, and then work 8–12 hours in the papermaking plant. My father worked at the paper mill for nearly 40 years. He received about five weeks of holidays each year, and we were well treated with a generous dental plan and university scholarships, as well as with lobsters in the summer and a large fir tree each Christmas.

Meanwhile, my mother cared for six children. Piecing together a life out of a labourer's salary, she sewed most of our clothes, pickled summer vegetables from my grandmother's garden for the winter, served beef and fish in an infinite variety of ways from cows reared by my grandfather and fish caught by friends of my father who were seasonal fishermen. My mother's days were filled with the regular family chores of cooking all meals 'from scratch', housecleaning, washing clothes in an old-fashioned wringer washer in our basement, hanging out loads and loads of laundry, and driving us to various activities when required. She also volunteered at church and school events, diligently brought our old clothes to what were called the 'low-rental houses' just down the street from the paper mill, and worked tirelessly to accommodate the countless relatives who drove down from Ontario to visit their New Brunswick homestead each summer.

Through all my growing up years until I took my first course in feminism at York University in the late 1970s, my belief was this: *My father worked. My mother did not work.* The simplicity of that belief and the way in which I did not challenge it still astound me now. Yet, I was not alone. For decades, sociology was concerned only with paid work and with men's work. In Canada in the mid-1970s, a major survey of sociological research on Canadian women pointed out that women's unpaid domestic work in the home had been almost completely ignored (Eichler, 1975). Eight years later, the same author concluded again that 'by and large housework is excluded from consideration in the social

Figure 8.1 Employment Rates of Women, 15–54, by Age of Youngest Child at Home

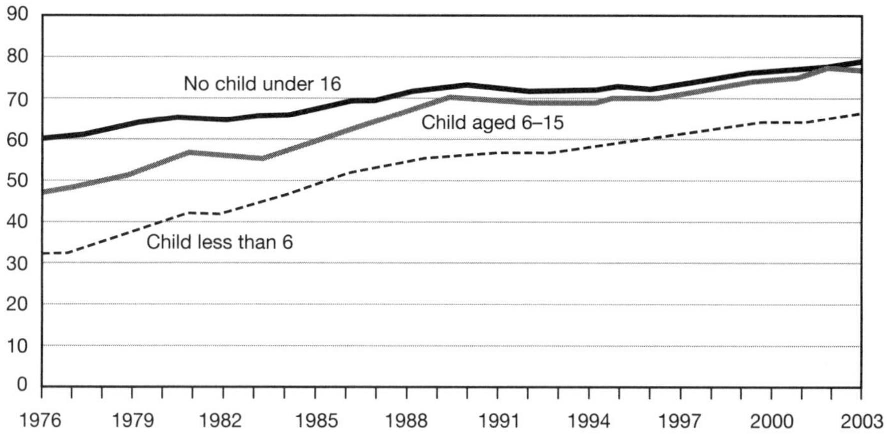

SOURCE: Statistics Canada (2003a).

sciences' (Eichler, 1983). Thus, housework, as a key form of unpaid work, was neither seen as 'work' nor viewed as worthy of study. Since the 1980s, however, all of that has changed and there has been tremendous interest in the study of paid and unpaid work, women's work and men's work, and an ever-expanding area of research and study that falls under the umbrella term of '**gender divisions of labour**' in paid and unpaid work.

Paid Work

The above description of my father's working life is what researchers have identified as the **standard employment relationship** wherein a worker has continuous full-time employment with the same on-site employer for all or most of his/her working life (Fudge and Vosko, 2001). This model of work has also been described as one of '48 hours for 48 weeks of 48 years' (Coote et al., 1990) or a 'male model of employment' (Brannen and Moss 1991). The word 'male' is inserted here for several reasons. First, this model of work has been described as 'male' because the continuous unbroken commitment to the labour market has been available mainly to men. Second, the financial remuneration given to women for their paid work has con-

sistently been less than that accorded to men. Third, women's employment has been marked by a dominant pattern of part-time employment while males have consistently worked full-time. Finally, the standard employment relationship has gradually given way to what researchers refer to as non-standard employment.

GENDER AND PAID WORK

The past several decades have witnessed dramatic international growth in the share of women who are part of the paid workforce. In 2003, 57 per cent of all Canadian women aged 15 and over had jobs, up from 42 per cent in 1976. There have been particularly sharp increases in the employment rate of women with children. In 2003, 72 per cent of all women with children under age 16 living at home were part of the employed work force, up from 39 per cent in 1976. Women with children are still less likely to be employed than women without children; that is, 79 per cent of women under age 55 without children had jobs while 63 per cent of women with children under age three were employed (Statistics Canada, 2003b). Figure 8.1 shows the employment rates of women by the age of the youngest child at home for the years 1976–2003.

GENDER AND WAGES FOR PAID WORK

A second reason for the argument that employment is characterized by a male model of work is that women's participation in the labour market, while increasing, has never been on an equal footing to that of men. This is best indicated in the fact that women's earnings continue to be less than those of men. According to a recent report from Statistics Canada, women's average hourly wages remain lower than men's in all occupations. The greatest male–female wage gap, however, occurs in blue-collar occupations where women earn 68 to 72 cents for every dollar earned by men. On the other hand, women's earnings are more comparable to their male counterparts (88 to 97 cents for every dollar earned by men) in the following occupations: natural and applied sciences, social sciences, education, government, religion, art, culture, health, and recreation and sport (Statistics Canada, 2003a). While women earn less than men in paid employment, the situation is even more aggravated for women who are both visible minorities and recently arrived immigrants (i.e., in Canada for less than seven years) (Palameta, 2004).

GENDER AND PART-TIME WORK

The labour market has male connotations because it is mainly men who work in full-time continuous work. Women of all ages are more heavily concentrated in part-time work. Many women, between the ages of 24–44 and between 45–64, are attracted to part-time service-sector jobs because of their responsibility for children as well as care of the elderly. For women ages 25–44, one in five worked part-time in 2002 while only a small minority of adult men (less than 5 per cent) did so. Women in the **sandwich generation** who are caring for young children as well as the elderly are also likely to work part-time in comparison to men. Table 8.1 shows the percentages of part-time workers in the labour force in 2002, by age and sex.

THE RISE OF NON-STANDARD EMPLOYMENT

A fourth and final point about standard employment, or a male model of work, is how a contrast-

Table 8.1 Employed Persons Working Part-time, by Age and Sex, 2002

	Women	Men
Workers aged:		
15–24	52.9	38.2
25–44	21.2	4.9
45–64	32.1	6.9
65 and over	59.4	35.3
Total	27.7	10.9
Total employed part-time (000s)	1,983.7	900.0
% of all part-time employment	68.8	31.2

SOURCE: Statistics Canada (2003c).

ing model has grown up rapidly alongside it. That is, while my father's work pattern was consistent with the dominant norm of (white) male employment in Canada after World War II, this model of paid work began to wane in the late 1970s when other forms of employment, largely filled by women as well as particular groups of men (i.e., men under 25, recent immigrants, and visible minorities), became common (Fudge and Vosko, 2001a, 2001b). Such employment has been variably termed as **non-standard employment** (Krahn, 1991, 1995), contingent employment (Polivka and Nardone, 1989), precarious employment (Vosko, 2000; Vosko et al., 2003), or temporary employment (Galarneau, 2005). Whatever its name, this is employment heavily characterized as part-time, temporary (e.g., short contracts, casual or seasonal work), or self-employment. Such jobs increased almost twice as rapidly as permanent employment in recent years and accounted for almost one-fifth of overall growth in paid employment between 1997 and 2003. What all of these jobs share are low wages, insecure working conditions, limited access to social benefits and statutory entitlements (i.e., Employment Insurance, maternity leave, and parental leave). What is notable as well is the marked distribution along gender lines. For example, in 2002 women accounted for over 6 in 10 of those employed in part-time temporary jobs or part-time self-employment and for nearly three-quarters of part-time permanent employees (Vosko et al., 2003)

Unpaid Work

Unlike paid work, the definitions and meanings of unpaid work are difficult to pin down. Unpaid work is largely invisible or unnoticed, difficult to measure, and has many subjective meanings that vary according to context. While there are many ways of categorizing unpaid work, most sociologists agree on several dominant types. These include: housework, child care, community and inter-household work, subsistence work, informal caregiving, and volunteer work. The first three categories are explored below.

HOUSEWORK

Several general points can be made about the first category of unpaid work. For one thing, housework is not a universal and homogeneous category. Its detailed composition varies between countries, regions, classes, and according to such factors as available technologies, number of children and income level. Second, housework has changed greatly during this century (Luxton, 1980; Cohen, 1983): while labour-saving devices have made some aspects of housework less onerous (i.e., laundering and dishwashing), growing consumption patterns within households and greater activity levels of children have led to new kinds of housework that entail household management, organization, and planning (Doucet, 2006; Taylor et al., 2004). Third, as Olivia Harris pointed out over two decades ago, the

Box 8.1 Who Pays for Housework Help?

Women more than men have become 'time poor' as their participation in paid work has gone up while their responsibility for housework has not decreased. Statistics Canada's analysis of the 1998 General Social Survey reveals that in families where both spouses work full-time, the woman is still responsible for daily housework such as meal preparation and cleanup, house cleaning, and laundry (Marshall, 1993b; Palameta, 2003). Furthermore, while Canadian households are increasingly paying for household cleaning services (10 per cent of husband-wife households in 2000), a key factor that determines the decision to hire domestic help is not only the household income but, even more important, the wife's share of the household income. According to a report from Statistics Canada:

> Buying domestic help is not just a matter of having sufficient household income. It is also matters whose income it is. Consider two husband-wife households, identical in every respect except that the husband makes 75 per cent of the income in one household while the wife makes 75 per cent in the other. . . . the second household will be roughly twice as likely to pay for home services. (Palameta, 2003: 15)

What these Canadian data reveal most poignantly is how woman's greater financial contribution to the household provides her with a greater rationale for easing her unusually large share of domestic labour. In 1989, American sociologist Arlie Hochschild wrote that working women are coming home to take on a *second shift* of work. Canadian women with good income levels are demonstrating that they are now attempting to avoid this second shift by putting some of their income towards housework relief.

degree to which housework is oppressive or burdensome differs greatly and will be influenced by income level as well as by the various forms of co-operation and collectivity between households (Harris, 1981).

CHILD CARE

In households with children, the care and upbringing of these children constitute a large part of parents' daily lives. While I am conceiving of housework and child care as two separate categories of unpaid work (see also Fox, 1998, 2001), they are obviously closely linked. Both kinds of work are usually performed for other household members and thus may be viewed as 'familial' work (Delphy, 1984). Moreover, some tasks (e.g., cooking for children) may constitute *both* housework and child-care activities. Finally, it is important to recognize that both housework and caring activities may have monotonous and routine aspects as well as rewarding and creative dimensions.

Several noteworthy distinctions can, however, be drawn between housework and child care. First, improved technology may have had an impact on household tasks (e.g., cooking and clothes washing) but has had little impact on caring activities, which are heavily reliant on human input. That is, while the majority of Canadian women do not, in comparison to women in the 1960s and 1970s, wash clothes by hand or with a time-consuming wringer washer and while most households often buy pre-packaged or takeout food to relieve the demands of cooking every night, the care of children cannot be replaced by technology. While parents may joke or complain that the television and computer have become technological babysitters, the fact is that an adult must still supervise their children regardless of what activities they are doing. Infants still require the same amount of time and attention as they have for generations, while many school-aged children have high levels of homework and varied levels of participation in extracurricular activities that require time, planning, and organization.

A second distinction between housework and child care is that housework allows for greater flexibility than child care; this is particularly the case with infants and young children where continuous care must be undertaken by household members or must be arranged and organized to be undertaken by others. When children are ill or emotionally troubled, parents often find that they are the ones who need to be with their child. Similarly, while certain aspects of housework can be put on hold, child care cannot. This was beautifully expressed by one particular woman, 'Laura', whom I interviewed in Britain in the early 1990s as part of a study on couples attempting to share housework and child care (Doucet, 1995, 2000, 2001). Laura made the point that every five years she went on strike over issues of housework. Quite simply, she stopped vacuuming, dusting, doing her husband's laundry, and cooking meals on the weekend. As she put it:

> Every five years I went on strike. I stopped doing certain things so that Richard would start doing more. And sure enough, he started doing more. But I never went on strike around the children. That would have been very unwise. I just would never take those risks with my children. But with housework? Absolutely!

Like Laura, historically and cross-culturally, women overwhelmingly have taken on the work and responsibility of caring for children. Indeed, many researchers have argued that, more than any other single life event, the arrival of children most profoundly marks long-term systemic inequalities between women and men (Brannen and Moss, 1991; Dowd, 2000; Fox, 1998, 2001). This is not to say that fathering and mothering have been static over time. Yet, while women have become secondary workers and wage earners for the household, and sometimes the principal breadwinners, they still remain as primary carers. Men, on the other hand, have moved from being primary breadwinners but have retained a secondary role in caregiving (Coltrane, 2000; Coltrane and Adams, 2001; Doucet, 2000, 2001; Robinson and Barret, 1986; Silver, 2000).

While the overwhelming majority of men have not come to share equally in the responsibilities for raising children, there has nevertheless been somewhat of a revolutionary change in father involvement, in Canada as well as in other Western countries. A good indication of Canadian men's increasing involvement in child care is perhaps best revealed in two sets of statistics. The first has to do with fathers at home on a long-term basis while the second has to do with fathers taking parental leave. With regard to the former, the most recent statistics from Statistics Canada suggest that stay-at-home fathers (about 111,000 of them in 2002) have increased 25 per cent in the past 10 years while stay-at-home mothers have decreased by approximately the same figure (Statistics Canada, 2002b). The second indication of father's increasing participation in the care of children relates to the recent extension of parental leave in Canada (from six months to one year) and the increased use of parental leave by fathers to care for infants. In a recent study by Statistics Canada, it was reported that in 2002 parental benefits taken by fathers increased by five times from what it was just two years earlier (Marshall, 2003; Pérusse, 2003).

COMMUNITY AND INTER-HOUSEHOLD WORK

An extension of both housework and child care is found in a category of work that has only recently come to be considered in sociological studies on unpaid work. In my own work (Doucet, 2000, 2001, 2004, 2006), I have used the term 'community responsibility' to refer to the extra-domestic, community-based responsibility for children. This work of parents *and others* appears in varied guises in a wide body of feminist and sociological research. Terms such as 'kin work' (Di Leonardo, 1987; Stack, 1974), 'servicing work' (Balbo, 1987), 'motherwork' (Collins, 1994, 2000), and 'household service work' (Sharma, 1986) describe domestic work as much wider—spatially, theoretically, and practically—

than simply housework and child care. This idea of community responsibility is also explored in the work of scholars working in developing countries, who point to complex webs of social relations within which domestic labour and parenting occur (Goetz, 1995, 1997; Moser, 1993; Scheper-Hughes, 1992). Moreover, black feminist scholars highlight how community networks and inter-household relations are integral elements of black motherhood (see Collins, 1991, 1994). Canadian author and filmmaker Sylvia Hamilton has illuminated community responsibility and inter-household work in the lives of African-Canadian women living in Nova Scotia (Hamilton, 1989).

In summary, both Canadian women and men engage in a considerable amount of unpaid work. Yet, what is the gender divide in unpaid work? It is now a well-recognized cross-cultural and historical fact that women take on the lion's share of unpaid work—whether housework, child care, inter-household work, subsistence work, informal caring, or volunteer work (Bianchi et al., 2000; Coltrane and Adams, 2001; O'Brien, 2005). In 2001 in Canada, about 21 per cent of women aged 15 and over devoted 30 hours or more to unpaid household work a week, compared with 8 per cent for men (Statistics Canada, 2003a). Moreover, Canadian statistics from the General Social Survey (1998) indicated that while women and men averaged a total of 7.2 hours a day on paid and unpaid work, there was a distinct gender division of labour, with women spending an average of 2.8 hours a day on paid work and 4.4 hours on unpaid work; the situation for men represented almost a perfect reversal of these numbers (see Figure 8.2).

Studying Paid and Unpaid Work

As noted earlier, it was not until the 1970s that unpaid work was accorded mention within academic studies, and more specifically within sociology. Three of the 'classic' empirical studies of housework (including child care) documented women's 'occupation' as domestic labourers within

Figure 8.2 Average Time Spent on Paid and Unpaid Work Activities by the Population Aged 15 and Over, 1998

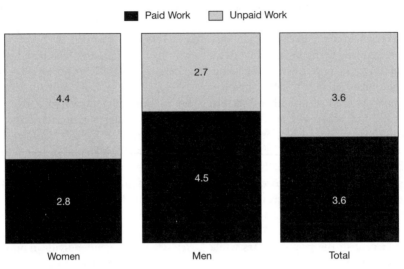

SOURCE: Statistics Canada General Social Survey.

their own homes (Lopata, 1981; Luxton, 1980; Oakley, 1974) and emphasized the isolating and monotonous nature of most housework tasks as well as the fact that housework is overwhelmingly women's work. While these early studies, and many more that followed, concluded that men did little unpaid domestic work, one criticism of early studies on housework and child care was that they did not fully investigate men's roles in domestic work. In contrast to Ann Oakley's early definition of housework as 'an activity performed by housewives within their own homes' (Oakley, 1974), many studies have sought to challenge the idea that only housewives do housework. Indeed, the past three decades have produced an astonishing number of case studies on gender divisions of labour, that is, on *who* does *what* in relation to unpaid and paid work. These studies generally fall under the rubric of 'gender divisions of labour' or studies on 'work-life balance' (Duxbury et al., 2004) or 'work–life integration' (Johnson et al., 2001).

Beginning in the 1970s, Canadian academic studies of gender divisions of labour within the household have collected basically three major types of data on the division of domestic work:

time (Meissner et al., 1975; Zuzanek, 2001), *tasks* (Blain, 1994; Marshall, 1993), and *responsibility* (Doucet, 2004, 2006; Luxton, 1980). All three of these areas of study have revealed constant movement and change but with women still putting in more time, taking on more tasks, and, most importantly, having the greatest responsibility for housework and child care. In focusing on work–life balance issues, Canadian researchers have employed a combination of large-scale surveys as well as in-depth interviews (Duxbury et al., 2004; Fast and Keating, 2001). These studies have pointed to how, while men have increasingly come to appreciate the importance of work–family balance, most of the balancing or juggling of home and work continues to fall on women.

In pointing out the persistent connection between women and the time, tasks, and responsibilities associated with caring for children and with domestic life more widely, and for their holding the weight of balancing work and family life, many researchers have also considered why gender differences persist in paid and unpaid work and why the progress towards gender equality or symmetry has been slow. Several explanations have repeatedly been put forth, including: differing gendered expectations of women and men in relation to earning and caring (Deutsch, 1999; Dowd, 2000; Pleck, 1985); **gender ideologies** (Deutsch, 1999; Hochschild, 1989); discourses of motherhood and fatherhood (Dienhart, 1998; Lupton and Barclay, 1997; Mandell, 2002); and the role of social networks in influencing women's and men's choices and decisions, particularly with regard to earning and caring (Barker, 1994; Bott, 1957; Doucet, 2000, 2001; Morris, 1985).

In addition to these findings on gender equality and gender differences, four key areas of study have been emphasized: the connections between paid and unpaid work; the relationship between paid and unpaid work and state policies; the differences and inequalities in paid and unpaid work; and, finally, the overarching question, 'What difference does difference make?'

CONNECTIONS BETWEEN PAID AND UNPAID WORK

Talcott Parsons most famously promoted within sociology the notion of complementary spheres of home and work and corresponding gender divisions of labour, with women taking on unpaid work in the 'private' sphere and men taking on paid work in the 'public' sphere (Parsons, 1967; Parsons and Bales, 1955). This dichotomy between home and work, paid and unpaid work, and a household model with men as breadwinners and women as homemakers, characterized to some extent the early stages of industrial capitalism where the reorganization of production physically separated the home from the workplace. As described earlier, it was a time when men left the home each morning to go to work while women stayed at home. Spatially, practically, and ideologically, the spheres seemed to be separate.

There are, however, several problems with this dichotomy between home and work and between paid and unpaid work. First, women, especially women in low-income households as well as African-Canadian women, have always worked outside the home (Carty, 1994). Cross-cultural research has clearly demonstrated that many working-class households have always required more than the male wage; thus, women have contributed to the maintenance of the household either by intensifying domestic and self-provisioning work inside the home, by earning money through the informal economy, or by earning a wage themselves (Bradbury, 1984, 1993; Tilly and Scott, 1987).

A second problem specific to the home/work distinction is the debatable extent to which a clear line of demarcation existed between home and work. This thesis is challenged by the fact that a considerable number of women, as well as men, have always been employed as outworkers or homeworkers. This false distinction between home and work is well captured in the concept of the 'household work strategy', which, as defined by Ray Pahl, is 'how households allocate their collective effort to getting all the work that they define has, or feel needs, to be done' (Pahl, 1984: 113). The household work strategy of each household blurs the distinction between home and work because it combines basically three kinds of work that can be done at various sites, including the household, the workplace, and within other households: (1) domestic work; (2) various forms of work in the informal or voluntary economy; and (3) paid employment in the formal economy. While Pahl developed his concept of the household work strategy within a British context, similar ideas have been developed in Canada by Meg Luxton and Bonnie Fox through the articulation of family households as sites of 'social reproduction' (Fox and Luxton, 2001), which refers to 'the activities required to ensure day-to-day and generational survival' (Luxton, 1998).

Since the 1980s, numerous books have appeared with titles including the words 'women, work, and family' wherein scholars have investigated the impact of women's labour force participation on gender roles within the household as well as the inter-relationship between the spheres of home and work (Lamphere, 1987; J. Lewis et al., 1988; Zavella, 1987). All of these studies have argued in varied ways that women's experiences of paid and unpaid work cannot be divided. By the late 1980s

Box 8.2 Measuring the Value of Unpaid Work

Kathryn Spracklin was in her kitchen in Montreal, making a snack for her son and listening to a radio interview with Evelyn Drescher, of Mothers Are Women (MAW). 'As a new mom, I'd been feeling that I wasn't being true to my idea of what a feminist should do, which was to work at a paid job', Spracklin recalls. 'Listening to that interview, I realized for the first time that maybe feminism wasn't just associated with making an income.' This insight moved her to join MAW, a Canadian activist group that believes there won't be real equality for women until the unpaid work they do in the home and community is counted and valued as real work.

A few years earlier, across the country in Saskatchewan, Carol Lees opened her front door to a census taker from Statistics Canada. Lees, a full-time mother of three, sparked a minor revolution that day when she politely refused to fill out the census form if it meant declaring that as an unpaid home-maker she didn't 'work'. 'People who work, both paid and unpaid, need to be valued', Lees explains. 'The census is a key instrument on which government policy is based. If you're not represented on the census, then you don't have a voice as public policy is developed, and policy isn't developed on your behalf' (Luxton and Vosko, 1998).

Lees eventually received a letter from Statistics Canada's chief statistician in Ottawa, threatening the full weight of the law, including fines and jail time, if she didn't fill out the form. Lees held her ground and founded the Canadian Alliance for Home Managers, which joined together with MAW and several other organizations to achieve dramatic results. Widespread media coverage was generated, and three questions about unpaid labour were added to the Canadian census in 1996. Meanwhile, most of the US remains oblivious to the social movement taking place just across the border. Something vital was missing from the 2000 US census: a specific count of full-time parents. In contrast, worldwide attention has been paid to the importance of counting unpaid labour, particularly that of women. In 1985, the Third UN World Conference on Women passed a resolution that directed countries to 'recognize the remunerated (paid) and unremunerated (unpaid) contributions of women in national economic statistics and the gross domestic product, especially those contributions of women in agriculture, food production, reproduction, and household activities.'

There is an enormous amount of untracked, unpaid labour. According to a 1995 UN Human Development Report, 'If these unpaid activities were treated as market transactions at the prevailing wages, they would yield huge monetary valuations—a staggering $16 trillion [of which] $11 trillion is the non-monetized, "invisible" contribution of women.' To put this figure into perspective, the official estimate of total paid global output is $23 trillion (UNDP, 1995).

The Platform for Action at the UN Beijing World Conference on Women in 1995 strengthened this issue, requiring governments to start efforts to measure and value unpaid work in official statistics. Australia, Germany, Israel, and Norway are among the countries that have followed the UN recommendations and started counting unpaid labour in their national statistics. In the US, however, neither the government nor women's organizations have taken any substantial action on this issue. It's a telling sign that a public information economist from the US Bureau of Labor Statistics told me, 'We don't specifically track stay-at-home moms because they aren't relevant to the labour force.'

Box 8.2 Measuring the Value of Unpaid Work (cont.)

Not relevant? Imagine the uproar if the government decided to call any other segment of the population irrelevant. The absence of full-time parents in US census data is especially disconcerting because the census is supposed to provide a snapshot of American life that drives public funding, political policy, consumer marketing, and much more. Invisibility in the census thus has rippling repercussions and long-term financial consequences. Full-time parents in the US are both unpaid and uncounted. Back in Canada, Kathryn Spracklin and Carol Lees celebrated 15 May 2001 as the day the Canadian census again asked those hard-won questions about unpaid labour. Lees reflects, 'I'm gratified to know that a housewife without any political training or skills could help make these changes.' Spracklin, now a policy analyst with MAW, says, 'Activists are still working to make sure the census data are used for positive policy that promotes equality and social justice.'

SOURCE: Adapted from Kristin Rowe-Finkbeiner, 'Count us in! Motherhood, feminism, and the US census', *Mothering* no. 111 (Mar.–Apr. 2002).

and early 1990s it became clear that the issue was not simply a woman's issue and that leaving men out was further solidifying the binary distinction between paid and unpaid work that these analyses were seeking to dissolve. While a few scholars picked up on the importance of examining men, work, and family in the early 1980s (C. Lewis, 1986; O'Brien, 1987), this crucial focus came to be part of mainstream sociological work on work and family in the 1990s and in the new millennium. Indeed, research on men as fathers, as domestic partners, and as carers has created a burgeoning literature (Coltrane, 1996; Coltrane and Adams, 2001; Dienhart, 1998; Dowd, 2000; Hobson, 2002; Lamb and Day, 2004).

CONNECTIONS BETWEEN PAID AND UNPAID WORK AND STATE POLICIES

While connections need to be emphasized between home and work, they also need to be drawn between home, work, and state policy. That is, in examining the 'choices' and actions of women and men as they negotiate paid and unpaid work—who stays home and who works, how housework is divided, and who takes responsibility for varied

aspects of domestic life, caring, and earning—we are reminded, as sociologists, that such actions, decisions, and 'strategies' must be situated in a wide set of social relations where women's and men's lives are structured differently. In this vein, state policies in relation to paid and unpaid work do matter. If we take the example of formal child care, Canada's report card has been mixed. In terms of the early years of child-rearing, Canada's approach to child care has come under heavy scrutiny in recent years. According to a study by the Organization for Economic Co-operation and Development, Canada's approach to child care provides 'basic babysitting, but not much else for working parents, and disregards the importance of early education' (Doherty et al., 2003; OECD, 2004). As a nation, Canada also invests less than half of what other developed nations devote to early-childhood education and has enough regulated child-care spaces for less than 20 per cent of children under six with working parents. This compares to the United Kingdom where 60 per cent of young children are in regulated care while in Denmark the figure is 78 per cent. The exception is the province of Quebec, which has a public child-care system, based on daycare centres and private home care and at a cost of only $7 a day. Quebec currently accounts for about 40 per cent of regulated child-care centres in Canada (see Chapter 14).

One positive aspect of state support for parenting is Canada's generous parental leave policy, which ranks as one of the best in the world. Also, according to the OECD, one of Canada's strengths is its Employment Insurance Act of 2001, providing paid parental leave for almost a year as a 'very important contribution to both equal opportunity for women and infant well-being and development' (OECD, 2004). While excellent, it nevertheless has its weaknesses in that its connection with Employment Insurance (EI) means that self-employed and part-time workers, who are a growing proportion of the workforce, are largely excluded from both maternity benefits and parental leave (Deven and Moss, 2005).

GENDER DIFFERENCES IN PAID AND UNPAID WORK: WHAT DIFFERENCE DOES DIFFERENCE MAKE?

In examining gender differences in paid and unpaid work as well as how ethnicity and class intersect with gender, the question 'Why does this matter?' can often arise. Indeed, this question is invariably asked by at least one student each year when I teach the sociology of gender: *What difference does it make that women do most of the unpaid work in society?* Another way to frame this question is to ask a question that I have often raised in my work: *What difference does difference make?* Drawing particularly on the work of feminist legal scholar Deborah Rhode, we can see that the issue of concern is not that of difference per se, but rather 'the disadvantages that follow from it' (Rhode, 1990). As phrased by Rhode: 'The critical issue should not be difference, *but the difference difference makes*' (Rhode, 1989).

Thus, what difference does difference make? It matters in several ways. First, ample scholarship has highlighted the economic, social, political, and personal costs to women of the gender imbalance in the 'costs of caring' (Folbre, 1994, 2001;

Ruddick, 1995) for the very young, the very old, the elderly, the sick, and the disabled in all societies. American journalist Ann Crittenden describes the gender disparity in care and the costs to women particularly well in her best-selling book, *The Price of Motherhood: Why the Most Important Job in the World Is Still the Least Valued.* She writes:

> The entire society benefits from well-raised children, without sharing more than a fraction of the costs of producing them. And that free ride on female labor is enforced by every major institution, starting with the workplace. (Crittenden, 2001)

In addition to this 'free ride' of unpaid labour that society reaps from women, this weighting of the balance of unpaid labour on the side of women has been very costly to the paid work opportunities for many women (Adams and Coltrane, 2004; Bianchi et al., 2000; Cohen, 2004; Coltrane, 2000; Crittenden, 2001; Folbre, 2001). These costs can include: occupational downgrading; loss of earnings, pensions, and benefits; economic vulnerability in cases of divorce; and long-term poverty for women (Arber and Ginn, 2004; Brannen and Moss, 1991; Folbre, 1994, 2001; Ginn and Arber, 2002; James et al., 2003).

A third point about the difference is that we must ask *which* women and *which* men are most affected. Aboriginal men, and men of ethnic minorities, particularly recent immigrants, are disadvantaged in paid work in comparison to males and females who are white and middle-class. Yet Aboriginal women and ethnic minority women are doubly disadvantaged because they are faced with inequalities in the labour market while still taking on extra shifts of unpaid work.

A further, conceptual problem entails a deepening of the gender division of unpaid work between women and men. This is an increasing pattern whereby middle-class families with ample economic resources rely on other lesser-paid women (e.g., nannies and housekeepers) for domestic work and child care (Bakan and Stasiulis, 1997;

Coltrane, 2003; Stasiulis and Bakan, 2005). Paying others to perform domestic services such as child care and housework ultimately passes on women's traditional domain from one group of women to another, thus hardening the boundaries that exist around gender and caring. A good example of this trend has been Canada's Live-In Caregiver program whereby thousands of women have come to Canada, mainly from the Philippines. Working as low-paid nannies with low pay and high levels of stress, these women highlight the tremendous inequalities between women based on ethnicity and citizenship rights (Spitzer et al., 2003). The end result is that work and homemaking remain as devalued 'women's work' wherein an ever-broadening lower tier of women are paid meagre wages to perform a 'modified housewife' role while other women do work that is more socially 'valuable'. As phrased eloquently by one author, this model seems to trap us into 'endlessly remaking the world in the same image: some people in the public sphere, the world of power, of importance, and some people in the private sphere, rocking the cradle but never really ruling the world' (Rothman, 1989).

Finally, it is important to point out that gender differences in unpaid work can also make a difference to men. While feminists have been calling for men's involvement in housework, child care, and informal caring partly to ease the gendered costs of caring and as one of the routes towards greater gender equality, men have also been busy documenting the personal and relational losses that they incur from not being fully involved in caring. Most of these claims are found in the burgeoning literature on fatherhood, which has drawn attention to the costs of stress and work–family conflict, the burden of being breadwinners, and the lack of opportunities to develop close emotional and relational attachments for men who are distant or absent fathers (Barnett et al., 1992; Bumpus et al., 1999; Milkie and Peltola, 1999; Pruett, 2000). Alternatively, scholars have pointed to the important generative effects for fathers who are highly involved with their children (Hawkins et al., 1993; Hawkins and Dollahite, 1996; Snarey,

1993). As summarized in a recent Canadian overview of fathering research, '[i]t is clear from the research that father involvement has enormous implications for men on their own path of adult development, for their wives and partners in the co-parenting relationship and, most importantly, for their children in terms of social, emotional and cognitive development' (Allen and Daly, 2002).

Conclusion

My household today has dramatically different configurations of paid and unpaid work to those undertaken by my parents in the 1960s and 1970s. Much of my unpaid work is invested in child care and the community responsibility for my three school-aged children as well as in housework and small bits of informal caregiving. My paid work consists of being a professor at a Canadian university. My paid and unpaid work occurs in relation to that of my husband, who, as a self-employed naturopathic doctor, varies his hours between full-time and part-time paid work. In addition to the housework, child care, and some parts of community responsibility that my husband takes on, he also takes on a fair bit of subsistence work in our household (painting, household repair, gardening, landscaping, and baking). Moreover, our paid and unpaid work have to be considered in relation to the larger structural and ideological changes that have occurred in Canadian society with regard to norms and practices for women and men at work and at home over the past three decades. Unlike my mother, I have used varied private services over the years to assist me with both child care and housework. Unlike my father, I have not been with only one employer but have worked in several different jobs and two careers over the past 25 years. The sites of where my paid work is done are multiple: university classrooms, my university office, my home office, and coffee shops where I read and write. My division of unpaid labour with my husband has been symmetrical, intertwining both equality and differences, with varying contributions from each of us at differing times depending on the ages of our children, the pressures from our respective jobs, our backgrounds, and personal inclinations. Our paid and unpaid work opportunities are also structured by class and ethnicity.

As detailed throughout this chapter, the dramatic changes in the paid and unpaid work patterns in my household are directly related to the tremendous changes in ideologies and family forms, as well as the varied types of paid and unpaid work that have proliferated in the past few decades (Cheal, 1999). Families continue to change and evolve and it could well be argued the traditional family model, which characterized the household where I grew up (with a breadwinner father and child-rearing mother), has been replaced by multiple new family forms. These new forms, which American sociologist Judith Stacey has named the 'postmodern family', include single-parent families (both single-father and single-mother families), blended families, two-household families with joint custody of children, cohabiting couples, lesbian and gay families, stay-at-home father families, and various sorts of two-income families (Stacey, 1990). This movement towards what David Cheal has called a 'convergence to diversity' and the 'destandardization of the family' (Cheal, 1991) exists alongside a parallel move towards non-standard employment models. This evolving diversity, complexity, and plurality in both paid and unpaid work will continue to pose exciting theoretical and methodological challenges to sociologists engaged in the study of work and family life (Cheal, 1991, 1999; J. Lewis, 2003).

Study Questions

1. Why is the standard employment model often considered to be a 'male' work model?
2. What types of unpaid work do you engage in? Do you consider these to be 'work'? Why or why not?
3. Why do scholars consider it important that men take on a fair share of society's unpaid work?
4. Look back to the generations of your parents and grandparents and reflect on how they structured their paid and unpaid work. What challenges and opportunities did women and men face? How was paid and unpaid work structured by gender, ethnicity, and class?

Glossary

Community responsibility and inter-household work The extra-domestic, inter-household community-based aspects of being responsible for children.

Gender divisions of labour The study of how labour is divided by gender in paid and unpaid work.

Gender ideologies A set of social beliefs about men and women's roles and relationships in varied social institutions.

Household work strategy According to Pahl (1984), this is defined as 'how households allocate their collective effort to getting all the work that they define has, or feel needs, to be done'.

Non-standard employment relationship Several types of work that are very different from the norm of a full-time, full-year, permanent paid job, including part-time employment, temporary employment, self-employment, or multiple job holding; also referred to as precarious employment or contingent employment.

Social reproduction '[T]he activities required to ensure day-to-day and generational survival' (Luxton, 1998).

Standard employment relationship A situation where the employee works full-time for one employer on the same premises and receives statutory benefits from that same employer; also called the male model of employment.

Websites

www.genderwork.ca/
The Gender and Work database at York University in Toronto explores how gender relations shape and are shaped by institutions such as labour markets, trade unions, and immigration. The site also examines the intersections between gender, race, class, age and disability.

www.worklifecanada.ca
The Guelph Centre for Families, Work, and Well-being at the University of Guelph conducts and disseminates research relevant to individual and family well-being and the interface between work and family.

www.lsbu.ac.uk/families/
The Families and Social Capital website has information on how families, work, and societies are changing. Based in the UK, the site includes linkages with other research centres throughout the world and is focused on some of the most innovative theoretical and empirical work on families, including the relationship between the dynamics of family change and processes of social capital.

Further Readings

Atlantis: A Woman's Studies Journal 28, 2 (2004). This special issue, 'Never Done: The Challenge of Unpaid Work', explores several issues critical to understanding unpaid work in Canada, such as gender roles, the structure of unpaid and paid work, and the role of states and markets in determining what work is paid and what is not.

Doucet, Andrea. 2006. *Do Men Mother?* University of Toronto Press. This book builds on international literature on fathering and mothering and the narratives of over 100 Canadian fathers who are primary caregivers of children, exploring the interplay between fathering and public policy, gender ideologies, community norms, social networks, and work–family policies.

Hughes, Karen. 2006. *Female Enterprise in the New Economy*. Toronto: University of Toronto Press. Using various methods, including interviews and quantitative data, Hughes examines the connections between an increasingly entrepreneurial economy and women's opportunities for economic success and security or for their increased risk of poverty and financial insecurity.

Lewis, Jane. 2003. *Should We Worry about Family Change?* Toronto: University of Toronto Press. Drawing on a wide range of literature, cross-national data, and policy approaches, Lewis unpacks the issues and controversies surrounding family change and highlights policy options that can increase the choices men and women make about their contributions to family life and to promote family responsibility.

Luxton, Meg, and June Corman. 2001. *Getting By in Hard Times: Gendered Labour at Home and on the Job*. Toronto: University of Toronto Press. Set against a backdrop of economic restructuring of the steel industry and the local economy in Hamilton, Ontario, this book draws on a wealth of survey data and interviews conducted over a decade.

Vosko, Leah F. 2000. *Temporary Work: The Gendered Rise of a Precarious Employment Relationship*. Toronto: University of Toronto Press. Rooted in archival data, Canadian statistics on temporary employment, comparative international literature, and qualitative interviews, this book is a significant contribution to our understanding of precarious or temporary employment in Canada and of changing global employment relations. Vosko demonstrates that temporary work is overwhelmingly 'feminized'.

References

Adams, Michele, and Scott Coltrane. 2004. 'Boys and men in families: The domestic production of gender, power and privilege', in Michael S. Kimmel, Jeff Hearn, and Robert W. Connell, eds, *The Handbook of Studies on Men and Masculinities*. Thousand Oaks, Calif.: Sage.

Allen, Sarah M., and Kerry Daly. 2002. 'The effects of father involvement: A summary of the research evidence', working paper. Carleton Place, Ont.: Father Involvement Initiative—Ontario Network.

Arber, Sara, and Jay Ginn. 2004. 'Aging and gender: Diversity and change', in C. Summerfield and P. Babb, eds, *Social Trends No. 34*. London: TSO.

Bakan, Abigail B., and Daiva Stasiulis, eds. 1997. *Not One of the Family: Foreign Domestic Workers in Canada*. Toronto: University of Toronto Press.

Balbo, Laura. 1987. 'Crazy quilts: Rethinking the welfare state debate from a woman's point of view', in Anne S. Sassoon, ed., *Women and the State*. London: Unwin Hyman.

Barker, Richard W. 1994. *Lone Fathers and Masculinities*. Avebury, UK: Aldershot.

Barnett, Rosalind C., Nancy L. Marshall, and Joseph H. Pleck. 1992. 'Men's multiple roles and their relationship to men's psychological distress', *Journal of Marriage and the Family* 54, 3: 358–67.

Bianchi, Suzanne M., et al. 2000. 'Is anyone doing the housework? Trends in the gender division of household labor', *Social Forces* 79, 1: 191–228.

Blain, Jenny. 1994. 'Discourses of agency and domestic labor: Family discourse and gendered practice in dual-earner families', *Journal of Family Issues* 15, 4: 515–49.

Bott, Elizabeth. 1957. *Family and Social Networks*. London: Tavistock.

Bradbury, Bettina. 1984. 'Pigs, cows and boarders: Non-wage forms of survival among Montreal families, 1861–1881', *Labour/Le Travail* 14 (Autumn): 9–46.

———. 1993. *Working Families: Age, Gender, and Daily Survival in Industrializing Montreal*. Toronto: McClelland & Stewart.

Brannen, Julia, and Peter Moss. 1991. *Managing Mothers: Dual Earner Households after Maternity Leave*. London: Unwin Hyman.

Bumpus, Matthew F., Ann C. Crouter, and Susan M. McHale. 1999. 'Work demands of dual-earner couples: Implications for parents' knowledge about children's daily lives in middle childhood', *Journal of Marriage and the Family* 61, 4: 465–76.

Carty, Linda. 1994. 'African Canadian women and the state: "Labour only, please"', in Peggy Bristow, ed., *We're Rooted Here and They Can't Pull Us Up: Essays in African Canadian History*. Toronto: University of Toronto Press.

Canadian Broadcasting Corporation. 2004. Indepth on-line news: 'Day Care in Canada', 25 Oct.

Cheal, David. 1991. *Family and the State of Theory*. Toronto: University of Toronto Press.

———. 1999. *New Poverty: Families in Postmodern Society*. Westport, Conn.: Greenwood.

Cohen, Philip N. 2004. 'The gender division of labor: "Keeping house" and occupational segregation in the United States', *Gender & Society* 18, 2: 239–52.

Collins, Patricia Hill. 1994. 'Shifting the center: Race, class and feminist theorizing about motherhood', in Evelyn N. Glenn, Grace Chang, and Linda R. Forcey, eds, *Mothering: Ideology, Experience and Agency*. New York: Routledge.

———. 2000. *Black Feminist Thought: Knowledge, Consciousness, and the Politics of Empowerment*, 2nd edn. London and New York: Routledge.

Coltrane, Scott. 1996. *Family Man: Fatherhood, Housework, and Gender Equity*. New York: Oxford University Press.

———. 2000. 'Research on household labor: Modeling and measuring the social embeddedness of routine family work', *Journal of Marriage and the Family* 62, 4: 1208–33.

———. 2003. 'Fathering: Paradoxes, contradictions, and dilemmas', in Lawrence H. Ganong, ed., *Handbook of Contemporary Families: Considering the Past, Contemplating the Future*. Thousand Oaks, Calif.: Sage.

——— and Michele Adams. 2001. 'Men's family work: Child-centered fathering and the sharing of domestic labor', in Nancy L. Marshall, ed., *Working Families: The Man of the American Home*. Berkeley: University of California Press.

Coote, Anne, Harriet Harman, and Patricia Hewitt. 1990. *The Family Way: A New Approach to Policy-Making*. London: Institute for Public Policy Research.

Crittenden, Anne. 2001. *The Price of Motherhood: Why the Most Important Job in the World Is Still the Least Valued*. New York: Henry Holt and Company.

Delphy, Christine. 1984. *Close to Home: A Materialist Analysis of Women's Oppression*. London: Hutchinson.

Deutsch, Francine M. 1999. *Halving It All: How Equally Shared Parenting Works*. Cambridge, Mass.: Harvard University Press.

Deven, Fred, and Peter Moss, eds. 2005. *Leave Policies and Research: Overviews and Country Notes*. Brussels: Centre for Population and Family Studies.

Dienhart, Anna. 1998. *Reshaping Fatherhood: The Social Construction of Shared Parenting*. London: Sage.

Di Leonardo, Micaela. 1987. 'The female world of cards and holidays: Women, families and the world of kinship', *Signs* 12, 3: 440–53.

Doherty, Gillian, Martha Friendly, and Jane Beach. 2003. *OECD Thematic Review of Early Childhood Education and Care: Canadian Background Report*. Paris: OECD.

Doucet, Andrea. 1995. 'Gender Equality, Gender Differences and Care: Toward Understanding Gendered Labor in British Dual Earner Households', Ph.D. thesis, University of Cambridge.

———. 2000. '"There's a huge difference between me as a male carer and women": Gender, domestic responsibility, and the community as an institutional arena', *Community, Work and Family* 3, 2: 163–84.

———. 2001. 'You see the need perhaps more clearly than I have: Exploring gendered processes of domestic responsibility', *Journal of Family Issues* 22, 3: 328–57.

———. 2004. 'Fathers and the responsibility for children: A puzzle and a tension', *Atlantis: A Women's Studies Journal* 28, 2: 103–14.

———. 2006. *Do Men Mother?* Toronto: University of Toronto Press.

Dowd, Nancy E. 2000. *Redefining Fatherhood*. New York: New York University Press.

Duxbury, Linda, Chris Higgins, and Karen L. Johnson. 2004. *The 2001 National Work–Life Conflict Study: Report Three—Exploring the Link between Work–Life Conflict and Demands on Canada's Health Care System*. Ottawa: Public Health Agency of Canada.

Fast, Janet E., and Norah C. Keating. 2001. *Informal Caregivers in Canada: A Snapshot*. Ottawa: Health Canada.

Folbre, Nancy. 1994. *Who Pays for the Kids? Gender and the Structures of Constraint*. London: Routledge, Chapman and Hall.

———. 2001. *The Invisible Heart: Economics and Family Values*. New York: New Press.

Fox, Bonnie. 1998. 'Motherhood, changing relationships and the reproduction of gender inequality', in Sharon Abbey and Andrea O'Reilly, eds, *Redefining Motherhood*. Toronto: Second Story Press.

———. 2001. 'The formative years: How parenthood creates gender', *Canadian Review of Sociology and Anthropology* 38, 4: 373–90.

——— and Meg Luxton. 2001. 'Conceptualizing family', in Bonnie Fox, ed., *Family Patterns and Gender Relations*. Toronto: Oxford University Press.

Fudge, Judy, and Leah Vosko. 2001. 'Gender, segmentation and the standard employment relationship in Canadian labour law, legislation and policy', *Economic and Industrial Democracy* 22, 2: 218–310.

Galarneau, Diane. 2005. 'Earnings of temporary versus permanent employees', *Perspectives on Labour and Income*. Ottawa: Statistics Canada.

Ginn, Jay, and Sara Arber. 2002. 'Degrees of freedom: Do graduate women escape the motherhood gap in pensions?', *Sociological Research Online* 7, 2.

Goetz, Anne Marie. 1995. 'Institutionalizing women's interests and accountability to women in development', *IDS Bulletin* 26, 3: 1–10.

———. 1997. 'Getting institutions right for women in development', in Goetz, ed., *Getting Institutions Right for Women in Development*. London: Zed Books.

Hamilton, Sylvia D. 1989. *Black Mother, Black Daughter*. Montreal: National Film Board of Canada.

Harris, Olivia. 1981. 'Households as natural units', in Kate Young, C. Walkowitz, and R. McCullagh, eds, *Of Damage and the Market: Women's Subordination in International Perspective*. London: CSE Books.

Hawkins, Alan J., and David C. Dollahite. 1996. *Generative Fathering: Beyond Deficit Perspectives*. Thousand Oaks, Calif.: Sage.

——— et al. 1993. 'Rethinking fathers' involvement in child care: A developmental perspective', *Journal of Family Issues* 14, 4: 531–49.

Hobson, Barbara. 2002. *Making Men into Fathers: Men, Masculinities and the Social Politics of Fatherhood*. Cambridge: Cambridge University Press.

Hochschild, Arlie R. 1989. *The Second Shift*. New York: Avon Books.

James, Estelle, Alejandra Edwards, and Rebecca Wong. 2003. *The Gender Impact of Pension Reform: A Cross Country Analysis*. Washington: World Bank.

Jenson, Jane. 2002. 'Against the current: Child care and family policy in Quebec', in Sonya Michel and Rianne Mahon, eds, *Child Care Policy at the Crossroads*. New York: Routledge.

Johnson, Karen L., Donna S. Lero, and Jennifer A. Rooney. 2001. *Work–Life Compendium 2001: 150 Canadian Statistics on Work, Family and Well-Being*. Guelph, Ont.: Centre for Families, Work and Well-Being, University of Guelph.

Krahn, Harvey. 1991. 'Non-standard work arrangements', *Perspectives on Labour and Income* (Statistics Canada) 4, 4: 35–45.

———. 1995. 'Non-standard work on the rise', *Perspectives on Labour and Income* (Statistics Canada) 7, 4: 35–42.

Lamb, Michael E., and Randal D. Day, eds. 2004. *Reconceptualizing and Measuring Father Involvement*. Mahwah, NJ: Lawrence Erlbaum Associates.

Lamphere, Louise. 1987. *From Working Daughters to Working Mothers: Immigrant Women in a New England Community*. Ithaca, NY: Cornell University Press.

Lewis, Charlie. 1986. *Becoming a Father*. Milton Keynes, UK: Open University Press.

Lewis, Jane. 2003. *Should We Worry about Family Change?* Toronto: University of Toronto Press.

———, Marilyn Porter, and Mark Shrimpton, eds. 1988. *Women, Work and the Family in the British, Canadian and Norwegian Offshore Oil Fields*. London: Macmillan.

Lopata, Helen. 1981. *Occupation: Housewife*. New York: Oxford University Press.

Lupton, Deborah, and Lesley Barclay. 1997. *Constructing Fatherhood: Discourses and Experiences*. London: Sage.

Luxton, Meg. 1980. *More than a Labour of Love: Three Generations of Women's Work in the Home*. Toronto: Women's Press.

———. 1998. *Families and the Labour Market: Coping Strategies from a Sociological Perspective*. Ottawa: Canadian Policy Research Networks.

——— and Leah F. Vosko. 1998. 'The census and women's work', *Studies in Political Economy* 56 (Summer): 49–82.

Mandell, Denna. 2002. *Deadbeat Dads: Subjectivity and Social Construction*. Toronto: University of Toronto Press.

Marshall, Katherine. 1993. 'Dual earners: Who's responsible for the housework?', *Canadian Social Trends* 31 (Winter): 11–14.

———. 2003. 'Benefiting from extended parental leave', *Perspectives on Labour and Income* (Statistics Canada) 4, 3: 5–11.

Marsiglio, William, et al. 2000. 'Scholarship on fatherhood in the 1990s and beyond', *Journal of Marriage and the Family* 62, 4: 1173–91.

Meissner, Martin, et al. 1975. 'No exit for wives: Sexual division of labour and the culmination of household demands', *Canadian Review of Sociology and Anthropology* 12, 4: 424–39.

Milkie, Melissa A., and Pia Peltola. 1999. 'Playing all the roles: Gender and the work balancing act', *Journal of Marriage and the Family* 61, 4: 476–90.

Morris, Lydia. 1985. 'Local social networks and domestic organisations: A study of redundant steelworkers and their wives', *Sociological Review* 33, 2: 327–42.

Moser, Caroline. 1993. *Gender Planning and Development: Theory, Practice and Training*. London: Routledge.

Oakley, Ann. 1974. *Housewife*. London: Allen Lane.

O'Brien, Margaret. 1987. 'Patterns of kinship and friendship among lone fathers', in Charlie Lewis and Margaret O'Brien, eds, *Reassessing Fatherhood: New Observations on Fathers and the Modern Family*. London: Sage.

———. 2005. *Shared Caring: Bringing Fathers in the Frame*. Manchester, UK: Equal Opportunities Commission.

Organization for Economic Co-operation and Development (OECD). 2004. *Early Childhood Education and Care Policy: Canada Country Note*. Paris: OECD.

Pahl, Ray E. 1984. *Divisions of Labour*. Oxford: Blackwell.

Palameta, Boris. 2004. 'Low income among immigrants and visible minorities', *Perspectives on Labour and Income* (Statistics Canada) 5, 4.

Parsons, Talcott. 1967. *Sociological Theory and Modern Society*. New York: Free Press.

——— and Robert F. Bales. 1955. *Family, Socialization and Interaction Process*. Glencoe, Ill.: Free Press.

Pérusse, Dominique. 2003. 'New maternity and parental benefits', *Perspectives on Labour and Income* (Statistics Canada) 4, 3: 12–15.

Pleck, Joseph H. 1985. *Working Wives, Working Husbands*. London: Sage.

Polivka, Anne E., and Thomas Nardone. 1989. 'On the definition of "contingent work"', *Monthly Labor Review* 112, 12: 9–16.

Pruett, Kyle. 2000. *Fatherneed: Why Father Care Is As Essential As Mother Care for Your Child*. New York: Broadview Press.

Rhode, Deborah L. 1989. *Justice and Gender: Sex Discrimination and the Law*. Cambridge, Mass.: Harvard University Press.

Robinson, Bryan E., and Robert L. Barret. 1986. *The Developing Father: Emerging Roles in Contemporary Society*. New York: Guilford.

Rothman, Barbara Katz. 1989. 'Women as fathers: Motherhood and childcare under a modified patriarchy', *Gender & Society* 3, 1: 89–104.

Ruddick, Sara. 1995. *Maternal Thinking: Towards a Politics of Peace*. Boston: Beacon Press.

Scheper-Hughes, Nancy. 1992. *Death without Weeping: The Violence of Everyday Life in Brazil*. Berkeley: University of California Press.

Sharma, Ursala. 1986. *Women's Work, Class and the Urban Household: A Study of Shimla, North India*. London: Tavistock.

Silver, Cynthia. 2000. *Being There: The Time Dual-Earner Couples Spend with Their Children*. Ottawa: Statistics Canada.

Snarey, John. 1993. *How Fathers Care for the Next Generation: A Four Decade Study*. Cambridge, Mass.: Harvard University Press.

Spitzer, Denise, Anne Neufeld, Margaret Harrison, Karen D. Hughes, and Miriam Stewart. 2003. 'Caregiving in transnational context: "My wings have been cut; where can I fly?', *Gender & Society* 17: 267–86.

Stacey, Judith. 1990. *Brave New Families: Stories of Domestic Upheaval in Late Twentieth-Century America*. Boston: Basic Books.

Stack, Carol. 1974. *All Our Kin: Strategies for Survival in a Black Community*. New York: Harper and Row.

Stasiulis, Daiva K., and Abigail Bakan. 2005. *Negotiating Citizenship: Migrant Women in Canada and the Global System*. Toronto: University of Toronto Press.

Statistics Canada. 2002. *Labour Force Survey, Annual Average 2002/Family Characteristics of Single Husband–Wife Families*. Ottawa: Statistics Canada.

———. 2003a. *The Canadian Labour Market at a Glance*. Ottawa: Statistics Canada.

———. 2003b. *Women in Canada: Work Chapter Updates*. Ottawa: Statistics Canada.

———. 2003c. *Women and Men in Canada: A Statistical Glance*. Ottawa: Statistics Canada.

Taylor, Janelle S., Linda L. Layne, and Danielle F. Wozniak. 2004. *Consuming Motherhood*. New Brunswick, NJ: Rutgers University Press.

Tilly, Louise A., and Joan W. Scott. 1987. *Women, Work and Family*. New York: Holt, Rinehart and Winston.

United Nations Development Program (UNDP). 1995. *The Human Development Report*. New York: Oxford University Press.

Vosko, Leah F. 2000. *Temporary Work: The Gendered Rise of a Precarious Employment Relationship*. Toronto: University of Toronto Press.

———, Nancy Zukewich, and Cynthia Cranford. 2003. 'Precarious jobs: A new typology of employment', *Perspectives on Labour and Income* (Statistics Canada) 4, 10: 16–26.

Zavella, Patricia. 1987. *Women's Work and Chicano Families: Cannery Workers of the Santa Clara Valley*. Ithaca, NY: Cornell University Press.

Zuzanek, Juri. 2001. 'Parenting time: Enough or too little?', *Canadian Journal of Policy Research* 2, 2:125–33.

CHAPTER 9

Family Poverty in Canada: Correlates, Coping Strategies, and Consequences

Don Kerr and Joseph H. Michalski

Learning Objectives

- To understand the nature and extent of family poverty in Canada.
- To recognize the demographic characteristics of low-income families and how the face of family poverty has changed in Canada over time.
- To be able to identify the main factors contributing to the dynamics of family poverty, including socio-demographic, economic, and political dynamics.
- To develop an appreciation for the coping strategies that low-income families use to deal with their relative lack of disposable income.
- To understand and be able to identify the most important consequences of family poverty.

Introduction

Although a rich country by international standards, Canada has its share of families who clearly experience economic hardships. Social inequality and poverty have long characterized Canadian social life, as families confront the daily struggle of making ends meet. In drawing international comparisons across countries with similar levels of socio-economic development, the research consistently finds that Canada falls somewhere between the United States—where levels of poverty and inequality are relatively high—and much of Continental Europe—where the incidence of poverty is moderated somewhat by more comprehensive welfare states (Picot and Myles, 2005; Rainwater et al., 2001; Smeeding et al., 2002). Thus, despite Canada's considerable wealth, many families face the challenges and even the stigma

associated with poverty in a context of relative affluence and economic prosperity.

The last two decades of the twentieth century were turbulent years for many Canadians, which coincided with some notable ups and downs in the North American economy. In examining trends in family income security, Torjman (1999) describes the period as involving both good news and bad news, or 'both crests and crashes'. For example, Canadians experienced two severe recessions, in the early 1980s and then in the early 1990s. In more recent years, however, Canada has witnessed a period of sustained economic growth, which has been translated into job creation, rising incomes, and reduced poverty (Statistics Canada, 2005). As for the future, it is difficult to project whether or not these gains will continue, or whether we can expect some of the economic turbulence of the past quarter-century to resurface. Rather than hazard any such guesses, the current chapter focuses on the available data to document what has been happening with respect to low-income families in recent years.

Although average family income has increased modestly in 'real' terms for several decades (i.e., after adjusting for inflation), many families continue to experience major financial setbacks. Picot et al. (1998) highlight three distinctive types of events as potential explanations: (1) 'demographic' events that influence the types of families and living arrangements in which Canadians share and pool income; (2) 'economic' events that influence the availability of jobs and the sorts of wages available in the labour market; and (3) 'political' events that influence the types of transfer payments that Canadians receive from government. The current chapter develops these themes further by demonstrating the relevance of family and **demographic changes** to recent poverty trends, while also considering some of the broader structural shifts in the Canadian economy and in government policies. For example, changes in family structures alone have generated some degree of economic uncertainty, especially for women and children.

We plan to demonstrate that family poverty tends to be linked to key events—not all of which can necessarily be predicted or controlled. Many low-income families thus struggle to survive and, in some cases, successfully escape poverty. The many potential negative consequences, however, should remind readers that poverty has potential costs not only to the families immediately affected, but for society at large.

Has the Problem of Poverty Worsened in Recent Decades?

In addressing the issue as to whether poverty has worsened in Canada over time, one must choose some form of statistical indicator with which to work. Yet in reviewing the literature, we encounter a multitude of different working definitions of poverty (Canadian Council on Social Development, 2002). For instance, some researchers have set poverty thresholds at relatively low levels by considering only the most basic of physical needs necessary for short-term survival in their definitions (Sarlo, 1996; Fraser Institute, 2001; Montreal Diet Dispensary, 1998). Others have set the bar much higher in pointing out that the long-term well-being of families implies much more than merely meeting their barest necessities (Federal-Provincial Working Group on Social Development Research and Information, 1998; Social Planning Council of Metropolitan Toronto, 1992).

For present purposes, we work with the most commonly cited poverty line in the Canadian literature: Statistics Canada's **low-income cut-offs (LICOs)** after tax. Owing in part to the credibility of Statistics Canada, many policy analysts, editorialists, and social scientists consider the LICOs to

be the preferred indicators. The LICOs are a reasonable compromise insofar as they fall somewhere near the mid-range of the many working definitions currently available. In addition, Statistics Canada's LICOs vary by family size and by five different sized urban and rural communities. For example, in 2004 the after-tax low-income threshold ranged from $20,844 for a family of four living in a rural locale to $31,865 for such families living in one of Canada's largest cities. In developing these LICOs, Statistics Canada has systematically examined spending patterns and disposable income, since families that spend an inordinate percentage of their income on necessities (food, shelter, and clothing) are likely to be experiencing economic difficulties.

Table 9.1 provides information on recent trends in income poverty in Canada (1980–2004). In addition, the table presents comparable information on median family income, or the midpoint in the income distribution where one-half of all families falls above and one half falls below. Thus we can move beyond a narrow focus solely on families at the bottom of the income distribution. The low-income rates and median incomes are further broken down by family type and number of earners per household. This provides us with some indication as to how people are adapting to some rather fundamental changes in family life over the last couple of decades, especially in terms of changing family structure and the manner in which households earn and pool their resources. The information in Table 9.1 has been adjusted for inflation, with all figures presented in constant 2004 dollars.

In reading Table 9.1, we can see how both income poverty and **median income** have fluctuated over time, while also varying in a rather pronounced manner by family type and number of earners. As mentioned previously, the last two decades of the twentieth century have been characterized by periodic ups and downs in the North American economy, with two particularly difficult periods during the early 1980s and early 1990s. For example, in considering all **economic families**, income poverty rose during the recession of

Table 9.1 Incidence of Low Income (after tax) and Median Income for Selected Family-Unit Types, 1980–2004

	Low-Income Rate					
	1980	1985	1990	1995	2000	2004
Economic families, two persons or more	8.8	9.9	9.1	11.0	9.0	7.8
Non-elderly families[a]	9.1	10.7	10.1	12.6	10	8.8
Married couples, one earner	7.7	9.4	9.9	11.7	10.2	8.9
Married couples, two earners	1.3	1.8	2.7	2.8	2.2	2.2
Two-parent families with children[b]	6.9	8.8	7.2	10.7	8.3	6.7
Two-parent families with children, one earner	12.6	17.0	16.9	21.4	22.2	18.4
Two-parent families with children, two earners	3.6	5.3	4.4	5.7	4.1	3.7
Lone-parent families[b]	44.2	49.7	44.3	45.0	32.3	31.7
Male lone-parent families	21.5	21.2	18.1	22.9	12.3	14.2
Female lone-parent families	47.7	53.5	48.6	48.5	36.3	35.6
Elderly families[c]	7.2	4.8	2.6	2.4	3.1	2.1
Unattached individuals	37.2	34.9	31.3	35	32.9	29.6

	Median Income					
	1980	1985	1990	1995	2000	2004
Economic families, two persons or more	60,900	57,600	60,100	56,100	61,200	63,100
Non-elderly families[a]	63,500	61,000	63,700	59,900	65,600	67,300
Married couples, one earner	48,700	48,900	46,700	44,400	47,600	52,200
Married couples, two earners	70,300	64,800	67,300	65,800	69,400	70,900
Two-parent families with children[b]	65,700	65,200	69,200	66,000	73,000	76,100
Two-parent families with children, one earner	51,300	51,000	48,600	46,800	48,000	48,300
Two-parent families with children, two earners	68,700	67,600	69,500	69,600	75,100	77,400
Lone-parent families[b]	25,400	22,200	23,500	24,200	31,800	31,000
Male lone-parent families	43,200	41,100	42,500	36,100	46,300	44,800
Female lone-parent families	23,900	20,900	21,200	23,100	28,300	28,900
Elderly families[c]	33,800	34,600	41,300	40,900	39,500	41,900
Unattached individuals	21,100	20,600	21,700	19,700	21,600	23,600

a Oldest adult less than 65 years of age.
b With single children less than 18 years of age. Children 18 years+ and/or other relatives may also be present.
c Head 65 years of age and over.

the 1980s (from 8.8 per cent in 1980 to 9.9 per cent in 1985), whereas median income fell (dropping from about $59,800 to $56,600). Both of these statistical indicators are influenced by the availability of jobs and wages in the Canadian labour market, i.e., by labour market events and macroeconomic conditions. The increased inci-dence of low income is not surprising in light of the double-digit unemployment and inflation of the early to mid-1980s, which exacted a heavy toll on many families and, in particular, on families of low or modest means.

The economic upturn of the late 1980s was translated into income gains and reduced poverty, both of which are reflected in Table 9.1. Unfortunately, these gains were once again washed out during a second **recession** in the early 1990s. Suggestive of the difficulties that many families encountered during this latter period, median income was lower in 1995 ($55,100) than at the beginning of the decade in 1990 ($59,000) and even lower than it was 15 years earlier in 1980 ($59,800). In working with these income data, many social scientists in the mid-1990s highlighted this lack of progress (Richardson, 1996; McFate, 1995; Kazemipur and Halli, 2000). In terms of low income, the incidence was once again somewhat higher in 1995 (11.0 per cent) than it was at the beginning of the 1980s (8.8 per cent in 1980).

In the early 1990s, the North American economy was characterized by persistently high rates of unemployment and a decline in real earnings, as was the case with the earlier recession. In addition, the political context shifted with the election of more fiscally conservative governments, both federally and across many provinces. Unemployment insurance and income assistance programs became more restrictive, which had a direct impact on the economic well-being of lower-income Canadians (Meyers and Cancian, 1996). Federal and provincial budgetary constraints compounded difficulties in the economy, as governments that had hitherto run large fiscal deficits reduced their direct transfers to families (Picot et al., 1998).

The economic situation in Canada has since improved, with declining rates of unemployment and poverty. In 2000, the unemployment rate fell to 6.8 per cent (the lowest level since 1976), in stark contrast to the 12 per cent peak only seven years earlier. The unemployment rate has stabilized over the first years of the twenty-first century, as macroeconomic conditions remain relatively favourable, especially in terms of Canada's record high **labour force participation rate** of about 67 per cent in 2004. That means that two-thirds of all Canadians aged 15 and older currently work in the labour force, either on a full-time or part-time basis (Statistics Canada, 2005). With respect to household earnings, the new norm consists of two wage earners per family rather than one.

Over the past decade, federal and provincial governments have managed to establish a greater balance between revenues and expenditures. Employment in the public sector has begun to grow again, while labour market conditions in North America have improved noticeably. As a result, Canadians across the income distribution have enjoyed gains, such that both upper-income and lower-income families have witnessed some improvement in their economic circumstances. Following a period of sustained economic growth and job creation, Canadians have made up the ground they lost during the two previous recessions. After adjusting for inflation, median family income in 2004 stood at $63,100, while the incidence of low income was relatively low at 7.8 per cent. Furthermore, data on income and unemployment for 2004 show that a smaller proportion of Canadians relied on government transfers as their primary means of support.

Low Income, Family Type, and Number of Earners

Despite the most recent gains suggested in Statistics Canada's income statistics, certain types of families clearly continue to be at a much higher risk of experiencing economic hardship. For example, Table 9.1 documents how the likelihood of low income has long been much higher for female-headed, lone-parent families. In 2004, the likelihood of a female-headed, **lone-parent family** being classified as poor was more than four times that of all families (at 35.6 per cent in contrast to 7.8 per cent) and almost six times that for two-parent families with children (at 6.7 per cent). Similarly, median income varied quite dramatically across family types as well. For instance, the median income of female-headed, lone-parent families ($28,900) was only 38 per cent of the median income of two-parent families with children ($76,100).

Many lone-parent families, the overwhelming majority of which involve mothers rather than fathers, continue to experience great economic hardship and are seriously over-represented among the poor. This observation is especially consequential in light of some of the remarkable changes in patterns of family formation that have characterized Canada (and most other Western countries) over the last few decades. Sociologists have come to appreciate the importance of residential living arrangements for the well-being of adults and children alike, and, in particular, with respect to how individuals earn and pool resources (Beaujot, 1999; Cheal, 1999). Rising rates of divorce, union instability, and non-marital fertility have contributed to a rapid increase in the proportion of families headed by a lone parent—which often implies little or no economic contribution coming from a non-resident parent. Although lone-parent families now comprise more than one in five families with children (or 22 per cent according to the 2001 census), among families with children classified as income poor, over half (53 per cent) are single-parent families (Statistics Canada, 2005).

Recent trends in family structure therefore have important implications for the economic vitality of families. By their very nature, single-parent families are at a disadvantage in a society where the dual-earner family has now become the norm. The traditional breadwinner family, with a clear gender division of labour, no longer exists in majority form. For example, in considering dual-parent families with children in 2000, 91 per cent of men and 76 per cent of women were employed (Sauve, 2002). Most dual-parent families currently have two earners, which confers upon them a clear economic advantage. The median income of two-earner families with a child was $77,400 in 2004, as compared to a median income of only $48,300 among such families with only one earner (see Table 9.1).

Even among families with particularly young children, there has been a major shift in the labour force participation of their parents. The majority of new mothers return to paid employment after a short respite to care for their newborns. Recent survey data have revealed that on giving birth to a child, over 80 per cent of Canadian women indicate that they plan to return to the labour force within two years (Marshall, 2003). While many women (and increasingly, some men) take advantage of parental leave, in most instances the absence from the labour force is temporary. On the other hand, lone-parent families obviously face disadvantages that dual-parent families do not regarding their ability to re-establish themselves in the labour market. For example, single parents often cannot easily share child-care responsibilities with a partner. The age of the children has a particularly important impact on labour force participation of lone parents due to the difficulties of simultaneously raising very young children and maintaining a full-time job. Thus, employment rates for female lone parents tend to rise sharply as their children age and depending on the availability of other caregivers or social supports (Woolley, 1998). These difficulties are often compounded by the shortage of suitable and affordable child-care spaces for preschool children as parents seek to re-enter the labour force (Cleveland et al., 1996).

Recent statistics indicate that about one in five female lone parents reports no involvement in the labour force, which almost guarantees economic hardship (Statistics Canada, 2005). Regardless of individual or family circumstances, welfare payments across Canadian provinces fall well below what most Canadians consider adequate for a reasonable standard of living (see Box 9.1). Lone parents frequently have fewer alternate sources of income to compensate for their lower incomes, as many receive absolutely no child support from former partners (Marcil-Gratton and Le Bourdais, 1999). While Canadian law has attempted to enforce the idea that absent parents should maintain financial responsibility for their children, the rates of default on child payments remain high. Among children whose parents have separated or divorced, about one in three of all custodial parents has absolutely no agreement on child support. For those separated parents who have such an agreement, a significant proportion (approaching one-half) regularly faces default (Marcil-

Gratton et al., 2000). In addition, most non-marital births (i.e., children born to women not in a marital relationship) involve little or no contact with the biological father after the birth, which obviously translates into an absence of child support payments.

Moreover, women as lone parents share the same disadvantages that other women face in the Canadian labour market in general (Caragata, 2003). Women continue to face obstacles in obtaining equal pay for work of equal value, although younger cohorts appear to have been making some significant gains as of late. If one fur-

ther considers the intersection of visible minority status and Aboriginal status with gender, the labour market access and earnings differentials become especially pronounced (Lee, 2000; Smith and Jackson, 2002). Beyond issues of race and ethnicity, part of the gender-based disadvantage reflects the incidence of low-income families headed by males and females: 14.2 per cent among male lone parents and 35.6 per cent among female lone parents in 2004. On average, male lone parents tend to be older than their female counterparts, much more likely to be employed, and, when working, earn a significantly higher wage.

Box 9.1 Why Has the Number of Welfare Recipients Declined in Canada?

Fundamental to Canada's social safety net is welfare or social assistance—Canada's income support program of last resort. Although some people think of welfare as though it were a single government entity or program, there are actually several different welfare systems in Canada. The reason for this is that each province and territory is responsible for the implementation and management of its own welfare programs. As a result, Canadian families face a patchwork of different policies and possible levels of assistance, depending on where they live.

These programs have complex rules relating to eligibility for assistance. Yet in reviewing these different programs, we find that one generalization certainly applies across jurisdictions: Canadian welfare programs are not particularly generous. The reality is that families that rely on welfare to make ends meet usually experience severe economic hardship. For example, in 2003, the welfare income for a lone-parent family with one child living in a larger metropolitan area in Canada ranged from a low of only $12,515 in Halifax to a high of $15,056 in St John's (National Council of Welfare, 2004).

Given such low levels of support, it is not surprising that when economic conditions improve, many persons reliant on welfare move directly into paid employment. This is precisely what happened during the latter 1990s and early 2000s, as the number of persons accessing welfare dropped significantly. For example, welfare use dropped from a peak of about 3.1 million in 1994 to 1.745 million by 2003 (see Figure 9.1). While many factors contribute to this decline, the fact that this occurred during a period of labour market gains is far from coincidental. As the number of jobs grew, many individuals and families escaped from welfare dependency—or managed to avoid it in the first place (Sceviour and Finnie, 2004). When provided the opportunity for employment rather than welfare, it is obvious that Canadians opt for employment.

Box 9.1 Why Has the Number of Welfare Recipients Declined in Canada? (cont.)

Despite the importance of improved labour market conditions, other factors might be raised to under-stand what may be happening. For example, welfare participation is particularly sensitive to changes in 'eligibility rules'. Several provinces introduced major changes in eligibility rules during the 1990s, which generally affected the total number of persons receiving benefits. Many of these changes occurred in highly politicized environments, as some politicians were elected using the argument that 'welfare fraud' was widespread. The Conservative governments of Ontario and Alberta were particularly active in introducing extensive case reviews and fraud investigations. Several other provinces quickly followed suit with similar programs (National Council of Welfare, 2004).

Benefit rates were reduced across most provinces with the logic that this would increase the incentive for persons to leave welfare. For example, the Tory government in Ontario shifted eligibility rules in the mid-1990s through the widely publicized 'spouse in the house rule' (Little, 2001). According to this rule, as soon as welfare recipients started living with someone of the opposite sex who earned an income, they automatically lost their benefits—despite the fact that federal family law defines persons as 'common-law' only after living together for three years. Eventually defined 'unconstitutional' by the Ontario Court of Appeal in 2002, the current policy is that a welfare recipient must have his or her benefits reassessed only after living with an income earner for three months.

Figure 9.1 Estimated Number of Persons Receiving Welfare in Canada, 1993–2003

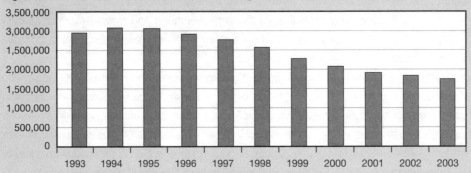

Source: National Council of Welfare (2004).

While relatively little is known of the economic situation of persons who left welfare over the past decade, some preliminary analyses have recently shed some light on the issue (cf. Morissette and Myles, 2003; Sceviour and Finnie, 2004; Frenette and Picot, 2003). The good news is that, in most cases, it appears that welfare-leavers have experienced some improvement in their economic situation. On average, the family income of welfare-leavers during the latter 1990s increased substantially, as these families are less likely to be income poor (Sceviour and Fennie, 2004). Yet for some families, an exit from welfare appears to have led to a worsening of their situation. In following persons who left welfare during the latter 1990s, Frenette and Picot (2003) have estimated that as many as one-third saw their household income decline—sometimes dramatically. One can only speculate as to the economic situation of these individuals and families that appear to have completely slipped through Canada's social safety net.

Poverty among Families in Later Life

Older Canadians can be characterized by their diversity in terms of life history, family characteristics, and economic statuses (Gee, 1995). With several additional decades of life experience, it is logical that older people tend to be less alike than younger people. In documenting the life history of the elderly, we observe considerable diversity of their life courses, work histories, and patterns of social interaction over a more extended length of time. As an example, some older people have managed to accumulate considerable wealth and property over their lifetimes, whereas others have relatively little. While some older Canadians benefit from a high income relating to their past investments and/or private pension plans, others are completely reliant on government transfers as they move into later life.

While acknowledging such diversity, we can also draw a few generalizations as to the living arrangements and relative economic status of older Canadians. Most of those aged 65 and older currently live in small households, either with their spouse, sometimes by themselves, and occasionally with an adult child. Whereas older men are more likely to be living with a spouse in later life, older women are far more likely to be living on their own. Widowhood is much more common for women than for men, as women outlive men by about five years on average and tend to marry men slightly their senior. Although women are more likely to outlive their husbands, men are more likely to marry on the event of their spouse's death. Thus women are much more likely to spend the last several years of their lives living by themselves—a reality that has direct ramifications for their economic well-being.

The expansion of the welfare state in Canada during the second half of the twentieth century had a dramatic impact on the economic well-being of elderly Canadians (Myles, 2000). Various programs were introduced and expanded, and these programs, including Old Age Security, the Guaranteed Income Supplement, the Canada Pension Plan, and the Quebec Pension Plan (among other benefits), significantly reduced the risk of sliding into poverty. When the Dominion Bureau of Statistics first started reporting information on the incidence of low income in Canada in the 1960s, Canadians aged 65 and older were more likely to be classified as income poor than any other age group. In fact, more than 40 per cent of elderly families were classified as having low income at that time (Podoluk, 1968). Since then, however, the rates of low income have declined substantially and have fallen to levels below that of other age groups (Statistics Canada, 2005).

Many of the income support programs that were expanded during the 1970s and 1980s were highly successful in reducing the likelihood of economic hardship among the elderly (Myles, 2000). Picot and Myles (2005) report that as recently as the late 1970s, the rate of low income (defined as less than half the median family income) among elderly households was just under 35 per cent. Two decades later, the elderly low-income rate had declined to less than 5 per cent—a more dramatic decline than for any other group in Canada. As there has been far less support to subsidize families at earlier stages of the life course, the incidence of poverty is now lower among families with at least one person over the age of 65 than it is among any other family or household types (with the exception of two-parent, dual-earner households). Although the median income of elderly families (at $41,900 in 2004) is lower than across all families, so too is average family size and the likelihood of income poverty. According to Statistics Canada, the incidence of low income in 2004 after taxes plummets to only 2.1 per cent among elderly families (Table 9.1).

While most families in later life can avoid poverty by pooling government transfers, even without savings or private pension plans, this option is not possible for the elderly who live alone. Just as older women are more likely to outlive their husbands, so too are they more likely to slip into poverty on the death of their spouse. About 17 per cent of unattached women aged 65 years or older who lived alone were classified as being in the low–income bracket in 2004, while 11.6 per cent of unattached older men were classified in this manner. Clearly, a great many unattached Canadian seniors remain vulnerable, as some have insufficient assets and pension plans to retire in comfort. Fundamental in this context is whether or not the elderly live in families, which again hints at the importance of family living arrangements and the manner in which individuals share resources in predicting low income and economic hardship (Cheal, 1999).

Low Income, Family Change, and Child Poverty

Public policy in Canada has been far less generous towards families at earlier stages of their life course than in subsidizing families at latter stages. The expansion of income support programs for the elderly has not been accompanied by anything comparable for young families with children. If anything, as governments expanded income support programs for older Canadians in recent decades, income support programs directed at younger families have become less generous. For example, during the 1990s, unemployment insurance and income assistance programs became more restrictive, which obviously had a greater impact on younger families (with or without children) than on elderly families. Moreover, the federal government also abandoned its universal Family Allowance program, further reducing the limited institutional support available for families with children.

In this context there has been a major shift in the age distribution of the poor in Canada. While in the 1960s elderly Canadians were about twice as likely as children to be classified as income poor, the situation these days has nearly reversed itself. The shift in the age distribution of poverty is arguably one of the most striking changes to characterize the distribution of family income over the last several decades (Cheal, 1999). This raises troubling questions relating to public policy and gen-

erational equity (Preston, 1984). Many of the aforementioned changes in the structure of the Canadian family—including the increased incidence of lone parenthood—have had a much greater impact on the economic well-being of children than on older age groups.

Poverty among Canadian children deserves special mention for a variety of reasons. First, children are particularly vulnerable because of their dependency on parents or caregivers for their economic well-being. Most research on income poverty, however, completely neglects the manner in which resources are shared within families, such as between spouses and between adults and children. The implicit assumption of an equal sharing of financial resources can potentially obscure important differences in the actual level of economic hardship experienced by individual family members (Phipps and Burton, 1995; Woolley, 1998). Yet the well-being of children ultimately depends on the judgement and goodwill of their parents, as well as the adults' decisions and options regarding family composition, work opportunities, and housing and community locations. Children have far less influence in these areas, despite the significance of such factors in shaping their economic well-being.

While poverty or low-income rates may appear to be somewhat stable in drawing comparisons over time, the actual distribution of individuals and families classified as poor will vary somewhat in response to different life events and especially in terms of changing family characteristics. In Canada, Finnie (2000) has shown that roughly half of those defined as 'poor' early in the 1990s escaped poverty within four years, even though a substantial minority remained poor for four consecutive years. Those at greatest risk for such 'persistent poverty' were single mothers with children. In addition, Picot et al. (1999) have concluded from their analysis of the Survey of Labour and Income Dynamics that divorces, separations, and remarriages have as great an impact on children entering or leaving poverty as does the changing labour market situation of their parents.

Shortcomings of Income-based Measures of Poverty

Income-based indicators of economic well-being have many well-known limitations, most of which have been discussed in detail elsewhere (Cotton et al., 1999; Hulchanski and Michalski, 1994; Ruggles, 1990; Wolfson and Evans, 1989). These measures tend to systematically under-report or exclude various types of in-kind public assistance, the sharing of resources and services across households and generations, the impact of exchanges in the informal economy, the bartering of goods and services, and various types of employment benefits such as extended medical insurance and drug plans. This is particularly problematic in documenting the economic well-being of Canadians in that these resources and entitlements can vary considerably across individuals and households.

For example, merely consider the economic situation of a college or university student temporarily earning a relatively low income, yet receiving generous non-declared income support from a parent or relative. This is a dramatically different situation from a young adult working full-time at a minimum wage job and without any such aid from a family member. Similarly, a young adult living precariously close to the poverty line in a low-wage and insecure job is in a vastly different situation from a young university graduate setting out in a career-type job with perhaps a temporarily low wage but with generous benefits, a pension plan, job security, and the promise of higher income. The aforementioned income statistics do not directly provide us with this sort of detailed information necessary to delineate such differences across individuals and households. In fact, there is currently a scarcity of comprehensive data at the national level that would allow us to carefully consider many of these issues, both cross-sectionally and over time.

Most income-based measures of income poverty also exclude information on wealth, which again varies in an important manner across households. Economists typically define wealth to mean the stock of assets held by a household or individual that either yields or has the potential to yield income. Wealth can take on a variety of forms and is typically defined as the difference between total assets and total debts. Total assets include all deposits, investments in mutual funds, bonds, and stock holdings, as well as registered retirement savings plans, locked-in retirement accounts, home-ownership, vehicles, etc. Total debts include mortgage debts, outstanding balances on credit cards, student loans, vehicle loans, lines of credit, and other money owed. While there is considerable income inequality in Canada, there is an even greater level of wealth inequality—which actually appears to have worsened somewhat over recent years (Statistics Canada, 2002). For example, in 1984 the top decile of all family households in Canada controlled 51.8 per cent of wealth, but by 1999 this had risen to 55.7 per cent (Morissette et al., 2002). Since 1999, Statistics Canada has not gathered more up-to-date information on the distribution of wealth across individuals and households.

While households classified as income poor are considerably more likely to have little wealth or property, clearly there is not a perfect association between income and wealth. For example, consider the economic situation of someone who has paid off his or her mortgage, has major investments in terms of securities and the stock market, and yet for whatever reason chooses to live on a relatively low income. Alternatively, consider a new immigrant to Toronto or to some other large city in Canada trying to establish him or herself in the labour market for the first time, without any property or investments. Rising housing costs also work against the interests of many, including new labour force entrants, whether they are newly arrived to Canada or have recently completed their education (Zhang, 2003). Once more, these sorts of disparities are not obvious when restricting ourselves exclusively to the distribution of income across families.

Just as wealth differs enormously across households and individuals, it tends to vary systematically by life cycle stage as well. In working with

Statistics Canada's 1999 Survey on Financial Security, Morissette et al. (2002) demonstrate major discrepancies by age group. Among families whose major income recipient was aged 25–34, median wealth in 1999 dollars was about $67,000, which compared to a median of over $300,000 for families whose major income recipient was aged 55–64. Everything else being the same, younger people not only tend to have lower incomes, but also typically have less overall wealth. Similarly, Morissette et al. (2002) have documented that median wealth varies in an important manner by education, immigration status, and number of years residing in Canada. There are also important differences in wealth as documented across family types (see Figure 9.2), in comparing lone-parent families with dual-parent families, elderly with non-elderly families, or households with or without children.

Lone-parent families reported a median wealth of only $4,000 in 1999, which contrasts sharply with dual-parent families with children aged 18 and over, who reported a median wealth of over $160,000. In fact, when we systematically examine differences in wealth across individuals and family types, the inequalities documented in terms of income largely become accentuated. The precariousness of certain types of households and families (e.g., lone-parent families or non-elderly individuals living alone) appears to be even more obvious when we consider differences in terms of assets and wealth. To the extent that those who left income poverty in recent years continue to work in low-wage, insecure jobs with relatively little wealth or property, they are clearly more vulnerable to economic downturns. Many Canadians could easily fall back into poverty with the loss of a low-income job and, in turn, have relatively little wealth to draw from in getting through the worst of economic times.

How Do Low-Income Families Cope with and Survive Poverty?

How do low-income families survive, particularly those with limited market incomes and/or meagre state transfers, such as social assistance? Several commentators have observed that the combination of economic factors, globalization, and the subse-

Figure 9.2 Median Wealth by Family Type, Canada, 1984 and 1999

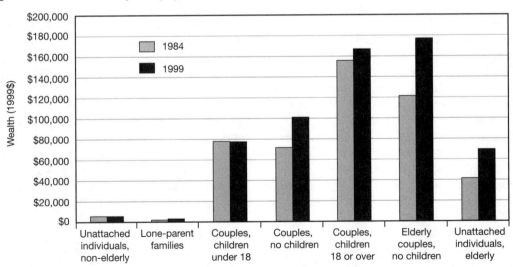

SOURCES: Morissette et al. (2002); Statistics Canada (2002).

quent restructuring of the Canadian welfare state has increased the vulnerability of large segments of the population (Caragata, 2003; Wilson, with Tsoa, 2001). Social assistance rates declined and eligibility requirements tightened across Canada during the 1990s, as the proportion of unemployed workers eligible for Employment Insurance benefits also fell significantly (Krahn and Lowe, 2002). At the same time, housing costs increased and created further economic pressures on the poor (Ontario Non-Profit Housing Association, 1999).

As a result, some argue that the 1990s bore witness to increasing activism at the local community level, with the emergence and expansion of a variety of support services and in-kind contributions. Both Chekki (1999) and Capponi (1999) argued that many agencies—soup kitchens, church and school programs, community centres, Salvation Army centres, and other charitable organizations—expanded their operations in the face of growing demands. In addition, Michalski (2003b) has demonstrated the importance of food banks as a supplemental source of support for low-income families that has expanded dramatically over the past two decades, but especially in the 1990s (see Box 9.2).

Box 9.2 What Role Do Food Banks Play in Helping To Sustain Low-Income Families?

The first food bank in Canada opened in Edmonton in 1981 as a stopgap measure to assist poor individuals and families on an emergency basis. Throughout the 1980s, the number of food banks continued to grow across Canada, such that by 1989 there were nearly 160 food banks located across the 10 provinces (Oderkirk, 1992). The number of food banks doubled over the next two years and expanded quite rapidly through the 1990s. In just two decades, the total number had grown to roughly 600 food banks working with more than 2,000 agencies dispensing groceries and/or serving meals in every province and territory in Canada (Wilson, with Tsoa, 2001). Table 9.2 indicates the extent of use of food banks in March 2003 as compared to six years earlier. It appears that food banks have become well entrenched as an increasingly pervasive response to hunger in Canada (Michalski, 2003b; Teron and Tarasuk, 1999).

More generally, food banks and emergency food programs are part of the bundle of coping strategies that many low-income individuals and families use to survive (Dachner and Tarasuk, 2001; Michalski, 2003a). Kennedy (1995) has demonstrated that in the Greater Toronto Area, the coping

Table 9.2 People Who Used a Food Bank in 2003, by Province

	People Who Used a Food Bank in March 2003	% Change from March 1997
Canada	777,869	+22
Newfoundland and Labrador	31,132	−11
Prince Edward Island	3,118	−16
Nova Scotia	20,263	+25
New Brunswick	18,875	+8
Quebec	216,000	+23
Ontario	308,452	+8
Manitoba	38,584	+70
Saskatchewan	16,792	−1
Alberta	48,743	+30
British Columbia	72,573	+23

SOURCE: Vanier Institute (2005).

Box 9.2 What Role Do Food Banks Play in Helping To Sustain Low-Income Families? (cont.)

strategies for low-income families include a vast array of budgeting and money-saving schemes, including public transit, bulk shopping, selling personal possessions, doing without telephones, forgoing recreation and entertainment, or even simply consuming less food or doing without altogether. While by no means a comprehensive service or welfare supplement, food banks are an additional source of support among a patchwork of low-income survival strategies (Tarasuk, 2001).

The available studies clearly indicate that those who access food banks in urban settings on average tend to have household incomes far below established poverty lines (Michalski, 2003b; Starkey et al., 1998). Their economic statuses are almost always quite precarious, with housing costs consuming the majority of available monthly income (Vozoris et al., 2001). The depth of their need has been measured more formally over time by comparing their disposable income with household needs (shelter costs, food, clothing, transportation, dental or special health needs, recreation, and so forth). In focusing on Toronto, Michalski (2003a) has estimated that the disposable income of food bank users actually declined significantly during the latter 1990s. In this context, it is not surprising that a proportion of Ontario residents has become increasingly dependent on public charity in meeting their most basic of needs.

Indeed, low-income families typically rely on a broad range of economic survival strategies. The available research demonstrates that these strategies vary at least in part in response to the degree of urbanization and, more specifically, the resource infrastructures available in different locales (Meert et al., 1997). The labour market represents one key structural dimension, with the commercial infrastructure providing a variable range of options for low-income households in their efforts to meet their basic needs (Iyenda, 2001). In addition, different locales provide distinct opportunities for exchanges, including a variety of non-market and non-governmental economic options such as household production, self-provisioning, and other forms of unpaid work, as well as community-based exchanges and the many non-profit organizations associated with the 'social economy' (Felt and Sinclair, 1992; Hulchanski and Michalski, 1994; Quarter, 1992).

Where job loss occurs and in high unemployment areas, families with limited resources compensate by reducing their expenses in general, receiving public assistance, retaining a stable residence, and cutting food expenditures (Yeung and Hofferth, 1998). Edin and Lein (1997) studied the importance of three additional strategies above and beyond employment income and welfare supports for sustaining low-income households: informal network supports from friends, family, and absentee fathers; side work in the formal, informal, and underground economies; and agency-based strategies from community groups and charitable organizations. Since neither welfare nor low-wage work provided adequate income for living for the families in their study, Edin and Lein (1997: 6) reported that 'all but one of the 379 mothers spoken to were engaged in other income-generating strategies to supplement their income and ensure their economic survival.'

In Ontario, Vozoris et al. (2002) have demonstrated that income from Ontario Works (welfare) alone proved insufficient to cover the core needs for households residing in market rental accommodations on a regular basis. Even if families were fortunate enough to live in rent-geared-to-income housing, a great many expenses beyond the bare necessities (e.g., school expenses, reading materials, gifts) routinely placed them in a deficit-spending position and thus unable to afford regularly a nutritious diet. Herein the importance of relying on informal sources of support or developing a range of alternative coping strategies cannot be overstated.

For example, the majority of food bank users indicated one specific coping mechanism involved simply being hungry at least once each month, while nearly half reported that their children were hungry at least that often as well (Michalski, 2003a). Other coping strategies included not having a telephone, walking rather than owning a vehicle or using public transportation, forgoing recreation, relying on charities, borrowing money or receiving cash advances, and financial or food gifts from extended family or friends in the past year. In summation, the research has confirmed that low-income families employ a range of adaptive strategies—informal support networks, unreported and underground work, self-production, and in-kind supports from voluntary and charitable organizations—in their ongoing struggles to secure the basic necessities of life (Bostock, 2001; Michalski, 2003a; Iyenda, 2001).

What Are the Consequences of Poverty?

Very briefly, we wish to consider an issue that has been examined more extensively than any other aspect of low-income families: what are the consequences of poverty? Many consequences are highly predictable and have been well documented. Others are not especially obvious or well understood. Health consequences, for instance, have long been associated with a relative lack of family resources and poverty in general. Social scientists have established that a direct relationship exists between socio-economic status (whether measured in terms of income levels or other measures of social class) and health status (Kosteniuk and Dickinson, 2003; Phipps, 2003). The groundbreaking Whitehall Study of British civil servants determined that those employed at the highest grades had about one-third the mortality rate of those in the lowest grades (Marmot and Smith, 1997). The study found that death rates were three times higher among junior office support staff as compared with senior administrators, even though these were all white-collar workers in the same offices and living in the same area of the country.

Interestingly, having a sense of control over one's work significantly relates to one's health status—a finding replicated in the second stage of the British research or the Whitehall II Study (Griffin et al., 2002). Higher incomes appear to be linked to improved health not simply as a result of the ability to purchase adequate housing, food, and other necessities, but also because of the enhanced sense of control and mastery that people have over their lives. Even the level of job insecurity or the threat of losing one's job apparently contributes to increased distress and a decreased sense of control—which have negative effects on self-reported health status.

The 1999 *Report on the Health of Canadians* found that Canadians in the highest income bracket were more likely to report their health as excellent and to live longer than those in the lower income brackets. The statistical evidence revealed further that the poor were at greater risk for most types of illnesses and almost all causes of death (Federal, Provincial and Territorial Advisory Committee on Population Health, 1999). Indeed, in their review of more than a dozen studies using eight data sets across four countries, Benzeval and Judge (2001: 1379) conclude the following: 'All of the studies that include measures of income level find that it is significantly related to health outcomes.'

Even more compelling has been the finding that childhood financial circumstances may be linked to adult health outcomes (Duncan and Brooks-Gunn, 1997). Obviously, many other factors may intervene and otherwise affect such long-term out-comes, but the impacts of sustained poverty and the likelihood that children and adolescents may be deprived of various social and economic advantages cannot be denied (Curtis et al., 2004). In fact, the research confirms that the relative disadvantages for children commence even before they are born, as poor children have significantly greater risks of being born prematurely and with lower birth weights, suffer greater intellectual impairment such as mental handicaps, and experience higher infant mortality rates (Wilkins and Sherman, 1998). By the time poor children have entered formal schooling, the evidence indicates that they have already fallen behind in terms of cognitive achievements and early academic performance.

Growing up in a poor family has consistently been linked to a variety of negative outcomes, including academic problems, psychosocial morbidity, and, more generally, a range of emotional and behavioural problems (Lipman and Offord, 1997). Adolescents who have experienced persistent poverty tend to have lower self-esteem and poorer school performance and attachment, engage in a range of risky or unhealthy practices (e.g., drugs and alcohol abuse), and commit more acts of delinquency and other forms of anti-social behaviour (McLeod and Shanahan, 1996).

Why should poverty have such negative effects on children, who are often quite resilient? Certainly many children *do* survive and even thrive in the long term *despite* their relatively deprived conditions. The main reason for having potentially negative short-term and long-term effects may be more the result of the problems and stressors that parents face in providing adequate financial, physical, and often emotional resources than anything else. Lone-parent mothers, for instance, often experience a high level of stress in meeting the requirements of both child care and income support. This often leads to poorer health outcomes for both parent *and* child, which in turn introduce additional obstacles to securing gainful employment (Baker, 2002). More generally, while the causal connections can be quite complex, recent research has shown that several home-related or environmental factors such as a difficult physical environment may also mediate the relationship between low income and intellectual development (Brannigan et al., 2002; Guo and Harris, 2000). Neighbourhood and community cohesion can serve to lessen the impact of family poverty, as the potential for additional social supports increases (Klebanov et al., 1994). Low-income families tend to live in poorer neighbourhoods and in lower-quality housing, which introduce additional obstacles as they attempt to provide children with the same types of services that most middle- and upper-income Canadians take for granted.

Conclusion

Despite Canada's considerable wealth, many families with low income remain in poverty and continue to face major challenges—even after a period of sustained economic growth and job creation. As of 2004, most statistical indicators would suggest that, in general, Canadians have made some progress lately in terms of rising family incomes and reduced poverty. In working with Statistics Canada's low-income cut-offs, we find that the country experienced five consecutive years (from 1996 to 2001) of declining low-income rates before stabilizing over the 2001–4 period (Statistics Canada, 2005). Over a similar time period, the number of persons reliant on welfare dropped by about 50 per cent from 1994 to 2004.

Yet a careful appraisal of the available statistics leads us to emphasize that not all is rosy, for some issues of considerable concern should not be downplayed or overlooked. As merely one example, the persistently high incidence of low income among recent immigrants (at about 2.5 times the levels observed for non-immigrants) offers one source of concern in a country increasingly dependent on immigration. The extremely high level of income poverty among female lone-parent families should not be overlooked either, particularly in view of the important consequences for the young. In addition, while most Canadian families witnessed income gains during the late 1990s and early 2000s, the evidence suggests that upper-income Canadians experienced the greatest gains. Statistics Canada (2005) reports a real (yet modest) upturn in income inequality over this period in terms of family income both 'before tax' and, to a lesser extent, 'after tax'.

As highlighted in this chapter, family change and demographic events have an impact on income poverty, especially to the extent that they influence the types of families and living arrangements in which Canadians share and pool income. Changing family structures in particular have generated some degree of economic uncertainty, especially for women and children. Whereas lone-parent families comprise about one in five families with children, among families classified as income poor, over half are single-parent families (Statistics Canada, 2005). Many of these changes observed in the Canadian family, in terms of non-marital fertility and marital instability, have had a greater impact on the economic well-being of women than they have on men. The consequences for children have been particularly important, as child poverty persists despite political pronouncements such as the House of Commons 1989 resolution to end child poverty by the year 2000. Canada has simultaneously witnessed a shift in the age distribution of the poor over past decades. In the 1960s, elderly Canadians were about twice as likely as children to be classified as income poor, but this situation has nearly reversed itself as the likelihood of poverty stands much higher among families with children.

In closing, two observations are worth repeating. First, it is useful to re-emphasize Frenette and Picot's (2003) finding that as many as one-third of all persons who left welfare during the late 1990s saw their household income decline—and rather precipitously in some cases. The evidence suggests that for a minority of families and individuals, an exit from welfare in recent years has actually led to a worsening of an already bad situation. Among those who continue to rely on welfare, there is no disputing the fact that in most cases their situations have worsened as benefit levels have been

nearly universally reduced across jurisdictions. Second, over this same period, there has been a substantial increase in the number of food banks in Canada, as well as other charities that serve meals and/or provide for other basic necessities. In a sense, food banks have become institutionalized during a period of more restrictive governmental income supports. These two observations are clearly linked, which implies that, especially among the poorest of the poor, there has been little improvement—and arguably some deterioration—in their relative situations.

Just as it is hazardous to forecast future economic trends, it is also extremely difficult to forecast 'political' events that might influence the types of transfer payments that Canadians receive from government. While both federal and provincial governments recently have managed to establish some balance between revenues and expenditures, it is unclear if this will lead to a 'reinvestment' in terms of income support for the most vulnerable of Canadians. Thus, while unemployment insurance and welfare payments became more restrictive during the late 1990s, little evidence suggests that governments are poised to reinvest in significant ways that might compensate for these policy changes. It is in this context that we recognize that the incidence of low income and poverty varies considerably, depending on family type and number of earners, as well as variations linked to age, life course stage, immigration, visible minority status, labour market conditions, and other factors.

The challenge of developing social policies or implementing social reforms aimed at further reducing the incidence of poverty must consider the above factors and the broader social context. In reworking income support policies or other transfers to families, with and without children, the current debate on a national child-care policy has particular relevance, especially in terms of assisting lone-parent females in gaining employment income. Other reforms of potential importance include direct transfers to families, since in a great many cases fathers are either unwilling or unable to provide child support. Some of the barriers that newcomers and visible minorities confront in attempting to access the labour market can be addressed through policy reforms, although silent forms of racism or social exclusion may never be amenable to government resolutions. Finally, still other problems that low-income families face may be more intractable, particularly in regard to dealing with certain unpredictable events and interpersonal decisions that shake families up or leave them vulnerable. Where family poverty cannot be prevented, however, the research points to the significance of a great many negative outcomes linked to living in poverty over a sustained period of time. From a social transfer standpoint, however, the costs associated with dealing with the long-term consequences of family poverty inevitably exceed the costs associated with reducing or preventing such poverty in the first place.

Study Questions

1. The last two decades of the twentieth century were turbulent years for many Canadians, with some noticeable ups and downs in the North American economy. Discuss these trends in terms of median income and income poverty, with particular attention to the two economic recessions of the early 1980s and 1990s and the economic recovery that occurred during the late 1990s.
2. Picot et al. (1998) highlight three distinctive types of events in the explanation of recent trends in terms of income poverty, including: 'demographic' events (that influence the types of families and living arrangements in which Canadians share and pool income), 'economic' events (that influence the availability of jobs and the sorts of wages available in the Canadian labour market), and 'political' events (that influence the types of transfer payments that Canadians receive from government). Discuss the relevance of each in reference to recent trends in the economic well-being and poverty of Canadian families.
3. The number of families living on welfare in Canada declined during the 1990s and early 2000s. What are some of the contributing factors responsible for this decline? Do you think that this trend will continue over the next several years? Why or why not?
4. Evidence suggests that one-third of all persons who left welfare during the late 1990s saw their household income decline—sometimes dramatically. Why do you think this occurred? How do you think these individuals and families cope with such economic hardship?

Glossary

Demographic changes Population shifts related to their size, distribution, and composition (e.g., ethnicities, age structure, family statuses, etc.), changes in them, and the components of such changes, that is, births, deaths, migration, and social mobility (change of status).

Economic family A group of two or more persons who live in the same dwelling and are related to each other by blood, marriage, common-law relationship, or adoption.

Labour force participation rate The proportion of the population 15 years of age and over that is in the labour force (that is, either employed or looking for work) in a specified reference period.

Lone-parent family One parent with one or more children who have never married, living in the same dwelling.

Low-income cut-offs (LICOs) Income levels at which families or unattached individuals are considered to be living in straitened circumstances. Statistics Canada currently produces LICOs before and after tax, which are periodically revised on the basis of changes in the average standard of living of Canadians. These are essentially 'relative measures' of low income that vary by family size and degree of urbanization.

Median income That point in the income distribution at which one-half of income units (individuals, families, or households) fall above and one-half fall below.

Recession A term given to a sharp slow-down in the rate of economic growth, as distinct from a slump or depression, which is a more severe and prolonged downturn. Two successive declines in seasonally adjusted real gross domestic product (GDP) would constitute a recession.

Further Readings

Duncan, Greg J., and Jeanne Brooks-Gunn, eds. 1997. *Consequences of Growing Up Poor*. New York: Russell Sage Foundation. Leading experts in the field discuss and interpret the research relating to the psychological, health, educational, and economic impacts of growing up in poor families.

McKeen, Wendy. 2004. *Money in Their Own Name: The Feminist Voice in Poverty Debate in Canada, 1970–1995*. Toronto: University of Toronto Press. The author presents a feminist perspective on social policy debates regarding poverty over the last three decades of the twentieth century, and also discusses the implications of 'women-friendly' social policies.

National Council of Welfare. 2004. *Poverty Profile*. Ottawa: National Council of Welfare. This volume provides national statistics on poverty for the year, along with poverty trends dating back to 1980, based on Statistics Canada data. The NCW examines poverty trends and factors linked to poverty, including poverty among groups of special interest.

Picot, Garnett, and John Myles. 2005. *Income Inequality and Low Income in Canada: An International Perspective*. Analytical Studies Research Paper Series 11F0019MIE2005240. Ottawa: Statistics Canada, Analytic Studies Branch. This is an overview of income inequality and low-income trends in Canada from an international perspective, establishing the extent to which Canada can be considered a low-income country as compared with other Western nations.

Statistics Canada, 2005. *Income in Canada*. Ottawa: Statistics Canada, catalogue no. 75-202-XIE. This definitive annual publication is the most reliable source of income statistics in Canada. Statistics Canada presents highlights and summary statistics on income and low income among Canadian families, along with some trend data.

Websites

www.ccsd.ca/

The Canadian Council on Social Development, a non-profit social policy and research organization, focuses on issues such as poverty, social inclusion, disability, cultural diversity, child well-being, and employment.

www.lisproject.org/

The Luxembourg Income Study is a non-profit co-operative research project with a membership of 25 countries, including Canada, on four continents: Europe, America, Asia, and Oceania. This research project regularly publishes comparative and international research on poverty across member countries.

www.campaign2000.ca/

Campaign 2000 is a cross-Canada public education movement to build Canadian awareness and support for the 1989 all-party House of Commons resolution to end child poverty in Canada by the year 2000.

References

Baker, Maureen. 2002. 'Child poverty, maternal health and social benefits', *Current Sociology* 50, 6: 823–38.

Beaujot, Roderic. 1999. *Earning and Caring in Canadian Families*. Peterborough, Ont.: Broadview Press.

Benzeval, Michaela, and Ken Judge. 2001. 'Income and health: The time dimension', *Social Science and Medicine* 52, 9: 1371–90.

Bostock, Lisa. 2001. 'Pathways of disadvantage? Walking as a mode of transport among low-income mothers', *Health and Social Care in the Community* 9, 1: 11–18.

Brannigan, Augustine, William Gemmell, David J. Pevalin, and Terrance J. Wade. 2002. 'Self-control and social control in childhood misconduct and aggression: The role of family structure, hyperactivity, and hostile parenting', *Canadian Journal of Criminology and Criminal Justice* 44, 2: 119–42.

Canadian Council on Social Development (CCSD). 2002. *The Canadian Fact Book on Poverty*. Ottawa: CCSD.

Capponi, Pat. 1999. *The War at Home: An Intimate Portrait of Canada's Poor*. Toronto: Viking.

Caragata, Lea. 2003. 'Neoconservative realities: The social and economic marginalization of Canadian women', *International Sociology* 18, 3: 559–80.

Cheal, David. 1999. *New Poverty: Families in Postmodern Society*. Westport, Conn.: Praeger.

Chekki, Dan A. 1999. 'Poverty amidst plenty: How do Canadian cities cope with rising poverty', *Research in Community Sociology* 9: 141–52.

Cleveland, Gordon, Morley Gunderson, and Douglas Hyatt. 1996. 'Child care costs and the employment decision of women: Canadian evidence', *Canadian Journal of Economics* 29, 1: 132–51.

Cotton, C., M. Webber, and Y. Saint-Pierre. 1998. *Should the Low Income Cutoffs Be Updated?* Ottawa: Statistics Canada, Catalogue no. 75F0002MIE–99009.

Curtis, Lori J., Martin D. Dooley, and Shelley A. Phipps. 2004. 'Child well-being and neighbourhood quality: Evidence from the Canadian National Longitudinal Study of Children and Youth', *Social Science and Medicine* 58, 10: 1917–27.

Duncan, Greg J., and Jeanne Brooks-Gunn, eds. 1997. *Consequences of Growing Up Poor*. New York: Russell Sage Foundation.

Edin, Kathryn, and Laura Lein. 1997. *Making Ends Meet: How Single Mothers Survive Welfare and Low-Wage Work*. New York: Russell Sage Foundation.

Federal, Provincial, and Territorial Advisory Committee on Population Health. 1999. *Statistical Report on the Health of Canadians*. Ottawa: Health Canada and Statistics Canada.

Federal Provincial Working Group on Social Development Research and Information. 1998. *Construction of a Preliminary Market Basket Measure of Poverty*. Ottawa: Federal Provincial Working Group.

Felt, Lawrence, and Peter Sinclair. 1992. '"Everyone does it": Unpaid work in a rural peripheral region', *Work, Employment & Society* 6: 43–64.

Finnie, Ross. 2000. 'The dynamics of poverty in Canada: What we know, what we can do', C.D. Howe Institute, Commentary No. 145 (Sept.).

Fraser Institute. 2001. *Measuring Poverty in Canada*. Vancouver: Fraser Institute.

Frenette, Marc, and Garnett Picot. 2003. *Life after Welfare: The Economic Well-Being of Welfare Leavers in Canada during the 1990s* (Research Report No. 192). Ottawa: Statistics Canada, Business and Labour Market Analysis Division, Catalogue no. 11F0019MIE.

Gee, Ellen. 1995. 'Families in later life', in Roderic Beaujot, Ellen M. Gee, Fernando Rajulton, and Zenaida Ravanera, eds, *Family Over the Life Course: Current Demographic Analysis*. Ottawa: Statistics Canada Demography Divison, 77–113.

Griffin, Joan M., Rebecca Fuhrer, Stephen A. Stansfeld, and Michael Marmot. 2002. 'The importance of low control at work and home on depression and anxiety: Do these effects vary by gender and social class', *Social Science and Medicine* 54, 5: 783–98.

Guo, Guang, and Kathleen Mullan. 2000. 'The mechanisms mediating the effects of poverty on children's intellectual development', *Demography* 37, 4: 431–47.

Hulchanski, David, and Joseph H. Michalski. 1994. *How Households Obtain Resources To Meet Their Needs: The Shifting Mix of Cash and Non-Cash Sources*. Toronto: Ontario Human Rights Commission.

Iyenda, Guillaume. 2001. 'Street food and income generation for poor households in Kinshasa', *Environment and Urbanization* 13, 2: 233–41.

Kazemipur, A., and Shiva Halli. 2000. *The New Poverty in Canada: Ethnic Groups and Ghetto Neighbourhoods*. Toronto: Thompson Educational Publishing.

Kennedy, Gerard. 1995. *The Circumstances and Coping Strategies of People Needing Food Banks*. Toronto: Daily Bread Food Bank.

Klebanov, Pamela Kato, Jeanne Brooks-Gunn, and Greg J. Duncan. 1994. 'Does neighborhood and family poverty affect mothers' parenting, mental health and social support?', *Journal of Marriage and the Family* 56, 2: 441–55.

Kosteniuk, Julie G., and Harley D. Dickinson. 2003. 'Tracing the social gradient in the health of Canadians: Primary and secondary determinants', *Social Science and Medicine* 57, 2: 263–76.

Krahn, Harvey J., and Graham S. Lowe. 2002. *Work, Industry, and Canadian Society*, 4th edn. Scarborough, Ont.: Thomson/Nelson.

Lee, Kevin. 2000. *Urban Poverty in Canada*. Ottawa: Canadian Council on Social Development.

Little, Margaret. 2001. 'A litmus test for democracy: The impact of Ontario welfare changes on single mothers', *Studies in Political Economy* 66: 9–36.

Lipman, Ellen L., and David R. Offord. 1997. 'Psychosocial morbidity among poor children in Ontario', in Duncan and Brooks-Gunn (1997: 239–87).

McFate, Katherine. 1995. 'Western states in the new world order', in McFate, *Poverty, Inequality, and the Future of Social Policy*. New York: Russell Sage Foundation.

McLeod, Jane D., and Michael J. Shanahan. 1996. 'Trajectories of poverty and children's mental health', *Journal of Health and Social Behavior* 37, 3: 207–20.

Marcil-Gratton, N., and Celine Le Bourdais. 1999. *Custody, Access and Child Support: Findings from the National Longitudinal Survey of Children and Youth*. Ottawa: Department of Justice Canada, Child Support Team.

———, ———, and Evelyn Lapierre-Adamcyk. 2000. 'The implications of parents' conjugal histories for children', *Canadian Journal of Policy Research* 1: 32–40.

Marmot, Michael G., and George Davey Smith. 1997. 'Socio-economic differentials in health: The contribution of the Whitehall studies', *Journal of Health Psychology* 2, 3: 283–96.

Marshall, Katherine. 2003. 'Benefiting from extended parental leave', *Perspectives on Labour and Income* 4: 15–25.

Meert, Henk, Pascale Mistiaen, and Christian Kesteloot. 1997. 'The geography of survival: Household strategies in urban settings', *Journal of Economic and Social Geography* 88, 2: 169–81.

Michalski, Joseph H. 2003a. 'The economic status and coping strategies of food bank users in the Greater Toronto area', *Canadian Journal of Urban Research* 12, 2: 275–98.

———. 2003b. 'Housing affordability, social policy and economic conditions: Food bank users in the Greater Toronto area, 1990–2000', *Canadian Review of Sociology and Anthropology* 40, 1: 65–92.

Montreal Diet Dispensary. 1998. *Budgeting for Basic Needs and Budgeting for Minimum Adequate Standard of Living*. Montreal.

Morissette, René, Xuelin Zhang, and Marie Drolet. 2002. *The Evolution of Wealth Inequality in Canada, 1984–1999*. Ottawa: Statistics Canada, Business and Labour Market Analysis Division, Catalogue no. 11–F0019.

Myles, John. 2000. 'The maturation of Canada's retirement income system: Income levels, income inequality and low income among older persons', *Canadian Journal on Aging* 19, 3: 287–316.

National Council of Welfare. 2004. *Poverty Profile 2001*. Ottawa: Minister of Public Works and Government Services Canada.

Oderkirk, Jill. 1992. 'Food banks', *Canadian Social Trends* 24, 6: 6–14.

Phipps, Shelley. 2003. *The Impact of Poverty on Health: A Scan of Research Literature*. Ottawa: Canadian Institute for Health Information.

——— and Peter Burton. 1995. 'Sharing within families: Implications for the measurement of poverty among individuals in Canada', *Canadian Journal of Economics* 28: 177–204.

Picot, Garnett, and F. Hou. 2003. *The Rise in Low-Income Rates among Immigrants in Canada*. Analytic Studies Research Paper Series 11F0019MIE2003198. Ottawa: Statistics Canada, Analytic Studies Branch.

——— and John Myles. 2005. *Income Inequality and Low Income in Canada: An International Perspective*. Analytical Studies Research Paper Series 11F0019MIE2005240. Ottawa: Statistics Canada, Analytic Studies Branch.

———, ———, and Wendy Pyper. 1998. 'Markets, families and social transfers: Trends in low income among the young and old, 1973–1995', in Miles Corak, ed., *Labour Markets, Social Institutions and the Future of Canada's Children*. Ottawa: Statistics Canada, Catalogue no. 890553–XPB, 11–30.

———, M. Zyblock, and Wendy Pyper. 1999. *Why Do Children Move into and out of Low Income: Changing Labour Market Conditions or Marriage and*

Divorce? Analytic Studies Research Paper Series 11F0019MIE1999132. Ottawa: Statistics Canada, Analytic Studies Branch.

Podoluk, Jenny. 1968. *Incomes of Canadians.* Ottawa: Dominion Bureau of Statistics.

Preston, Samuel. 1984. 'Children and the elderly: Divergent paths for America's dependents', *Demography* 21: 435–58.

Quarter, Jack. 1992. *Canada's Social Economy: Co-operatives, Non-Profits, and Other Community Enterprises.* Toronto: James Lorimer.

Rainwater, Lee, Tim Smeeding, and John Coder. 2001. 'Child poverty across states, nations and continents', in K. Vleminckx and Tim Smeeding, eds, *Child Well-Being, Child Poverty and Child Poverty in Modern Nations: What Do We Know?* Bristol, UK: Policy Press, 33–74.

Richardson, Jack. 1996. 'Canada and free trade: Why did it happen?', in Robert Brym, ed., *Society in Question.* Toronto: Nelson.

Ruggles, P. 1990. *Drawing the Line.* Washington: Urban Institute.

Sarlo, Christopher. 1996. *Poverty in Canada.* Vancouver: Fraser Institute.

Sauve, Roger. 2002. *The Current State of Canadian Family Finances.* Ottawa: Vanier Institute of the Family.

Sceviour, R., and Ross Finnie. 2004. 'Social assistance use: Trends in incidence, entry and exit rates', *Canadian Economic Observer* (Statistics Canada): 1–13.

Smeeding, Tim, Lee Rainwater, and John Coder. 2002. 'United States poverty in a cross-national context', in Sheldon H. Danziger and Robert H. Haveman, eds, *Understanding Poverty.* New York and Cambridge, Mass.: Russell Sage Foundation and Harvard University Press, 162–89.

Smith, Ekuwa, and Andrew Jackson. 2002. *Does a Rising Tide Lift All Boats?* Ottawa: Canadian Council on Social Development.

Starkey, Linda J., Harriett V. Kuhnlein, and Katherine Gray-Donald. 1998. 'Food bank users: Sociodemographic and nutritional characteristics', *Canadian Medical Association Journal* 158, 9: 1143–50.

Statistics Canada. 2002. 'Wealth inequality: 1984–1999', *The Daily* (Feb.), Statistics Canada.

———. 2005. *Income Trends in Canada.* Ottawa: Statistics Canada, Catalogue no. 75–202–XIE.

Tarasuk, Valerie S. 2001. 'Household food insecurity with hunger is associated with women's food intakes, health and household circumstances', *Journal of Nutrition* 131, 10: 2670–6.

Teron, Adrienne C., and Valerie Tarasuk. 1999. 'Charitable food assistance: What are food bank users receiving?', *Canadian Journal of Public Health* 90, 6: 382–4.

Torjman, Sherri. 1999. 'Crests and crashes: The changing tides of family income security', in Maureen Baker, ed., *Canada's Changing Families: Challenges to Public Policy.* Ottawa: Vanier Institute of the Family, 69–88.

Vozoris, Nicholas, Barbara Davis, and Valerie Tarasuk. 2002. 'The affordability of a nutritious diet for households on welfare in Toronto', *Canadian Journal of Public Health* 93, 1: 36–40.

Wilkins, Russell, and Gregory J. Sherman. 1998. 'Low income and child health in Canada', in David Coburn, Carl D'Arcy, and George M. Torrance, eds, *Health and Canadian Society: Sociological Perspectives.* Toronto: University of Toronto Press, 102–9.

Wilson, Beth, with Emily Tsoa. 2001. *Hunger Count 2001: Food Bank Lines in Insecure Times.* Toronto: Canadian Association of Food Banks.

Wolfson, M., and J. Evans. 1988. *Statistics Canada's Low Income Cutoffs: Methodological Concerns and Possibilities.* Ottawa: Statistics Canada, Analytic Studies Branch.

Woolley, Frances. 1998. 'Work and household transactions: An economist's view', in David Cheal, Frances Woolley, and Meg Luxton, eds, *How Families Cope and Why Policymakers Need to Know.* Ottawa: Canadian Policy Research Networks Study No. F12, 27–55.

Yeung, W. Jean, and Sandra L. Hofferth. 1998. 'Family adaptations to income and job loss in the US', *Journal of Family and Economic Issues* 19, 3: 255–83.

Zhang, Xuelin. 2003. *The Wealth Position of Immigrant Families in Canada.* Ottawa: Statistics Canada, Business and Labour Market Analysis Division, Catalogue no. 11F0019MIE2003197.

Part IV   **Diversity**

The dominant forms of behaviour in any society receive the most attention, but what about families that live outside the mainstream? Part IV takes a look at several groups of minorities in Canada and their family patterns: individuals who differ from the heterosexual norm; Aboriginals, immigrants, and visible minorities; and people with disabilities.

Doreen Fumia, in Chapter 10, examines the issue of same-sex marriage in Canada, how debates have both unsettled and reproduced mainstream notions of national identity, and changes in marriage law in Canada in the form of Bill C-38, the Civil Marriages Act, which shifted the definitions about which couples could legally say 'I do.' Central to Fumia's analysis is an understanding of Canada as a 'heterosexual nation' and what this means in light of changes in law and practice. She explores how concepts of 'normal' and 'abnormal' sexuality, of meaning and identity, demarcate heterosexual from homosexual relationships, and thus how lesbian and gay human rights claims to same-sex marriage limit the possibility for confronting a heterosexual nation where sexual orientation still leaves many people as 'others', outside the 'nation' looking in.

In Chapter 11, James Frideres discusses family patterns among ethnic minorities. He first presents a brief socio-demographic overview of each of three broad groups—Aboriginal peoples, immigrants, and visible minorities—by looking at such factors as age distribution, then explores socio-economic factors, including labour force participation, unemployment, and residence patterns. Frideres also examines family issues such as family structure and organization, and family conflict. Data are presented on lone-parent families and fertility, and he points out that many new immigrants and Aboriginal people live in households that are different from the standard nuclear organization typical of Canadian-born, non-visible minority families. Also considered are the role of gender and of young people, and intermarriage and mixed unions.

Michelle Owen, in Chapter 12, seeks to understand the impact that disability has on families. She begins by discussing the problem of defining disability, with a special focus on the social model of disability, and then discusses children and youth with disabilities, including their effects on their families. For example, she reports that the average household income for preschool and school-age children with disabilities is lower than the household incomes of their peers without disabilities. Owen finds fault with the general lack of support services for parental caregivers, and describes the often onerous parental caregiving responsibilities. Parents, too, are frequently disabled, and Owen explores the economic implications of parental disability in regard to child care, employment and learning, and domestic labour. The chapter ends with a review of issues pertaining to violence and abuse against women and children with disabilities.

CHAPTER 10

'I Do' Belong in Canada: Same-Sex Relationships and Marriage

Doreen M. Fumia

Learning Objectives

- To be able to distinguish between marriage as a private lived experience of two people and as a relationship between two people and the state.
- To learn about key events and debates that led to adoption of the Civil Marriages Act (Bill C-38) in Canada.
- To understand how same-sex marriage challenges a heterosexual nation.
- To identify debates that both enable and constrain attempts to secure sexual citizenship.
- To recognize the difference between human rights claims based on inclusion and those based on confronting heterosexism.

Introduction

Just as Adrienne Rich (1995) claimed in her groundbreaking work on motherhood that it is both a personal relationship and a public institution, so, too, is marriage. To view marriage as an institution is to step back from viewing it as a relationship *between* two people and, rather, view it as a relationship between two people and the state. Marriage relationships have been the concern of individual families and the state for different reasons at different points in history. When we focus on marriage as an institution, we are less interested in the specificity of any one couple and more interested in which couples fit into state regulations that define and protect family relations. In addition, it is important to point out that focusing on any relationship between the state and the people is always embedded in a broader discussion about the nation and its citizens.

Like heterosexual marriage, same-sex marriage, when viewed as an institution, is embedded in a broader discussion between the nation and its citizens, in this case its **sexual citizens** (see Richardson, 1998; Phelan, 2001). The term 'sexual citizens' refers to those who stake their claim to be non-heterosexual *and* legitimized in a society that privileges full citizenship participation based on identities inscribed through whiteness, masculinity, heterosexuality, middle-class status, and able-bodiedness (see Berlant, 1997; Sharma, 2000). This chapter examines same-sex marriage debates in Canada that establish sexual citizenship in ways that both unsettle and reproduce mainstream notions of national identity. It also discusses changes in marriage law in Canada in the form of Bill C-38, the Civil Marriages Act, which shifted the definitions about which couples could legally say 'I do.'

The chapter is divided into five broad sections. The first section explores some of the changing social needs that have produced changes in the institution of marriage and asks: What is marriage for? The second section addresses the subject of sexual diversity and how concepts of 'normal' and 'abnormal' sexuality are racialized in ways that have been effective in demarcating heterosexual from homosexual relationships. Section three examines how lesbian and gay human rights claims to same-sex marriage limit the possibility for confronting a heterosexual nation. In light of the discussion in section three, section four poses questions such as: How do gender, race, and class operate when the groom and groom or bride and bride, surrounded by all the signifiers of a grand heterosexual church wedding, are shown walking down the aisle on national television?

Which aspects of identity stand out more in the national imaginary when a normative white middle-class same-sex male couple walks down the aisle? Section five discusses more specifically the challenges that arise from confronting a heterosexual nation.

I now turn to explore some of the reasons why relationships and/or marriages between two people of the same sex are such a hotspot of contestation in the realm of public debate in Canada.

What Is Marriage For?

One scholar who writes about the historically varied and changing criteria for marriage and family relationships in the West is E.J. Graff (2004). Graff provides a historical overview of marriage and notes its changing status based on changing economic and social needs. She explains that in earlier historical periods, marriage was viewed as a contractual business relationship based on money matters for the family unit, such as the earning of income and the acquisition and preservation of property for income (farms), dowry, status of wives, and servants. According to Graff, in later periods of industrial and post-industrial capitalism less emphasis was placed on money as the basis for marriage and an increased emphasis was placed on psychological relationships and the importance of feelings. She notes that even with the emphasis on matters of the heart there continues to be economic interdependence.

The formalized regulation of 'coupledom' has concerned local communities and the state. Acceptable norms about how to recognize who is and who is not married have varied from simply declaring a commitment before God to signing documentation that is legally binding. More recently, there has been a departure from religious and legally formalized marriage and an increase in unmarried couples cohabiting in common-law relationships (see Box 10.1).

The Canadian state is interested enough in common-law relationships to track them in census polls. The terms 'cohabitation' and 'common-law relationship' are formally sanctioned by the state and now include the category of two non-related same-sex adults living together. Statistics Canada data from the 2001 census indicate that married couples accounted for 70 per cent of all

Box 10.1   Common-Law Relationships

You are in a common-law relationship if you live as a couple but are not married. The law recognizes common-law relationships between opposite-sex and same-sex couples after the couple has been in a marriage-like relationship for a certain amount of time. Under most federal laws, that time is one year. Under most provincial laws, that time is two years. In 1997, the Family Relations Act (R.S.B.C. 1996, c. 128) was amended to provide that for all purposes under that Act (except division of family property), 'spouse' includes unmarried persons of the same or opposite sex who are in a marriage-like relationship for at least two years. Although significant changes in applicable laws have extended many of the rights and responsibilities of marriage to common-law couples, there are still significant differences. For example, if you are in a common-law relationship, unlike marriage, there is no presumption that assets should be divided equally at the end of a common-law relationship.

SOURCE: www.bcfamilylaw.ca; accessed 11 May 2005.

families in 2001, down from 83 per cent in 1981. At the same time, the proportion of common-law couples rose from 6 per cent to 14 per cent. The 2001 census reported 5,901,400 married couples, 1,158,400 common-law couples, and 1,311,200 lone-parent families in Canada (www.statcan.ca; accessed 17 May 2005).

Cohabitation and common-law relationships are similar to, but not exactly like, marriage. Marriage is taken more seriously—in ways that have both legal and social ramifications—by banks, insurers, courts, employers, schools, hospitals, cemeteries, rental car companies, frequent-flyer programs, and more. Graff (2004: 49) remarks that 'marriage is a word that is understood to mean that you share not only your bedroom but the rest of the house as well. . . . [it] is the marker that allows the courts to assume that you two wanted your relationship to be respected after death.'

Marriage is now a publicly policed institution and an inner experience, and society wrestles with understanding the balance between public authority and the heart (Graff, 2004: 193). Marriage doesn't exist unless both parts happen—two human beings behave as married and everyone else treats them as such. What does matter is which side you think counts more. The decisions made about individual marriages will be quite different if you think marriage is a 'publicly conferred status or an immanent state' (ibid.). There are benefits and penalties attached to state-recognized relationships (for updates on benefits, visit government websites that provide information, such as www.government.ca and follow the links). Who gets to share and who does not affects capital, property, lottery winnings, insurance benefits, and personal income tax (which has both beneficial and non-beneficial effects). With an economy capable of operating without business contracts legally bound by marriage, other relationships become subject for possible state recognition.

The de-emphasis on money as the central factor in the institution of marriage has been followed by the erosion of other historical underpinnings that have been viewed as immoral practices, such as premarital sex and child-bearing outside marriage. One of the most significant shifts has been that of the heterosexual presumption that has underpinned marriage, 'one man + one woman = marriage', as a placard proclaimed at a March 2005 protest in Ottawa against same-sex marriage. What these shifts signal is a redefinition of the moral underpinnings of state-recognized relationships. The question that Graff asks in the title of her book is apt here: What is marriage for?

> [O]nce society got rid of the ideas that sex without babies is bad . . . once our philosophy and laws protect sex for pleasure and love, how can same-sex marriage be barred? (Graff, 2004: 84)

Beyond Love and Marriage

Marriage has been defined within notions of presumed heterosexuality (two opposite-sex adults) and heterosexual identities (masculine and feminine sex and gender roles; see Holloway, 1993; Rich, 1993; Valverde, 1993). While historical underpinnings have been openly and publicly challenged, they have by no means disappeared. Placards held by opponents to same-sex marriage in the Ottawa protest mentioned above read: 'Natural Marriage: 1 man, 1 woman'; 'DEFEND MARRIAGE: *children, churches, culture, CANADA!*' (Toronto Star, 7 Mar. 2005, A6). The presumed heterosexuality explicit in these words is absolute, national, and God-given. In some settings challenges make a difference, in others they are resisted and reaffirm the status quo. What is important to ask is, if presumed heterosexuality is being challenged, what is presumed to take its place?

Sexual identities are multiple and marked as different and marginal through notions of racialization and sexual difference. As sexual Others, we are identified not by who we are (for instance, professors, students, sales clerks, lawyers, union representatives) but, rather, by what we do (for instance, sexual acts). Therefore, when non-heterosexual relations are considered for legitimacy within the institution of marriage, **normalization**, that is, the ways in which identities are constituted within social norms, needs to be discussed. It is important to say a word about the terms used to identify non-heterosexual identities: lesbian, gay, bisexual, transgendered, transsexual, two-spirited, intersexed, and queer, hereafter referred to as LGBTIQ. While this acronym aims to identify the multiple identities that constitute non-heterosexual orientations, it is not meant to conflate the varying political and social struggles embedded in each identity. This chapter, because it addresses state-sanctioned same-sex relationships, focuses on identities represented in **human rights claims** within the frame of the Charter of Rights and Freedoms. For this reason, the subjects of the category 'same-sex marriage' are predominantly those who can fit into a normative notion of 'lesbian' or 'gay', which like other normative identities are assumed to share white middle-class values. When the terms 'lesbian' and 'gay' are unmarked and used without any qualifying signifiers to mark race, class, or specific sexual orientation such as transsexual, then mainstream identities of **whiteness**, middle-class status, and able-bodiedness are assumed (for discussion about unmarked social identities, see Berlant, 1997; Mackey, 2002). While important work theorizes sexual identities and refuses fixed categories of sex and/or gender (for instance, Butler, 1990; Beauvoir, 1989; Grosz, 1993; Wittig, 1993), the reference in this chapter to lesbians and gays is not meant to assume fixed identities as ontological truths. Rather, referring to 'lesbians and gays' is meant to note how these essentialized identities have monopolized the debates around same-sex relationships in ways that exclude other and more marginalized groups from the discussion. Therefore, I explicitly use the term 'lesbians and gays' in relation to current same-sex marriage debates in order to remain conscious of the exclusive specificity of who is able to say 'I do' in practice if not in law in Canada today.

IDENTITIES: NORMAL AND NOT

Social practices that aim to separate the normal from those viewed in society as not normal ensure that some people belong and others do not. In the West, scientific methods that arose in the late eighteenth and early nineteenth centuries racialized and sexualized some bodies as not normal (see Adams, 1997; Brock, 2003). At a time when race lines were being reinforced (due to challenges to racial segregation and anti-miscegenation laws), measuring and classifying the sexualized (mostly female), racialized body built upon earlier scientific approaches used to identify different species of humans (Gilman, 1992; Somerville, 1997). Regardless of racial makeup, non-heterosexuals come under the scientific gaze of racism. It is important to remember, however, that certain social attitudes towards homosexuality must not be viewed as the same thing as racism; the white homosexual is not the black heterosexual (hooks, 1989). Sexualized identities are racialized and they are multiple.

THE EMERGING SUBJECT OF SEXUAL DIVERSITY

The nineteenth-century homosexual became a personage, a past, a case history, and a childhood, in addition to being a type of life, a life form, and morphology with an indiscreet anatomy and possibly a mysterious physiology. Nothing that went into his [sic] composition was unaffected by his sexuality. . . . Homosexuality appeared as one of the forms of sexuality when it was transposed from the practice of sodomy onto a kind of interior androgyny, a hermaphrodism of the soul. The sodomite had been a temporary aberration; the homosexual was now a species. (Foucault, 1990: 43)

The homosexual as a social identity began to emerge in the late eighteenth and early nineteenth centuries. The history of lesbians and gays in North America is now well documented (e.g., Duberman et al., 1989; Katz, 1995; Khayatt, 1992; Kinsman, 1983; Lenskyj, 1990; McCaskell, 1988; Ross, 1995; Sedgwick, 1990). Uncovering this history developed as a way to make the presence of sexual minorities known and accepted, as in the campaigns that declare, 'We Are Everywhere' (slogan for the 1984 Toronto Pride Day celebration). Identifying historical figures, politicians, movie stars, sports figures, and family relatives as lesbian or gay has supported the effort to make an invisible presence visible. Those who write about sexually diverse identities contribute to an ongoing project of increasing the visibility of and legitimizing sexual minorities. Definitions of the homosexual individual shape legal and social debates. Brian MacDougall contends that such definitions are legally inscribed, based on sexual practices, personalities, and identities. MacDougall (2000: 24) argues that when the law wishes to marginalize or regulate a group it is easier to define and condemn supposed activities rather than their social status. For example, if Muslims are to be legally marginalized, rather than Muslims being explicitly excluded the veil is outlawed. If homosexuals are to be legally marginalized, sexual acts such as anal intercourse between two men (not between a man and a woman) are drawn on to punish homosexuals. MacDougall argues that various acts are emblematic of heterosexual activity while others are emblematic of homosexual activity. Through such a demarcation, heterosexuality is sustained as normal, whereas homosexual acts are used to define the homosexual as abnormal. MacDougall suggests that the socially defined differences among normal, unmentionable, tolerated, and deviant sexuality are not a reflection of the value of sexual acts. Sexual acts only gain meanings of normal and abnormal when invested with social norms. Jeffery Weeks argues that the social meaning given to sexual acts is based on regulation rather than pleasure. Weeks (1991: 11) articulates it this way:

> Our culture has all too readily justified erotic activity by reference to something else—reproduction or the cementing of relationships usually—and has ignored the appeal of the erotic as a site of freedom, joy and pleasure. One man touching another man's penis is not just engagement in pleasurable activity—he is in danger of becoming (or being) a homosexual.

At the same time that political, legal, and social challenges to presumed heterosexuality have been taking place, so, too, have epistemological debates about sexual identity.

'NORMAL' SAME-SEX RELATIONSHIPS

The boundary between what is and is not normal opens and constrains spaces in which to publicly declare a non-heterosexual identity, or in popular language, in which to 'come out'. Celebrating individual and group processes of coming out is tempered by what it leads to. Michelle Owen (2001) problematizes who benefits from the successful challenges aimed to secure legally sanctioned same-sex relationships. She poses the question: are sexual minorities queering the normal or normalizing the queer? Throughout the 1980s and 1990s social movements actively maintained a campaign to 'normalize' homosexuality based on court challenges, tracing histories, and publicly coming out of the closet. The 1990s community slogan that 'We Are Family', for example, communicates the normality of homosexual families modelled on a notion of a two-parent nuclear family unit. While insisting on the right to have a (non-heterosexual) family is a significant challenge to heterosexual norms, representing the lesbian or gay family as nuclear also risks reinscribing heterosexuality (and whiteness and able-bodiedness) as the norm. Even with the best intentions to find justice in the face of legalized discrimination, 'normalizing the queer', as Owen (2001) characterizes it, continues to exclude single-parent families, LGBTIQ people of colour who are assumed to carry a legacy of dysfunctional families, and LGBTIQ poor people who cannot afford to live up to middle-class family standards.

Owen contends that in the 1990s Canadian lesbian and gay activism primarily focused on same-sex relationships. Her question is: should queers be associated with family at all? Increasing literature and stories raising the visibility of lesbian mothers in Toronto and the rest of Canada (see Arnup, 1995; Epstein, 1998; Fumia, 1998, 1999) suggest that when the narratives of lesbian mothers are grounded in the experiences of white middle-class women, lesbian mothers emerge as an epistemological and privileged site (Owen,

2001: 87). Further, she demonstrates that when same-sex couples 'present themselves as "normal" in pursuit of formal recognition, the polarization of "family" and "not family" is effectively cemented' (ibid., 96). Other academic work joins that of Owen in expressing concern that the push to legitimize same-sex relationships falls into a trap of reinscribing heterosexist norms that underpin family units. Those who become politically legitimized by statute law may still lack **social legitimation**. Such heterosexist norms might overlook same-sex relationships temporarily as long as a solid attachment to whiteness, middle-class status, and able-bodiedness is maintained. That is, with the passing of Bill C-38, if you are a family that can assimilate to normalized notions of the family (Weston, 1991), then you will be recognized legally as a family. Which lesbian relationships can say 'I do'? We must think about whether, for example, a family headed by a lesbian mother who is drug-addicted and dependent on welfare will be accorded full state recognition (see Boyd, 1999, for a discussion about drug-addicted mothers). Brenda Cossman (1996) argues that family as a social construct is not the problem; rather, the problem lies in the legal and political system that demands people either fit into a presumed heterosexual unit or be excluded from the benefits of a legal family unit. Now that same-sex couples have the right to claim the benefits of a legal family unit, it will be interesting to observe which same-sex couples have access to social acceptance and belonging.

The Limits of Political Gains of Sexual Citizenship

Court challenges and human rights claims aimed at legitimating sexual minorities are limited because they reproduce social hierarchies of dominance and they structure benefits as available to some and not others. People need cultural and intellectual capital, access to resources, and time to be able to stake claims to rights promised. Social marginality constrains those opportunities. Those

constituted through marginal sexualities that are further marginalized through race, class, ethnicity, and/or disabilities may be excluded from or entirely invisible in the discussion around same-sex marriage. The most successful legal claims of same-sex relationship, especially prior to the passing of Bill C-38, have been by those who identify as lesbian or gay in ways that closely align with mainstream heterosexual, white, able-bodied, opposite-sex couples.

SURVIVAL OR SELF-DESTRUCTION BY ASSIMILATION?

The emphasis in court challenges has been placed on the right to be *included* rather than the right to be *different*, and lesbians and gays have shown themselves to be 'more' like everyone else than those further from the centre (Phelan, 2001). The normalized lesbian or gay appears to be better positioned to launch rights claims that promise inclusion than the excessively different transsexual, transgendered, intersexed, two-spirited, or queer. These strategies of inclusion have exclusions built into them.

Lauren Berlant (1997) contends we often turn to strategies of inclusion to gain legal rights and calls these strategies 'survival tactics'. The need for **survival tactics** of inclusion arises from the need to put in place laws that have the potential for protection against the violence of homophobia. Yet, survival tactics from within capitalist culture are critically motivated acts of commodity consumption (Berlant; 1997: 9). That is, survival tactics developed for inclusion into a dominant cultural centre rely on an economic positioning useful to capitalism. In Britain this has been referred to as the 'pink pound', and in the Canadian context I use the term 'lavender looney'. Thus, 'identity-based economic investment zones' are said to make marginalized social groups more central, more legitimate, and more powerful in capitalist society (ibid.). Is the publicity about the economic advantages of same-sex weddings helping or hindering sexual others to stake claims to legitimacy? Berlant cautions:

for all the importance of survival tactics, a politics that advocates the subaltern appropriation of normative forms of the good life makes a kind of (often tacit) peace with exploitation and normativity as well as with the other less happy and frequently less visible aspects of capitalist culture. (Ibid., 15)

Political strategies that seek to normalize sexual diversity in human rights claims in relation to commodity-based capitalism simultaneously exclude those who cannot stake claims to (upper) middle-class standards.

SEXUALITY MEETS UP WITH NATIONALITY

Along with the tension created by the benefits and disadvantages that arise from securing normative forms of the good life in a capitalist society is a false history of ex-privileged heterosexuality. Through this 'false history' a story emerges about how sexuality and nationality meet up in the public sphere. Berlant contends that identity is marketed in national capitalism as a property. That is, identity is something you can purchase a relation to or something you already own that you can express—'my masculinity', 'my sexual differences'. According to Berlant, identity is fundamentally sexual (ibid., 17). Further, Foucault (1990), Butler (1990), and Katz (1995) have argued that sexuality is the modern form of self-intelligibility. It is this very notion of identity being fundamentally sexual that creates the conditions of possibility for national identity to be viewed as heterosexual. And, in response to perceived threats to national identity amid public debates about same-sex relationships, a renewed urgency to protect heterosexual norms is presented by opponents to same-sex marriage. Berlant (1997: 17) has this to say:

[A] virulent form of revitalized national heterosexuality has been invented, a form that is complexly white and middle class. . . . I simply do not see why the nation has to have an official sexuality . . . that uses cruel and mundane strategies both to promote shame for non-normative

populations and to deny them state, federal, and juridical supports because they are deemed morally incompetent to their own citizenship.

Berlant here pointedly asks a very important question: Why does a nation have to have an 'official sexuality'? This question is aptly applied to debates around same-sex marriage, though national threats to identity are not limited to debates on this issue. Normalized heterosexual images regularly make their way into the public sphere. Take, for instance, the familiar heterosexual image of a politician posing with his or her opposite-sex spouse, or of a soldier kissing his or her opposite-sex spouse or partner farewell when heading off to battle on behalf of the nation. A nation that has a heterosexual identity is deeply troubled when such images are disrupted by non-heterosexual images that emerge to represent 'the family', 'the soldier', and 'the politician'. It is in this way that we can understand how private issues of sexual identity are indeed public issues of national identity.

Berlant agues that 'private' issues such as pornography, abortion, sexuality, reproduction, marriage, personal morality, and family values flash across people's faces in a collapse of the political and personal into a world of **public intimacy**. The citizen who once could find *himself* in colonial narratives of white, masculine, heterosexual dominance has not been displaced but rather has been destabilized. Amid public debates and increased visibility of racial and sexual minorities, he suffers from a destabilized national and cultural identity that in turn creates a need to restore stability.

The following quotation, from a letter to the editor opposing the Canadian Supreme Court decision to uphold the government's authority to change the definition of marriage, exemplifies how same-sex marriage is perceived as a particular kind of threat: 'Do we care enough about our children and the future of this country to fight for the survival of the traditional family?' (*Globe and Mail*, 11 Dec. 2004, A30). Here, securing national identity is propped up by analogies to the family. One of the most frequently quoted examples (even in Canada) of this analogy is United States Senator Daniel Patrick Moynihan's (racist and heterosexist) report, *The Negro Family: The Case for National Action* (1965). It blames black single-headed female households for the demise of the family. The deterioration of the family is, in turn, identified as a threat to the nation that could lead to its demise.

There are, however, other approaches that make connections between the healthy family and the healthy nation. Mary Louise Adams (1997) draws on the work of Stephanie Coontz to argue that when the Canadian nation is viewed as threatened by the instability of 'the family', as was the case after World War II, the response is to create a return to a romantic version of a nuclear, heterosexual two-parent family of *Leave It To Beaver* fame. Such an idealized notion of the family in fact never existed and is, rather, a romantic and nostalgic creation of our imagination. The purpose for its invention, both Coontz and Adams agree, is detrimental to the health of our real, lived experience of family, since no one can possibly live up to this image. However, it is useful in regulating citizens to understand 'the family' in relation to a white, heterosexual, middle-class standard.

The ability to adhere to and become a 'normal' subject of state-sanctioned relationships is not something that just anyone can decide to do. Privileges accruing from notions of what is 'normal' are reserved for those who either come by it 'naturally', that is, those who are white, heterosexual, able-bodied, and middle-class, or those who are able to assimilate to some semblance of those standards (e.g., whitened ethnicity and/or upward class mobility). For sexual citizens, being legitimated through a respectable institution such as marriage provides access to full citizenship. But as noted previously, this access is limited and precarious at best (Berlant, 1997; MacDougall, 2000; Owen, 2001; Weston, 1991). To understand how the possibilities of fully participating as a citizen are shaped, one must be able *consistently* to see one's identity reflected in the public displays of national identity.

(Re)Presenting the Groom and Groom: Sexual Citizens Walk Down the Aisle

Images shown in relation to national debates that playfully acknowledge the existence of sexual diversity in Canada, for instance during lesbian and gay PRIDE events, are presented by the media as highly sexualized and not 'normal'. Images shown in relation to national debates that acknowledge the formal, legal claims to sexual citizenship, such as same-sex marriage, are portrayed quite differently. On national television news in Canada, same-sex couples that walk down the aisle are representative of a universal white, middle-class national identity, albeit not heterosexual. White, able-bodied male couples don wedding clothes appropriate for their gender, and white able-bodied female couples don clothes appropriate for a modern woman.

The representation of sexual minorities in line for benefits to citizenship, in order not to destabilize an imagined national identity (Anderson, 1994), draws on 'survival tactics' that emphasize the sameness in support of heterosexual notions of marriage and traditional family values. Such representations also de-emphasize difference, thereby persuading the viewing public to tolerate and include a particular diversity marked by non-heterosexuality. Thus, complex and multiple sexual identities embedded in sexual diversity are traded for a degree of white middle-class respectability that can be applied against non-normative sexuality. The purpose served is to be recognized as part of a national imaginary.

The capacity to be reflected, even in part, in national identity is how we come to know whether or not we belong in the nation. Or, as Ghassan Hage (2000) says, whether we are simply objects to be moved around at will, maybe fitting one time and not another. Fitting into a nation and being able to participate fully as a citizen involves more than having legal documents. Hage argues that there are many reasons why 'people's experience and how they are able to deploy their claims to national belonging in everyday life is not always equated with formal citizenship' (Hage, 2000: 50). Having 'papers' can be both 'proof' of belonging at the same time it can signal 'proof' of national non-belonging to the dominant culture. For instance, in Canada during World War II a kind of discriminatory 'culturalistic logic' was used to justify the internment of Canadian citizens from Japan (Oikawa, 2000). In many cases, official documents for internees were not worth the paper they were written on and their cherished rights as Canadian citizens disappeared overnight.

Minority social status leaves people vulnerable to be moved around at national will. Seeking to be included both legally and in the national imaginary, without identifying the historical, social, and political reasons why groups have been excluded, fails to dismantle the systems that exclude (Bannerji, 2000). Seeking to be included without attending to the specific historical context of legacies of cultural domination, **heterosexism**, and colonialism makes it possible to believe that changing laws changes the everyday experiences of minorities living in Canada. The following discussion traces some of the recent changes in law that have opened the door for (some) **sexual minorities** to stake claims to citizenship in Canada (see Box 10.2). These changes, however, do not establish a cure for heterosexism or for unstable relationships between the state and sexual citizens.

Current public events, such as PRIDE Week in Toronto, have evolved from political intent on the part of those left out of or on the fringes of the nation to become incorporated in the polity. Attending the once-a-year Sunday PRIDE parade was at one time a conscious political decision that carried with it the risk of beatings, loss of employment, and the consequences of being 'found out' by friend and families. Now, except for those who consciously mark their bodies radically enough to be picked up by the media as the subjects of marginal sexual diversity, PRIDE celebrations have become a normative space of (hetero)sexual diversity. Any political intent to confront **national heterosexism** has been lost to consumerism, photo opportunities, and heterosexist voyeurism

that promote inclusion and traditional family values—even if those families are lesbian or gay. Some have referred to this shift as being one from 'outlaw' to 'in-law'. An important question has been raised internal to struggles for LGBTIQ movements that seek to represent those who are differently and complexly positioned as sexual minorities. What is achieved when PRIDE celebrations swing away from confronting traditional heteronormative relationships to normalizing same-sex relationships? While the scope of this chapter makes it impossible to consider this problem in depth, it is important to note that such questions reflect complex day-to-day experiences of people whose lives are constrained by issues such as race, class, disability, partner abuse, poverty, and immigration. In other words, the 'normal' is not so normal after all.

Bill C-38: Confronting National Heterosexism?

This chapter was initially written as the drama unfolded about whether or not same-sex marriage would become the law in Canada. For a brief moment it looked as though Bill C-38 would become law in 2005, then it seemed to be highly improbable. Debates about whether or not same-sex marriages would be legally sanctioned became a linchpin (along with the scandal created by the misappropriation of public funds being uncovered in the Gomery Inquiry, a.k.a., 'the sponsorship scandal') in a contestation about whether or not the federal Liberals would fall in a no-confidence vote. It appeared that the public shame arising, on the one hand, from the public charge of moral corruption in the sponsorship scandal and, on the other, public shame arising from the challenge to national (hetero)sexuality would be the demise of the Liberals and Bill C-38. At the eleventh hour, Prime Minister Paul Martin and New Democrat Party leader Jack Layton were conjured up as queer bedfellows when the Liberals agreed to barter power and politics with the left, thus enabling then Prime Minister Martin to maintain a tenuous hold on Liberal power. In this confusion,

Box 10.2 Key Events in Sexual Minorities Movements in Canada, 1980s–2005

1981   Sexual minorities confront police as they raid the bathhouses in Toronto and over 300 people are arrested. This is sometimes referred to as Canada's 'Stonewall'.

1985   The Parliamentary Committee on Equality Rights recommends that the Canadian Human Rights Act be changed to make it illegal to discriminate based on sexual orientation.*

1996   Bill C-33 is passed. It adds 'sexual orientation' to the Canadian Human Rights Act.

2000   Bill C-23 is passed. It recognizes same-sex couples as common-law partners and provides equality in over 68 federal statutes. Marriage, however, remains the lawful union of one man and one woman to the exclusion of all others and is reserved for heterosexual couples.

2001   The Canadian census includes the category: common-law same-sex relationships.

2003   The Ontario Court of Appeal rules that effective immediately, same-sex couples should be entitled to marry; denying them wedding licences, the Court determines, would be unconstitutional. Michael Leshner and Michael Stark become first couple to marry.

2004   On 9 December the Supreme Court of Canada decides that the federal government, not the provinces, has the authority to legislate the definition of marriage.

2005   Seven provinces (Ontario, Quebec, British Columbia, Manitoba, Saskatchewan, Nova Scotia, and Newfoundland and Labrador) and one territory (Yukon) deliver court decisions that provide equal marriage rights to same-sex couples.

2005   Since the legalization of same-sex marriages in seven provinces and one territory, 3,000 same-sex weddings have been registered. It is announced that the 2006 census will include a category, 'same-sex married spouse'.

1 February 2005   Legislation to make same-sex marriage legal in Canada is introduced (Bill C-38).** The Act is cited as the Civil Marriage Act.

29 June 2005   Bill C-38 passes final reading in the House of Commons with a vote of 158 to 133.

19 July 2005   Bill C-38 passes in the Senate with a vote of 47–21 (3 abstentions).

20 July 2005   Bill C-38 receives royal assent and becomes the law of the land.

*The provinces and territories changed their human rights laws to include sexual orientation as follows: Quebec, 1977; Ontario, 1986; Manitoba, Yukon, 1987; Nova Scotia, 1991; British Columbia, New Brunswick, 1992; Saskatchewan, 1993; Newfoundland and Labrador, Alberta, and Prince Edward Island, 1998 (Canadian Lesbian and Gay Rights Organization Archives).

**This enactment extended the legal capacity for marriage for civil purposes to same-sex couples in order to reflect values of tolerance, respect, and equality consistent with the Canadian Charter of Rights and Freedoms. It also made consequential amendments to other Acts to ensure equal access for same-sex couples to the civil effects of marriage and divorce. All parliamentary publications can be found at: <www.parl.gc.ca>.

Martin's former move to strike a committee to hear public consultations on Bill C-38, which would have delayed its passing into law or even endangered it, was reversed and instead the bill was quickly passed into law on 20 July 2005.

At the same time that these events were unfolding, the leader of the right-wing Conservative Party, Stephen Harper, a large part of whose political base rested in the religious right and on traditional heterosexual family values, vowed, if the Liberals lost power in a no-confidence vote and the Conservatives were elected to government, that he would do all in his powers to bring down Bill C-38. Harper's aim was to keep the nation heterosexual: marriage would be limited to one man and one woman. Over 100 Canadian lawyers wrote an open letter opposing Harper's political views based on legal grounds (www.law.utoronto.ca/samesexletter.html, accessed 18 May 2005). While Harper was unsuccessful at this time in his attempt to prevent any challenge to the heterosexual nation, his position demonstrates the unstable relationship between the state and sexual citizens. Same-sex debates indeed have not dwindled with the passing of Bill C-38. In the January 2006 election the Conservatives and Harper won a minority government. In June 2006, Harper announced that he will reopen the debate by putting the question to Parliament in the fall with an open vote on same-sex marriage. The meaning is clear. Even when the disruption of the heterosexual nation is legal, those who are socially conservative continue to call for a return to traditional heterosexual family values.

As these events unfolded, it was a reminder of two things. First, rights-based claims from the margins are always tenuous. And second, while Graff's question—'How can same-sex marriage be barred?'—follows a compelling logic, it ignores the fierce opposition based on religious beliefs, an opposition that continues to be given space in public debates. Even when there is a clear commitment to keep church and state separate, once a social issue arises that generates strong moral opposition *and* is viewed as a threat to the moral fabric of national identity, religion becomes the

vocal gatekeeper. Controversy over Bill C-38 was no exception. Yet, unlike other religious debates that have opposed legalizing same-sex relationships in the past, the religious debate this time both rejected and supported same-sex marriage. The two following quotations express opposition to Bill C-38 based on a Biblical interpretation of one man + one woman = marriage.

We've never believed the State can issue or declare a right that people can be married. . . . [Homosexuality] is a choice of form of relationship people want to live in. They make their choice but they have no right to call that marriage.
—Brian Rushfeldt, executive director of Canada Family Action Coalition

Canada is a nation which recognizes at its core, the supremacy of God, the rule of law, and the right of the people to be heard and represented by the laws of the nation. Any attempt to legally impose a particular ideology by the state damages civic life, distorts political liberalism, undermines constitutional consensus and places communities holding different views in permanent tension with the law and with each other.
—Tristan Emmanuel, executive director of Equipping Christians for the Public-square Centre (www.canadianchristianity.com; accessed 24 Feb. 2006)

On 9 April 2005 thousands of people opposed to same-sex marriage gathered on the Parliament Hill lawn in Ottawa. This protest was sanctioned by Stephen Harper, then leader of the Conservative Party (and currently Prime Minister of Canada), who 'denounced the federal plan to legalize same-sex marriage, telling the crowd that a Tory government would bring in legislation defining marriage as the union of one man and one woman' (Canada Press on-line, 11 Apr. 2005). Those in opposition to Bill C-38 further argue that marriage is not and never has been considered a human right, while religion is.

One religious leader who supports same-sex marriage, Rabbi David Mivasair, disagrees with religious groups that insist marriage is not a human right. Mivasair interprets the Bible (Genesis) to mean that it is not good for a person to be alone and asserts that the criteria for a marriage relationship sanctioned by God is that the couple be loving, not abusive, and have a commitment to each other to be together for life (www.canadian christianity.com; accessed 24 Feb. 2006). He further argues that what we understand today of same-sex relationships is not what the Bible talks about as an 'abomination' because when it was written 'there wasn't a real understanding of [same-sex relationships]. The Bible talks about a very ugly, distorted form of sexuality.'

Rabbi Mivasair was among many religious leaders who participated in nationwide rallies on 10 April 2005 to support gay marriage. In Toronto, a statement of support was issued by the Religious Coalition for Equal Marriage Rights, a multi-faith coalition that stated it wants to dispel the myth that people of faith must be opposed to same-sex marriage (Canada Press on-line, 11 Apr. 2005). The multi-faith coalition includes representatives from liberal and traditional faith communities across Canada, including the United Church of Canada, the Canadian Unitarian Council, the Muslim Canadian Congress, the Canadian Friends Service Committee of the Religious Society of Friends (Quakers), the World Sikh Organization, Canadian Rabbis for Equal Marriage, Metropolitan Community Church, Ahavat Olam Synagogue (Vancouver,) Church of the Holy Trinity (Anglican) in Toronto, Apostolic Society of Franciscan Communities—Canada, Saint Padre Pio Congregational Catholic Community (Toronto), and liberal and progressive members of the Buddhist, Catholic, First Nations, Hindu, Mennonite, and Muslim communities (www.canadianchristianity.com).

Another statement in support of Bill C-38 is worth mentioning since today Muslims are often wrongly viewed only as conservative and always in opposition to the lesbian and gay community. It was made by a prominent, admittedly left-leaning, Toronto Muslim leader, Tarek Fatah of the Canadian Muslim Congress. Fatah contends that 'There's something fundamentally contradictory about invoking hate and bigotry while invoking religion' (Canada Press on-line, 11 Apr. 2005).

To fight for human rights is to claim a space in the citizenship body of the nation. Alex Munter of Canadians for Equal Marriage understands this well. Echoing the proliferation of statements made by legal and political authorities that acknowledged the pains the government took to ensure no one would be forced to perform the religious rites of same-sex marriage against their will, Munter states, 'The equal marriage bill is a win-win for Canada, it ends exclusion and it protects religious freedom and that's why it deserves to be passed. It's a question of citizenship, are lesbian and gay Canadians entitled to full citizenship without exception?' (Canada Press, 11 Apr. 2005).

To be sure, Canadians are ambivalent about changing the heterosexual underpinnings of national identity. On the one hand, Canada has a commitment to keep church and state separate and keep the state out of the bedrooms of the nation, in the famous phrase of Pierre Trudeau. On the other hand, the Canadian state turns to religious voices to sway the public. Examples of ambivalence about a full commitment to sexual citizenship are not hard to find. For instance, just before Bill C-38 came into law Canada's nationally distributed newspaper, the *Globe and Mail*, reported 'nearly 90 per cent of Canadians live in provinces or in the territory where same-sex marriage is already legal' (*Globe and Mail*, 15 Apr. 2005, Section A). In the same article it declared that, according to polling done by Angus Reid, the majority of Canadians (52 per cent) reject Bill C-38 (www.angus-reid.com/polls). This ambivalence can be framed as the same conundrum evoked in moral arguments that claim to hate the sin and love the sinner. It is an ambivalence that those of us who seek sexual citizenship must constantly be wary of. To trust rights based on seeking inclusion is always dangerous territory, for if efforts to be included fail, then the right to stand up and say 'I do' fails.

Data collected in 2003 by Professor Reginald Bibby of the Vanier Institute of the Family (www.vifamily.ca; accessed 13 Apr. 2005) further indicate the ambivalence inherent in confronting a heterosexual nation:

> About one in three Canadians currently expresses both approval and acceptance of homosexual acts, while 40 per cent say they neither approve of nor are willing to accept such behaviour. Although more than two-thirds of our respondents would be willing to accept that their child was gay, only one out of every four parents would approve. Some 25 per cent of parents have told us that they would neither approve of nor find acceptable their child's homosexuality.

In addition, 58 per cent of respondents in the Bibby study indicated that the traditional family arrangement is ideal—a married man and woman with at least one child. The findings of the Bibby study were reported in the *Globe and Mail* with the headline, 'Married With Children Preferred' along with a subheading stating: 'Study says even those who don't live in one still favour the traditional nuclear family' (6 Dec. 2004). No matter how much it may seem like our human rights laws reflect a nation that is tolerant of sexual diversity, prevailing traditional views about the healthy nation, and the citizens who live in it, continue to reflect normative notions of a white, middle-class, able-bodied heterosexual citizenship.

Conclusion

The legitimacy of formalizing same-sex relationships as marriage remains unstable, and this unstable rapprochement reveals the still insecure relationship between sexual minorities and citizenship. Previous to same-sex marriage becoming the law of the land in July 2005, it was adopted by seven provinces and one territory. Bill C-38 became a point of national interest, important enough to be deployed as a 'tool of shame' by a

right-wing party and a 'tool of negotiating power' by a left-wing party. It became the focus of the Liberal government's ability to maintain a healthy nation. The passing of Bill C-38 does show that lesbians and gays have made respectable gains in staking claims to sexual citizenship. It must be remembered, however, that confronting national heterosexuality, while seemingly successful at this point in Canada's history, has its limits.

This chapter has highlighted the limits of human rights claims to same-sex marriage when strategies aim to assimilate to normalized heterosexual notions of marriage and traditional family values rather than confront heterosexism. These limits shape the inclusion and exclusion of who is and is not in line for access to the benefits those rights offer. Whose relationships will the state legitimate and respect, even after death? More marginal sexual minorities are in the shadow of human rights claims made by white middle-class lesbians and gays. Recognizing a modern form of self-intelligibility as a sexual self does not secure a place in the national imaginary. There are always overlapping and contradictory national imaginaries and I have argued that historical, social, and political accounts indicate that some are hegemonic over others. That is, some national representations carry with them the weight of cultural, economic, and political dominance of certain groups.

Increased visibility of sexual minorities and changing laws make it impossible to ignore the fact that there have been significant changes in the social struggle to re-imagine family units. However, it would be foolish to be persuaded that Canada is past debating fundamental concerns such as: are heterosexual traditional marriage and relationships assumed to be morally superior to same-sex marriage and relationships? Questions as basic as whether the state has any business in the bedrooms of the nation are not passé. The paradox is best encapsulated by the fact that at the same time as the people living in Canada have access to state-sanctioned same-sex relationships, the majority of Canadians reject same-sex marriage legislation and still believe that the traditional heterosexual family with children is ideal. This reality will not change immediately.

I always ask students in the university classes I teach if there is any such thing as a nuclear family norm in Canada today. Most often the question is pushed back at me. 'No. Just look around.' Their answer is that the face of families has changed so drastically that there is no one norm. Backup for their beliefs arises from their view of marriage as a personal reflection of their own individual, moral, tolerant, and inclusive perspective. These views are articulated by students saying 'it doesn't matter what people do as long as they don't hurt anybody else', by their reference to television programming,[1] such as *Will & Grace*, *Queer Eye for the Straight Guy*, and *Queer as Folk*, that reflects more tolerant societal attitudes, and by their referring to same-sex human rights legislation as proof that Canada no longer views the traditional heterosexual nuclear family model as the only acceptable family unit.

In teaching, even before I launch into the argument that marriage is both private experience and public institution, I ask students if their relatives—parents, siblings, aunts, uncles, grandparents—accept same-sex relationships or marriage, or would be accepting if they were to go home and announce that they were involved in such a relationship. Their answers become more elaborate, qualified, and less assured. When I ask them to consider their response if a child of theirs announced that he or she was identified with any of the following sexual or gendered identities—lesbian, gay, bisexual, transgendered, transsexual, two-spirited, intersexed, or queer—they struggle much more as they examine the penalties that come with discrimination based on the differential

social positioning each of these identities carries. The ambivalences created by the disjuncture between same-sex marriage as a public institution and as a personal experience confuse the landscape of sexual citizenship. Same-sex couples can now say 'I do' in Canada. Yet what are the conditions placed on social belonging once the legal document of marriage is procured within its heavily coded frame of heterosexist presumptions?

There is danger in believing we have come far enough because we not only give up struggles that have not yet been won, but we also fail to recognize the limits placed on sexual minorities, not only in law, but in the ways in which the law is interpreted and practised as well. Ultimately, when we neglect to distinguish between inclusion and difference and ignore the effects that sexual difference creates, we fail to heed Berlant's caution to notice the resurgence in demarcating the normal/abnormal divide so important to maintaining a white, heterosexual, middle-class, and able-bodied nation. Even after the political struggle over same-sex marriage has ended, other battle lines will be drawn when public issues of legitimizing sexual diversity reappear in the media. The current public homophobic diatribes freely reported in the national media in response to the claims sexual minorities are making on the national landscape are not unlike those I have encountered in other research in the public setting of education (Fumia, 2003). These violent words do two things. First, they inform me of my insecure and marginal place, as a lesbian, in the national imaginary. And second, they tell me that political struggles to eradicate national heterosexism have most certainly not been achieved.

Note

1. While television programming is important to LGBTIQ history (see Gay and Lesbian Milestones in the Media at <http://religioustolerance.org/hom_medi.htm> for an overview of lesbians and gays on television and in film), often the roles are played by people who are straight and the script and plot reflect heterosexual presumptions about what it means to be lesbian or gay.

Study Questions

1. What does E.J. Graff mean when she asks: What is marriage for?
2. What does it mean to be legally declared a citizen yet not experience social citizenship?
3. What is the difference between common-law relationships and same-sex relationships?
4. Why is same-sex marriage so hotly contested?

Glossary

Heterosexism Rather than the term 'homophobia', which is suggestive of a fear (phobia), heterosexism aims to target the presumption of heterosexual norms as the main reason that sexual minorities are discriminated against.

Human rights claims Rights are entitlements to do something without interference from other people. Human rights belong to everyone by virtue of being human, although only some members of society have access to certain rights. When people contend that they are denied entitlements to rights they believe are owed to all humans, they fight for laws and policies to ensure they have access to them.

National heterosexism Western societies are steeped in normative notions that reflect their colonial histories of discovery and conquest (in Canada the history of English and French Christian white settlers is commonly understood). Thus the nation comes to be defined within norms, beliefs, and values that travelled from the homelands to the colony. One of these norms is heterosexuality, a term that defines the national norm and in so doing discriminates against non-heterosexuals.

Normalization A complex process by which concepts, social practices, identities, or ideas are assumed to be normal. This assumption of 'normal' is based on beliefs informed by moral discourses of right and wrong, rather than contextualized through specific political, cultural, and social histories that represent a wide array of values and beliefs.

Public intimacy We usually think of intimacy as belonging to the private sphere of interpersonal relationships. Lauren Berlant (1997) uses the term to mean that intimate sexual relations are very much the concern of the state. An example of public intimacy is reflected in the 1967 statement by Pierre Trudeau that 'there's no place for the state in the bedrooms of the nation.'

Sexual citizen Someone who is not identified, by herself or by others, as heterosexual and who may have documents that prove a legal status, yet nonetheless remains outside the social privileges accrued from social belonging (e.g., the ability to freely discuss one's relationship or to express affection in public). A sexual citizen can also be someone who demands to be included in the citizenship body as not heterosexual.

Sexual minorities People who identify on the basis of non-heterosexuality, including those who identify as lesbian, gay, bisexual, trans-identified, two-spirited, intersexed, or queer.

Social legitimation Although a social group may gain political legitimation from the state, through laws and policies, which can result in benefits such as lower taxes or increased mobility in society, social approval or legitimation may still be withheld. For example, while the Canadian state legally legitimates same-sex marriage, polls indicate that it is not socially legitimated by the majority of Canadians.

Survival tactics A term used by Berlant (1997), who contends that while we might question actions deployed by activists, we must understand the conditions under which people fight for their rights. For instance, it may be problematic for some sexual minorities to seek recognition through the institution of marriage since many sexual minorities do not gain from it and many do not want it. However, for some, recognition of same-sex marriage is emblematic of acceptance by the state, friends, and family—in short, it allows some to survive the penalties of non-recognition.

Whiteness A subordinate term is always defined in relation to its dominant counterpart. Identifying 'whiteness', usually the dominant, unmarked term that serves to subordinate racial terms, destabilizes the non-visible minority (i.e., those of European ancestry are the dominant One that defines all Others).

Further Readings

Adams, Mary Louise. 1997. *The Trouble with Normal: Postwar Youth and the Making of Heterosexuality*. Toronto: University of Toronto Press. Adams connects dominant views about what it is to be 'normal' with a time in history when, post-World War II, Canada was undergoing rapid social and economic changes. She grounds her discussions about 'the making of heterosexuality' in Toronto schools in theories of moral regulation, normalization, and governmentality.

Foucault, Michel. 1990. *The History of Sexuality*. New York: Vintage Books. This account of sexuality, and the identification of 'the homosexual' as a (sub)species of 'man', covers long and complex histories. One of the many arguments advanced by Foucault is that censorship of sexuality increases rather than decreases people's desire to discuss and practice it.

Graff, E.J. 2004. *What Is Marriage For? The Strange Social History of Our Most Intimate Institution*. Boston: Beacon Press, 2004. Graff argues that marriage in Western societies has changed so much over the years that it challenges us to think about its social purpose. Building on a history of marriage, she asserts that there is no longer a reason to deny same-sex couples the right to marry.

MacDougall, Brian. 2000. *Queer Judgments: Homosexuality, Expression, and the Courts in Canada*. Toronto: University of Toronto Press, 2000. This book documents human rights-based court challenges that contribute to the rich and diverse history of the struggle for recognition of same-sex relationships in Canada. Along with this history, MacDougall also provides thought-provoking and critical analysis of seeking sexual minority rights.

Websites

www.egale.ca
EGALE (Equal Rights for Gays and Lesbians Everywhere) seeks to advance equality and justice for lesbian, gay, bisexual, and trans-identified people and their families. It posts both current and archival materials about LGBT issues in Canada.

www.clga.ca
The Canadian Lesbian and Gay Archives, established in 1973, documents and preserves lesbian and gay history in Canada (and beyond). It offers public access to collected histories, personal records, photographic collections, moving images, posters, audiotapes, and artifacts.

http://samesexmarriage.ca
This website of the organization Equal Marriage for Same Sex Couples includes contemporary, historical, and legal information about same-sex marriages, as well as reporting about events in queer communities, for example, a photo documentary of the first same-sex wedding in Canada.

http://religioustolerance.org
This website of Ontario Consultants on Religious Tolerance discusses religious, moral, and political debates in Canada and elsewhere.

References

Adams, Mary Louise. 1997. *The Trouble with Normal: Postwar Youth and the Making of Heterosexuality*. Toronto: University of Toronto Press.

Anderson, B. 1994. *Imagined Communities*. London: Verso.

Arnup, Catherine. 1995. *Lesbian Parenting: Living with Pride and Prejudice*. Charlottetown: Gynergy Books.

Bannerji, Himani. 2000. *The Dark Side of the Nation: Essays on Multiculturalism, Nationalism and Gender*. Toronto: Canadian Scholars' Press.

Beauvoir, Simone de. 1989 [1949]. *The Second Sex*. New York: Vintage Books.

Berlant, Lauren. 1997. *The Queen of America Goes to Washington City: Essays on Sex and Citizenship*. Durham, NC: Duke University Press.

Boyd, Susan C. 1999. *Mothers and Illicit Drugs: Transcending the Myths*. Toronto: University of Toronto Press.

Brock, Deborah, ed. 2003. *Making Normal: Social Regulation in Canada*. Scarborough, Ont.: Thomson/Nelson.

Butler, Judith. 1990. *Gender Trouble: Feminism and the Subversion of Identity*. New York: Routledge.

Coontz, Stephanie. 1992. *The Way We Never Were: American Families and the Nostalgia Trap*. New York: Basic Books.

Cossman, Brenda. 1996. 'Same sex couples and the politics of family status', in Janine Brodie, ed., *Women and Canadian Public Policy*. Toronto: Harcourt Brace & Company, 223–53.

Duberman, Martin, Martha Vicinis, and George Chauncey. 1989. *Hidden from History: Reclaiming the Gay and Lesbian Past*. New York: Meridian.

Epstein, Rachel. 1998. 'Parent Night will never be the same: Lesbian families challenge the public school system', *Our Schools/Ourselves*: 91–119.

Eskridge, William N., Jr. 1997. 'A jurisprudence of "coming out": Religion, homosexuality, and collisions of liberty and equality in American public law', *Yale Law Journal* 106, 8: 2411–74.

Foucault, Michel. 1990. *The History of Sexuality*. New York: Vintage Books.

Fumia, Doreen. 1998. 'By any (m)other name: Once married mother lesbians', *Canadian Women's Studies Journal* 18, 1 and 2: 41–5.

———. 1999. 'Marginalized motherhood and the mother-lesbian subject', *Journal of the Association of Research on Motherhood* 1, 1: 86–98.

———. 2003. 'Competing for a Piece of the Pie: Equity Seeking and the Toronto District School Board in the 1990s', Ph.D. thesis, University of Toronto.

Gilman, Sander. 1992. 'Black bodies, white bodies: Toward an iconography of female sexuality in late nineteenth century art, medicines and literature', in J. Donald and A. Rattansi, eds, *'Race,' Culture and Difference*. London: Open University Press, 171–97.

Graff, E.J. 2004. *What Is Marriage For? The Strange Social History of Our Most Intimate Institution*. Boston: Beacon Press.

Grosz, Elizabeth. 1993. 'Bodies and knowledges: Feminism and the crisis of reason', in Linda Alcoff and Elizabeth Potter, eds, *Feminist Epistemologies*. New York: Routledge, 187–215.

Hage, Ghassan. 2000. *White Nation: Fantasies of White Supremacy in a Multicultural Society*. New York and London: Routledge.

Holloway, Wendy. 1993. 'Heterosexual sex: Power and desire for the other', in Bonnie Fox, ed., *Family Patterns/Gender Relations*. Toronto: Oxford University Press, 195–203.

hooks, bell. 1984. *Feminist Theory: From Margin to Center*. Boston: South End Press.

———. 1989. *Talking Back: Thinking Feminist, Thinking Black*. Boston: South End Press.

Katz, Jonathan. 1995. *The Invention of Heterosexuality*. New York: Dutton.

Khayatt, Didi Madiha. 1992. *Lesbian Teachers: An Invisible Presence*. New York: State University of New York Press.

Kinsman, Gary. 1983. 'The social construction of homosexual culture: Heterosexual hegemony and homosexual resistance', Ph.D. thesis, University of Toronto.

Lenskyj, Helen. 1990. 'Beyond plumbing and prevention: Feminist approaches to sex education', *Gender and Education* 2, 2: 217–30.

McCaskell, Tim. 1988. 'The bath raids and gay politics', in Frank Cunningham et al., eds, *Social Movements/ Social Change: The Politics and Practice of Organizing*. Toronto: Between the Lines, 169–88.

MacDougall, Brian. 2000. *Queer Judgments: Homosexuality, Expression, and the Courts in Canada*. Toronto: University of Toronto Press.

Mackey, E. 2002. *The House of Difference: Cultural Politics and National Identity in Canada*. Toronto: University of Toronto Press.

Moynihan, Daniel Patrick. 1965. *The Negro Family: The Case for National Action*. Washington: Department of Labour, Office of Planning and Policy Research.

Oikawa, Mona. 2000. 'Cartographies of violence: Women, memory and the "subjects" of the internment', *Canadian Journal of Law and Society* 15, 2: 39–70.

Owen, Michelle K. 2001. '"Family" as a site of contestation: Queering the normal or Normalizing the queer?', in Terry Goldie, ed., *In a Queer Country: Gay and Lesbian Studies in the Canadian Context*. Vancouver: Arsenal Pulp Press, 86–102.

Phelan, Shane. 2001. *Sexual Strangers: Gays, Lesbians and Dilemmas of Citizenship*. Philadelphia: Temple University Press.

Rich, Adrienne. 1993. 'Compulsory heterosexuality and the lesbian experience', in Henry Abelove et al., eds, *The Lesbian and Gay Studies Reader*. New York: Routledge, 227–54.

———. 1995. *Of Woman Born: Motherhood as Experience and Institution*. New York: Norton.

Richardson, Diane. 1998. 'Sexuality and citizenship', *Sociology* 32, 1: 83–100.

Ross, Becki. 1995. *The House That Jill Built: A Lesbian Nation in the Formation*. Toronto: University of Toronto Press.

Sedgwick, Eve. 1990. *The Epistemology of the Closet*. Berkeley: University of California Press.

Sharma, Nandita. 2000. 'Race, class, gender and the making of difference: The social organization of "migrant workers" in Canada', *Atlantis: A Women's Studies Journal* 24, 2 (Spring): 5–15.

Somerville, Siobhan B. 1997. 'Scientific racism and the invention of the homosexual body', in Roger N. Lancaster and Micaela di Leonoardo, eds, *The Gender Sexuality Reader: Culture, History, Political Economy*. New York: Routledge, 37–52.

Valverde, Mariana. 1993. 'Heterosexuality: Contested ground', in Bonnie Fox, ed., *Family Patterns/ Gender Relations*. Toronto: Oxford University Press, 189–94.

Weeks, Jeffery. 1991. *Against Nature: Essays on History, Sexuality and Identity*. London: Rivers Oram Press.

Weston, Kath. 1991. *Families We Choose: Lesbians, Gays, Kinship*. New York: Columbia University Press.

Wittig, Monique. 1993. 'One is not born a woman', in Henry Abelove et al., eds, *The Lesbian and Gay Studies Reader*. New York: Routledge, 103–9.

CHAPTER 11

Building Bridges: Aboriginal, Immigrant, and Visible Minority Families in the Twenty-First Century

J.S. Frideres

Learning Objectives

- To understand the social and economic position of immigrant, Aboriginal, and visible minority families in Canadian society.
- To identify the social structure and organization of different types of families.
- To learn about the challenges facing Aboriginal, immigrant, and visible minority youth.
- To find what people intermarry and why.
- To understand the role of gender in minority families.
- To discover patterns of conflict in minority families.

Introduction

Families are the framework of social life and prepare new members to participate in the social, spiritual, and economic aspects of their society. Through the experiences within the confines of the family all of us begin to take on a sense of who and what we are and what directions our lives will take. Through the family we become firmly rooted in time and place and, as such, families are the critical social unit in our society that mediates knowledge, cultural beliefs, and traditions from one generation to the next. However, families have evolved in structure and form and there is, contrary to popular belief, no single structure that represents the norm for society. Nevertheless, we are a nation of families.

Adding to the complexity of family structure is the increasing number of ethnic groups that make up Canada. As immigrants enter Canada, individuals are required to adapt to a new cultural environment that generates a high level of uncertainty

and stress. Immigrants must quickly learn different aspects of the host culture in order to manage their daily activities (Sharlin and Voin, 2001). Moreover, many immigrants left their home culture with different conceptions as to what a family is and the roles individuals play in the family, and thus they find Canadian culture very different. Adaptation to Canadian culture requires fundamental adjustments in the relationship between husband and wife, parents and children, adults and their elderly parents and even in-laws (Laaroussi, 2006). A primary source of conflict occurs between family members who hold traditional cultural values and those who may challenge and even reject these traditional values and who, consequently, may be more willing to accept Canadian egalitarian principles. In short, the values of the family are threatened, and the harmony and consensus in other areas of the family's core are at risk. Other sources of conflict within the family include downward social mobility, particularly that of the husband, and the increasing importance of the wife's economic contribution to the family. Family adjustment also is difficult for individuals whose language, customs, and values are different from those of mainstream Canadians. If individual family members are unable or unwilling to change or accept alternative values, conflict within the family may result (McAdoo, 1993).

Prior to immigrating to Canada, immigrants have experienced family life, and these experiences from their homeland have forged their core values and ideologies. These values and ideologies are shaped by their family, kinship ties, and social location in the community as well as by the values embedded in their home culture. However, immigrating can amputate long-standing social networks and secondary ties from the immigrant's relational world. Nevertheless, immigrants are resourceful, and many have developed 'fictive kin' to support their efforts to integrate and adapt to Canadian society. These fictive kin are family-type relationships not based on blood or marriage but rather on religion or close friendship ties. They substitute for actual kin linkages and constitute a type of **social capital** that facilitates their incorporation into the host society (Ebaugh and Curry, 2000).

For most immigrants, issues surrounding the family continue to be of concern when they settle in Canada. Through these family arrangements they provide one another with a variety of resources ranging from sponsorship to the necessities of daily life, e.g., job referrals, short-term and crisis financing, and child care. These social networks provide stability for families as well as play an important functional role for the individuals and their community. Older members of the family can provide social, economic, and psychological resources and support to others in the family that allows them to fulfill some of their traditional responsibilities. Younger members can contribute economically as well as play the role of 'broker' between cultures until integration is more complete. In the case of Aboriginal families, grandparents and other kin in the community were looked to for providing care and **socialization** of young children. However, over time these supportive networks have been severed and Aboriginal communities have found it difficult to provide families with social support.

The assumption of homogeneity within cultures or ethnic categories, which lead to comparisons among groups, must be tempered by careful and nuanced analysis in order to identify the subtleties of differences. As Walters et al. (2002) point out, in many respects living in a family is the same in all cultures. Relationships between members of the family are negotiated on a short- and long-term basis and most relationships within families are hierarchical. Typically, the female primarily carries out work in the home while supporting the family is the responsibility of both parents (even if the wife does not have employment outside the home), and

individuals and families change or develop in predictable ways over the life cycle. However, within these broad 'universals' there are important differences within and among groups. It will be our task to present the differences and similarities among the three categories of families (immigrant, visible minorities, Aboriginal) portrayed in this chapter.

The Diverse Canadian Family: Demographic Profile

The social and demographic attributes of people have direct and indirect implications for the study of the family. The availability of marriage partners, the age distribution of the group, and the number of children born to families are just some of the factors that are important in the study of the family. As such, a brief socio-demographic overview of each of the three groups is a necessary first step.

IMMIGRANTS

The ethnic mix of Canadian society continues to increase in diversity in terms of ethnicity, nationality, race, and religion. Early immigrants to Canada were from the United States, the United Kingdom, and Western Europe and nearly all were 'white' and held Judeo-Christian religious beliefs. Even with the massive immigration in the late nineteenth and early twentieth centuries, most of the immigrants to this country fit this profile because Canada's immigration policy prioritized immigrants from Europe. However, with the passage of new immigration rules in the 1960s, overt **discrimination** against non-white source countries was eliminated. As a result, immigrants from around the world have come to Canada to find a better life for themselves and their children. Over the past decade, over 2.2 million immigrants were admitted to Canada and today we find that one in 10 families in Canada is comprised of recent immigrants.

The source of immigrants also has shifted over time. Table 11.1 shows that before 1961 over 40 per cent of immigrants came from two source countries and over 80 per cent came from only 10 countries. However, by 2001, just over half of all

Table 11.1 Top 10 Countries of Birth for Immigrants to Canada, before 1961 and 1991–2001

Before 1961	1991–2001
UK (24.3%)	China (10.8%)
Italy (16.5%)	India (8.5%)
Germany (10.8%)	Philippines (6.7%)
Netherlands (8.9%)	Hong Kong (6.5%)
Poland (5.0%)	Sri Lanka (3.4%)
United States (3.9%)	Pakistan (3.2%)
Hungary (3.1%)	Taiwan (2.9%)
Ukraine (2.4%)	United States (2.8%)
Greece (2.3%)	Iran (2.6%)
China (1.8%)	Poland (2.4%)

SOURCES: Adapted from 2001 Census, Analysis Series, *Canada's Ethnocultural Portrait: The Changing Mosaic*, Catalogue no. 96F0030XIE2001008 (Ottawa: Statistics Canada), 39; J. Reitz, ed., *Host Societies and the Reception of Immigrants* (San Diego: University of California, 2003).

immigrants came from 10 countries, and only three countries—China, Poland, and the United States—were among the primary source countries for both periods (Informetrica Limited, 2001).

In regard to recognizing diversity, Canada officially adopted a **multiculturalism** policy in 1971 and the Multiculturalism Act was proclaimed in 1988. In 2001, the proportion of Canada's population born outside the country reached its highest level in 70 years, at 18.4 per cent. Canada's immigration policy is guided by three objectives: family reunification, development of a strong economy, and support for our international obligations and humanitarian goals with respect to refugees.

The age distribution of recent immigrants is very different from that of the Canadian-born population, with two-thirds of the immigrants of ages 15–44 and only 14 per cent under the age of 15. The proportion of women in the immigrant population is similar to that of the Canadian-born population. However, when comparing specific ethnic groups, there are wide variations. For example, among recent immigrants from the Philippines,

62 per cent are women. At the opposite end of the spectrum, immigrant women from Iraq (41 per cent) and Ethiopia (46 per cent) make up a smaller proportion of total immigration from those countries. These figures have implications for potential mate selection and the propensity for inter-ethnic marriages.

The number of children produced by Canadian women has varied over time but the overall trend has been towards significantly lower birth rates. However, for new immigrant women, the fertility rate in the past five years has been 3.1 children per woman, significantly higher than the rate of immigrant women who arrived 10 years ago, which is 1.5. This shows that fertility rates among immigrant women start to decline after they arrive in Canada and eventually reach those of women who were born in Canada. The fastest decline is among women from Southern Europe. While Asian women have shown a steep decline in the number of children they have, the number of children per woman is still much higher than the overall population—1.89 compared to 1.47 for native-born Canadian women. On the other hand, women from other countries, such as South Asia (2.5), Africa (2.4), and Central/West Asia and the Middle East (2.2), far exceed this rate.

Recent immigrants are similar to Canadian-born individuals in that most live in nuclear families with no relatives other than parent(s) and children. However, recent immigrants are still more likely to live in extended families. One reason may be cultural although a substantial portion of this may be a result of financial necessity. Recent immigrants are poorer than the Canadian-born and many elderly immigrants are 'sponsored' by their families. Under Canadian law, sponsored immigrants arriving in Canada are not eligible for government transfer payments or welfare benefits for up to 10 years after arrival. Consequently, many of them choose to live with their relatives or sponsors. Overall, the propensity for immigrants to live in households of three or more generations is about four times that of their Canadian-born counterparts. However, immigrants from different countries of origin vary significantly in this regard, e.g., 40 per cent of South Asians live in three-generation households compared to 2 per cent of Canadian-born.

VISIBLE MINORITIES

The term 'visible minorities' represents a subset of both native-born and immigrant Canadians. Under the Employment Equity Act (1986), the concept of 'visible minority' was created in law and is defined as 'persons, other than Aboriginal peoples, who are non-Caucasian in race or non-white in colour'.

A majority of recent immigrants are visible minorities and, as such, have contributed to the changing social landscape of Canadian society. During the period 1996–2001 the Canadian population grew by 3.9 per cent while the visible minority population grew by 25 per cent—73 per cent of all immigrants coming to Canada in the 1990s were members of visible minority groups. Over the past two decades, this population has increased substantially, reaching 13.4 per cent of the total population by 2001. Chinese are the largest visible minority group today and when combined with South Asians and blacks, they make up two-thirds of the visible minority population (see Table 11.2). The majority of the growth in the visible minority population within Canada is through immigration, e.g., Chinese, 75 per cent, and South Asian, 70 per cent, although for groups such as Japanese (35 per cent) and blacks (58 per cent), who have long histories in Canada, their

growth is based to greater extent on natural increase (i.e., they are more likely to be Canadian-born) and not so much on immigration. Today, the majority of visible minorities live in either Ontario or British Columbia. This new 'rainbow' population in Canada has led to new conceptions about how Canadians view themselves and how others are defined within our society (Pendakur, 2000).

Since the concept was created, it has taken on both legal and social significance, and visible minority status is now one of the four designations (women, disabled, visible minority, Aboriginal) that must be taken into consideration by government and the private sector in regard to employment practices such as hiring and promotions. The political justification for such a classification is that all these groups are seen to experience similar types of barriers to employment and other services.

Visible minorities have very high rates of living in households of three or more generations—compared to the Canadian-born, visible minorities are 20 times more likely to live in extended family units. In addition, because of this and their high poverty rates, they also tend to have the highest rates of crowding in housing units of any group with the exception of Aboriginal peoples.

ABORIGINAL PEOPLES

Aboriginal peoples, as identified in the Constitution Act, 1982 (section 35), are comprised of three separate groups: Indians (sometimes called First Nations), Métis, and Inuit. All of these groups have

Box 11.1 Visible Minorities in Canada

Visible minorities are defined by the Employment Equity Act as persons other than Aboriginal peoples who are non-Caucasian in race or non-white in colour. The following groups are included under this Act: Chinese, South Asians (e.g., East Indian, Pakistani, Punjabi, Sri Lankan), blacks (e.g., African, Haitian, Jamaican, Somali), Arab and West Asians (e.g., Egyptian, Iranian, Lebanese), Filipinos, Southeast Asians (e.g., Indonesians, Vietnamese, Cambodian), Latin Americans, Japanese, Koreans.

Table 11.2 Visible Minority Population by Age, 2001

	0–14	15–24	25–64	65 and older	Total
Black	195,120	110,615	313,900	32,580	652,215
South Asian	228,345	139,805	492,250	45,720	906,120
Chinese	195,255	157,730	574,600	101,810	1,029,395
Korean	19,525	21,110	55,445	4,585	100,665
Japanese	12,735	10,980	39,670	9,830	73,215
Southeast Asian	50,125	32,775	106,620	9,355	198,875
Filipino	68,795	44,485	177,005	18,295	308,580
Arab/West Asian	76,580	50,805	163,830	12,705	303,920
Latin American	48,450	38,550	122,630	7,240	216,870
Other*	47,275	27,785	88,695	8,925	172,680

*Includes visible minorities not included elsewhere and multiple visible minorities.
SOURCE: Adapted from Statistics Canada, at: <www.statcan.ca:80/english/Pgdb/demo50a.htm>; Citizenship and Immigration Canada, *Facts and Figures, 2001* (Ottawa: Public Works Canada); Ethnic Diversity Survey (Ottawa: Heritage Canada, 2002).

been subjected to a variety of policies and programs of the government since well before Confederation. For Indians, the Indian Act was first enacted in 1876 and brought together many pieces of legislation dating prior to Confederation that impacted Indian people. The Indian Act also created new powers for the federal government, e.g., the reserve system began with the Act and this complex and evolving control mechanism still exists. The Act affects Indians from birth to death and from bedroom to boardroom and its contents cover almost every kind of behaviour of Aboriginal peoples.

Today, over one million individuals identify themselves as Aboriginal (see Table 11.3) and account for just over 3 per cent of the total Canadian population. When compared to the numbers 20 years ago, this represents an increase of over 25 per cent. Such an increase is the result of decreased death rates, continued high birth rates, legal changes as to who can be a 'registered Indian', and more individuals willing to identify themselves as Aboriginal. There are differences among the three subgroups on a number of demographic and social factors, but overall this category remains remarkably homogeneous with regard to their marginal position in Canadian society.

The Aboriginal population is young, with nearly one-third of all Aboriginal people in Canada under the age of 14. The median age is 24.7 (compared to 37.7 for the general Canadian population), reflecting a fertility rate of well in excess of 3.4, which is over twice the national rate. The rate of natural increase for Aboriginals is about 20 per 1,000 people, while for the total Canadian population the rate is 5.1. At the same time, the death rate for Aboriginals is almost half of that for the general population—in part due to the higher average age of the general Canadian population. Nonetheless, life expectancy among Aboriginal people is about five years less, for both women and men, than for the total Canadian population, a result of relatively poor living conditions and high suicide rates among other factors.

Overall, the Aboriginal peoples of Canada occupy the lowest levels of education, occupation, labour force participation, and income. Moreover, their participation in almost every institutional order of Canadian society is marginal and they continue to struggle to maintain their culture and traditions (Frideres and Gadacz, 2005).

Table 11.3 Size and Growth of Aboriginal Ancestry and Aboriginal Identity Population, Canada, 1996–2001

	2001	1996	% Growth 1996–2001
Total Aboriginal ancestry	1,319,890	1,101,960	19.8
Total Aboriginal identity	976,305	799,010	22.2
Indian	608,850	529,040	15.1
Métis	292,310	204,115	43.2
Inuit	45,070	40,220	12.1
Multiple response	30,080	25,640	17.3

Sources: Adapted from 2001 Census, Analysis Series, *Aboriginal Peoples of Canada: A Demographic Profile* (Ottawa: Statistics Canada, Catalogue no. 96F0030XIE2001007), 20; J. Frideres and R. Gadacz, *Aboriginal People in Canada* (Toronto: Pearson Education, 2005).

Aboriginal people have a long history of their family organization and structure being under attack from the dominant society. For example, soon after the signing of the numbered treaties in the late nineteenth century, residential schools were established and young Aboriginal children were forced to attend and live apart from their families (immediate and extended). During this time, intense assimilation procedures were enforced, so that young people were not allowed to speak their native language at the schools and the cultural and spiritual practices of their people were banned, and many young Native people were exploited economically and/or sexually. Nearly three generations of Aboriginal people were subjected to programs that systematically destroyed the structure and functioning of Aboriginal families, climaxed by the 'Sixties Scoop' when thousands of children from dysfunctional (according to Euro-Canadian norms) Aboriginal families were removed from their homes and sent to distant foster homes and for adoption.

This short review of the three groups provides a 'snapshot' of their position in Canadian society.

It shows different histories, demographic profiles, and different strategies to deal with the new post-colonial efforts of the Canadian government. We now turn to specific issues that are germane to family and present a comparative assessment with regard to these issues. We begin with the issue of how family is linked to the structure and organization of Canada.

Socio-economic Location in Canadian Society

The socio-economic status of individuals has a great impact on the structure and functioning of the family. Those individuals who have a reasonable income can obtain adequate housing, provide social amenities for family members, achieve higher educational goals, and develop interpersonal skills. On the other hand, for those families who live in poverty, family quality of life is marginal in almost every dimension. These issues are important not only because they impact on the current family but have far-reaching implications for the children as they reach adulthood and create their own families.

In reviewing the three target groups included in this chapter, we find that for recent immigrants and Aboriginals the labour force participation rate is about 50 per cent. The unemployment rate for these two groups is about 20 per cent (triple the overall Canadian rate), although in some areas it may be as high as 60 per cent (Teelucksingh and Galabuzi, 2005). Thus, it is no surprise that about one-third of Aboriginals live in poverty. Visible minorities experience a median after-tax income gap of over 13 per cent compared to the overall Canadian income. Data show that the proportion of recent immigrants with family incomes below the poverty line rose to nearly 36 per cent by 2000 (Picot, 2004; Frenette and Morissette, 2003). Overall, recent immigrants have low-income rates 2.5 times those of Canadian-born residents (Pendakur, 2000; Li, 2001). In summary, only four out of 10 highly educated immigrants will find a job within one year that uses their skills, and the

Figure 11.1 Percentage of Native-born, Recent Immigrant, and Aboriginal Children Exposed to Risk Factors

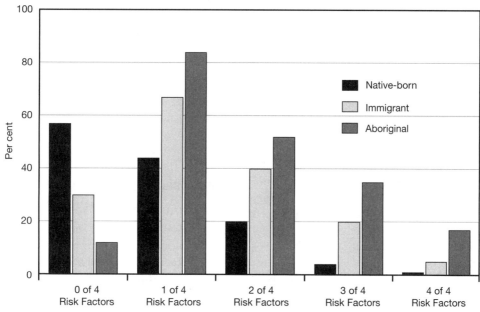

Risk Factors:
1. Having a mother who has not graduated from high school.
2. Living in economic deprivation.
3. Living in a linguistically isolated household.
4. Living in a one-parent family.

poverty rate for visible minority persons is between 40 and 50 per cent. Employed visible minority members earn about 79 cents for every dollar earned by a Canadian-born, non-visible person, and one in every five visible minority immigrants with a university education was in the poorest 20 per cent of Canadians.

Socio-economic factors in a child's family can have major impacts on the child's well-being and future development, including their future employment possibilities, income, and success in functioning in families of their own. Statistics Canada shows that in 2000, one-third of the children who had at least one parent immigrating to Canada in the past decade were living in poverty. As Figure 11.1 points out, children of different groups experience various risk factors at a differential rate.

On virtually every measure of hardship, children from immigrant, visible minority, and Aboriginal families fare less well than children in families of Canadian-born parents. Children of immigrants are more than four times as likely to live in crowded housing while Aboriginals are nearly 10 times more likely. Immigrant and Aboriginal children are more likely to have poorer health and to live in families that are worried about being able to afford food for their children.

RESIDENCE

Where families reside has important consequences for their employment, development of networks (social capital), and ability to draw on community support. The residential patterns of immigrants in Canada are clear. Over 80 per cent of all immigrants reside in British Columbia, Quebec, and Ontario, and within these provinces over 75 per cent live in Vancouver, Montreal, and Toronto. Immigrants cited two principal reasons for choosing major urban centres: a family member or close friend living in the area and the perception of greater employment opportunities. As a result of this pattern, immigrants now make up a significant percentage of the populations of major urban centres. Toronto is a good example, where over 50 per cent of the total population is foreign-born.

Today nearly half of the Aboriginal population live in urban areas, with more than one-quarter living in 10 metropolitan areas across Canada. This population is much more mobile than the non-Aboriginal population and statistics show that nearly one-quarter of the Aboriginal population move in the span of one year (compared to about 10 per cent for non-Aboriginals). This high level of mobility creates many challenges for Aboriginal families in the areas of education, social services, housing, and health care.

With the increase in the number of visible minorities comes the expansion of visible minority neighbourhoods in urban centres (Hou, 2004). While the level of concentration has not achieved the extent of segregation in many American cities, there has been a noticeable rise in ethnic concentrations over the past quarter-century. The number of ethnic/racial neighbourhoods that can be defined as 'concentrated' has increased from six in 1981 to nearly 300 in 2001. This 'overexposure' to members of their own group has both short- and long-term implications for selecting marriage partners, job opportunities, and socialization techniques (Hou and Picot, 2003). These neighbourhoods are generally poor, have recent immigrants, and contain a high proportion of visible minorities. However, these concentrations are not 'ghettos', such as are common to cities in Europe and the United States. Even when families can afford to leave, many remain because of their affiliation or development of networks/friendships within the community. For example, in Vancouver large concentrations of Chinese are a result of voluntary decisions to reside within the newly formed Chinese community. These concentrations create social networks in the neighbourhood, develop social capital, and produce high levels of **institutional completeness**.

These types of ethnic communities allow the groups to develop a hybrid type of identity and maintain social control mechanisms over family and community members. Second, these neighbourhoods can provide social capital for families and build dense networks to support their social and economic goals. Moreover, the emergence of ethnic enclaves transforms the physical and social attributes of the neighbourhood, challenges the way of life established by previous residents, and generates tension in local space.

Family Issues

FAMILY STRUCTURE AND ORGANIZATION

How are families arranged and structured? What are the roles each of the members of the family play? These are important considerations for researchers and policy-makers to consider when looking at families, perhaps especially those of marginal groups within society. For example, what is the parental arrangement in families? It is estimated that nearly half the children born since 1980 will spend at least part of their childhood with fewer than two parents in the home. And among those with two parents, frequently one is a step-parent. These are major changes in family structure over the past half-century. Since the 1950s, when less than 10 per cent of the children were living with only one parent, the rate has now doubled. For the period of 1985–99, nearly 20 per cent of the children born had 'unstated paternity' and over 30 per cent of the Aboriginal children born to Aboriginal women under 20 during this period had an unstated paternity (Clatworthy, 2003). Most European and Asian families follow a patrilineal kinship structure, meaning that kinship is traced through the father's line. On the other hand, for many Aboriginal groups a matrilineal (tracing kinship through the mother's line) kinship structure is the norm. However, over the years, the dominant Euro-Canadian group has sought to impose its own policies onto Aboriginal peoples. Nevertheless, people in many First Nation communities still recognize the importance and power of women and respect 'powerful women' who support the community.

According to data from the 2001 census, 80 per cent of Aboriginal families consist of husband and wife, compared to 86 per cent for non-Aboriginals and 87 per cent for immigrants. Just over 17 per cent of Aboriginal families were female lone-parent while 12 per cent of non-Aboriginal families were headed by female single parents. In terms of marital status, over half of the total Aboriginal population has never married, while over one-third are married. For non-Aboriginals, 38 per cent have never married and just less than half are married. The separation and divorce rates of Aboriginal and non-Aboriginal Canadians are comparable, although the percentage of Aboriginal people who are widowed is much lower than that for the non-Aboriginal population (3.2 per cent vs 7.5 per cent).

Birth and fertility rates for Aboriginal people are much higher than for the non-Aboriginal population (25 live births annually vs 12 per 1,000 women and 3.2 children per woman ages 15–45 vs 1.6). Young children (under the age of 14) of Aboriginal origin tend to have family structures different from those of non-Aboriginal Canadians. For example, 83 per cent of young children of non-Aboriginal origin live with two parents. However, in the case of Aboriginal peoples on reserves, less than two-thirds of young children resided in a two-parent context, and in an urban setting less than half lived in a two-parent home. Conversely, twice as many Aboriginal children lived with a lone parent as did non-Aboriginal children. In urban areas, over 5 per cent of young Aboriginal children lived away from their parents—compared to 0.6 per cent for non-Aboriginals. An increasing number of Aboriginal children are being placed under institutional care. For Aboriginals, there has been an increase from 4 to 6 per cent over the past decade, while for non-Aboriginals the institutional care rate is less than one per cent.

Has the organization of families changed over time? The organization of the Aboriginal family was profoundly changed during the twentieth century in two separate actions. First was the establishment of residential schools, where young Aboriginal children (estimated at 125,000) were forcibly removed from their families and sent to live in boarding schools. This removal was part of a larger 'assimilation policy' that the federal government supported, and its intent and result were to keep children from learning their traditional language or culture. This has led to the underdevelopment of parenting skills by several generations. The large-scale involvement of the provincial governments in social services for Aboriginal people in the 1960s and 1970s meant that Aboriginal children were once again forcibly removed from their families and sent to non-Aboriginal families. Steckley and Cummins (2001) show that, in 1964 alone, over one-third of the young Aboriginal population in BC were removed from Aboriginal homes.

In terms of household activity, Aboriginal and non-Aboriginal Canadians reveal similar patterns for such activities as housework, child care, and care to seniors. For example, nearly 80 per cent reported no care for seniors, nearly 50 per cent had no children under their care, and about 10 per cent did not involve themselves with household work. For those who did engage in these activities, again, the patterns for Aboriginal and non-Aboriginal were similar.

When immigrants come to Canada, they are faced with a decision as to how they will cope with their new social environment. They can try to preserve the culture of their origin, they can try to become 'Canadian' as quickly as possible, or they can try to develop a hybrid that incorporates both the 'old' and the 'new'. Regardless of the strategy they choose, immigrant families find ways to cope with the new norms, values, and behaviours of Canadian society. Rer-Strier (1996) identified three coping strategies employed by immigrants: unicultural, rapid assimilation, and bicultural. The first strategy involves the parents remaining as the primary socializing agents. The second strategy is for parents to withdraw as the chief socializing agent and defer to other agents in the new country, e.g., teachers, social service professionals. A third strategy involves encouraging the child to live in a bicultural world, whereby in the home and for family-related activities the parents are the chief socializing agents but outside the home the children are expected to conform to the culture of their new environment. Each strategy involves risks and benefits, although the traditional unicul-ture strategy has the highest risk for immigrant families because retaining one's 'home' culture while residing in Canada results in a lack of inte-gration and reduces social and economic opportu-nities (Brandon, 2004).

New forms of family have emerged over time. One new form of family—the 'split household'—is somewhat unique to Asians (particularly natives of Hong Kong, Singapore, South Korea, and Taiwan). The split-household family is organized according to time and space so that over time the family is distributed over a long dis-tance or wider expanse of space. This strategy of transnationalism is a process by which immi-grants build social networks that link the country of origin with their country of settlement. This new form of family is particularly suited to the entrepreneurial population of Asia. In this form of the family, parents 'parachute' into the Canadian residence when business allows (Pe-Pua et al., 1998; Waters, 2001).

Many new immigrants and Aboriginals live in households that are different from the standard nuclear organization typical of Canadian-born, non-visible minority families. Our research has identified three different types of extended family. First, in the 'upward extended' family parents or older relatives of the head of household also live in the household. In other families, 'downward extended' families occur where the children and/or grandchildren of the head of household live in the same residence. Finally, there are those extended households that are called 'horizontal extended' families, in which, for example, the sibling or close relatives (e.g., cousins) of the head of household live in the same house. Immigrant and refugee families use all three forms of extended families while Canadian-born families tend to use only the upward extended family structure.

FAMILY CONFLICT

Prior research has identified three conflict patterns in families. One pattern emerges when the husband takes on the instrumental role and the wife takes on the emotional role. Over time, if one becomes more isolated, lonely, or dependent on the other, the other person will see the second as 'ignorant and a burden' and this will lead to spousal conflict. A sec-ond scenario is when women get new opportuni-ties after marriage and this new situation, e.g., a job outside the home, gives her self-confidence to challenge the traditional power distribution and role allocation (Darvishpour, 2003). Alternatively, if the man experiences a status change that decreases his power in the family, he may try to maintain dominance by, among other things, referring to old norms and rules that legitimize relations as they were before. A third pattern of conflict arises between generations within a family. Generational conflicts are endemic to all families, regardless of their ethnicity. The general basis for such conflict is the fact that the children are growing up in a differ-ent social milieu from that in which their parents were raised. In the case of Canadian-born families, the discontinuity is minimal but nevertheless evi-dent. However, immigrants and Aboriginal people may find that they are living in a society that has many different cultural rules from those during their own childhoods, for example, the shift from an age-graded society in which respect for one's elders was a given to the contemporary twenty-first-century Canadian society that stresses individ-ual equality and glorifies youth. In addition, young immigrants and Aboriginals tend to assimilate rap-idly. As such, cultural gaps between the generations become more pronounced and visible. For exam-ple, some Hispanic traditions promote family co-operation that is the antithesis of Canadian values of individualism. Young immigrants are then faced with making a decision about living in a unicul-tural or bicultural world. At the same time, older immigrants have similar problems to deal with. In Vietnamese and Aboriginal cultures, for example, where elders are important family members, they may find themselves marginalized because they don't speak an official language and/or are not consulted on important family decisions.

Economic necessity for many immigrant and Aboriginal families requires that women and/or children enter the labour market. This tends to reverse the 'provider' role that may be expected in their homeland. Immigrant women and children are able to enter the labour market more quickly than men because of the availability of low-paying jobs for females/youth, and thus they become the principal breadwinners for the family. In turn, they take on the status and power that accompanies the 'provider' role. This inversion of roles, if not dealt with skilfully and with sensitivity, can create hostility and resentment within families and create stress and health problems, e.g., depression, violence, alcoholism, for all members of the family.

None of the above situations may create more than minor episodic bouts of conflict and can be resolved in a short time and with minimal resources. However, when conditions escalate or become chronic, the conflict may turn to physical or emotional abuse inflicted on family members by other family members.

Raj and Silverman (2002) found a paucity of research on the prevalence of intimate partner violence in immigrant communities but suggest community organizations feel that violence against immigrant women has reached 'epidemic proportions'. Qualitative studies by Macleod and Shin (1990), Husaini (2001), and Dosanjh, Deo, and Sidhu (1994) looked at family violence in the South Asian community and found that it was a serious concern. Moreover, they found that battered immigrant women are less likely than non-immigrant women to seek both informal and formal help for intimate partner violence. In cases where spouses have been sponsored, many experience what is called 'sponsorship debt' (Cote et al., 2001). Others have found that cultural barriers to receiving help often come from community/religious leaders who compel women to stay in abusive relationships and not to speak publicly (Smith, 2004). They fear that disclosure to outsiders promotes criticism of their culture or ethnicity. Finally, immigrant women are less likely to seek help due to isolation, lack of language skills, fear of deportation, lack of information with respect to available services, and lack of culturally sensitive or safe services available to them (Merali, 2006). Values implicit in existing mainstream services often clash with the values of many immigrant women. For example, services offered by mainstream service organizations focus on individual rights and empowerment while immigrant women come from a cultural system that believes the values of the community should be of central concern. Finally, mainstream service agencies have few connections with immigrant communities and thus are ineffective in dealing with ethnocultural community issues. On the other hand, Brownridge and Halli (2003) show that the pattern is not universal. They found that immigrant families from 'developed' nations have a lower prevalence of violence than Canadian-born families.

Elder care is one of the greatest challenges facing an aging Canadian population and families play an important role in providing this care. The demand for elder care services is currently being met through three different types of organizational arrangements. Informal support, the most common, consists of uncompensated services provided by family members and friends. Medical health-care workers funded by the state provide the second type of service. Finally, there is independent living within long-term care. Under this type of care, health-care workers provide services either in an institutional setting or at the aging individual's home. Immigrants and Aboriginal peoples are more likely to engage in informal support while native-born Canadians tend to use long-term care facilities. Immigrants and Aboriginals argue that there are few culturally sensitive care facilities and thus only they understand the cultural significance of certain types of care. This is changing as some cities are opening ethnic elder care facilities. All three of our target groups utilize state-funded health services when the aging relative requires major health care. Nevertheless, providing care for the elderly causes psychological, emotional, and economic burdens for families and thus places seniors at an increased risk of being victims of abuse. Like family assaults against children and youth, rates of elder abuse have escalated 35 per cent over the past five years.

Elder abuse by ethnicity is rarely mentioned in the literature on family, but an Ontario Native Women's Association study carried out in 1989 found that abuse of older adults was identified as a serious problem in some First Nation communities (Ontario Advisory Council on Senior Citizens, 1993). The Family Violence Initiative Report (2002) shows that Aboriginal women and men experience higher levels of spousal violence compared with non-Aboriginal peoples (20 per cent compared with 7 per cent). Aboriginal women were three times more likely than non-Aboriginal women to report having been assaulted by a current or former spouse and spousal homicide is more than eight times higher than for non-Aboriginal women. This study also found that nearly half of the children in these communities have been physically abused by a family member (La Rocque, 1994). While these data are for status Indians, there is every indication that domestic violence is just as problematic for other Aboriginal women.

Familial violence seems to increase when factors such as economic and social deprivation, alcohol and substance abuse, the intergenerational cycle of violence, and overcrowded and substandard housing are evident. For Aboriginal families, the breakdown of healthy family life is linked to residential school upbringing and the loss of traditional values, and family violence is a partial consequence of colonization, forced assimilation, and cultural genocide—the learned negative cumulative multi-generational actions as well as the behavioural patterns practised by the dominant group to weaken and destroy the harmony and well-being of the Aboriginal community.

An issue related to family violence is suicide. While this involves only one person, it is clear that in many cases family milieu is a major causal factor and the suicide has an impact on the rest of the family. For the general Canadian population, the suicide rate is just over 13 per 100,000 people. On the other hand, for immigrants, the rate is almost half the overall Canadian rate (7.9) while for Aboriginal peoples it is more than double (27 per 100,000). While suicides for the general population and for Aboriginals often involve youth, for immigrants it is highest in the older population. These differences may reflect different community and social support systems.

The Role of Gender in Family

The role of women in the family is an important issue that has short- and long-term consequences for all involved. However, men and women immigrants are treated differently as they settle into Canada, and how well each immigrant is able to integrate depends on a number of factors such as entry status (defined as being 'independent' or 'dependant'), involvement in the labour market, and the level of social networks (Boyd and Grieco, 2003). An independent immigrant has access to language-training programs, job-training programs, and a host of other programs that support **immigrant integration** into Canadian society; dependants have no access to these services. In Canada, most women enter as dependants and thus this places barriers for them to integrate, e.g., they do not have access to language programs. It also impedes their involvement in the labour market, leaves them subject to abuse with no avenue of escape, and limits access to resources. Canadian-born women are more likely to be active participants in the labour market than immigrant women. In addition, their participation does not involve taking on low-paying jobs and learning one of the official languages as well as specific technical or social skills.

Migration also can alter the status and relations between husband and wife and between parent and child. Participation in the labour market by females can bring about an increase in social mobility, economic independence, and relative autonomy. This in turn may change the distribution of power in the family, leading to greater authority and participation in household decision-making by family members that have not traditionally had that role. At the same time, labour force participation by women may increase the burden they must carry, e.g., caregiving and housework.

Previous research pictures immigrant women as passive victims of their culture (men being the oppressors) and their surroundings. While this stereotype is especially common for specific ethno-cultural groups, e.g., Muslim women, it is an over-simplified view that reflects the **ethnocentrism** of the researchers. First of all, Canadian women are equally oppressed in various ways. Second, it ignores the fact that women and men have their own centres of power and competence and the stereotypes underestimate the woman as an active agent. Third, this stereotype also ignores the fact that people from the same country or ethnocul-tural group do not constitute a homogeneous group and that within some immigrant families there are conditions for an equal relationship. Finally, this stereotype often leads to a focus on the problems of 'women' and seldom on their pos-sibilities and freedom of action. In general, immi-gration to Canada has led to a dramatic increase in power resources for many immigrant women.

In Aboriginal communities there has and con-tinues to be a gender split on a number of commu-nity issues. Men occupy major economic and political positions in the community even though they generally have less education and training than women. As Aboriginal women have taken on more and more responsibility on the reserves, legal and social issues have taken on a 'gender' perspec-tive. Over time these gendered views of the world have become public and major conflicts have pit-ted men against women.

YOUTH

Overall, young people from all ethnic groups engage in similar activities—watching television, listening to music, and spending time with their friends. At the same time, youth from the groups we have studied in this chapter have different experiences in growing up. For example, nearly three-quarters of immigrant youth are involved in

the labour force to support their families and they are expected to participate in family enterprises when required. This affects their ability to spend time on social and extracurricular activities as well as on academic pursuits. In other cases female youth will be treated very differently from their Canadian-born counterparts.

In 2001, nearly one-quarter of all Canadian chil-dren up to the age of 17 were recent immigrants or were born in Canada to immigrant parents. These youth face diverse linguistic, psychological, and socio-economic challenges in their lives. Their complex needs with respect to health, education, social services, and the justice system are linked and are played out in the home, at school, and in the community (Ngo and Schleiffer, 2005). They want to be accepted by the mainstream culture but at the same time they want to maintain and affirm their own personal identity. In their cultural adjust-ment, they often experience cognitive and emo-tional changes. In addition, immigrant youth have to struggle with the changing dynamics within their families. Issues such as a clash of cultures, chang-ing roles in the family, and changes in family rela-tionships have been identified as problematic for youth. For example, since young people tend to learn English/French and understand Canadian culture earlier than their parents, they become aware of Canadian expectations much earlier than their parents. Having some expertise in Canadian culture, they are expected to act as interpreters for their parents and this 'role reversal' has important impacts on family dynamics.

Linguistic and cultural barriers pose challenges for youth to understand school routines, educa-tional rights and responsibilities, and school cus-toms. Moreover, parents are unaware of social support services and their imagined role in the edu-cation process may differ from the expectations of the schools. Data from the National Longitudinal Survey of Children and Youth reveal that children of immigrant parents start school with low achieve-ment levels in reading, writing, and mathematics. However, their performance generally reaches or exceeds the performance of children of Canadian-born parents before they complete elementary school. Children whose mother tongue was neither English nor French have higher dropout rates as they move from elementary to middle school. Nevertheless, the academic performance of immigrant youth who achieve Grade 10 is equal to that of Canadian-born students.

Visible minority youth encounter barriers to full integration and thus remain within the confines of their group. In schools, there is a clear spatial division (segregation) of groups in a variety of contexts, such as in the cafeteria and in school activities. In addition, when outside the school and within the larger community, visible minority youth must confront other issues. For example, their detention rate by the police is seven times higher than for other Canadians, and incarceration rates for visible minorities are twice as high as for non-visible minorities (Derouin, 2004). Despite the official rhetoric and Canada's long history of receiving immigrants, young immigrants to the country often perceive a general non-acceptance of immigrants (or visible minorities) by people within their community and the media. They see systemic social barriers that face them and their parents in securing employment or in gaining recognition of their professional qualifications, which often results in **underemployment**.

INTERMARRIAGE/MIXED UNIONS

Most Canadians marry or live common law with persons of the same or similar ethnic or cultural group. However, this pattern is changing and since the 1960s the number of intermarriages has increased. Today over 3 per cent of all unions in Canada involve a visible minority and a non-visible minority (or a different visible minority) partner. While these absolute numbers are low, they represent a 55 per cent increase since 1981 and our overall intermarriage rate is one of the highest in the world, which perhaps is not surprising when we consider that a constitutionally recognized 'people', the Métis, are the offspring of unions between Euro-Canadian colonizers and Aboriginal peoples. Of mixed unions in Canada, just over half were

non-visible minority men and visible minority women. The actual rate of intermarriage varies by ethnic group. Japanese have the highest rate of intermarriage with 70 per cent marrying outside their ethnic community, followed by Latin Americans, 45 per cent, and blacks, 43 per cent. At the other end of the scale, South Asians have the lowest rate of mixed unions (13 per cent), followed by Chinese (16 per cent) and Koreans (18 per cent). In terms of raw numbers, the most common union was between blacks and non-visible minorities followed by Chinese and non-visible minorities. (Note that according to Statistics Canada definitions, Aboriginal Canadians are not considered to be a visible minority and therefore are not included in these and the following statistical data.)

Another form of intermarriage focuses on the native/foreign-born status of the individual spouses. Over half of marriages involving immigrants reveal that both partners are recent immigrants, 13 per cent consist of one recent immigrant and one earlier immigrant, and in 16 per cent one recent immigrant and one Canadian-born spouse are joined. On the other hand, 40 per cent of immigrants who came to Canada prior to 1981 are married to a Canadian-born spouse. Today, 7 per cent of foreign-born couples are mixed racial unions, while only 2 per cent of Canadian-born couples are mixed. Canadian-born visible minority couples are more likely to be a mixed union than with the same visible minority. However, the longer foreign-born visible minorities are in Canada, the more likely they are to be in a mixed union. We also find that no matter which group we compare, mixed unions are much more likely to be common law rather than formal marriages.

There are a number of reasons for the increase in intermarriages. First, the social and geographical mobility of people means more opportunity to meet people from different backgrounds. Second, because of the increased diversity in Canada, people have greater opportunities in school, work, and other social places to meet individuals from diverse backgrounds. Third, with the increasing numbers of immigrants from across the world, residents have a larger pool to draw upon for potential marriage partners. In the case of Aboriginal people, females tend to move from rural to urban settings with their children and enter the labour force, thereby increasing their chances of bonding with non-Aboriginal persons. Fourth, a multicultural society such as Canada has reduced the level of prejudice, discrimination, and social distance of immigrants, visible minorities, and Aboriginals in Canada.

While a majority (86 per cent) of Canadians have not experienced discrimination, well over one-third of visible minorities have encountered discrimination in Canada. Nevertheless, Canadians demonstrate a growing openness to other cultures. Still, many in Canadian society would not feel comfortable if their son or daughter married someone from certain other groups. For example, two-thirds of Canadians would feel very comfortable if their child married a Euro-Canadian while only 52–3 per cent would feel that way if their child married a black or Chinese and 37 per cent if they married a Muslim. These factors suggest that 'race' is not the sole factor involved. There are significant generational differences in views on mixed unions. While one-quarter of Canadians between the ages of 18 and 29 expressed some discomfort with marriage to Muslims, this figure increases to over 50 per cent for those over the age of 60. In the case of Chinese, 20 per cent of those over 60 felt 'uncomfortable' if their child married one whereas less than 10 per cent of those in the 18–29 group responded that way (Jedwab, 2004).

Traditional perspectives view intermarriage as more difficult, unstable, and conflictual than marriages within one's own culture. The assumption is that intermarriage is a 'stressor' and that exposure to stress undermines marital adjustment. However, the choice of intermarriage and the subsequent success of that marriage depends on several factors. For example, intermarriage couples are more flexible and resourceful in dealing with individual differences, they have dealt with family objections, and finally, in practically all cases they have married for 'love', which is associated with greater marital stability. Nevertheless, major social contextual factors are associated with intermarriage success. The level of prejudice and community acceptance, the availability of same-ethnic/race marital partners, and the structure of personal social networks are the most important factors. Openness to marriage with those from other communities is considered a measure of acceptance of diversity.

Conclusion

The easing of divorce law and other social changes in Canadian society have brought about a major shift in how marriage and the family are viewed. In addition, changes in immigration policy have opened the door to immigrants from around the world and created a racial, ethnic, and religious diversity in our society. This diversity has led to different organizations of family as well as to various processes of socialization. Communities and schools have been overwhelmed by this diversity and only recently are developing strategies for integrating families from diverse backgrounds. Over time more Aboriginal people have moved off reserves and now are a major force in the urban centres. In all these cases, families have had to adapt and integrate into Canadian society. As such, parents still interpret the world to their children and in turn the children learn how to cope with the dynamics of integration and adaptation to Canadian culture. Relatives and kinship relations (real or fictive) form networks of social and economic care and interdependence. In some cases these systems span three or four generations. At the same time, the nature and structure of communities provide more or less support for families. Institutions such as health and social services and the court system also are trying to adapt to incorporate Canada's growing diversity while maintaining equality and justice.

Finally, the backgrounds (human capital) of parent(s) are important in establishing the level of functionality for families. For example, immigrant families with high education attainment and secure jobs, and who are not visible minorities, find the adjustment less problematic than those without this human capital. Nevertheless, families develop the structure of their children's basic values, and this schema is part of a group's 'culture'. As such, it becomes the basis by which family and individual experiences are processed and evaluated. It is, in short, a world view that serves as a framework for evaluating experiences and gives stability and order to family life. Unfortunately, these structures do not converge across cultural groups and allow all to apply the same schema to each of life's challenges.

Study Questions

1. Compare the social attributes of the three groups examined in this chapter with the general Canadian population.
2. How do families differ among the three groups under consideration?
3. How does the socio-economic status of a family impact its role and function?
4. How does domestic violence impact a family?
5. Why do individuals engage in mixed unions?

Glossary

Discrimination Negative or positive behaviour towards a person based on attitudes held towards the group to which that person belongs.

Ethnocentrism Bias or preference for one's own way of life or culture, as reflected in one's thinking and actions.

Immigrant integration The extent to which immigrants are able to participate in the social, economic, and political structure of the host country to which they moved.

Institutional completeness The development of many institutions, e.g., banking, shopping, education, religion, to meet the needs of members of a particular ethnic group.

Multiculturalism A policy that Canada adopted in 1971 to support the cultural development of ethnocultural groups and to help members of ethnocultural groups overcome barriers to full participation in Canadian society.

Social capital The social networks and trust that allow for community members to co-ordinate their activities for mutual benefit.

Socialization The process by which individuals learn the norms and mores of a society.

Underemployment Inability to obtain a job commensurate with one's education/training qualifications.

Further Readings

Baker, M., ed. 1996. *Families: Changing Trends in Canada.* Toronto: McGraw-Hill Ryerson. This volume looks at family organization and structure over the past 100 years. Individual contributors to the book look at changes in a variety of dimensions of the family.

Eichler, M. 1997. *Family Shifts: Families, Policies, and Gender Equality.* Toronto: Oxford University Press. The author analyzes reproductive technology and how the Canadian family has changed over time, and demonstrates how shifts in government policy have reflected and led this change.

Frideres, J., and R. Gadacz. 2005. *Aboriginal People in Canada,* 7th edn. Toronto: Prentice-Hall Canada. Provides a comprehensive assessment of both the history and current status of Aboriginal people in Canadian society, with 'facts and figures' on a number of topics, e.g., health, language, crime, and demography.

Halli, S., F. Trovata, and L. Driedger, eds. 1991. *Ethnic Demography: Canadian Immigrant Racial and Cultural Variations.* Ottawa: Carleton University Press. This volume, from an interdisciplinary perspective, addresses a number of issues confronting immigrant families as they attempt to adapt and integrate into Canadian society.

Websites

www.statcan.ca/start.html
The Statistics Canada website provides information on Canada's people, economy, and government. Up-to-date information on families is available and new publications on the topic are presented. The site also includes official Canadian census data on families.

www.hrsdc.gc.ca/en/home.shtml
Human Resources and Skills Development deals with human capital issues and how people obtain skills in Canada. The focus is on labour programs for families as well as homelessness and youth programs. The department provides information on workplace activities for Canadians and commissioned reports can be accessed here.

www.metropolis.net
The Canadian government's Metropolis Project has established five regional centres focusing on immigration and integration of immigrants, including families, into Canadian society. Each centre has an extensive archive identifying research papers.

www.ainc-inac.gc.ca/index_e.html
Historical, statistical, and legal aspects of Aboriginal people are part of this federal government website.

References

Boyd, M., and E. Grieco. 2003. 'Women and migration: Incorporating gender into international migration theory', unpublished paper.

Brandon, P. 2004. 'The child care arrangements of preschool-age children in immigrant families in the United States', *International Migration* 42, 1: 65–88.

Brownridge, D., and S. Halli. 2003. 'Double advantage? Violence against Canadian migrant women from developed nations', *International Migration* 41, 1: 29–46.

Clatworthy, S. 2003. *Factors Contributing to Unstated Paternity*. Ottawa: Strategic Research and Analysis Directorate, Indian and Northern Affairs Canada.

Cote, A., M. Kerisit, and M. Cote. 2001. *Sponsorship for Better or for Worse: The Impact of Sponsorship on the Equality Rights of Immigrant Women*. Ottawa: Status of Women Canada.

Darvishpour, M. 2003. 'Immigrant women challenge the role of men: How the changing power relationship within Iranian families in Sweden intensifies family conflicts after immigration', *Journal of Comparative Family Studies* 33, 2: 271–96.

Derouin, J. 2004. 'Asians and multiculturalism in Canada's three major cities', in C. Andrews, ed., *Our Diverse Cities* no. 1 (Spring): 58–62.

Dosanjh, R., S. Deo, and S. Sidhu. 1994. *Spousal Abuse in the South Asian Community*. Vancouver, mimeo.

Ebaugh, H., and M. Curry. 2000. 'Fictive kin as social capital in new immigrant communities',

Sociological Perspectives 43, 2: 189–209.

Frenette, M., and R. Morissette. 2003. *Will They Ever Converge? Earnings of Immigrant and Canadian-born Workers over the Last Two Decades*. Ottawa: Statistics Canada Analytical Studies Research Paper Series.

Frideres, J., and R. Gadacz. 2005. *Aboriginal People in Canada*, 7th edn. Toronto: Prentice-Hall Canada.

Health Canada. 2002. *The Family Violence Initiative: Five-Year Report*. Ottawa: National Clearinghouse on Family Violence.

Hou, F. 2004. *Recent Immigration and the Formation of Visible Minority Neighbourhoods in Canada's Large Cities*. Ottawa: Statistics Canada.

——— and G. Picot. 2003. *Visible Minority Neighbourhood Enclaves and Labour Market Outcomes of Immigrants*. Ottawa: Statistics Canada.

Husaini, Z. 2001. *Cultural Dilemma and a Plea for Justice: Voices of Canadian Ethnic Women*. Edmonton: Intercultural Action Committee for the Advancement of Women.

Informetrica Limited. 2001. *Canada's Recent Immigrants*. Ottawa: Citizenship and Immigration Canada.

Jedwab, J. 2004. 'Diversity of marriage: Canadian opinion on cross-cultural marriage', unpublished paper.

Laaroussi, M. 2006. 'Le nous familial vecteur d'insertion pour les familles immigrantes', *Canadian Themes* (Spring): 72–5.

LaRocque, E. 1994. *Violence in Aboriginal Communities*. Ottawa: Royal Commission on Aboriginal Peoples.

Li, P. 2001. 'The market worth of immigrants' educational credentials', *Canadian Public Policy* 27, 1: 23–38.

McAdoo, H., ed. 1993. *Family Ethnicity*. London: Sage.

Merali, N. 2006. 'South Asian immigration to Canada through arranged marriages', *Canadian Issues* (Spring): 38–41.

Ngo, H.V., and B. Shleifer. 2005. 'Immigrant children and youth in focus', *Canadian Issues* (Spring): 29–33.

Ontario Advisory Council on Senior Citizens. 1993. *Denied Too Long: The Needs and Concerns of Seniors Living in First Nation Communities in Ontario*. Toronto.

Pendakur, R. 2000. *Immigrants and the Labour Force*. Montreal and Kingston: McGill-Queen's University Press.

Pe-Pua, R., et al. 1998. 'Astronaut families and parachute children: Hong Kong immigrants in Australia', in E. Sinn, ed., *The Last Half Century of Chinese Overseas*. Hong Kong, 279–97.

Picot, G. 2004. *Deteriorating Economic Welfare of Immigrants and Possible Causes*. Ottawa: Statistics Canada.

Raj, A., and J. Silverman. 2002. 'Violence against immigrant women', *Violence Against Women* 8, 3: 367–98.

Reitz, J. 2001. 'Immigrant success in the knowledge economy: Institutional changes and the immigrant experience in Canada, 1970–1995', *Journal of Social Issues* 57: 579–613.

Rer-Stier, D. 1996. 'Coping strategies of immigrant parents: Directions for family therapy', *Family Process* 35: 363–76.

Sharlin, S., and V. Moin. 2001. 'New Immigrants' perception of family life in origin and host cultures', *Journal of Comparative Family Studies* 32, 3: 405–18.

Smith, E. 2004. *Nowhere to Turn? Responding to Partner Violence against Immigrant and Visible Minority Women*. Ottawa: Canadian Council on Social Development.

Steckley, J., and B. Cummins. 2001. *Full Circle: Canada's First Nations*. Toronto: Prentice-Hall.

Teelucksingh, C., and G. Galabuzi. 2005. *Working Precariously: The Impact of Race and Immigrant Status on Employment Opportunities and Outcomes in Canada*. Ottawa: Canadian Race Relations Foundation.

Walters, L., W. Warzywoda-Krusznska, and T. Gurko. 2002. 'Cross-cultural studies of families: Hidden differences', *Journal of Comparative Family Studies* 33, 3: 433–50.

Waters, J. 2001. 'Migration strategies and transnational families: Vancouver satellite kids', RIMM Working Paper, No. 01–10, Vancouver.

CHAPTER 12

Lack of Support: Canadian Families and Disabilities

Michelle Owen

Learning Objectives

- To be able to distinguish between the medical and social constructionist models of disability.
- To understand the impact disability has on Canadian families.
- To recognize the role gender plays in the lives of people with disabilities.
- To describe the relationship between poverty and disability.
- To identify the factors that put people with disabilities at increased risk of abuse.

Introduction

> Too many Canadian children and families face inordinate difficulties because they live with the stresses, the acquired poverty, the health issues, the exclusion and the other markers of disability, even though these issues are becoming more widely recognized in Canada. (Roeher Institute, 2000b: vii)

Disability affects many Canadians and their families. Some 3.6 million people (12.4 per cent of the 2001 census population, or one in eight) have disabilities (Cossette and Duclos, 2002), and approximately 11 million people (36 per cent) without disabilities have a family member with disabilities (Environics Research Group, 2004; see Figure 12.1). These include 2.6 million people whose parents have disabilities, 1.3 million people whose children have disabilities, and half a million people whose spouses/partners have disabilities (Rietschlin, 2005). In addition, 2.8 million adult Canadians (12 per cent of the 1996 population)

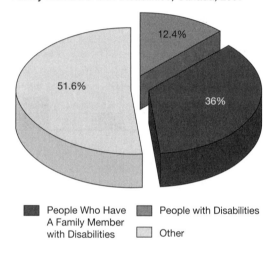

Figure 12.1 People with Disabilities and People with Family Members with Disabilities, Canada, 2001

12.4%

51.6%

36%

People Who Have A Family Member with Disabilities

People with Disabilities

Other

provide some support to a family member with disabilities (Government of Canada, 2004).

We are an aging society, and rates of disability increase with age. In this sense, all people without disabilities can be considered TABs (temporarily able-bodied). While 10 per cent of working-age adults (ages 15–64) report having a disability, seniors have a rate four times higher: 'More than three in ten younger seniors (aged 65 to 74) have disabilities, as do more than half of older seniors (75 and over)' (Government of Canada, 2004: 9).

Canada has one of the highest life expectancies in the world, and women live longer than men in Canada (82.2 years versus 77.1) and are thus more apt to experience disabilities (14.7 per cent versus 13.1 per cent) (Des Meules et al., 2003). According to the 2001 Participation and Activity

Figure 12.2 Rates of Disability in Canada, 2001

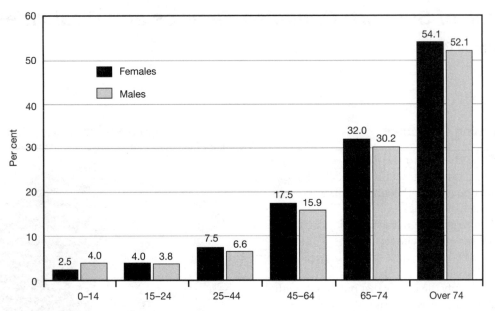

SOURCE: Statistics Canada (2002a).

Limitation Survey (PALS), 13.3 per cent of females in Canada have disabilities, compared to just 11.5 per cent of males (Statistics Canada, 2002a). Figure 12.2 shows the rates of disability for males and females in Canada. Furthermore, women with disabilities have lower incomes than men with disabilities and have a greater likelihood of being recipients of social support (Health Canada and Women's Health Bureau, 1999).

Women and girls with disabilities are oppressed by sexism and **ableism** (and in some cases racism, classism, homophobia, etc.). Fawcett (1996: 151) writes:

> Compared to their male counterparts, women with disabilities have lower rates of participation in the labour force, higher rates of unemployment when they are in the labour force, lower employment earnings, less access to the more generous income support programs, and higher rates of poverty overall.

Women with disabilities are also more marginalized than women without disabilities, and Aboriginal women with disabilities face 'triple jeopardy' (Demas, 1993a: 89). Disability compounds the risk of lone parenthood and violence for women (Fawcett, 1996), as well as **familialism** or the oppression of women in the nuclear family (Blackford, 1999).

Defining Disability

There are no easy definitions of 'disability', and the terminology used in disability activism and studies has been hotly debated. Defining words is a political act, as feminist and critical race theorists have struggled to highlight. Some people use a wheelchair or a cane and are noticeably disabled, while others have chronic illnesses or mental health issues that are not so readily apparent. These are sometimes referred to as **visible and invisible disabilities**, a distinction that of course only makes sense if one is sighted. Some disabilities are permanent (paraplegia), while others are temporary (broken limbs) or they come and go (relapsing/remitting multiple sclerosis). Who is disabled and what counts as disability is constantly changing.

The Office for Disability Issues (2001: 42) lists four distinct ways of defining disability:

> The *biomedical perspective* sees disability as a disease, disorder, medical condition or biological 'abnormality' within the individual. The *functional perspective* understands disability as a restriction in ability to perform certain standard tasks in a way considered 'normal'. The *social/environmental perspective* presents disability as the result of barriers in the social environment that prevent persons with disabilities from participating fully in community, work and learning. Finally, the *human rights perspective* focuses on respect for human dignity and on protection against discrimination and exclusionary practices in the private and public spheres.

The 2001 **Participation and Activity Limitation Survey (PALS)** considered people to have a disability if they reported a physical or mental condition or a health problem that restricted the ability to perform activities that are normal for their age in Canadian society (Government of Canada, 2004). A national post-censal survey on people with disabilities, PALS included information on children (aged 14 and under) and adults (aged 15 and over) who had a disability according to the above definition (Office for Disability Issues, 2001).

At present, PALS is the most up-to-date resource on disability in Canada. It is important to note, however, that the data from PALS exclude persons living in institutions, on First Nations reserves, and in the three northern territories. This means that disability among Aboriginal people, with a rate 1.5 times higher than that of non-Aboriginal Canadians (Government of Canada, 2004), is not fully explored.

The federal government acknowledges that the concept of disability is always shifting and thus 'defining disability is not an easy task' (Government of Canada, 2002: 10). Although national survey data rely on self-identification for a broader range of individuals, much like many community-based organizations and activists, benefits and disability-oriented programs use a far more limiting definition. The Charter of Rights and Freedoms does not unequivocally define disability, although it does specifically prohibit discrimination against persons with physical and/or mental disabilities.

Whenever a definition is not explicitly given by a piece of legislation, it is up to the courts to determine scope and limitations. For example, a 2001 Quebec Supreme Court decision was that 'various ailments such as congenital physical malformations, asthma, speech impediments, obesity, acne and, more recently, being HIV positive, constitute grounds of discrimination' (Office for Disability Issues, 2003: 14–15). The focus of this ruling is on how society treats (or mistreats) people with non-conformist bodies, which is an example of social model theorizing.

THE SOCIAL MODEL OF DISABILITY

The **social model of disability** can be understood as 'the relationship between a person with impairment and the environment, including attitudes, beliefs, climate, architecture, systems and services' (Hurst, 2005: 65). It is useful to distinguish between two social models: the materialist or radical, and the idealist or rights interpretation (Sheldon, 2005: 118–19). According to Alison Sheldon, while a radical social model focuses on capitalism as 'the root cause of disablement', rights-based analyses lead to 'short-term policy reforms and sticking-plaster solutions' (ibid., 118, 121). From her perspective, the impact of globalization must be taken into account as we theorize disability.

The Union of Physically Impaired Against Segregation (UPIAS) (1976) in Britain was perhaps the first to make an unambiguous distinction between personalized physical **impairments** and the social experience of disability: 'In our view it is society which disables physically impaired people. Disability is something imposed on top of our impairments by the way we are unnecessarily isolated and excluded from full participation in society. Disabled people are therefore an oppressed group in society' (cited in Oliver, 1996: 33).

Hence, since the 1970s, disability activists and theorists have put forth a social constructionist model of disability that identifies barriers as being systemically rather than biologically based (Crowe, 1996). As Jenny Morris (2001: 1) writes:

> Disability is the disadvantage or restriction of activity caused by a society which takes little or no account of people who have impairments and thus excludes them from mainstream activity (therefore, disability, like racism or sexism, is discrimination and social oppression).

Thus, the social model of disability has much in common with analyses that theorize race and gender as being social constructions and not as biological or 'natural'. This notion is encapsulated in Simone de Beauvoir's 1949 statement: 'One is not born, but rather becomes a woman' (1989 [1949]: 267).

The emphasis in defining 'disability', therefore, has shifted from a medical model of (ab)normality (Malec, 1993) to a focus on social structures. This has been a significant move in the rethinking of disability and the beginning of political action. Previously, the concept of disability was centred on individual impairments and people with disabilities were 'othered' because of their difference from the ableist norm. Within the social model external obstacles, as opposed to individual characteristics, are viewed as disabling (Block and Keys, 2002). For example, the lack of a ramp is the problem, not the fact that someone uses a wheelchair.

Despite the progressive thrust of the social model of disability, gender differences have been an ongoing source of tension. However, as Thomas (1999) maintains, experiences of disability are always shaped by gender. A number of academics and activists have struggled for recognition of the double discrimination faced by people who are marked as both 'women' and 'disabled' (see Wendell, 1996). The concept of **gendered disablism** (Thomas, 1999: 28) is increasingly receiving recognition. Unfortunately, other differences, such as race (ibid.) and sexuality (Tremain, 1996), have received far less attention.

THEORETICAL/METHODOLOGICAL FRAMEWORKS

Although this chapter is based in the social model of disability, it is important to acknowledge some of the critiques of this mode of theorizing, such as the denial of bodies and pain (Wendell, 1996). A cross-disability perspective has been employed, rather than focusing on any one disability or type of disability. This encompasses so-called 'visible' and 'invisible disabilities', including physical disabilities (mobility, visual, hearing), mental health issues, chronic illnesses, and intellectual disabilities. Self-identification is critical in this context, as it shifts the power of naming away from those in authority and contributes to our cultural identity. Finally, the phrase 'persons with disabilities' is used rather than 'disabled persons' in order to signal that people have many identities. While this phraseology is more common in the Canadian context than the British, it is by no means standard.

Children and Youth with Disabilities

Statistics Canada (2002a) reported that in 2001 there were approximately 5.5 million Canadian children aged 14 and under. Of this total, 180,930 or 3.3 per cent had disabilities, representing 2.5 per cent of girls and 4.0 per cent of boys. Boys 14 or younger are more likely than their female counterparts to have disabilities that limit activity, but once they move into the next age category (15–24) this prevalence disappears (Cossette and Duclos, 2002). Eighty-five per cent of children with disabilities were 5–14 years old, with incidence of disability consistently increasing with age of the child. This was found to be true regardless of gender (Statistics Canada, 2002a).

DEMOGRAPHICS

While in the past they might have been institutionalized, children with disabilities are increasingly likely to live at home with their families rather than in institutions (Roeher Institute, 2000a). A disturbing trend since the late 1990s was recently exposed in Ontario, however, of parents relinquishing custody so their children could receive needed government-funded supports and services.

Of the population of children with disabilities in Canada, only 14.5 per cent (26,210) are preschoolers (Statistics Canada, 2002a). According to Behina and Duclos (2003), 57.5 per cent of children with disabilities in this age group had mild to moderate disabilities, while 42.5 per cent had severe to very severe disabilities. Nearly half of preschoolers with disabilities had more than one type of disability.

The most common type of disability among preschoolers is developmental delay (68 per cent), including delays in intellectual and/or physical development and other delays such as speech impairment (Cossette and Duclos, 2002). Chronic health conditions such as asthma, severe allergies, heart conditions or disease, kidney condition or disease, cancer, epilepsy, cerebral palsy, spina bifida, cystic fibrosis, muscular dystrophy, fetal alcohol syndrome, etc. were the next most prevalent type of disability causing activity limitations for this age group (62.6 per cent) (Statistics Canada, 2002a).

The majority (85.5 per cent or 154,220) of all children with disabilities are school age (Statistics Canada, 2002a). According to the 2004 *Advancing the Inclusion of Persons with Disabilities* report, the most common type of disability for school-age children (5–14) (bearing in mind that many have more than one disability) is activity limitations caused by chronic conditions (65.3 per cent) (Government of Canada, 2004). The second most common type is learning disabilities (64.9 per cent), with this being more prevalent for boys (68.9 per cent) than girls (58 per cent) (Statistics Canada, 2002a). Speech-related disabilities (43.3

per cent) are the third most common disability for school-age children (Government of Canada, 2004). Over half (57.4 per cent) of children with disabilities in Canada are considered to have 'mild to moderate disabilities', with Quebec and Ontario having the highest incidences of children with severe to very severe disabilities (45.8 per cent and 45.7 per cent of children with disabilities, respectively) (Statistics Canada, 2002a).

IMPACT OF CHILDREN WITH DISABILITIES ON FAMILIES

Many parents of children with disabilities experience considerable frustration, largely stemming from a lack of supports rather than from dealing with their child's disability (Roeher Institute, 2000b). In some cases, children are placed in residential or foster care due to inadequate family supports (Howlett, 2005). Family breakdown is not uncommon, and children with disabilities are over-represented in female-headed lone-parent families (Fawcett, 1996) compared with other children (18.1 and 14.1 per cent, respectively) (NPHS, 1996, as cited in Roeher Institute, 2000b).

Family Income, Employment, and Poverty

The average household income for preschool and school-age children with disabilities is lower than the household incomes of their peers without disabilities (Table 12.1). Having a child with a disability does not only influence income, but can also impact the employment situation of families. Many families of children with disabilities (nearly 62 per cent of families with preschool children and 54 per cent of those with school-age children) report that their child's condition has impacted the family's employment situation (Government of Canada, 2004). The impact was found to be positively correlated to the severity of the child's disability—while 40 per cent of families of children with mild to moderate disabilities reported an impact on their employment, this proportion almost doubled to 73 per cent in families having children with severe to very severe disabilities (Benhia and Duclos, 2003).

Table 12.1 Average Household Income of Canadian Children, 2001

Age	Children with disabilities	Children without disabilities
0–4	$54,660	$66,138
5–14	$63,366	$72,069

SOURCE: Statistics Canada, Participation and Activity Limitation Survey, 2001, as cited by Office for Disability Issues (2003).

Compared with fathers, mothers are most likely to be responsible for providing, arranging, and advocating for care for their children with disabilities (Roeher Institute, 2000a). Hence, women are more likely than men to experience an impact on their employment due to their child's disability (Government of Canada, 2004). Impacts on employment included: working fewer hours (34 per cent), changing hours of work (32 per cent), not taking a job (28 per cent), quitting a job (19 per cent), and turning down a promotion and/or better job (17 per cent) (Statistics Canada, 2002b).

Children with disabilities, as we have seen, are more likely to be poor than other children (Roeher Institute, 2000b). This trend also goes in the opposite direction: 'Children living in poverty are 2.5 times more likely than children in high-income families to have a problem with vision, hearing, speech or mobility' (Ross and Roberts 1999, as cited in Roeher Institute, 2000b: 5). According to the Roeher Institute, *poverty can lead to disability* in a number of ways. People living in impoverished conditions have little access to nutritious foods, both during pregnancy and as children grow. Poor people tend to live in areas or circumstances that may increase the risk of injury and also tend to have less access to health services as well as lower literacy levels, all of which have been linked to increased rates of disability and/or ill health (ibid.). Labelling is a concern for these children, as well: 'Poor children, like children who are from visible minorities, are also more likely to be

labelled as having a disability than children from more privileged families' (ibid., 6).

The Roeher Institute also suggests that *disability can lead to poverty*. Families with children with disabilities are more likely to experience 'family breakdown' and the corresponding reduced family income. Parents of children with disabilities also experience increased barriers to participation in the paid labour force. For example, families with disabilities must contend with costs that families without disabilities do not face, including those related to 'tutors, special diet, special clothing, transportation, babysitting, medications, supplies and equipment, and home adaptations' (ibid.).

Some parents have no other alternative than to care for their children full-time rather than participate in the paid labour force. According to the 1996 National Population Health Survey, young people with disabilities are more than twice as likely as young people without disabilities to live in familial environments that depend on government, not employment, for their main source of income (16.9 per cent compared with 8.1 per cent) (ibid.). 'For many families of children with disabilities it makes more sense to use social assistance than to take a job with low wages, since they are entitled to receive more disability-related supports when on welfare' (ibid., 6). Because social assistance can provide these disability supports, many parents of children with disabilities simply cannot 'afford' to work.

Aboriginal families of children with disabilities living on reserves experience unique problems related to social assistance. Due to federal guidelines for support, social assistance on reserves tends to be lower than elsewhere. These families do not receive any disability supports and often subsequently move off reserve to access these supports, or else go without or have to pay for these supports themselves (ibid.).

Only the provincial governments of Quebec, Prince Edward Island, and Newfoundland and Labrador provide income support provisions for parents caring for children with disabilities (ibid.). As a result, many parents of children with disabilities in other provinces and territories, who want to participate in the paid labour force, find this next to impossible given their caregiving responsibilities. According to Roeher Institute (2000a), 50 to 60 hours of a parent's week was spent providing disability-related supports to their child(ren).

Employers are not required to accommodate people caring for their children with disabilities, so parents are forced to alter their commitments to their jobs or leave the paid workforce entirely, with very little government assistance (Roeher Institute, 2000b). In Canada, a monthly supplement called the Child Disability Benefit (CDB) is available to parents of children with disabilities. It has a maximum amount per child, as well restrictions based on the age of the child, the length of time received, the type of disability, and the severity of the child's disability. The CDB is a tax-free benefit of no more than $2,000 per year, which is only available for 'low- and modest-income families, who care for a child under age 18 with a severe and prolonged mental or physical impairment' (Canada Revenue Agency, 2005, para. 2).

THE DEARTH OF SUPPORTS FOR CHILDREN WITH DISABILITIES

Housework, Family Responsibilities, and Personal Activities

Although having a child with a disability creates additional demands for parents, nearly 60 per cent of parents of preschool children and almost 80 per cent of school-age children with disabilities report not needing additional help with housework and family responsibilities (Government of Canada, 2004). Parents of preschool children with disabilities are more likely than parents of school-age children with disabilities to report needing additional help with housework and family responsibilities. Parents of children with severe to very severe disabilities were more likely than parents of children with mild to moderate disabilities to report unmet needs (Government of Canada, 2004).

Cost is a major factor preventing parents of school-age children with disabilities from getting the assistance they require—71 per cent cited cost as a reason for not receiving the help they need (Government of Canada, 2004). One parent of a child with a disability describes this frustration: 'I want them to have a life. They need opportunities to develop. This is not possible for me to do without needed supports and services' (Roeher Institute, 2000b: 1).

Family access to disability-related supports can be difficult and fraught with problems. According to the Roeher Institute, families report that eligibility screening is too rigid and does not sufficiently take individual family circumstance and disability-related costs into consideration. In addition, access to services seems to vary between families and regions. Families also report being discouraged by long waiting lists and not being able to afford short-term relief care, transportation, and equipment.

Since the late 1990s, the disparity of supports in Canada has left some families caring for children with disabilities with no option other than to temporarily relinquish guardianship over their children. According to the report of the Ontario ombudsperson, up to 150 families in Ontario signed temporary custody agreements with the Children's Aid Society in order to obtain supports needed by their children with severe disabilities. Douglas Elliott, a lawyer representing many of these families in a class-action lawsuit, argued that 'many parents were concerned their children would not continue receiving care once legal custody was restored. Parents had turned to a children's aid society because that was the only way to obtain treatment' (Howlett, 2005: A13).

Parental Caregiving Responsibilities

Due to the inadequacy of support services, parents and other familial caregivers are often forced to fill the gap themselves. This can result in what a 2003 Canadian study has termed 'caregiver strain' (Duxbury and Higgins, 2003, cited in Pappone, 2005). People in the workforce who are caring for aging parents or children with disabilities are vulnerable to a variety of problems, including depression, fatigue, family conflict, and financial problems.

Research illustrates the multiple responsibilities of parents of children with disabilities: nurses, advocates, trainers and educators, and service co-ordinators (Haverstock, 1992, cited in Roeher Institute, 2000b). One parent interviewed encapsulates this sentiment: 'I'm everything—I'm the playmate, storyteller, therapist, disciplinarian, advocate, cook, and parent' (ibid., 10).

As in other Canadian families, women perform the majority of caregiving duties for children with disabilities (Government of Canada, 2004). According to Bowman and Virtue (1993, cited in Roeher Institute, 2000b) mothers are up to 10 times more likely than fathers to be the primary caregivers for children with disabilities. Moreover, the federal government of Canada reports that only 30 per cent of children with disabilities receive equal help from both parents (Government of Canada, 2004).

Parenting does not end when a child grows up and/or leaves home, particularly for some children with disabilities. And, as Heather Hewett's story (see Box 12.1) emphasizes, a number of people besides parents are included in the 'networks of support' for a person with a disability (Hewett, 2004). Although Hewett is writing in an American context, her description of the 'intricate web' that allows her sister to live interdependently is relevant for Canadians.

Home and Respite Care

Access to **home care** varies across Canada and even within provinces and territories. To date, there is no 'consistent or coherent home care coverage, nor standards defining access to basic services' (Roeher Institute, 2000b: 9). A 2005 report by the Council of Canadians with Disabilities identifies these jurisdictional issues as problematic (Krogh and Ennis, 2005).

Box 12.1 A Sister's Story

My 31-year-old sister has Down syndrome. She lives in her own house, three miles away from my 70-something parents, and she works part-time busing tables at a local café. An extended network of people help her live on her own: my mother, her full-time advocate and teacher; my father, her biggest fan and supporter; her caseworker, Alicia, who oversees the coordination of her social services; her live-in house companion, Eleanor; her habilitation training specialist, Delores, who helps teach her skills such as balancing her checkbook; her speech pathologist, Judy; her boss, David; her 80-something best friend, Ellen, who gives her rides around town; and finally, her close friends Laurie and Elizabeth, two middle-aged dance therapists who listen to her and provide her with an endless supply of hugs. Then, of course, there's me, but I live thousands of miles away.

From my vantage point, it is particularly evident how much of my sister's daily existence depends on this extended family of friends and professional caregivers. In this respect, her life is not so different from that of other families in our country. Many families rely on similar (though not always as extensive) networks of support; it is just that in my sister's case, the intricate web holding her up cannot be ignored. It is there, in plain view, for all who look.

SOURCE: Hewett (2004).

Families also report needing more **respite care**—those services that give parents/guardians a break from their caregiving responsibilities. The Roeher Institute (2000a), in a study of 50 families of children with disabilities, found that 90 per cent identified respite care as one of the most crucial supports needed for them and their children but this need was not being met. Access to respite care is particularly difficult for families in rural areas, as well as for children with exceptional support needs.

Child Care

The federal Office for Disability Issues (2001) reported that approximately 20 per cent of parents of preschool children with disabilities were refused child-care or babysitting services due to their child's impairment. This percentage was not found to vary significantly based on severity of disability.

Although the deficiency of child care in Canada is a concern for all Canadians, for parents of children with disabilities accessing child care can be even more difficult. Child-care facilities are not required to include children with disabilities, although some do. When child-care centres accept children with disabilities, it is usually done on a child-by-child basis, with some children with disabilities accepted and others not (Roeher Institute, 2000b).

According to Roeher Institute, the problem is inadequate funding—centres would be more inclusive if there were enough money. Getting their children into daycare is not the only problem. The Roeher Institute explains that even when they have managed to secure child care, parents may encounter difficulties in getting their child to the centre and back home again, rigid hours of operation and inflexible curricula, and a lack of training among staff about disability (ibid., 14).

Parents with Disabilities

Social stigma and moral regulation surround parenting by people with disabilities, especially women, who are most affected by medical proce-

dures designed to control fertility and reproduction. In the past, women with disabilities have been denied the right to have children through forced sterilization and chemical birth control (Ridington, 1989). Increasingly, women's lives are subject to a process of 'geneticization', with common conditions being labelled genetic diseases (Lippman, 1993: 40). Moreover, abortion is currently prohibited for sex selection but not for the elimination of disability (ibid., 62). Prenatal screening and testing have in fact become routine, opening the doors to a new type of eugenics (Peters and Lawson, 2002).

MOTHERING CHALLENGES

'Mothering or even fathering with a disability is assumed to be potentially "damaging" for children . . . [and] family "dysfunction" is presumed to be inevitable' (Blackford, 1999: 281). It is not uncommon for mothers with disabilities to face disbelief and discrimination regarding pregnancy and parenting, or to have their custody challenged. For example, adaptive measures such as lifting babies by clothing and harnesses on wheelchairs are not always understood or well received by the able-bodied public (Auliff, 2001).

Blackford (1999: 280) argues, however, that 'through the intimate experience of caring for and knowing a person with a disability, and through feeling cared-for and understood by a person with a disability, oppression associated with disability prejudice and with familialism [restrictive ideas about what constitutes the 'family'] is reduced.' In addition, children of parents with a disability learn to respect difference and are exposed to a more egalitarian family environment, as well as gain a profound awareness and recognition of the lived experience of space and the body (ibid.).

Canadian women with disabilities over 45 years of age are less likely to be married than men with disabilities (Des Meules et al., 2003). In the 25–44 age range, women with disabilities in this country are more likely than women without disabilities to be single, divorced, separated, or widowed (see Table 12.2).

Table 12.2 Relationship Status of Men and Women Aged 25–44, with and without Disabilities, 1991

	Single (%)	Married (%)	Divorced, Separated, or Widowed (%)
Women with disabilities	20.2	62.5	17.4
Women without disabilities	15.4	76.4	8.1
Men with disabilities	29.7	59.2	11.1
Men without disabilities	22.2	72.8	5.0

SOURCE: Fawcett (1996).

Women with disabilities have a higher rate of lone parenthood (16 per cent) than women without disabilities (8 per cent) and are more likely to be caring for dependent children on their own (Fawcett, 1996). While the above figures are dated, no comparable statistics have been published from PALS. Moreover, even if there have been significant reductions in the percentage of women with disabilities who are divorced, separated, widowed, and/or lone parents, it is reasonable to assume that the disparity between women with disabilities and the other three groups would not have been eliminated between 1991 and the present.

Despite the challenges, the number of Canadian women with disabilities who are mothers is increasing (Blackford et al., 2000). According to Blackford et al., the needs of expectant mothers with chronic illnesses and/or disabilities are not being met by current models of prenatal care and education. The authors suggest, 'If prenatal education is individualized and culturally respectful, education can be a medium to address the empowerment needs of marginalized expectant mothers' (ibid., 899).

In their research, Blackford and her colleagues interviewed eight mothers with disabilities who had given birth to a child within the past two years about their maternity experiences. They found that the women noted six areas of prenatal care that needed improvement: learning resources for self-care, opportunities to voice anxiety, supportive relationships, communication within the family, information pertaining to postnatal care, and special circumstances.

INFORMAL CAREGIVING

According to the Canadian government's 2004 *Advancing the Inclusion* report, 70 per cent of persons with disabilities need assistance with everyday activities (including washing, eating, personal hygiene, and transportation), with women (79 per cent) being more likely to require help with these activities than men (59 per cent). Age is also a factor, with seniors needing more assistance than working-age adults or children (Government of Canada, 2004).

Although the most common source of assistance in everyday activities is family (1.9 million Canadians with a disability report receiving assistance from a family member), more than one-quarter of people with disabilities say that their friends and families are unable to provide these informal care services. Usually one family member, typically a woman, provides the majority of informal care services: 'The role of informal caregiver can be challenging, especially since many caregivers are also employed, are lone parents or have responsibilities besides helping a person with a disability. Caregivers may need support to keep providing quality care to people with disabilities' (ibid., 19).

Working-age adults with disabilities are more likely to receive informal care from family members who live with them than from any other resource. According to government of Canada, 'Informal caregivers often face long-term financial repercussions in the form of, for instance, turning down career opportunities, being unable to update skills, saving less for retirement and experiencing reduced working hours, pay and pension benefits' (ibid., 20). Re-entering the workforce after a period of full-time caregiving has also proven to be difficult for these caregivers and the 2004 government report suggests improved access to respite care, as well as better workplace accommodations for caregivers, to better support these familial caregivers.

For Aboriginal Canadians with disabilities, supports to family caregivers are even more limited. Insufficient reimbursement and/or respite care services exist for family caregivers of Aboriginal people with disabilities, even when the caregivers themselves have disabilities. The Aboriginal Reference Group on Disability Issues (1997) cautions: 'In many rural and remote communities there are no respite service providers at all. Lack of respite services is likely to lead to family deterioration and by extension to community deterioration' (cited ibid., 23).

EMPLOYMENT AND LEARNING

Working-age adults with disabilities are only half as likely as other Canadians to find viable employment (Statistics Canada, 2002a). Moreover, workers with disabilities earn less than workers without disabilities, and women with disabilities in Canada continue to earn less than men without disabilities. In 1998 Canadian women with disabilities had an average income of $7,190, compared to $13,700 for men with disabilities. The average household income of persons with disabilities is 74 per cent of the income of persons without disabilities, and persons with disabilities 'can be doubly disadvantaged by extra costs related to disability' (Government of Canada, 2002: 44).

People with disabilities who are parents of young children experience even more difficulty in finding paid employment opportunities because of their child-care responsibilities (Office for Disability Issues, 2003). This issue is particularly prevalent among mothers with disabilities. Fawcett (1996: 163) explains, 'The greater likelihood of being a lone parent, coupled with lower participation rates among lone parents, contributed to the lower likelihood of labour force participation among women with disabilities.'

Post-secondary education narrows the gender gap in labour force participation, as well as the wage gap, for persons with disabilities:

> Among persons with disabilities whose highest level of education was primary school, or less, the participation rate for women was about 53 per cent that of men (25.3 per cent participation rate for women, compared to 48.2 per cent participation rate for men). [However], women's participation rates as a proportion of men's rose to about 92 per cent for those with either a non-university post-secondary diploma (67.6 per cent participation rate for women, compared to 73.4 per cent participation rate for men) or a university degree (69.8 per cent participation rate for women, compared to 76 per cent participation rate for men). (Ibid., 153–4)

According to more recent figures, women with disabilities are now surpassing their male counterparts in regard to completing college (women: 60.8 per cent; men: 39.2 per cent) and university (women: 59.2 per cent; men: 40.8 per cent) (Statistics Canada, 2002b).

IMPACT OF DEPENDENT CHILDREN ON LABOUR FORCE PARTICIPATION

Similar to other Canadian women, the labour force participation of women with disabilities is largely influenced by their (unpaid) domestic labour responsibilities, including the care of dependent children. According to the 2001 PALS, 'among the 84,000 children whose families' employment situation was affected, mothers (71 per cent) most often experienced such impacts on their employment because of their child's condition' (Government of Canada, 2002).

The age of dependent children is often a factor:

> Women with disabilities who had children under the age of six were less likely to be in the paid labour force than those who had no dependent children or had school-aged children. Among women aged 25 to 34 with disabilities, for example, 68.2 per cent of those who had no dependent children were in the paid labour force; for those with children under age six, the figure dipped to 59.8 per cent, and for those with children over age five, it was 62.9 per cent. (Fawcett, 1996: 158)

Fawcett (1996) found a more pronounced distinction among Canadian women *without* disabilities in the 25–34 age group. Women in this age group having no dependent children had the highest rate of labour force participation, while those with pre-school children experienced the lowest participation rate. This suggests that women without disabilities may be likely to enter or re-enter the paid workforce once their children are in school. This pattern was less pronounced among women *with* disabilities, in part because older women with disabilities who never had children were more likely to have a severe disability (which is also limiting to their labour force participation) than women of ages 25–34 without children or ages 35–44 with children.

The impact of having children under the age of six could also be found in women who were employed. Employed women aged 15–64 with disabilities who had children were more likely than other women with disabilities to require some form of job redesign or accommodation (ibid.). In addition, parents of young children with disabilities reported turning down advancement opportunities, working fewer hours, not taking a job, altering their working hours, or having to resign (Government of Canada, 2003). This suggests, according to Fawcett, that the interaction of child-care responsibilities with employment responsibilities affected the higher rate of job accommodation.

DOMESTIC LABOUR

Women with disabilities are more likely than men with disabilities to perform most of the basic household chores. This was found to be true, regardless of severity of disability or living arrangements. In this vein, 'men with disabilities were much more likely to have assistance with household chores—whether it was required for the disability or not' (Fawcett, 1996: 165). Men with disabilities were also more likely than women with disabilities to report needing assistance with meal preparation, even if it was not required as the result of their disability.

In Fawcett's words, 'While the majority of both women and men with disabilities did not require assistance with basic household chores strictly because of their disability, the majority of men were likely to receive assistance anyway; the majority of women were not' (ibid., 167). The assistance received by men with disabilities may have been from a family member inside or outside of the household, a friend outside the household, or hired help through a service or agency.

Assistance with household chores was very much related to whether or not the individual lived alone or with others. Those who lived with others received much more assistance than those who lived alone (ibid.). Women with disabilities who live with other people were more likely to perform their own meal preparation.

Blackford (1999: 279) found that although oppression in families where a parent has a disability certainly exists, strengths can be gained from the experience: 'In organizing the social relations of family life when a parent has a chronic illness like multiple sclerosis, family members often learn to do it differently.'

Violence and Abuse

The Roeher Institute (1994: v) characterizes violence against people with disabilities as being comprised of both systemic discrimination and overt and subtle forms of abuse. The Roeher Institute's research shows that people with disabilities are more likely than people without disabilities to experience physical abuse, sexual abuse, psychological and emotional abuse, neglect and acts of omission, and financial exploitation (ibid., v–vi).

A number of factors put people with disabilities at a higher risk for violence: negative attitudes of others, social isolation, reliance on others for care, lack of control, and socialization to be compliant. Gender and poverty are also cited as risk factors (ibid., vii). And, as Block and Keys (2002: 37) point out, 'Disability, poverty, and minority status are linked and intensify the already negative relationship between economic status and the existence of a disability.' Disability makes the already challenging task of reporting even more difficult, particularly if the abusers are caregivers.

CHILDREN

It has been estimated that, in Canada, children with disabilities are the victims of abuse up to 10 times more frequently than children without disabilities (Sobsey, 1994, cited in NCFV, 2000). 'Among children with disabilities . . . research has found that 39 to 68 per cent of girls, and 16 to 30 per cent of boys are subjected to sexual abuse before the age of 18' (Bunch and Crawford, 2000: 18). Children with mental or developmental disabilities are especially vulnerable (BC Institute against Family Violence, 1996; Government of Canada, 2004).

Although they are more likely than other children to be victims of abuse, violence against children with disabilities has received little attention. For children with disabilities, some forms of abuse are so subtle that they are not easily recognized by the law. The Roeher Institute (2000b: 18) reports that 'abuse may come in the form of restricted movement, invasive "therapy" or rough handling while receiving personal care (e.g., for washing, feeding, grooming, using the toilet) . . . abuse could come at the hands of parents, teachers, health professionals and others.'

Violence against children with disabilities varies by gender, as well as by type of disability. While girls are at particular risk for sexual assault, boys are more likely to be physically abused and neglected (Canadian Mental Health Association, 1993, cited in Roeher Institute, 1995). 'Girls with intellectual disabilities are twice as likely as boys to be sexually abused before the age of 18 years' (ibid., 19). Children who are deaf also experience higher levels of abuse than other children, as do children with physical disabilities.

Where children with disabilities are most vulnerable is debatable. DAWN Toronto's (1995: 32) research concluded: 'The most dangerous place for her [girl with a disability] to be is in her own home. . . . If a girl with a disability is sent to foster homes or institutions, she still faces a high risk of sexual and physical assault.' However, other sources maintain that Canadian children who have been institutionalized due to physical and/or intellectual impairments have an increased risk of maltreatment (NCFV, 2000). And although protective measures are now in place to prevent this from recurring, children living in institutions continue to be victimized more often than other Canadian children (Doe, 1999).

Children with disabilities are at an elevated risk for abuse, in part because of the difficult circumstances common to their families (Roeher Institute, 2000b). According to the Roeher Institute's 1994 report for the National Clearinghouse on Family Violence (cited ibid., 18):

> Children with disabilities are more likely to be abused within their families when their families experience isolation (which may be increased by demands of caregiving), are overwhelmed by the demands of caregiving, lack opportunity to develop effective coping skills, or engage in difficult caring activities while lacking respite and other supports.

The report goes on to state that additional stresses such as unemployment, as well as a family history of abuse, use of corporal punishment, or substance abuse, can all contribute to the risk of abuse.

The authors suggest that this kind of abuse is more prevalent where negative social attitudes towards disability are prominent (Roeher Institute, 1994).

Child abuse is an issue of power. The risk of children with disabilities experiencing abuse is often intensified because of their increased levels of dependency and vulnerability (NCFV, 2000). Their vulnerability is heightened because of social stereotypes about their impairments. For instance, children with disabilities may experience social isolation within their own families or peer groups due to a family member or friend's negative attitudes towards disability. For example, a child may be left out of a family game, without any accommodations being made to include the child, because of assumptions of the child's inability to participate successfully. Social isolation can lead to an increased vulnerability to abuse (NCFV, 2000).

The murder of Tracy Latimer is one of the most high-profile cases involving a child with a disability (Box 12.2). On 24 October 1993, Robert Latimer, a Saskatchewan farmer, killed his 12-year-old daughter Tracy by using a hose to feed carbon monoxide from his truck's exhaust pipe into the cab where he had placed her. She was born with cerebral palsy and was unable to perform many of the so-called activities of daily living without assistance.

WOMEN

DAWN Toronto (1995: 32) characterizes violence against women and girls with disabilities as a crisis, estimating that over two-thirds of women with disabilities experience physical or sexual assault before they reach puberty. The Canadian Research Institute for the Advancement of Women (CRIAW) states that 'Violence is a major cause of injury to women, ranging from cuts and bruises to permanent disability and death' (CRIAW, 2002: 6). Women who are physically or sexually abused as adults or children are at greater risk of a variety of health problems, including chronic pain, anxiety, and clinical depression (ibid., 7).

Box 12.2 Tracy Latimer

It was true that Tracy had cerebral palsy, that she experienced pain and would have encountered more but it was not true that it was constant or excruciating as [her mother] Laura's testimony said. Like other children disabled at birth, Tracy knew no other life. This was the life she had been given, and she enjoyed it, valued it and fought to keep it, just as most able-bodied people value their lives.

The communication book entries written by Laura and read for the Crown during the second trial showed Tracy relished these simple pleasures at least until Tuesday, October 19, the date of the last entry, five days before her life was taken from her. Laura's entry that day read, 'Tracy was good, ate and drank fine [sic] Tracy was good, ate really well, had a bath, Bob [Tracy's father] bathed her.' It was the day Robert Latimer decided on using exhaust fumes to kill her.

In able-bodied people pain is a symptom, but in Tracy it was a death sentence carried out by her father and condoned by her mother, the defence attorney, the judges and juries and most media and their audiences. It was not her intermittent pain that was the predominant issue in either trial. It was her disability. Because she couldn't speak, the assumption was that she couldn't comprehend and, if she couldn't comprehend, her death really wasn't as monstrous as the killing of someone who could.

Source: Enns (1999: 46–7).

Family violence impacts more on women with disabilities than on any other group in our society. According to the National Clearinghouse on Family Violence (1993a: 3), women and children with disabilities are 'one of the most highly victimized groups in our society' and violence and/or fear of violence are 'the most critical issues facing women with disabilities'. They are 'particularly vulnerable to threats to their physical safety, and to psychological and verbal abuse and neglect' (Government of Canada, 2002: 54).

Sobsey (1988, cited in NCFV, 1993a) estimates the rate of abuse for persons with disabilities as 150 per cent that of individuals without disabilities of the same gender and age. Although men with disabilities are more likely to be abused than men without disabilities, 95 per cent of victims of spousal assault are women (including women without disabilities) (NCFV, 1993a).

Violence against women with disabilities often comes in the form of family violence. This can include 'physical, psychological or sexual maltreatment, abuse or neglect of a woman with disabilities by a relative or caregiver. It is a violation of trust and an abuse of power in a relationship where a woman should have the right to absolute safety' (ibid., 1). Women with disabilities who live in institutions (who are more dependent on a higher number of people) may be at an even greater risk.

Like women without disabilities, violence against women with disabilities is usually perpetrated by someone known to the victim, someone in their inner circle, their 'family'. Women with disabilities are particularly vulnerable, however, because they often depend on a variety of people to help them in carrying out their everyday lives—'attendants, interpreters, homemakers, drivers, doctors, nurses, teachers, social workers, psychiatrists, therapists, counsellors, and workers in hospitals and other institutions' (ibid., 2). Thus the 'family' of a woman with a disability includes 'not only parents, husbands, boyfriends and other relatives, but also friends, neighbours and caregivers' (ibid.).

BARRIERS TO OBTAINING HELP

It can be exceedingly difficult for a woman with a disability to leave an abusive relationship. In addition to reduced self-esteem, a woman with disabilities who reports violence may risk poverty or loss of housing, fear that she will not be believed, face further violence or institutionalization, and could lose her children (ibid.). Research suggests that up to 90 per cent of incidents of abuse against people with disabilities do not get reported (BC Institute against Family Violence, 2003). Social attitudes about disability, not the individual's impairment, are the largest contributor to the increased vulnerability to abuse experienced by women with disabilities (NCFV, 1993a).

Society oppresses women with disabilities through *infantilization* (persons with disabilities are viewed and treated as if they are children or are assumed to be lacking in intelligence); *compliance requirements* (they may be punished for assertiveness and trained to be passive and compliant at all times); *the assumption of non-sexuality* (women with disabilities are often not educated about their sexuality, which could result in 'an inability to distinguish between abusive behaviour and normal or necessary forms of touching'; *presumptions of incompetency* (women with disabilities may be considered incompetent by members of police or the courts, particularly if they require assistance in communicating); and finally, *lack of credibility* (when women with disabilities *do* report abuse, they may not be believed). These oppressive ideas about women with disabilities effectively increase their risk for violence (ibid.).

Conclusion

There is a real lack of support for Canadian families living with disabilities. Disability affects many Canadians and their families: some 3.6 million people have disabilities and approximately 11 million people without disabilities have a family member with disabilities. And the rate of disability is higher for women and Aboriginal people than for other Canadians. Moreover, we are an aging society, and rates of disability increase with age.

Disability and poverty are inextricably intertwined: disability leads to poverty and poverty leads to disability. The average household income for families with preschool and school-age children with disabilities is lower than the household incomes of their peers without disabilities. Family breakdown is not uncommon, and children with disabilities are over-represented in lone-parent families. Children with disabilities, especially those with mental or developmental disabilities, are at increased risk of violence. Cost is a major factor preventing parents from getting the assistance they require. Working-age adults with disabilities are only half as likely as other Canadians to find viable employment, and they have lower average incomes than people without disabilities.

Women with disabilities are more likely than men with disabilities to perform most of the basic household chores. Compared with fathers, mothers are most likely to be responsible for providing, arranging, and advocating for care for their children with disabilities. Child care is the primary barrier to participation in the paid workforce for parents (especially mothers) of children with disabilities. Women with disabilities are more likely than women without disabilities to be single, divorced, separated, widowed, and lone parents of dependent children. Parenting, especially mothering, with a disability is surrounded by social stigma. Violence against women with disabilities often comes in the form of family violence.

The social model of disability identifies barriers as being systemically rather than biologically based. From this perspective, the obstacles that prevent a full life are the problem, not disabilities themselves. Canadians with disabilities clearly need increased support in order to thrive as family members. For example, increased public funds are needed for social assistance, disability supports, health needs, home care, respite care, child care, accessible transportation, adequate housing, education and training, etc. One of the difficulties, as outlined in this chapter, is inconsistency across jurisdictions. This matter needs to be addressed by all levels of government immediately.

In addition, social perceptions regarding families and disabilities must be radically altered. Despite progress in many areas, modern Canadian society is still marked by a strong sense of what is (and is not) 'normal'. This is most evident when it comes to ideals of the perfect body. Ask yourself what you would think if you saw a child with cerebral palsy in a classroom full of non-disabled children? Or two young people with intellectual disabilities holding hands and kissing? What about a mother breast-feeding a baby in her wheelchair? These are images that are not yet common, but hopefully will be one day.

Study Questions

1. What are the implications of the social model of disability?
2. How is disability defined in Canada?
3. In what sense are many people 'TABs' (temporarily able-bodied)?
4. What ableist assumptions underpin the organization of paid and unpaid labour?
5. How does sexism (ageism/racism/heterosexism, etc.) intersect with ablesim?
6. What barriers are faced by people with visible disabilities versus so-called invisible disabilities?
7. Why are people with disabilities so vulnerable to violence? Who is particularly at risk?

Glossary

Ableism The belief that people without disabilities have more worth than people with disabilities. This view may be explicit or implicit.

Familialism According to functionalists the so-called 'traditional' nuclear family remains the ideal. This conservative model is based on rigidly gendered roles, and women are expected to provide physical and emotional care to the rest of the family.

Gendered disablism The notion that gender and disability are interlocking and intersecting sites of oppression. Disability is always gendered. There is no generic experience of disability outside of gender (as well race, class, sexuality, etc.).

Home care The in-home paid or unpaid assistance provided to a person with a chronic disability or illness, allowing the person with the impairment to remain living at home.

Impairments Characteristics, features, or attributes that may or may not be the result of illness, disease, or injury, for example: mobility impairments, depression, cancer, being hard of hearing, psychological impairments, etc.

Participation and Activity Limitation Survey (PALS) The most recent (2001) large-scale survey to collect information on persons in Canada (excluding those in institutions, in the territories, and on First Nations reserves) whose everyday activities are limited due to a physical or mental health problem or illness.

Respite care Short-term, temporary care, sometimes including overnight, designed to give families that include people with disabilities a break from caregiving.

Social model of disability From this view society is regarded as disabling for persons who have impairments. According to this model, disability refers to the social, environmental, and attitudinal oppression faced by persons with non-conformist bodies.

TABS (temporarily able-bodied) The notion that anyone may become disabled at any time. Unlike other identity categories, the line between 'disabled' and 'not disabled' is constantly in flux. This is particularly the case in an aging society.

Visible and invisible disabilities Visible disabilities are easily discerned by a second party or, in other words, their barriers are 'visible', for example, using a wheelchair, walker, prosthesis, or oxygen. Invisible disabilities—which are not readily apparent—can include debilitating fatigue, pain, heart problems, depression, or neurological damage. A person may have both visible and invisible disabilities.

Websites

www.disabilitystudies.ca
This site is sponsored by Canadian Centre on Disability Studies, a consumer-directed, university-affiliated centre dedicated to research, education, and information dissemination on disability issues.

www.canadian-health-network.ca
The Canadian Health Network is a national, non-profit, bilingual web-based health information service. Its goal is to help Canadians stay healthy and prevent disease. Information pertaining to living with a disability in Canada is provided: click 'Living with Disabilities' under 'topics.'

www.ccdonline.ca
This bilingual website provides information on the issues at the forefront of the agenda of the Council of Canadians with Disabilities (CCD). CCD advocates at the federal level for the elimination of inequality and discrimination in the lives of men and women with disabilities. Members include national, regional, and local advocacy organizations controlled by persons with disabilities.

www.disabilityweblinks.ca/pls/dwl/dl.home
Disability Weblinks is a Canadian government search engine for disability-related information. Information can be searched by keyword and programs can be viewed based on jurisdiction and topic. The home page has a link to EnableLink, an on-line community for people with disabilities.

www.dawncanada.net
DisAbled Women's Network (DAWN) Canada is a national feminist organization controlled by and comprised of women who self-identify as women with disabilities. This website includes profiles of women with disabilities, special initiatives, related links, and an e-mail discussion group.

www.pwd-online.ca

Persons with Disabilities Online is a bilingual website affiliated with the government of Canada, which aims to provide integrated access to information, programs, and services for persons with disabilities, their families, their caregivers, service providers, and all Canadians.

Further Readings

Enns, Ruth. 1999. *A Voice Unheard: The Latimer Case and People with Disabilities*. Halifax: Fernwood. Enns uses the disability perspective to discuss the much-debated murder of Tracy Latimer by her father. Included are accounts by other Canadians with disabilities and an examination of the legal case through court documents. The book also presents an overview of the history of people with disabilities and their efforts in advocacy.

Fawcett, Barbara. 2000. *Feminist Perspectives on Disability*. Harlow, UK: Prentice-Hall. Fawcett uses the social model of disability extensively to examine the similarities between disability rights and feminist movements.

Roeher Insitute. 2000. *Count Us In: A Demographic Overview of Childhood and Disability*. North York, Ont.: Roeher Institute. Provides both a quantitative and qualitative overview of children with disabilities in Canada, their household, social, and economic status, and the variety of issues their families face. Attention is paid to access to disability supports, linking disability and poverty and violence against children with disabilities.

Wendell, Susan. 1996. *The Rejected Body: Feminist Philosophical Reflections on Disability*. New York: Routledge. Wendell criticizes past feminist theorizing about the body for favouring the able-bodied experience and, for the most part, ignoring the experience of disability. The book sets out to teach feminist scholars why disability is of importance to their work by pointing to disability studies as a significant but often overlooked feminist ally.

References

Auliff, Lily. 2001. 'Bringing up baby: Mothering with a disability', *WeMedia* 5, 1 (Jan.–Feb.): 66–9.

BC Institute against Family Violence. 1996. Overview of Family Violence. At: <www.bcifv.org/about/overview/3.shtml>.

Beauvoir, Simone de. 1989 [1949]. *The Second Sex*. New York: Vintage Books.

Behnia, Behnaz, and Édith Duclos. 2003. *Participation and Activity Limitation Survey, 2001: Children with Disabilities and Their Families*. Ottawa: Statistics Canada, Housing, Family and Social Statistics Division.

Blackford, Karen A. 1999. 'Caring to overcome differences, inequities, and lifestyle pressures: When a parent has a disability', in K.A. Blackford, M. Garceau, and S. Kirby, eds, *Feminist Success Stories*. Ottawa: University of Ottawa Press, 279–87.

———, Heather Richardson, and Sarah Grieve. 2000. 'Prenatal education for mothers with disabilities', *Journal of Advanced Nursing* 32, 4: 898–904.

Block, Pamela, and Christopher Keys. 2002. 'Race, poverty and disability: Three strikes and you're out! Or are you?', *Social Policy* 33, 1: 34–8.

Canada Revenue Agency. 2005. 'About the Child Disability Benefit (CDB)'. Ottawa: Government of Canada. At: <www.cra-arc.gc.ca/benefits/faq_cdb-e.html#q1>; accessed 22 July 2005.

Canadian Research Institute for the Advancement of Women. 2002. *Violence against Women and Girls Fact Sheet*. Ottawa: CRIAW/ICREF.

Cossette, Lucie, and Édith Duclos. 2002. *Participation and Activity Limitation Survey: A Profile of Disability in Canada, 2001*. Ottawa: Minister of Industry, Statistics Canada.

Crawford, Cameron. 2002. *Learning Disabilities in Canada: Economic Costs to Individuals, Families and Society*. North York: Roeher Institute.

DesMeules, Marie, Donna Stewart, Arminée Kazanjian, Heather McLean, Jennifer Payne, and Bilkis Vissandjée, eds. 2003. *Women's Health Surveillance*

Report: A Multi-dimensional Look at the Health of Canadian Women. Ottawa: Canadian Institute for Health Research. At: <www.phac-aspc.gc.ca/publicat/whsr-rssf/pdf/CPHI_WomensHealth_e.pdf>; accessed 15 May 2005.

DisAbled Women's Network (DAWN) Toronto. 1995. 'The risk of physical and sexual assault', *Abilities: Canada's Lifestyle Magazine for People with Disabilities* 22 (Spring): 32–3.

Doe, Tanis. 1999. 'Ecological view of prevention of violence', at: <http://members.shaw.ca/dewresearch/others.html>, accessed 17 Mar. 2005.

Enns, Ruth. 1999. *A Voice Unheard: The Latimer Case and People with Disabilities*. Halifax: Fernwood.

Environics Research Group. *Canadian Attitudes towards Disability Issues: 2004 Benchmark Survey*. Ottawa: Office for Disability Issues. Available at: <www.sdc.gc.ca/asp/gateway.asp?hr=/en/hip/odi/documents/attitudesPoll/benchmarkSurvey/toc.shtml&hs=pyp>.

Fawcett, Gail. 1996. *Living with Disability in Canada: An Economic Portrait*. Hull, Que.: Human Resources Development Canada.

Gignac, Michel. 2002. *Guide to Family Support Needs*. Drummondville, Que.: Office des personnes handicapées du Québec, Direction des communications.

Government of Canada, Office for Disability Issues. 2002. *Advancing the Inclusion of Persons with Disabilities: A Government of Canada Report*. Ottawa: Government of Canada, Dec.

———. 2004. *Advancing the Inclusion of Persons with Disabilities: A Government of Canada Report*. Ottawa: Social Development Canada.

Hendler, Darlene M. 1998. *Family Therapy with Families Who Have Special Needs Children*. Ottawa: National Library of Canada.

Hewett, Heather. 2004. 'My sister's family'. *The Scholar and Feminist Online: Young Feminists Take on the Family*, guest eds J. Baumgardner and A. Richards. At: <www.barnard.edu/sfonline/family/hewett_01.htm>; accessed 7 May 2005.

Howlett, Karen. 2004. 'Families of disabled children to reunite Monday, judge says', *Globe and Mail*, 4 June, A13.

Hurst, Rachel. 2005. 'Disabled Peoples' International: Europe and the social model of disability', in Colin Barnes and Geof Mercer, eds, *The Social Model of Disability: Europe and the Majority World*. Leeds: Disability Press, 65–79.

Irwin, Sharon Hope, and Donna S. Lero. 1997. *In Our Way: Child Care Barriers to Full Workforce Participation Experienced by Parents of Children with Special Needs—and Potential Remedies*. Wreck Cove, NS: Breton Books.

Johnson, Karen L., Donna S. Lero, and Jennifer A. Rooney. 2001. *Work-Life Compendium 2001: 150 Canadian Statistics on Work, Family & Well-Being*. Guelph, Ont.: Centre for Families, Work and Well-Being, Human Resources Development Canada.

Krogh, Kari, and Mary Ennis. 2005. *A National Snapshot of Home Support from the Consumer Perspective: Enabling People with Disabilities to Participate in Policy Analysis and Community Development*. Winnipeg: Council of Canadians with Disabilities.

Lippman, Abby. 1993. 'Worrying—and worrying about—the geneticization of reproduction and health', in G. Basen, M. Eichler, and A. Lippman, eds, *Misconceptions*, vol. 1. Quebec City: Voyaguer Publishing, 39–65.

Malec, Christine. 1993. 'The double objectification of disability and gender', *Canadian Woman Studies* 13, 4: 22–3.

Morris, Jenny. 2001. 'Impairment and disability: Constructing an ethics of care that promotes human rights', *Hypatia* 16, 5: 1–16.

Morris, Marika. 2001. *Gender-Sensitive Home and Community Care and Caregiving Research: A Synthesis Paper*. Ottawa: Women's Health Bureau, Health Canada.

National Clearinghouse on Family Violence (NCFV), Family Violence Prevention Division. 1993a. *Family Violence against Women with Disabilities*. Ottawa: Health and Welfare Canada. At: <www.phac-aspc.gc.ca/ncfv-cnivf/familyviolence/pdfs/fvawd.pdf>.

———. 1993b. *Family Violence and People with a Mental Handicap*. Ottawa: Health and Welfare Canada. At: <http://dsp-psd.pwgsc.gc.ca/Collection/H72-22-13-1993E.pdf>.

———. 2000. *Abuse of Children with Disabilities*. Ottawa: Health and Welfare Canada. At: <www.phac-aspc.gc.ca/ncfv-cnivf/familyviolence/html/nfntsdisabl_e.html>.

———. 2004. *Violence against Women with Disabilities*. Ottawa: Health and Welfare Canada. At: <www.phac-aspc.gc.ca/ncfvcnivf/familyviolence/html/femdisabus_e.html>.

Office for Disability Issues. 2001. *Disability in Canada: A 2001 Profile*. Gatineau, Que.: Human Resources Development Canada.

———. 2003. *Defining Disability: A Complex Issue.* Gatineau, Que.: Human Resources Development Canada.

Pappone, Jeff. 2005. 'Tech workers in "sandwich generation" often most squeezed', *Ottawa Business Journal*, at: <www.ottawabusinessjournal.com/305596806034971.php>; accessed 4 May 2004.

Peters, Yvonne, and Karen Lawson. 2002. *The Ethical and Human Rights Implications of Prenatal Technologies: The Need for Federal Leadership and Regulation.* Winnipeg: Prairie Women's Centre of Excellence.

Ridington, Jillian. 1989. 'Beating the odds: Violence and women with disabilities', Vancouver: DAWN Canada, at: <www.dawncanada.net/odds.htm>; accessed 28 Sept. 2004.

Rietschlin, John. 2005. Personal communication, Office for Disability Issues, 24 Aug.

Roeher Institute. 1994. *Violence and People with Disabilities: A Review of the Literature.* North York, Ont.: Roeher Institute, for the National Clearing House on Family Violence.

———. 1995. *Harm's Way: The Many Faces of Violence and Abuse against Persons with Disabilities in Canada.* North York, Ont.: Roeher Institute.

———. 2000a. *Beyond the Limits: Mothers Caring for Children with Disabilities.* North York, Ont.: Roeher Institute.

———. 2000b. *Count Us In: A Demographic Overview of Childhood and Disability.* North York, Ont.: Roeher Institute.

Sheldon, Alison. 2005. 'One world, one people, one struggle? Towards the global implementation of the social model of disability', in Colin Barnes and Geof Mercer, eds, *The Social Model of Disability: Europe and the Majority World.* Leeds: Disability Press, 115–40.

Statistics Canada. 1997. 'Who cares? Caregiving in the 1990s', *The Daily*, 19 Aug. At: <http://epe.lac-bac.gc.ca/100/201/301/daily/daily-h/1997/97-08/97-08-19/d970819.htm>.

———. 2002a. *2001 Participation and Activity Limitation Survey: A Profile of Disability in Canada, 2001—Tables.* Ottawa: Statistics Canada.

———. 2002b. *2001 Participation and Activity Limitation Survey: Education, Employment and Income of Adults with and without Disabilities—Tables.* Ottawa: Statistics Canada.

Thomas, Carol. 1999. *Female Forms: Experiencing and Understanding Disability.* Philadelphia: Open University Press.

Tremain, Shelley, ed. 1996. *Pushing the Limits: Disabled Dykes Produce Culture.* Toronto: Women's Press.

Wendell, Susan. 1996. *The Rejected Body: Feminist Philosophical Reflections on Disability.* New York and London: Routledge.

Acknowledgement

Thanks to Gary Annable and Carly Johnston for their assistance.

Part V   Problems, Policies, and Predictions

The last section of this book considers a diverse selection of topics—family violence, family policy in Canada, and the future of the Canadian family.

Aysan Sev'er, in Chapter 13, discusses the issues involved in defining violence and abuse in families and reviews the various theories that have been used to explain family violence and abuse, including individual pathology models, social learning theories, stress and crisis theories, and feminist explanations of violence. Sev'er examines the available data on violence against women and spousal homicide, and discusses problems inherent in the collection of such data. The chapter then examines the consequences of abuse for women and children, and Sev'er suggests that perhaps the most enduring consequences of abuse are psychological. She concludes that the powerlessness and dependency cycles in families that make children, women, and aged persons vulnerable to maltreatment can be broken. Awareness must be translated into programs for educating and promoting non-violent solutions in social relationships, as well as into social policies that can break the cycle of abuse.

Social policies concerning families have a central importance in Canadian life. They determine how families are defined and formed, which family members are entitled to governmental support, and the amount and type of support that families receive. Catherine Krull, in Chapter 14, examines family policy in Canada with a special focus on those measures that relate to families with children under the age of 18 years. Canada, she points out, lacks a comprehensive national family policy. Rather, family policies consist of a piecemeal set of programs and policies that either directly or indirectly have an impact on families. Examples of such policies include paid maternity and parental leaves and child and family benefits. The effectiveness of child and family benefits in reducing poverty is discussed, and Krull explains that large disparities in poverty rates exist between family types. In considering child care in Canada, she argues that a government-supported quality child-care program based on universality has remained elusive. In this context she reviews Quebec's family policies, as Quebec is the only province to currently have universal, subsidized daycare. Krull concludes that the rest of Canada has an opportunity to use and build on Quebec's example in the future.

The final chapter in *Canadian Families Today* offers a view to the future. Margrit Eichler, in Chapter 15, discusses issues involved in making predictions about the future of family life, examines past predictions by family sociologists and other experts about the future of the family and how successful they were, and considers the basis on which such predictions are made. Eichler explores which bases for prediction seem to yield more solid results. She concludes that overall there have been a number of spectacular misprognoses—that the family is a dying institution and that gender roles within the family are unchanging and unchangeable—as well as some surprisingly accurate predictions on such matters as the nature of sexual relations inside and outside of marriage, cohabitation, fertility, and new reproductive technologies. She draws the conclusion that identifying societal changes and reflecting on their importance for the family are the most useful predictive analyses for family studies but also the most difficult. Eichler concludes her chapter by making some predictions of her own.

CHAPTER 13

All in the Family: Violence against Women, Children, and the Aged

Aysan Sev'er

Learning Objectives

- To understand and be able to define different types of abuse.
- To learn about existing theories of abuse.
- To distinguish the strengths and weaknesses of the theories of abuse.
- To appreciate the incidence and consequences of wife/partner, child, and elder abuse.
- To know about possible interventions at the social and structural levels of society.

The Loving Family

Folk wisdom, religions, conservative politicians, movies, the media, the music industry, and children's stories often portray family life as warm and loving. Family as the 'heart in a heartless world' has a great allure. From childhood on, North Americans are bombarded with literary or visual depictions of love between family members. The vision is so potent that we even project 'traditional family' characteristics onto the animal or imaginary worlds. Bambi, the Lion King, Shrek, and other products of the imagination live within familial love and devotion.

There is some truth to this positive bias since many families are indeed close and loving. Nevertheless, positive generalizations tend to hide the severe power differences among family members that are inherent in differences of gender and age (Eichler, 1997). Researchers refer to the undesirable side of the coin as the 'dark side of the family' (Straus et al., 1986; Gelles, 1987, 1994), where power differences can translate into mental, physical, and/or sexual abuse and even murder.

This chapter reviews the basic definitions of abuse and introduces theories that explain violence within intimate relationships. We then focus on the most frequent types of violence: the abuse of female partners, child abuse, and elder abuse. Violence within families extends to dating relationships, same-sex couples, and caregiving institutions. Some men, also, are victimized by their partners. However, this chapter will focus on the most frequently and most seriously targeted members of families—women, children, and the elderly. Statistics Canada (1999) reports that 88 per cent of all victims of spousal violence reported to police are women. The chapter concentrates on Canadian patterns, with some US findings, and concludes with some suggestions as to where to start in order to stop the violence.

Defining Violence

UNITED NATIONS DEFINITION

Intimate violence against women has been defined in the United Nations Declaration on the Elimination of Violence Against Women (UN, 1993) as 'any act of gender-based violence that results in, or is likely to result in, physical, sexual, or psychological harm or suffering to women, including threats of such acts, coercion, or arbitrary deprivation of liberty, whether occurring in public or in private life'. Within this context, 'physical, sexual, and psychological violence in the family, including battering, sexual abuse of female children in the household, [and] marital rape', are considereda violation of human rights (UN, 1993, Articles 1 and 2).

LEGAL DEFINITIONS

In the Canadian Criminal Code violence within the family is subsumed under sections 444-446 (assault, assault with a weapon, aggravated assault and sexual assault). The Criminal Code requires both an 'intent' and an 'act' for an incident to be considered a crime. For example, neither hurting someone by accident nor contemplating to hurt someone will be considered a punishable crime.

GENERAL DEFINITIONS

It is always useful to understand how dictionaries and data collection agencies have defined the important terms with which one is concerned, and for our purposes these are **abuse**, **violence**, **spousal violence**, and **neglect**.

- *Abuse*. Dictionary definitions of 'abuse' include bad practice or custom and using harsh and insulting language. By connoting a violation of customs, the term hints at the relationship between the abuser and the abused. By reference to insults, there is recognition that the induced hurt can be psychological.
- *Violence*. Dictionary definitions of violence include rough force in action, rough treatment, harm or injury, and unlawful use of force. Like the Criminal Code definition of assault, the definition of violence emphasizes both the act itself and the outcome (harm or injury).
- *Spousal violence*. Statistics Canada defines spousal violence as 'cases of murder, attempted murder, sexual and physical assault, threats, criminal harassment, and other violent offences in which the accused person is a spouse, ex-spouse, or common-law partner of the victim' (Statistics Canada, 2003).
- *Neglect*. Neglect includes commissions (acts that put dependants at risk/injury) or omissions (neglect to prevent risk/injury). The subtypes of neglect are abandonment, failure to provide food, medical care, and the emotional well-being of children. Neglect is the

most common form of abuse, especially when the relationship is a one-sided dependency (child on parent), when it is repeated, and when the consequences are (or could have been) severe. Thus, neglect includes observable harm or imminent risk of harm to children and elders (Rose and Meezan, 1995).

Feminist research and theory have played a large part in creating a greater awareness of the hierarchical power within most families, and consequently feminists question the generic terms of abuse. For example, rather than 'domestic abuse' or 'family violence', which fail to identify the most likely perpetrators or targets, they insist on such terms as 'woman abuse', 'wife abuse', 'violence against female partners', and 'child abuse' or 'elder abuse'. They insist that violence within families: (1) is not random; (2) is not one-time, but cyclical; (3) is often severe; and (4) that, in general, perpetrators of violence are men and victims are women, children, and the aged (Sev'er, 2002a; Statistics Canada, 2003).

In this chapter, I will use 'abuse' and 'violence' interchangeably. Unless otherwise stated (e.g., child or elder abuse), 'violence' means intimate partner abuse against the woman partner. As in the Statistics Canada (2003) definition, intimate partners may include married or common-law spouses or ex-spouses, but not dating or other transient relationships.

TYPES OF VIOLENCE

Physical violence approximates the Criminal Code definition of assault, where one person (usually a man) intentionally and repeatedly hurts another (usually a woman, a child, or an elder). At the extreme, murder (intimate **femicide**, infanticide, filicide) is the outcome (Sev'er, 2002a).

Intimate sexual violence occurs when someone forces another (most likely a woman) to engage in sexual activity or intercourse against her/his consent or will (Mahoney and Williams, 1998). It can also take the form of inflicting pain or exposing the partner to unwanted pregnancy or sexually transmitted diseases. Sexual violence against children ranges from sexual touching, molestation, and incestuous rape to participation in the making of child pornography (Bergen, 1998b; Kendall-Tackett and Marshall, 1998; Sev'er, 2002a). A child is less likely to understand 'consent' or 'will' in reference to sexual abuse and may indeed come to desire the inappropriate sexual attention. Efforts to distinguish sexual violence towards children, therefore, usually refer to the age at which molestation began, or to the age when the child might (however incorrectly) be assumed to be capable of leaving the parental home.

Psychological abuse targets the mind and the soul of a person. It is very common, but also controversial. Some scholars argue that hurtful name-calling, put-downs, and constantly dismissing a woman or a child can be just as devastating as hits or punches (Sev'er, 1996, 2002a; DeKeseredy and MacLeod, 1997). Others avoid the term 'abuse' for verbal behaviour, preferring concepts such as '**controlling behaviours**' (Dobash and Dobash, 1992, 1998). The fear is that by expanding the boundaries of violence to include verbal/psychological abuse, one may inadvertently de-genderize the concept. Women typically attempt to control situations of abuse and to defend themselves through verbal reaction and confrontation.

The literature also includes economic abuse and spiritual abuse as types of abuse. The first refers to one partner's (most likely a woman) lack of access to resources and opportunity to partake in the family's financial decisions. Spiritual abuse occurs when one partner (or parent) forces another to practise a different belief system.

Theories about Interpersonal Violence

Theories are logically interrelated statements that order, describe, explain, and predict the causes and consequences of personal or social problems. Theories are generally abstract and vary on the micro/macro continuum. Some seek the causes of events within the person, some focus on social interaction, and still others concentrate on the structural domains. To understand the complex phenomenon of violence, we have to consult a range of theoretical orientations.

INDIVIDUAL PATHOLOGY MODELS

Gender-neutral theories see violence stemming from personal weakness or pathology. Theories of psychopathology are capable of explaining violence perpetrated by a few, clinically troubled individuals (e.g., notorious killers like 'Son of Sam' and Jeffrey Dahmer), but they are weak in explaining violence within families. Some gender-neutral views include a religious belief that humans are inherently disposed to wrongdoing that can be altered through acceptance of and adherence to certain beliefs.

Single-trait explanations such as alcohol/drug dependencies are common. Indeed, statistics show a close link between addictions and violence against women (Dugan and Hock, 2000: 21; Jacobson and Gottman, 2001). For example, a Canadian survey showed that drinking was involved in approximately 50 per cent of all violent relationships. Moreover, men who were heavy drinkers were six times more likely to assault their female partners than were their non-drinking counterparts (see Rodgers, 1994; Johnson, 1996). Although this link is not disputed, alcohol consumption cannot be considered the cause per se of intimate abuse for the following reasons:

- Not all men who drink, abuse.
- Abusive men do not abuse their partners or children each time they drink.
- Abusive men do batter their partners or children when they are not drinking.
- Some men who are non-drinkers also abuse.
- Some alcoholics who stop drinking continue to abuse (Gelles, 1993; Gelles and Straus, 1988).

One intrapersonal theory of violence classifies the victimizers as 'cobras' or 'pit bulls' (Jacobson and Gottman, 2001). Cobras are anti-social, cruel, egotistical men who enjoy hurting a variety of people, including their partners. They exploit and hurt people without remorse because they lack empathy. Cobras generally have charismatic personalities but are capable of severe forms of assault, including murder. Pit bulls, on the other hand, confine their violence to their family. They are jealous, possessive, and fear abandonment. Once pit bulls sink their teeth into their partners, it is extremely difficult to get them to let go (ibid.).

Other intrapersonal theories focus on the victims of violence. The 'blaming the victim' theories stem from Sigmund Freud's (1974 [1920]) perception of women as masochistic, emotionally immature, and deviant. For Freud, women are 'deficient men', both biologically (lacking a penis) and morally (never successfully completing their identification process). Ironically, strong women are also seen as maladjusted, and as taunting and 'castrating' the men in their lives. In other words, whether women were strong or weak, Freud saw them as the engineers of their own distress. A disturbing resurrection of these damaging stereotypes is evident recently (see Kelly and Radford, 1998; Russell and Bolen, 2000; Steed, 1994).

Intrapersonal theories have little explanatory power in understanding a widespread and often gendered phenomenon like men's violence against women, children, and elders. Gelles and Straus (1988) inform us that only about 10 per cent of intimate violence against partners is due to some kind of clinical pathology. Although numbers are unreliable, only a small proportion of abusers of children and elders have clinical problems. This leaves most intra-family abuse to be explained through factors other than individual pathology (Sev'er, 2002a).

Freud's convoluted logic about psychosexual development falls outside the general orientation of this chapter. Nevertheless, his views have profoundly influenced perceptions about women and probably still fuel stereotypical judgements. The dangers of Freudian assertions are obvious. First, by either blaming the victim or by seeing her as helpless, Freud directs the social gaze away from the perpetrators. He even switches the roles around

by depicting the abusers as the victims of their wives' 'castrating' behaviour, or by portraying little girls as the 'sexual aggressors' in incest. Second, by concentrating on women's real or imagined weaknesses, Freud has fuelled negative stereotypes. Third, by personalizing the problems, Freud has failed to challenge the social-structural context of violence, such as poverty, inequality, and patriarchy (DeKeseredy and MacLeod, 1997; Sev'er, 2002b). In sum, although intrapersonal theories provide some insight into general violence, they are not useful in addressing the causes of violence by intimates.

SOCIAL LEARNING THEORIES

Social learning theories see aggression as a learned behaviour. Causes of violence are sought within interaction with significant others and in the rewards and punishments certain types of behaviour engender (Bandura, 1973). Learning may be gender-specific. For example, the intergenerational transmission theory suggests that girls who experience violence are more likely to become victims of partner violence in their adult lives whereas male-child witnesses and victims of violence may become abusers themselves (Levinson, 1989; Scully, 1990).

Intergenerational transmission is extremely important when one considers the fact that children witness violence against their mothers in about 40 per cent of violent marriages (Fantuzzo and Mohr, 1999; Fantuzzo et al., 1991; Juristat, 1999; Lehmann, 1997; Ney, 1992; OAITH; 1998; Rodgers, 1994; Wolfe, Zak and Wilson, 1986). Moreover, many children (especially girls) are victims of violence or sexual violence (Kendall-Tackett and Marshall, 1998). To understand child abuse, Finkelhor (1986, 1988) extended the learning theory to what he calls the **dysfunctional learning model** (DLM). The components of DLM are traumatic sexualization and feelings of betrayal, powerlessness, and stigmatization. All of these dimensions have serious consequences in the adult lives of child victims.

A branch of learning theories focuses on male peer support (Godenzi et al., 2000) and highlights the intragenerational transmission of violence (violent peers, subcultures of violence). For example, DeKeseredy (1990) has shown how male peers cultivate unrealistic expectations among themselves, especially under stressful situations (e.g., unemployment). Males may cajole their peers to develop standards of hurtful, degrading, and destructive interaction patterns in dealing with women. Peers may also reward misogynist acts and punish those who deviate from macho expectations (DeKeseredy and MacLeod, 1997; Godenzi et al., 2000). There is substantial support for male peer support models, especially among college students (DeKeseredy, 1990; DeKeseredy and Kelly, 1993; Schwartz and DeKeseredy, 1997).

Despite their wide appeal, there are legitimate challenges against learning theory arguments. Kaufman and Zigler (1993) show that transmission of violence is mediated by biological, socioeconomic, and cultural factors. For example, although some abusive men may have been witness to or victims of violence in their childhood, a larger proportion of abused children do *not* become abusers. In contrast, some boys who were never abused become abusive men. Although it is reasonable to argue that learning takes place in almost all situations, what exactly is learned— aversion to or acceptance of what is being modelled by the parent—will vary.

Learning theories in general and male peer support models in particular are inadequate in explaining child and elder abuse. For example, even in the macho subcultures, there are strong taboos against child molestation, but some men molest children anyway. Moreover, elder abuse is surrounded by dependencies, shame, and isolation, and societal values that devalue age. The latter issues require an explanation other than early or peer socialization.

STRESS AND CRISIS THEORIES

A version of the frustration/aggression theory proposes that family violence is the outcome of stress. However, families differ in how they deal with stressful events. In what is called the ABCX model, Hill (1958) proposed that events (A), mediated by family's resources (B) and the meanings associated with the event (C), will lead to a particular outcome (X). For example, a pregnancy (A) may be seen as a blessing in one family (positive B/C), but a crisis in another (negative B/C). A more current version of the model (double ABCX) purports that the history of the family's ability to deal with the same or a similar event/ crisis will also affect the outcome, sometimes exacerbating, other times cushioning, the impact (McCubbin and Patterson, 1983).

Dependency theory also asserts that violence against an aging parent results from stress that the latter's escalating debility and need for care engender. Especially where resources are scarce, the physical and economic dependency of the parent is deemed overly taxing to the caregivers. However, Pillemer (1993) transposes the causal direction suggested by the dependency theory. Instead, he contends that the abusive adult children are the ones who are dependent on their aging parents: abuse serving as a means to usurp parental resources. Either way, the incongruence in the relationship (dependent parent or dependent adult child) is seen as the cause of abuse.

Stress theories of violence are alluring. There is no doubt that skills, resources, past experiences, and emotional or economic dependencies of families determine coping skills. However, there are major problems with stress theories. First, by not asserting violence as a moral wrong regardless of personal or social conditions that engender it, they imply resignation to the unavoidability of violence, especially among those who lack resources. Second, stress theories de-genderize (and sometimes, de-age) interpersonal abuse. For example, mothers under stress may physically abuse their children, but it is extremely rare that they sexually abuse them. Father figures may do both, with or without stress. Young children do not abuse their parents, but some older children do. Older women are still most likely to be abused by their male partners, whereas both older men and older women are equally likely to be abused by their sons. Thus, stress theories ignore the fact that regardless of stress, coping skills, or resources, disproportionately more men abuse their partners, children, and parents.

Third, stress theories are blind to cultural variations. In patriarchal cultures where age correlates with status, abuse of elders is less likely, regardless of day-by-day strain. In cultures where the aged are marginalized, they easily become scapegoats for other people's frustrations. Thus, stress theories never adequately address structural or cultural dimensions.

Feminist Explanations of Violence

Numerous are the feminist explanations of men's violence towards intimate partners (Dobash and Dobash, 1979; Flax, 1976; Mitchell, 1973; Yllö and Bograd, 1988), although an in-depth coverage of their variation falls outside the goals of this chapter. Marxist feminism, socialist feminism, and radical feminism provide some of the examples. Noteworthy is that these theories converge on seeking the roots of violence in social structures without disregarding the role of interpersonal or intrapersonal processes.

Feminists criticize the gendered distribution of power and resources, a differentially valued division of labour, and the role of a patriarchal system that protects these inequalities. In feminist explanations, the triangulation of gender, power, and control determines relations in work, politics, law, health, and education as well as male dominance within coupled relationships. Because of this perceived linkage, the UN Declaration on Violence Against Women holds the signatory states accountable for eliminating all forms of inequality in education, work, and family realms.

A premise of radical feminism is the eradication of violence against women. Radical feminists underscore the fact that even men who do not directly harass, abuse, or otherwise subjugate women benefit from the male social status quo (Bart and Moran, 1993; Brownmiller, 1975; MacKinnon, 1982; O'Brien, 1981; Rubin, 1983; Russell, 1989). Through their groundbreaking

Duluth project, Pence and Paymar (1993) proposed a conceptual model for the interrelated dimensions in the cycle of violence. The model suggests that power-seeking men intimidate, emotionally abuse and degrade their partners, isolate them, minimize their complaints, or blame them as the instigators of their own suffering. Men use children against their partners and/or directly hurt children. Men also use coercion and threats to silence their partners.

Feminist theories, especially radical feminist assertions, are quite robust in explaining the abuse of female partners, female children, and older women. Their combined assertions on control of resources and control of women's sexuality explain why men abuse and how they get away with it. Feminists place violence on a continuum, where personal experiences interrelate with social, educational, political, legal, criminal, and economic dimensions. Extended versions also examine social constructions of masculinity, including male sexual socialization (Bowker, 1998; Seymour, 1998), and are particularly relevant to the understanding of male violence against women and children. However, feminist assertions are less robust in dealing with men's violence towards male intimates (sons, aged fathers, etc.). With a few exceptions (Sev'er, 2002a), they are also shy in addressing women's own violence. Moreover, only recently have feminist theories expanded to address race, ethnicity, and culture (see MacLeod and Shin, 1990). Table 13.1 shows the major assertions of violence theories and their applicability.

Violence and Society

Violence crosses over boundaries of ethnicity, race, education, income, sexual orientation, marital status, and physical ability (Crawford and Gartner, 1992; DeKeseredy and MacLeod, 1997; DeKeseredy and Schwartz, 1997; Koss and Cook, 1993; Renzetti, 1998). Nevertheless, poor, uneducated, and/or immigrant or refugee women may be more isolated and thus more vulnerable to social conditions that fuel violence (MacLeod and Shin, 1990;

Table 13.1 Explanatory Power of Theories of Violence

Type of Theory	General Assertions*	Explanatory Power		
		Wife Abuse	Child Abuse	Elder Abuse
Intrapersonal – Individual pathology – Addictions – Freud's psychoanalytic	Cause: Individual pathology or addictions Creates typologies to predict violence Blames women as weak or as domineering	Low	Low	Low
Social Learning – General social learning – Intergenerational transmission – Dysfunctional learning – Male peer support	Cause: Modelling or imitation Evaluates the rewards or punishments Emphasizes the behaviour of significant others Emphasizes gendered learning Emphasizes macho male-peer cultures	High	High	Low
Stress and Crisis Models – ABCX model of stress – Double ABCX model	Cause: Inability to deal with stress Emphasizes resources and perceptions Emphasizes earlier experience/coping	Low	Medium	High

Feminist Theories
– Marxist feminism
– Social feminism
– Radical feminism
– Power and control model
	Cause: Power difference between family
	  members and patriarchal legitimization
	Emphasizes unequal division of labour
	Emphasizes different access to opportunities
	  and resources
	Emphasizes patriarchal structures
	Emphasizes sexual and reproductive subjugation
	  of women
		High	High	Medium

*Assertions correspond to general types, not individual theories.

Box 13.1 Abuse of Women by Male Partners and Intimate Femicide

In 1996, Mark Vijay Chahal murdered his estranged wife Kalwinder and eight other members of her family during Kalwinder's sister's wedding. Chahal then turned the gun on himself. Chahal had repeatedly abused Kalwinder during their troubled marriage, and stalked and threatened her after their separation. Outstanding peace bonds barring him from approaching his estranged wife did not prevent the bloody rampage ('A family gone', *Toronto Star*, 7 Apr. 1996, A1).

On a warm summer day in 2000, a completely naked Gillian Hadley ran out of her house, carrying her one-year-old baby in her arms. She was trying to escape her estranged husband who ambushed her while she was taking a shower. Gillian's last act was to hand over her baby to a bewildered neighbour before she was shot to death by Ralph Hadley (*Toronto Star*, 23 Oct. 2000, B1; *Toronto Star*, 24 Oct. 2000, A1).

Richie and Kanuha, 2000) or may come from a culture where violence is condoned.

A national study involving 12,300 women, the Violence Against Women Survey (VAWS, 1993), reported that 29 per cent of women had experienced violence at some point in their lives. Forty-one per cent of women who had suffered abuse from a former partner reported 11 or more incidents of violence (ibid.). In the most recent Canadian General Social Survey (GSS, 2000), an estimated 1.2 million people (549,000 men and 690,000 women) faced some form of intimate violence between 1995 and 1999. Although the reported violence was similar (8 per cent by women and 7 per cent by men), the consequences of violence were more severe for women (Pottie-Bunge, 1998). Moreover, 65 per cent of the assaulted women stated that they were victimized more than once, while 26 per cent were victimized more than 10 times. Four out of 10 women reported experiencing some form of injury, and 15 per cent claimed that they required medical attention as a result of violence. Younger women and women in common-law relationships reported both more frequent and more severe abuse (GSS, 2000).

Termination of relationships does not guarantee the termination of violence. On the contrary, relationships that were not violent sometimes become violent at the onset of a separation (Johnson, 1995; Kaufman-Kantor and Jasinski, 1998; Kurz, 1996; Sev'er, 1997, 1998). Other findings also attest to the increased risk engendered by separation (Freeman and Vaillancourt, 1993; Crawford and Gartner; 1992; Fleury et al., 2000; Gartner et al., 2001; Jacobson and Gottman, 2001; Johnson, 1995; Kurz, 1995, 1996; Rodgers, 1994; Sev'er, 2002a; Wilson and Daly, 1993). The General Social Survey (2000) also found termination of relationships as a strong predictor of violence. Twenty-six per cent of men and women who had had contact with a former partner reported having been beaten, 19 per cent sexually assaulted, 19 per cent choked, and 17 per cent threatened with a gun. Violence committed against women was more severe (beaten or sexually assaulted, etc.) than the

violence against men (kicked, hit, etc.). These statistics partially explain why women are afraid to leave their violent partners (Glass, 1995).

HOMICIDE DATA

In the most extreme cases, women are killed by their partners and the likelihood of murder sharply increases during or shortly after separation (Campbell, 1992; Crawford and Gartner, 1992; Ellis and DeKeseredy, 1997; Jacobson and Gottman, 2001; Johnson and Chisolm, 1990; Kurz, 1995, 1996; Wilson and Daly, 1993). In their analysis of Canada's homicide data between 1974 and 1992, Wilson and Daly (1994) report 1,435 cases where women were killed by their husbands, and show that separation presented a sixfold increase in homicide risk (Wilson and Daly, 1993; Gartner et al., 2001). Women under the age of 25 were at greatest risk of becoming homicide victims (GSS, 2000; Statistics Canada, 2003).

The most current violence statistics (Statistics Canada, 2003) show a slight decline in spousal murders since the mid-1990s, but the fact remains that women are three-and-a-half times more likely to be killed by a spouse than men are (Statistics Canada, 2003).

PROBLEMS WITH NUMBERS

Official Reports

The General Social Survey (2000) estimates the total number of victims of spousal violence between 1995 and 1999 to be 1.2 million. However, only 27 per cent of these incidents (338,000) were reported to the police, either directly by the victim (71 per cent) or by someone else (29 per cent). From these estimates, we can deduce that almost three-quarters of victims *do not* report the violence they suffer. The following reasons will demonstrate why the actual rates of violence may be much greater than shown in official records.

In North America, family relationships have been increasingly designated to a private sphere (Eichler, 1997). This ideology is reflected in physical barriers such as large yards, fences, gated communities, security systems, etc. Thus, a selective blindness exists about what goes on behind closed doors and why four of the most under-reported crimes—incest, child abuse, elder abuse, and woman abuse—are committed within families (Gartner and Macmillan, 1995).

Fear of the perpetrator, immature age, feelings of shame, lack of social support, family pressure, misconceptions, and distrust towards police are also responsible for low rates of reporting. Most women do not call the police; those who call do so only if the attack was severe, if their own or their children's lives were in danger, or only after repeated beatings (Finkelhor, 1993; Kurtz, 1995; Sev'er, 2002a). Language restrictions may make immigrant and minority women even more reluctant to report their experiences (Finkelhor, 1993; Huisman, 1996; Johnson and Sacco, 1995; Koss et al., 1987; MacLeod and Shin, 1990; Rodgers, 1994).

Data from Women's Shelters

Since the 1970s, the number of shelters for abused women in Canada has grown to about 500 (Juristat, 1999; OAITH, 1998, 1999; Statistics Canada, 2003), with thousands more in the US. Shelters routinely compile information on the characteristics of women and children who seek refuge. However, although the reliability of data from shelters is very high, shelter-based findings are problematic for purposes of generalization. The following characteristics are over-represented among shelter clientele:

- They are preponderantly younger women, with young children.
- Most of the women are literate, but not highly educated.
- They are unemployed or employed in low-paying jobs with lower socio-economic status.
- Overwhelmingly, the women are urban dwellers.

Shelter data also over-represent certain groups (black and Aboriginal) but under-represent others (women from the Middle East and Asia) (Huisman, 1996). In sum, although shelters provide extensive information about violence against women and children, these data skew our information in regard to older, more affluent, or immigrant women (OAITH, 1998).

The Standardized Conflict Tactics Scale (CTS)

Measuring abuse is a problem, because the person whose experience matters most is often contested (Currie, 1998). So far, the Conflict Tactics Scale (CTS) from the New Hampshire school remains the most frequently used tool of measurement (Gelles and Straus, 1988). This instrument defines violence in gender-neutral terms as an act carried out with the intention of causing pain or injury to another person (ibid., 1988). Some questions are concerned with such terms as throwing something; pushing, grabbing, or shoving; slapping; kicking, biting, or hitting; hitting or trying to hit with something; beating up; threatening with a knife or a gun; and using a knife or a gun. The violent acts are listed in ascendance of severity. Respondents (both sexes) are asked whether any of these events happened to them within an identified span of time (last year, ever, etc.).

Despite its extensive use, the CTS is insensitive to intent, context (who hit who first, i.e., whether the act was offensive or defensive), frequency, sexual forcefulness, or the severity of consequences (a slap may leave a bruise or break a jaw). Due to measurement problems, the CTS fails to differentiate chronic and severe abuse of women from a random hit or a slap of a male partner (Currie, 1998; Dobash et al., 1992; Kelly, 1997). Studies using the CTS often find symmetry between men's and women's violence (Steinmetz, 1977–8), but feminists insist that men and women are not equal combatants (Dobash et al., 1992; Kelly, 1997; Pagelow, 1985; Sev'er, 2002a).

Consequences of Abuse of Women and Children

Consequences of violence can be physical and psychological. Physical consequences can range from cuts, bruises, lacerations, broken bones, induced miscarriages, and mutilations to death.

Repeated violence also leaves emotional scars. Women victims of abuse report chronic pain, sleeping problems, eating disorders, chronic depression, and an increased propensity for attempted suicides (Stark and Flitcraft, 1996). Women victims of violence also are more likely to abuse both legal and illegal drugs (Sev'er, 2002a). What also needs to be underscored is that the parenting skills of abused women may be seriously compromised (Levendosky and Graham-Bermann, 2001; Orava et al., 1996).

Gender and age hierarchies and privacy norms that shield families from social scrutiny can function, ironically, to make young children vulnerable. In its most common form, abuse takes the form of neglect. Increasing numbers of studies suggest that the effects of neglect may be cumulative (English et al., 2005, Kaufman-Kantor and Little, 2003). In 2002, an emaciated five-year-old Jeffrey Baldwin died, covered with sores and weighing only as much as an average 10-month-old baby would weigh. In 2006, his maternal grandparents were convicted of second-degree murder for Jeffrey's starvation death. The little boy had been placed under his grandparents' care following allegations of physical abuse by his natural parents. Unfortunately, rather than finding comfort, he spent his tragic life 'in a cold, urine-soaked, feces-coated dungeon', with occasional scraps of food, and water he drank from the toilet. He was so emaciated that he was never able to stand upright or walk. In passing his sentence, the judge called Jeffrey's demise the worst case of neglect in the history of Ontario (Coyle, 2006). In this case, the parents, grandparents, neighbours, friends, and even the child-protection agencies failed this boy.

Other forms of child abuse are physical, sexual, and/or psychological and can disproportionately victimize female children (Statistics Canada, 2003). Most North American scholars interpret child abuse as a gross violation of Article 19 of the United Nations Convention on the Rights of the Child. Article 19 states that all children have a right to protection from all forms of violence (UNICEF, 2000). Ironically, section 43 of the Criminal Code still allows teachers, parents, or parent substitutes to use force in disciplining a child under their care, and most Canadians are reluctant to repeal this controversial section.

Box 13.2 Child Abuse and Murder

In Ontario a Durham Region couple tortured their two adoptive sons for a period of 13 years. The two boys were repeatedly tied up, left alone, beaten, and locked in cribs that were turned into cages. They often consumed their own feces to cover up accidents during long periods of confinement. The abusive couple received only a nine-month jail term despite a public outcry (Roy, 2004).

Tom Dewald from Chatham, Ontario, drowned his daughter Jennifer (12) and son Christopher (10) by holding their heads under water. Initially, he claimed that the whole thing was a tragic accident. However, when his estranged female companion demanded the truth, Dewald confessed that he did away with his children in order to rekindle their relationship. During the breakup, the companion had mentioned tensions between herself and Dewald's son, never imagining that he would actually kill his children in an insane attempt to get back with her (Harries, 1999).

In Canada, a national survey brought the issue of child abuse to the forefront when more than 53 per cent of girls and more than 30 per cent of boys under the age of 21 reported experiencing at least one incident of sexual molestation (Government of Canada, 1984; Duffy and Momirov, 1997). A national study also found that 50 per cent of all female respondents experienced at least one incident of sexual molestation before reaching the age of 16 (Freeman and Vaillancourt, 1993). Currently, 60 per cent of all assaults in Canada are committed against girls, of which one-third are by close family members (Statistics Canada, 2003). In 2001, 11- to 14-year-old girls were victims in 79 per cent of the reported family-related sexual offences (Statistics Canada, 2003).

A long list of researchers (Bagley and King, 1991; Wolak and Finkelhor, 1998; Fantuzzo et al., 1991; Fantuzzo and Mohr, 1999; Jacobson and Gottman, 2001; Jaffee et al., 1990; Reppucci and Haugaard, 1993; Russell and Bolen, 2000; Zima et al., 1999) conservatively estimate that 10–11 per cent of America's female children are subjected to some form of sexual assault or are witnesses to violence against their mothers. In light of what can be asserted regarding the intergenerational transmission of violence, the implications of these findings are overwhelming (Health Canada, 1996; Graham-Berman and Levendosky, 1998).

In 2001, 51 Canadian children were murdered by their fathers/stepfathers, mothers/stepmothers, or siblings (Statistics Canada, 2002). This is a sharp rise from the corresponding 2000 figure of 37. Since these figures reflect the solved homicides where the accused is known, unsolved cases or cases misclassified as accidents may push the number of murdered children higher.

As alarming as the stated numbers are, the true incidence of child abuse is certainly larger and open to surmise. Neglect is difficult to detect unless it reaches extreme proportions such as resulted in Jeffrey Baldwin's death. Younger children may not have the language to report abuse and older children may be too frightened to do so. Thus, child abuse remains a grossly under-reported crime.

Other problems with official reports include:

- Strong taboos exist against talking about children and sexuality, even when children are sexually victimized.
- Young children may be threatened or dissuaded from disclosing the abuse, or they may be blamed or disbelieved.
- Strongly positive biases about parent–child relations and social norms regarding family privacy may deter observers (neighbours, teachers) from reporting the abuse.
- In young children, injury from out-of-the-ordinary sources may be difficult to identify and hard to prove.
- Most mothers of abused children are also victims of violence, which reduces their ability to intervene. Sometimes, abused women themselves use violence against their children.

Researchers have repeatedly found that pregnancy is a very vulnerable time for women (Kurz, 1995; 1996; Sev'er, 2002a). This means that via abuse of the mother, child abuse may start before the child's birth. Effects of abuse will vary according to age, severity, duration of abuse, and the relationship of the abuser to his/her victim (Finkelhor, 1988). The variation notwithstanding, some of the most heart-wrenching consequences of abuse are those suffered by very young children. Physical abuse may lead to cuts, bruises, infected sores, malnutrition, broken bones, and death. With sexual abuse, where many more girls than boys are victimized, abuse may produce genital tears, infections, sexually transmitted diseases, and/or unwanted pregnancies. Perhaps the most enduring consequences of abuse are psychological—the angst of eating disorders, self-hatred, self-blame, feelings of worthlessness, inability to trust, inability to form relationships, and problems with sexual intimacy, in either of the directions of promiscuity or of frigidity (Fantuzzo et al., 1991; Kendall-Tackett and Marshall, 1998; Sev'er, 2002a).

Elder Abuse

Although definitions of senior abuse may vary, most fall into the categories of physical, emotional, sexual, economic, and neglect (Department of Justice, 2003; Health Canada, 1999). Often, victims suffer more than one type of abuse. In 2001, the reported rate for senior female victimization was 49 per 100,000 older women as compared with 40 senior males per 100,000 older men. Although Canadians aged 65 and older are the least likely age group to be victims of violent crimes, those who are victimized by family members are on the rise (Lindsay, 1999; Statistics Canada, 2003). Older females are most likely to be victimized by their spouses, which signifies wife abuse that has grown old. However, in all age categories, male relatives were four to 10 times more likely to use violence against senior Canadians than female relatives.

Between 1974 and 2001, 100 older women and 100 older men were killed by their relatives (Statistics Canada, 2003: 24). Women were more likely to be killed by a spouse (53 per cent of women, 24 per cent of men). Thirty-six per cent of men who killed their wives committed suicide (as opposed to 27 per cent suicides among younger men who kill their spouses). Men were more likely to be killed by their sons (24 per cent of women, 43 per cent of men) or by other family members (18 per cent of women, 29 per cent of men). In 2003, five mothers and four fathers were killed by their daughters.

The Hidden Nature of Abuse of Seniors

DeKeseredy (1996) refers to seniors as 'hidden victims', since they may be isolated and immobile and may have reduced physical or mental capacity. Moreover, older adults may be physically, emotionally, and/or economically dependent on their abusers, just as children are and, to a significant extent in patriarchal society, as women often are. Elderly victims may remain silent, especially if the abuser is a son or a daughter. Moreover, disbelief, shame, or fear of further victimization may prevent older victims from reporting the violence they experience (Statistics Canada, 2003). In Canada, reported cases of elder abuse range from 4–5 per cent of the 65+ population. Given the strength of factors that suppress reporting, this may be the peak of an iceberg (Neysmith, 1995; Patterson and Podnieks, 1995; *Toronto Star*, 21 Feb. 1998, M3; *Toronto Star*, 23 June 1998, A9).

Box 13.3 Elder Abuse

On 15 May 1999, David Patten (44) bludgeoned to death his parents, Claire (72) and Manus Patten (80), with a shovel. The flowers David gave to Claire on Mother's Day were still on the windowsill. David was unemployed and lived with his parents for the last several years (*Toronto Star*, 15 May 1999, A2; *Toronto Star*, 17 May 1999, B3).

Dr Stephen Golesic (41), a doctor in Timmins, Ontario, was ordered to donate $8,000 to charity after pleading guilty to charges of failing to provide the basic necessities of life to his mother. Mary Golesic (72) suffered from Alzheimer's, was extremely emaciated and incontinent, and had bronchial pneumonia. She lived and died in the basement of her son's house. Witnesses underscored the stench and filth of her living conditions (*Toronto Star*, 13 Oct. 1995, A10).

Most researchers believe that older women victims of abuse are not well served by the shelters and transition houses, which are geared towards younger victims with dependent children (Sev'er, 2002b; Patterson and Podnieks, 1995). Shelters may not be structurally designed to accommodate the special needs of older women and noise may be stressful for older residents (*Toronto Star*, 23 June 1998, A9). Moreover, shelters are not equipped to deal with couples who may both be victimized by their sons or daughters. The lack of access to shelters, transportation, or communication assistance may also contribute to the under-reporting of elder abuse.

CONSEQUENCES OF ELDER ABUSE

In some cultures and societies—for instance, historically in China and among many Canadian Aboriginal groups, age often confers status, since the younger generations are routinely socialized into showing respect for their elders. Abuse does occur in such societies, but the norms against it are likely to be stronger. In contrast, those individuals in North America who revere money, power, mobility, and physical perfection may marginalize people weakened through age. A preoccupation in Euro-Canadian society and in North America more generally with individuality and the emphasis on nuclear versus extended forms of family also contribute to the alienation of the elders from the younger generations in a family, as does the fact that extended families often do not live in the same community or nearby communities as they once did. Abuse may increase isolation and feelings of shame and worthlessness, and isolation may increase abuse, creating a vicious cycle (Neysmith, 1995; Patterson and Podnieks, 1995).

Senior victims of violence may suffer more injuries than other victims. Moreover, injuries may have more serious consequences for seniors. They may take longer to heal or may precipitate death— a broken hip can be a cause of death in an elder person, for example. The federal Department of Justice (2003) reports that 37 per cent of seniors who were subjected to abuse suffered injuries, and 2 per cent suffered major injuries or death. Feelings of despair may also push a senior into taking his or her life. However, the largest proportion of abuse is through neglect.

Discussion and Conclusions

Despite the positive biases about family relations, a dark side may shadow family life. Partner, child, and elder abuse is widespread in Canada. What can be done at the personal, social, and structural levels to combat intimate abuse? For preventative or interventional answers, insights from the discussed theories will be helpful.

As we saw, individual pathology theories are not much help, since only a negligible number of offenders have clinical pathologies. However, partners who are extremely jealous, highly controlling, and abusive in the early stages of interpersonal relationships are likely to continue or even escalate their abuse in the future. Parents or partners who use drugs or alcohol are also more likely to revert to violence. Yet none of these individual factors accurately predicts the type or severity of violence.

The social dynamics of violence, especially when they intersect with gender, suggest more promising opportunities for change. Development of attitudes, perceptions, prejudices, and behaviour takes place throughout one's life, but learning is most crucial, perhaps, in early childhood. Mass media and other symbolic agents of socialization have the potential to build or to blur the boundaries of acceptable and unacceptable behaviours. Training grounds for violence include exposure to violence of family members, peers, and the media (Hatty, 2000). If learning theory is correct, when significant others that the child looks up to use violence, the propensity to use violence will increase (Health Canada, 1996). Children may see their abusive fathers, bullying peers, or sports heroes rewarded for their unacceptable behaviour. Thus, it is crucial for parents and educators, mentors in sports and entertainment, and leaders in all public roles to emphasize respect for others and tolerance for resolving differences in non-violent ways. Moreover, this educative responsibility must go beyond just words and include modelling of non-violence.

As the power and control model suggests, abuse finds a fertile ground in family relationships where there is an imbalance of power. Balancing the power between historically powerless groups (children, women, the elderly) and men may transcend family boundaries and require political and judicial interventions at the state level. The state responsibility for ending systemic abuse falls within the United Nations declaration on violence.

The necessary agents of intervention include police forces who have specialized in family violence and prosecutors and judges sensitive to gender issues for victims' cases. Availability of shelters, short- and long-term affordable housing, quality child care, and access to counselling may help to provide a way out for the victims. The rebuilding of the welfare state to include a guaranteed annual income would also be a significant step in removing the assumption of economic dependency inherent in a patriarchal society, and this dependency too often traps victims in abusive relationships. We must also keep in mind that the criminal justice system should be the last resort in dealing with interpersonal violence (Dobash et al., 1995; Pence and Paymar, 1993). As English and her colleagues remind us (2005), policy changes to protect the vulnerable are crucial, but must be carefully crafted to avoid turning the poor into scapegoats.

Elder abuse may be a sleeping monster, awaiting awakening through the demographic rise of the 65+ population (Statistics Canada, 2003). Aging Canadians increasingly find themselves isolated and considered obsolete in our youth- and power-oriented culture. When aging parents become a challenge for their adult children, the latter may have few positive role models to emulate. Adult women's lives may be sandwiched between parents and children/grandchildren. In other words, intergenerational stress and conflict may be compacting both structural and gendered problems towards the later stages of life.

This chapter has suggested that the powerlessness and dependency cycles in families that make children, women, and aging adults vulnerable to maltreatment can be broken. Awareness must be translated into programs for educating and promoting non-violent solutions in social relationships, and into policies that can break the generational cycle of abuse.

Study Questions

1. Define and compare different types of abuse.
2. Why do feminists object to the concept of psychological abuse?
3. Which theoretical orientation best explains wife/partner abuse? Why?
4. What are some consequences of child abuse?
5. Why is elder abuse one of the most under-reported crimes?

Glossary

ABCX model A stress theory that predicts a causal link between events, meanings associated with events, resources, and outcomes.

Abuse Violation of custom, injurious behaviour, or the use of harsh and insulting language.

Controlling behaviours As used by feminists, a term that refers to men's psychological domination over women's behaviour, especially language, clothing, social contacts, and work.

Dysfunctional learning model (DLM) Finkelhor's assertion that child abuse is betrayal that leads to trauma, powerlessness, and stigmatization.

Femicide Murder of women by men.

Neglect Failure to provide care or necessities for someone in need of care; applies both to omissions and commissions.

Social learning theories Theories that predict links between modelling, rewards, punishments, and such behaviour as aggression.

Spousal violence Murder, attempted murder, sexual and physical assault, threats, criminal harassment, or other violent offence by a spouse or partner.

Violence Rough force in action, rough treatment causing harm or injury, and unlawful use of force.

Websites

www.unhcr.ch/huridocda/huridoca.nsf/(Symbol)/ A.RES.48.104.En?Opendocument
This United Nations site includes the Declaration on the Elimination of Violence Against Women, as well as information on all kinds of violence in work, health care, and family life.

http://canada.justice.gc.ca/en/ps/fm
The federal Justice Department offers strategies to eliminate violence within the family as well as detailed statistical information and provincial comparisons.

www.citizenship.gov.on.ca/owd/english/facts/ preventing.htm
The Ontario Women's Directorate, an agency within the provincial government, presents detailed statistical information on violence against women in Ontario and facts on women's stays in shelters.

www.statcan.ca/Daily/English/030623/d030623c.htm
Statistics Canada's *The Daily* publishes detailed statistical reports on various issues, and this site allows searches by topic and date. It also includes excellent yearly reports on intimate violence, especially for the years 1999, 2002, and 2003.

www.statcan.ca/Daily/English/050615/d050615a.htm
This Statistics Canada site provides the latest information on Canadian shelters and the characteristics and experiences of women who use them.

www.un.org/womanwatch
Woman Watch, a UN research arm and website, tracks reproductive, health, and violence issues that the world's women face.

Further Readings

Bergen, Raquel K.; ed. 1998. *Issues in Intimate Violence.* Thousand Oaks, Calif.: Sage. A collection of 18 theoretical and analytical articles on abuse of women and children.

Jasinski, Jana L., and Linda M. Williams. 1998. *Partner Violence: A Comprehensive Review of 20 Years of Research.* Thousand Oaks, Calif.: Sage. Seven articles that review two decades of work on intimate violence. Most of the work represented here is from the US.

Krane, Julia. 2003. *What's Mother Got to Do with It?* Toronto: University of Toronto Press. Shows how state ideologies shift the responsibility of child sexual abuse away from the perpetrators by holding mothers responsible for protecting their children.

Sev'er, Aysan. 2002. *Fleeing the House of Horrors: Women Who Have Left Their Abusive Partners.* Toronto: University of Toronto Press. Analyzes the struggles of 39 women who have left their abusive partners and proposes a model of post-violence adjustment.

References

Bagley, Christopher, and Kathleen King. 1991. *Child Sexual Abuse: The Search for Healing*. London: Tavistock.

Bandura, Albert. 1973. *Aggression: A Social Learning Analysis*. Englewood Cliffs, NJ: Prentice-Hall.

Bart, Pauline B., and Eileen G. Moran. 1993. *Violence against Women: The Bloody Footprints*. Newbury Park, Calif.: Sage.

Bergen, Raquel K., ed. 1998a. *Issues in Intimate Violence*. Thousand Oaks, Calif.: Sage

———. 1998b. 'The reality of wife rape: Women's experiences of sexual violence in marriage', in Bergen (1998a: 237–50).

Bowker, Lee H., ed. 1998. *Masculinities and Violence*. Thousand Oaks, Calif.: Sage.

Brownmiller, Susan. 1975. *Against Our Will: Men, Women and Rape*. New York: Simon and Schuster.

Campbell, Jacqualine C. 1992. '"If I can't have you, no one can": Power and control in homicide of female partners', in J. Radford and D.E.H. Russell, eds, *Femicide: The Politics of Woman Killing*. New York: Twayne, 99–113.

Coyle, Jim. 2006. '"A miserable existence" eked out behind the closed door of a bedroom', *Toronto Star*, 8 Apr., 1.

Crawford, Maria, and Rosemary Gartner. 1992. *Woman Killing: Intimate Femicide in Ontario, 1974–1990*. Toronto: Women We Honour Action Committee.

Currie, Dawn H. 1998. 'Violent men or violent women: Whose definition counts?', in Bergen (1998a: 97–111).

DeKeseredy, Walter S. 1990. 'Male peer support and woman abuse: The current state of knowledge', *Sociological Focus* 23: 129–39.

———. 1996. 'Patterns of family violence', in M. Baker, ed., *Families: Changing Trends in Canada*. Toronto: McGraw-Hill, 249–72.

——— and Katharine Kelly. 1993. 'The incidence and prevalence of women abuse in Canadian university and college dating relationships', *Canadian Journal of Sociology* 18: 137–59.

——— and Linda Macleod. 1997. *Woman Abuse: A Sociological Story*. Toronto: Harcourt Brace.

——— and Martin D. Schwartz. 1997. *Sexual Assault on the College Campus: The Role of Male Peer Support*. Thousand Oaks, Calif.: Sage.

Department of Justice Statistics. 2003. 'Abuse of older adults: A fact sheet'. At: <http://canada.justice.gc.ca/en/ps/fm/adultsfs.html>; accessed 27 Sept. 2004.

Dobash, Emerson R., and Russell P. Dobash. 1979. *Violence against Wives: A Case against Patriarchy*. New York: Free Press.

——— and ———. 1992. *Women, Violence and Social Change*. New York: Routledge.

——— and ———, eds. 1998. *Rethinking Violence against Women*. Thousand Oaks, Calif.: Sage.

———, ———, Kate Cavanagh, and Ruth Lewis. 1995. *Research Evaluation of Programmes for Violent Men*. Manchester, UK: Violence Research Unit.

———, ———, Margo Wilson, and Martin Daly. 1992. 'The myth of sexual symmetry in marital violence', *Social Problems* 39, 1: 71–91.

Duffy, Ann, and J. Momirow. 1997. *Family Violence: A Canadian Perspective*. Toronto: Lorimer.

Dugan, Meg K., and Roger R. Hock. 2000. *It's My Life Now: Starting Over after an Abusive Relationship*. New York: Routledge.

Eichler, Margrit. 1997. *Family Shifts: Families, Policies, and Gender Equality*. Toronto: Oxford University Press.

Ellis, Desmond, and Walter S. DeKeseredy. 1997. 'Rethinking estrangement, interventions and intimate femicide', *Violence Against Women* 3, 6: 590–609.

English, Diana J., Richard Thompson, J. Christopher Graham, and Ernestine C. Briggs. 2005. 'Toward a definition of neglect in young children', *Child Maltreatment* 10, 2: 190–206.

Fantuzzo, John W., and Wanda K. Mohr. 1999. 'Prevalence and effects of child exposure to domestic violence', *Future of Children* 9, 3: 21–32.

———, L.M. Depaola, L. Lambert, T. Martino, G. Anderson, and S. Sutton. 1991. 'Effects of interpersonal violence on the psychological adjustment and competencies of young children', *Journal of Counselling and Clinical Psychology* 59, 2: 258–65.

Finkelhor, David. 1986. *A Sourcebook on Childhood Sexual Abuse*. New York: Sage.

———. 1988. 'The trauma of child sexual abuse: Two models', *Journal of Interpersonal Violence* 2, 4: 348–66.

———. 1993. 'The main problem is still underreporting, not overreporting', in Gelles and Loseke (1993: 273–87).

Flax, Jane. 1976. 'Do feminists need Marxism?', *Quest* 3 (Summer): 46–58.

Fleury, Ruth E., Criss M. Sullivan, and Deborah I. Bybee. 2000. 'When ending the relationship does not end the violence', *Violence Against Women* 6, 12: 1363–83.

Freeman, M.P., and M.A. Vaillancourt, eds. 1993. *Changing the Landscape: Ending Violence, Achieving Equality*. Ottawa: Minister of Supply and Services, Canadian Panel on Violence against Women.

Freud, Sigmund. 1974 [1920]. *Introductory Lectures on Psychoanalysis*. Middlesex, England: Penguin.

Gartner, Rosemary, Myrna Dawson, and Maria Crawford. 2001. 'Confronting violence in women's lives', in B.J. Fox, ed., *Family Patterns, Gender Relations*, 2nd edn. Toronto: Oxford University Press, 473–90.

Gelles, Richard J. 1987. *The Violent Home*, updated edn. Newbury Park, Calif.: Sage.

———. 1993. 'Alcohol and other drugs are associated with violence—They are not its cause', in Gelles and Loseke (1993: 182–96).

———. 1994. 'Introduction: Special issue on family violence', *Journal of Comparative Family Studies* 25, 1: 1–6.

——— and D.R. Loseke, eds. 1993. *Current Controversies on Family Violence*. Newbury Park, Calif.: Sage.

——— and Murray A. Straus. 1988. *Intimate Violence: The Causes and Consequences of Abuse in the American Family*. New York: Touchstone Books.

General Social Survey (GSS). 2000. 'Family violence', *The Daily*. Ottawa: Statistics Canada.

Glass, Dee Dee. 1995. *All My Fault: Why Women Don't Leave Abusive Men*. London: Virago Press.

Godenzi, Alberto, Walter S. DeKeseredy, and Martin D. Schwartz. 2000. 'Toward an integrated social bond/male peer support theory of woman abuse in North American college dating', unpublished paper.

Government of Canada. 1984. *Sexual Offences against Children*. Ottawa: Minister of Supply and Services.

Graham-Berman, Sandra A., and Alytia A. Levendosky. 1998. 'Traumatic stress symptoms in children of battered women', *Journal of Interpersonal Violence* 13, 1: 111–28.

Harries, K. 1999. 'Father admits drowning children', *Toronto Star*, 18 Mar., B12.

Hatty, Suzanne E. 2000. *Masculinities, Violence and Culture*. Thousand Oaks, Calif.: Sage.

Health Canada. 1996. *Wife Abuse: The Impact on Children*. Ottawa: National Clearinghouse on Family Violence.

———. 1999. *Abuses and Neglect of Older Adults*. At: <www.hc-sg.gc.ca/hppb/familyviolence/html/agenegle.html>; accessed 27 Sept. 2004.

Hill, Robert. 1958. 'Generic features of families under stress', *Social Casework* 49: 139–50.

Huisman, Kimberly A. 1996. 'Wife battering in Asian American communities', *Violence Against Women* 2, 3: 260–83.

Jacobson, Neil S., and John M. Gottman. 2001. 'Anatomy of a violent relationship', in A.S. Skolnick and J.H. Skolnick, eds, *Family in Transition*, 11th edn. Boston: Allyn and Bacon, 475–87.

Jaffee, Peter G., David A. Wolfe, and Susan K. Wilson. 1990. *Children of Battered Women*: Newbury Park, Calif.: Sage.

Jasinski, Jana L., and Linda M. Williams, eds. 1998. *Partner Violence: A Comprehensive Review of 20 Years of Research*. Thousand Oaks, Calif.: Sage.

Johnson, Holly. 1995. 'Risk factors associated with non-lethal violence against women by marital partners', in C.R. Block and R. Block, eds, *Trends, Risks and Interventions in Lethal Violence*, vol. 3. Washington: National Institute of Justice, 151–68.

———. 1996. *Dangerous Domains: Violence against Women in Canada*. Toronto: Nelson.

——— and P. Chisolm. 1990. 'Family homicide', in C. McKie and K. Thompson, eds, *Canadian Social Trends*. Toronto: Thompson Educational Publishing, 168–9.

——— and Vincent Sacco. 1995. 'Researching violence against women: Statistics Canada's national survey', *Canadian Journal of Criminology* 37: 281–304.

Juristat. 1999. Canada's Shelters for Abused Women. Canadian Centre for Justice Statistics. Catalogue no. 85–002–XPE, vol. 19, 6.

Kaufman, John, and Edward Zigler. 1993. 'The intergenerational transmission of abuse is overstated', in Gelles and Loseke (1993: 209–21).

Kaufman-Kantor, Glenda, and Jana L. Jasinski. 1998. 'Dynamics and risk factors in partner violence', in Jasinski and Williams (1998: 1–43).

——— and Liza Little. 2003. 'Defining the boundaries of child neglect: When does domestic violence equate with parental failure to protect?', *Journal of Interpersonal Violence* 18, 4: 338–55.

Kelly, Katharine D. 1997. 'The family violence and woman abuse debate: Reviewing the literature, posing alternatives', in A. Sev'er, ed., *Cross-Cultural Exploration of Wife Abuse*. Lewiston, NY: Edwin Mellen, 27–50.

Kelly, Liz, and Jill Radford. 1998. 'Sexual violence against women and girls: An approach to an international overview', in Dobash and Dobash (1998: 53–73).

Kendall-Tackett, Kathleen, and Roberta Marshall. 1998. 'Sexual victimization of children: Incest and child sexual abuse', in Bergen (1998a).

Koss, Mary P., and Sarah L. Cook. 1993. 'Facing the facts: Date and acquaintance rape are significant problems', in Gelles and Loseke (1993: 104–19).

———, Christine A. Gidycz, and Nadine Wisniewski. 1987. 'The scope of rape: Incidence and prevalence of sexual aggression and victimization in a national sample of higher education students', *Journal of Consulting and Clinical Psychology* 55, 2: 162–70.

Kurz, Demie. 1995. *For Richer, For Poorer: Mothers Confront Divorce*. New York: Routledge.

———. 1996. 'Separation, divorce and woman abuse', *Violence Against Women* 2, 1: 63–81.

Lehmann, Peter. 1997. 'The development of post-traumatic stress disorder (PTSD) in a sample of child witnesses to mother assault', *Journal of Family Violence* 12, 3: 241–57.

Levendosky, Alytia A., and Sandra A. Graham-Bermann. 2001. 'Parenting in battered women: The effects of domestic violence on women and their children', *Journal of Family Violence* 16, 2: 171–92.

Levinson, David. 1989. *Family Violence in Cross-Cultural Perspective*. Newbury Park, Calif.: Sage.

Lindsay, Colin. 1999. *A Portrait of Seniors in Canada*, 3rd edn. Ottawa: Statistics Canada, Catalogue no. 89–519–XPE.

McCubbin, H.I., and J.M Patterson. 1983. 'Family transition: Adaptation to stress', in H.I. McCubbin and C.R. Figley, eds, *Stress and the Family*, vol. 1: *Coping with Normative Stress*. New York: Brunner/Mazel, 5–25.

Mackinnon, Catharine A. 1982. 'Feminism, Marxism, method and the state: An agenda for theory', *Signs* 7 (Spring): 515–44.

MacLeod, Linda, and Maria Shin. 1990. *Isolated, Afraid, and Forgotten: The Service Delivery Needs and Realities of Immigrant and Refugee Women Who Are Battered*. Ottawa: National Clearinghouse on Family Violence.

Mahoney, Janis, and Linda M. Williams. 1998. 'Sexual assault in marriage: Prevalence, consequences and treatment of wife rape', in Jasinski and Williams (1998: 113–62).

Mitchell, Julie J. 1973. *Women's Estate*. Toronto: Random House.

Ney, Philip G. 1992. 'Transgenerational triangles of abuse: A model of family violence', in E.C. Viano, ed., *Intimate Violence: Interdisciplinary Perspectives*.

Bristol, UK: Taylor and Francis, 15–26.

Neysmith, Sheila. 1995. 'Power in relationships of trust: A feminist analysis of elder abuse', in M. MacLean, ed., *Abuse and Neglect of Older Canadians: Strategies for Change*. Toronto: Thompson.

O'Brien, Mary. 1981. *The Politics of Reproduction*. Boston: Routledge.

Ontario Association of Interval and Transition Houses (OAITH). 1998. *Falling Through the Gender Gap: How Ontario Government Policy Continues to Fail Abused Women and Their Children*. Toronto: OAITH.

———. 1999. *Ten Years for Montreal: Still Working for Change*. Toronto: OAITH.

Orava, Tammy A., Peter J. Mcleod, and Donald Sharpe. 1996. 'Perceptions of control, depressive symptomatology and self-esteem of women in transition from abusive relationships', *Journal of Family Violence* 11: 167–86.

Pagelow, Mildred D. 1985. 'The battered husband syndrome: Social problem or much ado about little?', in N. Johnson, ed., *Marital Violence*. London: Routledge & Kegan.

Patterson, Christopher, and Elizabeth Podnieks. 1995. 'A guide to the diagnosis and treatment of elder abuse', in M. Novak, ed., *Aging and Society: A Canadian Reader*. Toronto: Nelson.

Pence, Ellen, and Michael Paymar. 1993. *Education Groups for Men Who Batter: The Duluth Model*. New York: Springer.

Pillemer, Karl. 1993. 'The abused offspring are dependent: Abuse is caused by the deviance and dependence of abusive caregivers', in Gelles and Loseke (1993).

Pottie, Bunge V., and A. Levett. 1998. *Family Violence in Canada: A Statistical Profile*. Ottawa: Canadian Centre for Justice Statistics.

Renzetti, Claire M. 1998. 'Violence and abuse in lesbian relationships: Theoretical and empirical issues', in Bergen (1998a: 117–28).

Reppucci, N. Dickon, and J. Jeffrey Haugaard. 1993. 'Problems with child sexual abuse: Prevention programs', in Gelles and Loseke (1993: 306–22).

Richie, Beth E., and Valli Kanuha. 2000. 'Battered women of colour in health care system: Racism, sexism and violence', in A. Minas, ed., *Gender Basics: Feminist Perspectives on Women and Men*, 2nd edn. Belmont, Calif.: Wadsworth.

Rodgers, Karen. 1994. *Wife Assault in Canada: The Findings of a National Survey*. Juristat 14, 9. Ottawa: Canadian Centre for Justice Statistics, Statistics Canada.

—. 2000. 'Wife assault in Canada', in Statistics Canada, *Canadian Social Trends*, vol. 3. Toronto: Thompson Educational Publishing, 237–42.

Rose, Susan J., and William Meezan. 1995. 'Child neglect: A study of the perceptions of mothers and child welfare workers', *Children and Youth Services Review* 17, 4: 471–86.

Roy, C. 2004. 'Relatives get off easier for abuse, survey finds', *Toronto Star*, 7 July, B2.

Rubin, Lillian B. 1983. *Intimate Strangers: Men and Women Together*. New York: Harper and Row.

Russell, Diana E.H. 1989. 'Sexism, violence and the nuclear mentality', in Russell, ed., *Exposing Nuclear Fallacies*. New York: Pergamon, 63–74.

—— and Rebecca M. Bolen. 2000. *The Epidemic of Rape and Child Sexual Abuse in the United States*. Thousand Oaks, Calif.: Sage.

Schwartz, Martin D., and Walter S. DeKeseredy. 1997. *Sexual Assault on the College Campus: The Role of Male Peer Support*. Thousand Oaks, Calif.: Sage.

Scully, Diana. 1990. *Understanding Sexual Violence*. Boston: Unwin.

Sev'er, Aysan. 1996. 'Current feminist debates on wife abuse: Some policy implications', *Sonderbulletin* (Berlin: Humboldt University Press): 121–37.

—. 1997. 'Recent or imminent separation and intimate violence against women: A conceptual overview and some Canadian examples', *Violence Against Women* 3, 6: 566–89.

—, ed. 1998. *Frontiers in Women's Studies: Canadian and German Perspectives*. Toronto: Canadian Scholars' Press.

—. 1999. 'Exploring the continuum: Sexualized violence by men and male youth against women and girls', *Atlantis* 24, 1: 92–104.

—. 2002a. *Fleeing the House of Horrors: Women Who Have Left Their Abusive Partners*. Toronto: University of Toronto Press.

—. 2002b. 'A feminist analysis of flight of abused women, plight of Canadian shelters: Another path to homelessness', *Journal of Social Distress and the Homeless* 11: 307–24.

Seymour, Anne. 1998. 'Aetiology of the sexual abuse of children: An extended feminist perspective', *Women's Studies International Forum* 21, 4: 415–27.

Stark, Evan, and Anne Flitcraft. 1996. *Women at Risk: Domestic Violence and Women's Health*. London: Sage.

Statistics Canada. 1999. *Family Violence in Canada: A Statistical Profile*. Catalogue no. 85–224–XIE.

At: <www.statcan.ca/Daily/English/990611/d990611a.htm>.

—. 2002. 'Homicides', *The Daily*, 25 Sept.

—. 2003. *Family Violence in Canada: A Statistical Profile*. Catalogue no. 85–224–XIE. Ottawa: Canadian Centre for Justice Statistics. At: <www.statcan.ca/Daily/English/030623/d030623c.htm>.

Steed, Judy. 1994. *Our Little Secret: Confronting Child Sexual Abuse in Canada*. Toronto: Random House.

Steinmetz, Suzanne K. 1977–8. 'The battered husband syndrome', *Victimology: An International Journal* 2: 499–509.

Straus, Murray, and Richard J. Gelles. 1990. *Physical Violence in American Families: Risk Factors and Adaptations to Violence in 8145 Families*. New Brunswick, NJ: Transaction.

—, —, and Suzanne K. Steinmetz. 1986. 'The marriage license as a hitting license', in A.S. Skolnick and J.H. Skolnick, eds, *Family in Transition*, 5th edn. Boston: Little, Brown, 290–303.

UNICEF. 2000. *A World Fit for Children: Millennium Development Goals Special Session on Children Documents the Convention of the Rights of the Child*. New Delhi, India: UNICEF.

United Nations (UN). 1993. Declaration on the Elimination of Violence Against Women (DEVAW). At: <www.un.org/womanwatch/daw/devaw>; accessed 24 May 2001.

Violence Against Women Survey (VAWS). 1993. *The Daily* Statistics, 18 Nov. Ottawa: Statistics Canada, Catalogue no. 11–001.

Wilson, Margo, and Martin Daly. 1993. 'Spousal homicide risk and estrangement', *Violence and Victims* 8: 3–15.

—— and ——. 1994. 'Spousal homicide', *Juristat* 14: 1–15.

Wolak, Janis, and David Finkelhor. 1998. 'Children exposed to partner violence', in Jasinski and Williams (1998: 73–111)

Wolfe, D., L. Zak, and S. Wilson. 1986. 'Child witness to violence between parents: Critical issues in behaviour and social adjustment', *Journal of Abnormal Child Psychology* 14, 1: 95–102.

Yllo, Kersti A., and Michel Bograd, eds. 1988. *Feminist Perspectives on Wife Abuse*. Newbury Park, Calif.: Sage.

Zima, Bonnie T., Regina Bussing, and Maria Bystritsky. 1999. 'Psychological stressors among sheltered homeless children: Relationship to behavioural problems and depressive symptoms', *American Journal of Orthopsychiatry* 69, 1: 127–33.

CHAPTER 14

Families and the State: Family Policy in Canada

Catherine Krull

Learning Objectives

- To understand the evolution of Canada's family policies within a liberal welfare state.
- To understand the ideology and implications of a universal approach versus a targeted approach to family policies.
- To become aware of how progressive Quebec's family policies are and how they might serve as a model for the rest of Canada.
- To get a better comprehension as to why Canada's targeted family policies have not yet eradicated child poverty as promised by Parliament in 1989.
- To be aware that the fight for a universal subsidized child-care program is not a recent phenomenom, but that feminists and advocacy groups have been working for such a program for the past three and half decades.
- To become conscious of the reasons why state intervention is necessary if parents, especially mothers, are to have better balance between employment and family responsibilities, and to recognize the implications that such a balance has on achieving gender equity.
- To appreciate the challenges that governments and family policy-makers face in Canada in developing the new child-care measures.

Introduction

In Canada, the state[1] has always been involved with families to some degree. It determines who can marry, at what age they can marry, and whether marriages can end. In a general sense, the state relies on families to care for and support its individual members and on its adult members to reproduce the population, thereby perpetuating Canadian cul-

ture and ensuring an adequate number of taxpayers, consumers, and labour force members (Baker, 1994). And just as the state relies on families, Canadian parents rely on the state for economic and social support to facilitate a healthy family life, for example, in balancing child care with paid work. **Family policy**, therefore, has central importance in Canadian life—determining how families are defined and formed, which family members are entitled to governmental support, and the amount and type of support that families can receive.

Family policy does not necessarily mean a cohesive policy; rather, it usually includes an array of policies and programs that either directly or indirectly have an impact on families. In this chapter, family policy will be more narrowly defined to include only those measures that directly relate to families with children under the age of 18 years. Such measures include:

> direct and indirect cash transfers for families with children (e.g. family allowances, means-tested family benefits, tax relief for dependent children); benefits related to work and granted to workers with family responsibilities (e.g. maternity and paternity leave, children-care leave); services to families (e.g. day-care centres, after-school care); other services and benefits for families with children in the field of housing, education, and health; and legislation directly affecting families (e.g. abortion, divorce, child alimony). (Gauthier, 1998: 3)

Although the federal and provincial governments have been involved in Canadian family life for more than a century, the country still lacks a comprehensive national family policy; rather, there exists a piecemeal set of programs and policies that either directly or indirectly have an impact on families. Moreover, state intervention in Canada has tended to be minimal in comparison to many other countries, especially in terms of the day-to-day functioning of families. The state has tended to limit itself primarily to situations of child abuse, child neglect, and limited family financial resources; and even in these situations, intervention has varied by gender and for different income and cultural groups (Baker, 2001). Moreover, state intervention has diverged significantly from province to province.

Governments at every level have consistently been criticized for their ambivalence and lack of agreement about their role in family matters, and for their insistence that matters such as child care and child development are the responsibility of individuals rather than the state (O'Hara, 1998). Beauvais and Dufour (2003) charge that there is a 'hierarchy of help' in Canada when it comes to assisting families—the first level of response is left up to the labour market, the second is a family responsibility; if these two levels fail to meet family needs, the state will involve itself in only a limited and targeted way. However, this hierarchical system prevents women from full participation in the labour force and, as such, impedes their progress for equality and independence.

The lack of a cohesive national family policy is due to several factors. Like citizens of other countries, Canadians are faced with new policy challenges as they attempt to address an aging population and increasing globalization. When governments make policy, they must take into consideration the conflicting viewpoints of family-oriented public interest groups—electors who put them in office—and these debates impede the development of a cohesive national policy. 'While the left seeks to include previously excluded interpretations of needs, the right aims to redefine what constitutes legitimate needs, who has the authority to define them, and how they are to be satisfied in ways that challenge social rights and the state's obligation to meet them' (Evans and Wekerle, 1997: 13). In addition, as Canada is a federal state,

there arises a unique constitutional impediment to the development of a cohesive national family policy. Different levels of government—federal, provincial, and territorial—have assumed different responsibilities. The federal government has tended to focus on income support, whereas provincial and territorial governments have concentrated on providing welfare assistance and other services, with a strong emphasis on child protection (O'Hara, 1998).

In its approach to family policy, Canada falls somewhere between the countries of Western Europe and the United States. It mirrors Western Europe in terms of its investment in health and education and in some of the family benefits offered by the federal government (for instance, maternity and parental leave and child tax benefits); and although these benefits are at a lower level than those enjoyed by the Western Europeans, they are at a higher level than in the United States. However, in one crucial area, Canada is the same as its southern neighbour: it shares a shameful history of extremely high child poverty rates (ibid., 9).

To understand the present state of family policy in Canada, three questions pose themselves. How have Canadian family policies evolved in the recent past? What are the strengths and weaknesses of these policies? And in response to criticism, how has the state decided to involve itself in the process of producing more effective policy? In answering these questions, an important point needs to be made. The province of Quebec provides a stellar example of government policies that both put a priority on family and serve as a potential model that the rest of Canada could follow to develop a cohesive national policy. Despite budgetary constraints on public finance, but confronting the increasing needs of families, the various levels of government began serious and promising discussions in late 1990s about creating a national family policy. But the process remained arduous: 'Canadian governments are beginning—sometimes hesitantly, sometimes enthusiastically, sometimes not at all—to see their role as one of sharing with parents in the responsibility for the well-being of all children' (Jensen and Thompson, 1999: 2–3).

Canada's Family and Child-related Policies

MATERNITY AND PARENTAL/ADOPTION LEAVE BENEFITS

Paid maternity and parental leaves occupy a central place in Canada's **liberal welfare state**. In specific terms, these policies are meant to assist Canadians in balancing family and employment. However, Canada has not had the best track record in this regard. Although all of Western Europe, Australia, New Zealand, and Japan adopted some form of paid maternity leave legislation by 1939, it took Canada until 1971 to offer women such assistance. The reason was that 'the responsibility of protecting pregnant women at work and compensating them for the loss of earnings was not seen as a governmental responsibility' (Gauthier, 1998: 197).

When the legislation was finally passed, the responsibility for **maternity benefits** (and later parental/adoption leave) was divided between the federal and provincial/territorial governments. The provinces and territories were obligated to determine the length and conditions of maternity leave, while financial replacement fell under the jurisdiction of the federal government's Unemployment Insurance [UI] program. If they had been paying UI premiums, working mothers were initially given 15 weeks of paid leave and received approximately 67 per cent of their regular salary as unemployment benefits. And if they so chose, these women had the option of taking two additional weeks of unpaid leave. Women adopting a child were finally made eligible to receive benefits in 1984. The provinces also offered unpaid maternity leave and, although unpaid, it nevertheless was beneficial because these mothers were guaranteed the right to return to the same or an equivalent job (Jensen and Thompson, 1999: 13).

Bowing to pressure from women's groups, the federal government introduced 10 weeks of **parental leave** in 1990, which could be taken by either parent or shared between them; the parent who took leave received unemployment benefits equalling 60 per cent of her/his regular salary. In 1996, eligibility for maternity benefits changed from being based on the number of weeks worked to the number of hours, but now women only received a maximum of 55 per cent of their regular salary with a maximum benefit of $413 per week (Baker, 2001; OECD, 2004). In a comparative study on international family policies, Gauthier (1998) found that when both the duration of the leave and maternity pay were taken into consideration, Canada was among the lowest of 22 industrialized countries.

In January 2001, the federal government doubled the amount of time that new parents could receive benefits, from 25 to a maximum of 50 weeks (Government of Canada, 2005). While maternity leave remained the same (15 weeks at 55 per cent of insurable earnings), parental leave increased from 10 to 35 weeks at 55 per cent of insurable earnings. To be eligible for the maximum, parents had to have worked a minimum of 600 hours of insurable employment in the previous 12 months. At present, a mother can add the parental leave to her maternity leave—giving her 50 weeks of paid leave—or she can take maternity leave (15 weeks), return to her employment, and the father could then take the 35-week parental leave. Another advantage of the new parental leave benefits is that parents can earn up to 25 per cent of their weekly benefits in part-time work without being penalized. In its October 2004 report card on Canada's childcare system, the Organization for Economic Co-operation and Development (OECD) praised Canada for its enhanced parental leave, stating that 'this has been a tremendous breakthrough for Canadian parents and infants' (OECD, 2004: 55).

FROM UNIVERSAL TO TARGETED CHILD AND FAMILY BENEFITS

The federal government has been financially supporting Canadian families in some way or another since 1918, when it introduced the Child Tax

Exemption, which allowed breadwinners with dependent children an annual fiscal deduction on their income tax (Baker, 2001; Lefebvre and Merrigan, 2003). In 1945, a monthly Family Allowance was paid to women with children at home. These two contributions were important because they were universal. In other words, they offered financial assistance to all families with dependent children. Family Allowance was also significant because it was paid directly to mothers, which for many women at this time was the only source of income that was theirs alone. These two universal contributions, the Child Tax Exemption and Family Allowance, became known as 'child and family benefits' (Baker, 2001) and developed as the pillars of Canadian family policy (Lefebvre and Merrigan, 2003).

By the late 1980s, Ottawa had become quite concerned about the country's high child poverty rates. Throughout that decade, child poverty rates in Canada ranged from 15.7 to 20.6 per cent—rates that were among the highest in the industrial world and second only to the United States (O'Hara, 1998). In 1989, a resolution was unanimously passed in the House of Commons to achieve the goal of eradicating child poverty by the year 2000. The next year, Canada signed the United Nations Convention on the Rights of the Child, a treaty that committed all signatories to protect and ensure children's rights and to hold themselves accountable for this commitment before the international community.

Between 1988 and 1993, the Conservative government of Brian Mulroney took measures that completely transformed family benefits with the goal of reducing child poverty. 'Discussions of poverty focused almost exclusively on 'child poverty,' as children were always seen as the deserving poor, whereas adults drawing social benefits were often suspected of defrauding the welfare system' (Baker, 2001: 276). The child tax deduction was cancelled in 1988 and replaced with a non-refundable child tax credit, a device that minimized significantly the amount received from wealthier families. In 1993, the Conservative

government abolished both Family Allowance and the non-refundable tax credit and introduced the Child Tax Benefit (CTB). The CTB paid low-income families an annual amount for each child, an additional supplement for each subsequent child under seven years of age, and a Working Income Supplement (WIS). These changes marked a monumental change in Canada's approach to family policy—universal benefits (designed to assist all families with dependent children) were substituted with targeted benefits (designed to assist low-income families).

In 1998, the Liberal government of Jean Chrétien developed the National Child Benefit (NCB). The NCB included the Canada Child Tax Benefit (CCTB)—just a new name for the previous CTB—and the National Child Benefit Supplement (NCBS), which replaced the WIS. In adhering to the parliamentary commitment to reduce poverty, only low-income families can receive the maximum annual basic amount. As of 2003 and after several amendments, the CCTB pays an annual maximum of $1,169 per child to families whose net income does not exceed $33,487. If they are not claiming the child-care deduction, parents are entitled to an additional $232 for each child under the age of seven. The maximum annual NCBS benefit currently pays families whose net income does not exceed $21,529: $1,463 for the first child and $1,254 for the second child (National Council of Welfare, 2004b).

The federal government has promised to gradually raise the CCTB to a maximum of $3,243 per child per year by 2007 (Canadian Council on Social Development, 2004: 6). But despite this promised increase in the CCTB, the NCBS may be fully or partially clawed back by provincial and territorial governments if families are receiving provincial social assistance (welfare). Therefore, while New Brunswick and Newfoundland and Labrador continue to allow welfare families to collect the full amount allotted by the NCBS, the supplement is fully or partially clawed back in British Columbia, Saskatchewan, Ontario, Prince Edward Island, Nunavut, and the Northwest Territories.

Nova Scotia, Quebec, Manitoba, and Alberta have recently reduced the amount of their clawbacks (National Council of Welfare, 2004a). The irony is that the federal government increases child benefits but allows provinces to reduce or deny them altogether for families on social assistance, the families most in need given that the welfare rates are well below the poverty line in every province in Canada (National Council of Welfare, 2004a).

Assessment of Canada's Child and Family Benefits

IMPACT OF MEASURES ON CHILD POVERTY

Canada's current child benefits have come under a great deal of criticism. Feminists argue that they represent a step backward for women in terms of their full and equal participation in the labour force. McKeen (2001: 187) suggests that 'the

move from universal entitlement to means testing on the basis of family income limits women's access to benefits, encourages familial dependency, and turns back progress in the effort to make the recognition of individual autonomy an important policy objective.' In essence, Canada's efforts since 1989, when Parliament promised to work towards eliminating child poverty by the year 2000, have failed dismally. In 1989, when the resolution passed, the child poverty rate was 14.9 per cent. Yet, poverty rates have been higher than the 1989 rate for every single year since then, not lower as promised. As Figure 14.1 indicates, child poverty rates increased after 1989 until they reached a high of 21.1 per cent in 1996. After this time, they decreased to 15.6 per cent in 2001. Although the rates have come down, the 2001 rate is still higher than it was in 1989 when Canada promised to eradicate child poverty.

Figure 14.1 Poverty Rates for Children under 18, Canada, 1980–2001

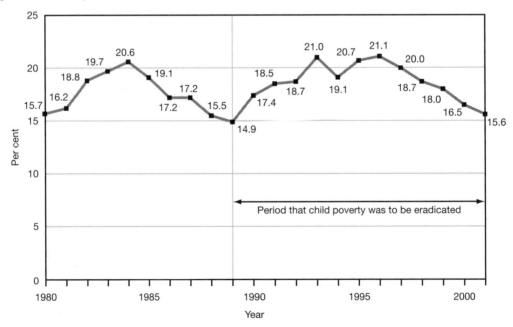

SOURCE: National Council of Welfare (2004b).

Critics of Canada's current NCB program are concerned that focus on impoverished children rather than on impoverished families relieves governments from both the responsibility to alleviate the causes of poverty and the provision of appropriate measures like providing employment for the parents of impoverished children (O'Hara, 1998: 9). Lefebvre and Merrigan (2003) demonstrate that poor children are poor because their parents are poor. Likewise, Jensen (2003) argues that in focusing solely on children, the rights and concerns of adults have become marginalized. Once children have left the nest, poor parents are no longer entitled to benefits and risk falling into deeper poverty. It is essential to point out that these critics do not advocate that governments should not invest in children. Rather, the prescription is that they cannot do so to the exclusion of adults and, in particular, single mothers, who are more likely to be impoverished.

Large disparities in poverty rates exist between family types. In 2001, the poverty rates were 9.5 per cent for two-parent families, 19.3 per cent for families headed by single-parent fathers, but 42.4 per cent for families headed by single-parent mothers (National Council of Welfare, 2004b). Despite decreasing over the past two decades, poverty rates for single-parent families headed by mothers remain twice that of such families headed by fathers and account for more than 90 per cent of poor single-parent households. In addition, the poverty rate for families headed by single mothers under the age of 25 jumps to 74 per cent (ibid.). Not surprisingly, there is also a fair amount of provincial variability in these rates. Manitoba and New Brunswick had the highest poverty rates in 2001 for families headed by single-parent mothers (54.7 per cent and 52.6 per cent, respectively), whereas Ontario and Alberta had the lowest (38.3 per cent and 39 per cent, respectively) (ibid.).

While two-parent families have by far the lowest poverty rates of all family types, these can differ depending on how many earners there are in the family. The poverty rate in two-parent families is 2.2 per cent for those with three or more employed family members, 5.1 per cent for those with two employed family members, but 28 per cent where only one person is employed (ibid.). Although being employed offsets poverty to some degree, having only one earner in a family is not adequate for most families. The Canadian Council on Social Development (2005: 3) reports that approximately half of all low-income children in Canada live in families where the parent or parents worked all year and still could not rise above the poverty line.

Of course, the poverty rate, which measures the risk of poverty within any given group, is important in judging policy. But so, too, is the number or percentage of poor families that exist in Canada. According to the National Council of Welfare (2004b: 110):

> One of the myths about child poverty is that since single-parent families have high poverty rates, most poor children must live in single-parent families. That has never been the case for any of the years on record. The largest number of poor children has always been the number living in two-parent families.

For example, although two-parent families have a relatively low poverty rate (10.8 per cent), children living in two-parent families accounted for 57 per cent of all poor children in Canada. In terms of non-two-parent families, 3 per cent of low-income children lived in families headed by single fathers, 36 per cent lived in families headed by single mothers, and 4 per cent were in other living arrangements (ibid.).

In May 2002, Canada participated in the United Nations General Assembly Special Session on Children and, along with many other countries, signed the UN Declaration on 'A World Fit for Children'. In ratifying this document, the federal government promised to develop a national plan of action based on Canada's unique circumstances that took into consideration four priority areas: promoting healthy lives; providing quality education;

protecting children against abuse, exploitation, and violence; and combatting HIV/AIDS. In 2004, Ottawa released its plan, 'A Canada Fit for Children', that reaffirmed the federal government's commitment to make children and families a national priority (see full report on-line at www.sdc.gc.ca).

Despite these efforts, critics claim that the government is still not doing enough. For example, the Canadian Council on Social Development has estimated that although the government's social investment has had some impact in that it kept 570,000 children out of poverty, CCTB benefits would need to be increased to $4,900 per child for real progress on child poverty (CCSD, 2004: 6). The National Council of Welfare echoes these concerns, charging that despite government promises to give priority to child poverty and work towards eliminating it, it has done little outside of gradually increasing child benefits. The Council has repeatedly urged the government for 'an integrated and coherent family policy in Canada that includes affordable, accessible child care and development' (National Council of Welfare, 2004b: 132).

Andrew Armitage, the Director of the School of Social Work at the University of Victoria, similarly asserts that Canada's current measures 'constitute one of the weakest social policy responses to family need that can be found in Western developed countries' (Armitage, 2003: 76). Government policies have obviously been inadequate—more than one million children live in poverty; one-third of all Canadian children experience poverty for at least one year; one in four workers (two million adults) are in low-wage employment; low-income couples with children remain, on average, $9,000 below the poverty line; the child poverty rate for female lone-parent families has risen above 50 per cent; the child poverty rates for children in Aboriginal, immigrant, and visible minority groups are more than double the average for all children; and 2003 was a record year for food bank use, of which over 300,000 users were children (CCSD, 2004: 1, 5). The critics have a point. Canadian families need better policy from their government.

IMPACT OF MEASURES ON CHILD CARE

One area where better policy can be helpful concerns child care. Despite all political discourse and efforts to this end over the past 35 years, little has been done to provide affordable quality child care. Women have constituted a large part of the workforce for several decades, yet for countless working women the challenge of balancing work and family responsibilities remains daunting. 'Many are *forced out of the labour force* to care for young children because they cannot afford to pay for child care or they do not have sufficient guarantees of return to employment. Conversely, others are virtually *forced back into employment* because they cannot sustain the income loss associated with taking even a limited unpaid parental leave' (Jensen and Thompson, 1999: 19). Today, fathers have taken on more child-care and domestic responsibilities than in the past and, as a consequence, they, too, can find the act of balancing work and family overwhelming. Parents often feel it their responsibility to overcome the challenges and problems encountered in trying to find equilibrium between family life and their employment. This message is reinforced by society—one just has to look at the numerous self-help books in any bookstore that offer advice on how to be more creative with time management so to better balance family and work (see Box 14.1).

Regulated child care has always been a provincial and territorial jurisdiction. It follows that policy, child-care services, and funding for child care vary considerably across jurisdictions. And with the exception of Quebec, subsidies are targeted to low-income families, leaving all other families to face exorbitant costs without help. Many parents cannot afford high-quality care, yet the effect that child care has on children ultimately depends on the quality of that care (McCloskey, 2001).

While feminists and advocacy groups have long recognized the urgent need for a government-supported quality child-care program based on universality, it has remained elusive. As early as 1970, the Royal Commission on the Status of Women stressed the importance of a subsidized national

Box 14.1   A Sample of Recently Published Self-Help Books on Balancing Employment and Family Responsibilities

Work-Life Balance in the 21st Century by Diane Houston (Palgrave, 2005).

How She Really Does It: The Secrets of Success from Stay-At-Work Moms by Wendy Sachs (HarperCollins Canada/Da Capo, 2005).

What's Wrong with Day Care: Freeing Parents to Raise Their Own Children by Charles Siegel (University of Toronto Press, 2005).

The Frazzled Factor: Relief for Working Moms by Karol Ladd and Jane Jarrell (W Publishing Group, 2005).

From Work-Family Balance to Work-Family Interaction: Changing the Metaphor by Diane F. Halpern (Lawrence Erlbaum Associates, 2005).

If You've Raised Kids, You Can Manage Anything: Leadership Begins at Home by Ann Crittenden (Gotham Books, 2004).

Going Back to Work: A Survival Guide for Comeback Moms by Mary W. Quigley and Loretta E. Kaufman (St Martin's Press, 2004).

7 Myths of Working Mothers: Why Children and (Most) Careers Just Don't Mix by Suzanne Venker, Foreword by Laura C. Schlessinger (Spence Publishing Company, 2004).

Home-Alone America: The Hidden Toll of Day Care, Behavioral Drugs, and Other Parent Substitutes by Mary Eberstadt (Penguin USA, 2004).

Work-Family Challenges for Low-Income Parents and Their Children by Ann C. Crouter and Alan Booth (Lawrence Erlbaum Associates, 2004).

I Love My Life: A Mom's Guide to Working from Home by Kristie Tamsevicius (Wyatt-MacKenzie Publishing, 2003).

The Mom Economy: The Mother's Guide to Getting Family-Friendly Work by Elizabeth Wilcox (Berkley Trade, 2003).

Working Mothers and Juvenile Delinquency by Thomas Vander Ven (LFB Scholarly Publishing, 2003).

Flex Time: A Working Mother's Guide to Balancing Career and Family by Jacqueline Foley, Foreword by Sally Armstrong (Avalon Publishing Group, 2003).

Working Women Don't Have Wives: Professional Success in the 1990s by Terri Apter (St Martin's Press, 1995).

Survival Tips for Working Moms: 297 Real Tips from Real Moms by Linda Goodman Pillsbury (Perspective Publishing, 2003).

Starting in Our Own Backyard: How Community Life Can Solve the Work-Family Crisis by Ann Bookman (Routledge, 2003).

child-care program: 'the time is past when society can refuse to provide community child care services in the hope of dissuading mothers from leaving their children and going to work' (in Jensen and Thompson, 1999: 12). The Royal Commission on Equality in Employment raised the subject again in 1984: 'Child care is not a luxury, it is a necessity. Unless government policy responds to this urgency, we put women, children and the economy of the future at risk. . . . policy should not be permitted to remain so greatly behind the times' (Armitage, 2003: 119). In 1982, a federally funded National Daycare Conference was held. The Katie Cooke Task Force, an outcome of the Conference, pushed for a universal daycare system for the next few years.

In 1988, the Canada Child Care Act was introduced in Parliament; it proposed an additional 200,000 subsidized child-care spaces, doubling the number of existing spaces, which accommodated only 13 per cent of children needing care. The bill was not passed by the House of Commons (Armitage, 2003). The issue became politicized, especially given the supposed desire of each federal party in Parliament to end child poverty by 2000. Therefore, in 1993, the opposition Liberals provided a detailed proposal for a national child-care program in their party manifesto, the so-called 'Red Book'; but nothing came of it after they won the general election that year. The reason was simple. Daycare remained expensive—'while child care makes for good electioneering, delivering child care is a somewhat daunting enterprise' due to its enormous expense (Krashinsky, 2001: 3). Families with two preschool children spend almost 23 per cent of their gross annual income on government-regulated daycare (Jensen and Thompson, 1999: 12).

By the late 1990s, talks on this matter resumed between the federal and provincial governments, culminating in a series of agreements that moved forward a national agenda for a universal child-care package. In 2003, the Multilateral Framework on Early Learning and Child Care underscored an emerging federal-provincial consensus on the necessity of such a program (CCSD, 2004: 7). However, for the Liberal government, now led by Paul Martin, costs remained an issue.

Little progress had been made by the autumn of 2004 when the OECD published its study of Canada's child-care system, part of an overall review of such systems in 21 leading industrialized countries. Although the OECD lauded Canada's enhanced parental leave program, it found the country's child-care system severely underfunded with no overarching goals, the training of many child-care workers to be poor, and the problem of high staff turnover at many centres. Canadian parents were also expected to pay more for child care than in other countries, and despite Canada having one of the highest percentages of employed mothers the Canadian government contributed half of what other developed countries in Europe did on child care. Less than 20 per cent of Canadian children under the age of seven had a space in a regulated centre, an extremely low figure compared to other industrialized countries such as Belgium (63 per cent), Denmark (78 per cent) France (69 per cent), Portugal (40 per cent), and the UK (60 per cent) (OECD, 2004: 7). The OECD report concluded:

> During the 90s, growth in early childhood services slowed significantly in Canada. . . .The result is a patchwork of economic, fragmented services. . . . In the same period, other OECD countries have been progressing toward publicly managed, universal services focused on the development of young children . . . [which are] expected to play a significant role with respect to social cohesion, the alleviation of the effects of child poverty, improved child health and screening, better parenting and family engagement in education. (Ibid., 6)

Among its many recommendations, the OECD suggested that Canada double its child-care spending to the average of other OECD countries and that the federal and provincial governments each pay 40 per cent of daycare costs, leaving parents responsible for the remaining 20 per cent. It was also strongly recommended that child-care workers be given better training and that child care be integrated with kindergarten.

Many Canadians were shocked by these findings. The federal NDP leader, Jack Layton, lamented that the OECD's report is 'a stinging indictment of Paul Martin's choice to break his child care promises. . . . If he had kept his first promise 11 years ago, the international community wouldn't be looking at Canada and saying we've failed' (CBC News, 2004). The Child Care Advocacy Association of Canada responded with a report urging the federal government to commit at least $10 billion for day-care within 15 years (CBC News, 2005). For its part, the Canadian Council on Social Development also argued for substantially increased funding from the federal government and a commitment that a developmentally focused child-care system be implemented that achieved the principles of universality, quality, accessibility, and inclusion (CCSD, 2004: 9). Many critics of the current system also suggested that the rest of Canada should look at Quebec as a model to build a national cohesive family policy (Canadian Policy Research Networks, 2003; Jensen, 2002; Krull, 2003; OECD, 2004).

Quebec's Family Policies: An Example to Follow

In this context, Quebec's family policies have been distinct from those in the rest of the country in both their evolution and their success. There are several reasons for this. Until 1997, Quebec's family policies had been geared towards promoting population growth: a pro-natal strategy of 'strength in numbers' (often referred to as *la revanche des berceaux*—'the revenge of the cradle') as a means of overcoming Quebec's subordination to English Canada and safeguarding Québécois culture. Second, there has been more government intervention and a stronger focus on universal support for families than in the rest of Canada. In this way, Quebec has moved beyond being a 'liberal' welfare society, like Canada and the United States, and

is moving towards a more heavily state interventionist model—similar to those in **social democratic states** such as Scandinavian countries—but with its own distinctive characteristics. Finally, Quebec is unique in that, since 1997, it has had a comprehensive family policy directed at strengthening families, assisting parents in balancing paid work and family responsibilities, and promoting parental employability—all of which are still lacking in the rest of Canada.

QUEBEC'S PRO-NATAL POLICIES

In the past two decades, there have been two major strategies to Quebec's family policy—pro-natalism (1988–97) and strengthening families (1997–present). Its **pro-natal policies** were in part a reaction to the many changes that occurred to family life as a result of the province's Quiet Revolution during the premiership of Jean Lesage (1960–6). Quebec's new nationalism, often referred to as the 'Quiet Revolution' because it 'quietly' but radically transformed and secularized Québécois society, generated liberal values, advanced the French language and education for both sexes, and provided an environment conducive to feminist reform (Behiels, 1986; Comeau, 1989; Thomson, 1984). Consequently, beginning in the 1960s, Quebec society witnessed historic changes to family life and to the status of women, including sharp increases in cohabitation, divorce, and births to unmarried women, as well as substantial declines in religiosity, marriages, and births (Krull, 2003; Langlois et al., 1992). With a decrease from an average of five children per woman in 1959 to its current level of 1.47 children per woman (Krull, 2003; Maximova, 2004: 3), Quebec nationalists were concerned that if the population continued to decline, Québécois culture could be in jeopardy.

Advocating direct government intervention, politicians and demographers proposed a monetary incentive program to elevate fertility levels. In a population-engineering effort unprecedented in North America, the Quebec government implemented three programs of direct financial assistance in 1988: allowances for newborns that, after amendments, paid women $500 for a first birth, $1,000 for a second, and $8,000 for third and subsequent births; a family allowance for all children under 18 years; and additional allowances for children under six years. Three rules underscored these programs: universality; monetary increases according to the rank—first, second, and so on—of the child; and more money for young children.

Reactions to the policies varied (Baker, 1994; Gavreau, 1991; Hamilton, 1995; Krull, 2003; Lavigne, 1986). Non-interventionists argued that fertility decisions were individual, not governmental, responsibilities. Feminists charged that Quebec's pro-natal policies marginalized women, reducing them to objects of demographic policy (Maroney, 1992). Social interventionists supported government action, not through pro-natalist intervention but through social policies to improve female equity and assist families. Of particular importance were policies to decrease tensions between employment and family responsibilities. These critiques coincided with a growing awareness that Quebec's incentive policies were not producing expected birth increases—families with three or more children remained atypical. Importantly, policies favouring third and subsequent children were viewed increasingly as contrary to the needs of most families.

From Pro-Natalism to Pro-Family

Quebec radically transformed its family and child support programs in 1997. It created the Ministère de la Famille et de l'Enfance (Ministry of Families and Children) and gave it a budget of $500 million. The new ministry's agenda was threefold (Ministère de la Famille et de l'Enfance, 1999). The first objective was to establish a unified child allowance program for low-income families—the amount of allowances would depend on the number of dependent children under 18 years, family type (single-parent, two-parent), and income (a threshold of $15,332 for single-parent families; $21,825 for two-parent families). This allowance was meant to supplement the CCTB, which Quebec

found to be insufficient for a family to survive. The second objective was to implement a maternity-parental leave insurance plan whereby parental remuneration increased during and following pregnancy. The third objective was to provide a network of government-regulated, highly subsidized ($5 per day) child-care facilities that offered a quality educational program to children from birth to kindergarten age. Parents who qualified for an income supplement program had only to pay $2 per day. By September 1997, all but the parental insurance plan had been implemented.

These three policy initiatives demonstrate the Quebec government's efforts at strengthening families and distinguish Quebec's strategy from those in the rest of Canada, the United States, and many European countries. Presently, Quebec is the only province to have universal subsidized daycare. Although the amount that parents pay increased from $5 per day to $7 per day in January 2004, the amount is negligible compared to the amounts paid in other provinces (Ministère de l'Emploi, de la Solidarité sociale et de la Famille, 2005). The average monthly cost of daycare in Ontario is about $715 compared to $140 in Quebec (Ross, 2006: 2). And in this equation, the portion of cost assumed by the Quebec government is $31 per day, or 82 per cent of the overall cost (Hamilton, 2004). Parents on social assistance are not charged for the first 23.5 hours per week and, if they enrol in an employability program, they are not charged for additional hours. To facilitate child care, employees can also take an annual maximum of 10 days away from work for family reasons.

In developing universal policy initiatives like low-cost child-care services, a range of tax credits, and full-day kindergarten for five-year-olds, Quebec can no longer be classified as a liberal welfare state (Dandurand and Kempeners, 2002; Jensen, 2002). Policy initiatives in liberal welfare states, such as the rest of Canada and the United States, favour targeting specific kinds of families, such as those with low incomes, rather than supporting all of them. Moreover, liberal welfare states are reluctant to involve themselves in the day-today activities of family life, including the problems involved with balancing paid work and family life. In this way, based on its child-care and family policy initiatives, Quebec is moving towards the more heavily state interventionist model—social democracy—of the Scandinavian countries (Beauvais and Dufour, 2003).

Quebec's family allowance is also innovative. While it targets low-income families with children under 18, the amount paid out is inversely related to the number of adults living in the house: the more adults in the household, the less received in benefits. Thus, single-parent families receive the most in benefits and tax breaks. The design decisions 'reflect nothing of the "moral panic" about lone mothers characterizing some liberal welfare states in the years of welfare reform. Nor do they reproduce the neutrality of programmes that do not take into account the particular difficulties faced by lone parents' (Jensen, 2002: 310). In 2002, the province passed Bill 112, a law that commits the Quebec government to develop an anti-poverty action plan with the goal of cutting poverty rates in half by 2012. It also requires the provincial government to make public a progress report every three years.

Critics charge that these new initiatives fall short of a universal, non-gender-specific program that assists all types of parenting. The family allowance program provides targeted assistance aimed almost exclusively at working low-income families. However, families with a net income of less than $10,000 benefit only marginally since the increase in family assistance is offset by a reduction of a similar amount in social assistance and families with a net income of $25,000 or higher now receive less family assistance than they did with the previous pro-natal policies (Baril et al., 2000: 4–5). Moreover, there are not enough regulated daycare spaces to keep up with demand—only one in five Quebec children has access to daycare space (the national average is one in eight children) (CBC News, 2005). Consequently, Quebec daycares have long waiting lists (parents might wait for several years) and one of the highest ratios

of children to daycare workers (Thompson, 1999: F7; see also Government of Quebec, 1999: Sections 4.4–4.7). Some critics charge that although the new policies promote the financial incentive for parents to work, they have inadvertently limited women's choices by offering more assistance to families with employed mothers than to those in which the mother stays at home (Vincent, 2000: 3). And although not overt, pro-natal objectives continue to impinge on policy. Quebec's Family Minister in 2005, Michelle Courchesne, said of the proposed parental leave plan: 'We feel that this sort of program will encourage . . . families to give birth, and maybe to have more children' (in Wyatt, 2005: A5).

Yet, despite these limitations, Quebec continues its efforts to strengthen families and increase the employability of parents. Since March 2004, Quebecers no longer pay provincial sales tax on diapers, baby bottles, and nursing items, and a new child assistance program has recently replaced family allowances, the non-refundable tax credit for dependent children, and the tax reduction for families (Ministère de l'Emploi, de la Solidarité sociale et de la Famille, 2005; Régie des rentes du Québec, 2005). This new family assistance program, paying out more than the three previous ones together, disburses funds every three months to families with children under the age of 18. Two-parent families whose net income does not exceed $42,800, as well as single-parent families with an income ceiling of $31,600, can receive an annual stipend of $2,000 for the first child, $1,000 each for second and third children, and $1,500 for each subsequent child (Régie des rentes du Québec, 2005). In both cases, the amount paid decreases in a ratio determined by a family's net income exceeding the thresholds. In some circumstances, single-parent families can obtain an additional $700 per year; and in one special case, regardless of parental income, families qualify for a monthly supplement of $119.22 for each child with a disability (Ministère de l'Emploi, de la Solidarité sociale et de la Famille, 2005).

Efforts were also stepped up in 2005 to ensure the employability of parents. A work premium was introduced to encourage low-income parents to remain employed. As with the new child assistance program, the amount of the premium depends on net income and family type to an annual maximum of $2,800 per year for two-parent families and $2,190 for single-parent families (Ministère de l'Emploi, de la Solidarité sociale et de la Famille, 2005). In May 2004, Quebec announced that under a special arrangement with the federal government it would 'offer a comprehensive parental-leave programme with increased benefits by Jan. 1, 2006, which is estimated to cost as much as $1 billion a year' (Séguin, 2004).

Quebec's family policies remain the most innovative and ambitious in Canada (CPRN/RCPPP, 2003; Krull, 2003; Lefebvre and Merrigan, 2003; OECD, 2004; Ross, 2006). In fact, the Canadian Policy Research Networks (CPRN/RCPPP) claims that 'Quebec provides North America's only example of an integrated approach to family policy. It stands as proof that there is room in market-oriented countries for progressive public policies designed specifically for families' (2003: 2). The rest of Canada can take some lessons from Quebec in designing effective national policy directed at strengthening families. Perhaps the strongest lesson that can be learned is the benefit of assisting *all* families to better balance employment and family responsibilities, and that families are strengthened not simply by supplementing incomes with small amounts of money but by increasing employability. For the Ministère de la Famille et de l'Enfance: 'Poverty is less present in families with full-time jobs. This is why the government has chosen to fight against it not only through providing financial support to the poorest families but also in the field of employment by offering parents conditions making it easier to balance family and job responsibilities' (quoted in Jensen, 2002: 311). Quebec's progress is recognized internationally. In its otherwise unfavourable report card on child care in Canada, the OECD praised the 'extraordinary advance made by Quebec, which has launched one of the most ambitious and interesting early education and care policies in North America' (OECD, 2004: 55).

On the Horizon: New Initiatives

With a policy modelled on Quebec's subsidized daycare program, the Liberal Party led by Paul Martin promised during the 2004 federal election campaign to create 250,000 child-care spaces by 2009. On 5 October 2004, just as the OECD findings were being made public, the Martin government used the occasion of the Speech from the Throne to tell Canadians: 'For a decade, all governments have understood that the most important investment that can be made is in our children. . . . Parents must have real choices: children must have real opportunities to learn' (Office of the Prime Minister, 2004). The next day, Prime Minister Martin laid out his government's commitment to 'a strong, Canada-wide program of early learning and care for our children, which is the single best investment we can make in their future and in ours' (ibid.).

By November 2004 the federal and provincial governments agreed on a series of principles for a national child-care program: quality, universal inclusion, accessibility, and a developmental focus (Galloway, 2004). Reaching agreement was actually not difficult, as these principles were essentially the same as those proffered consistently for 35 years: from the proposals of the 1970 Royal Commission on the Status of Women, to those of advocacy groups and the Quebec government in the 1980s and after, to the Liberal 'Red Book'. The problem lay in the details. Even before the principles were agreed, the Quebec government made public its position that it wanted 'the right to opt out of any national daycare program with full compensation' since it already had an established child-care system and it only needed additional federal funds to make its own improvements (Séguin and Galloway, 2004).

In February 2005, federal, provincial, and territorial ministers convened in Vancouver to give form to the four principles for a national child-care program. The issue of funding proved a sticking point, as did concern from some provinces about 'a national system' that failed to 'recognize provincial and territorial jurisdiction' (Galloway, 2005a; Matas, 2005). But not all provinces opposed federal ideas, and discussions explored topics like procedures of accountability, the funding of child-care centres, family child-care homes, pre- and nursery schools, and whether there should be 'a national vision for provincial and territorial systems' or 'a shared vision for a national system'. A draft agreement talked about 'shared vision' and accepted the 'inclusion of children with special needs and aboriginal children' in any system. But a firm national program proved impossible to achieve as both the Alberta and Quebec governments indicated that they would take federal funds but develop unique programs that reflected their particular circumstances—they might spend their allotment in other programs. Other provinces also had quibbles, so that only Manitoba and Ontario were willing to accept a full federal scheme. Ministers agreed to meet sometime after the announcement of the federal budget on 22 February, and Ken Dryden, the federal Minister of Social Services, allowed that he might permit agreements between the federal government and individual provincial governments.

In their 2005 budget, the federal Liberal government allocated $5 billion over five years to develop a national system of early learning and child care, adding the proviso that 'federal support will need to be ongoing beyond these initial years' (Galloway, 2005b). But desirous of wanting to get a country-wide system into place, the federal government declared that the 'provinces will have access to $700 million [the first year's disbursement] in child-care funds to spend virtually as they please.'

By the fall of 2005, all 10 provinces finally entered into agreement with the federal government—although the conditions for receiving federal funding varied from province to province. However, the national child-care program re-emerged as a divisive yet central political issue during the federal election campaign of December 2005–January 2006. Paul Martin again stressed the importance of a national system of regulated daycare, promising to more than double his gov-

ernment's $5 billion commitment if the Liberals remained in power. Stephen Harper and the Conservative Party, on the other hand, promoted a policy of paying parents $1,200 annually per pre-school child, arguing that this would enable parents the freedom of choosing their own child-care options. Interestingly, men and women were divided over these competing visions of child care. According to a survey by the Strategic Council, women tended to favour the Liberal policy of a national child-care program whereas men typically preferred the Conservative proposal for parents receiving federal funds directly (Laghi, 2005: A4).

On 23 January 2006 the Conservative Party formed a minority government, and in April the new government introduced its family allowance program, which pays $1,200 annually per pre-school child. This policy has been heavily criticized. Some critics see it as a step backwards, comparing it to that of Mackenzie King's 1945 Family Allowance (*Globe and Mail*, 2005). The Child Care Advocacy Association of Canada (CCAAC) argued that cancelling the federal-provincial agreements on child care 'sets back the development of a national child care program for years to come, leaving families with young children to fend for themselves. Breaking federal-provincial child care agreements would be a breach of public trust and would lead to a cut of almost $4 billion from child care funding' (www.buildchildcare.ca). The CCAAC urged Canadians to sign an open letter to Stephen Harper and the provincial premiers asking him to honour the promise of a national child-care program by protecting the early learning and child-care agreements between the government of Canada and the provinces. Within a few months, over 32,500 people signed the letter.

The Caledon Institute, a think-tank that focuses on Canadian child care, has also chastised the Conservatives for its child-care allowance policy, particularly because it eliminated the young-child supplement of the Canada Child Tax Benefit. Ken Battle, the Institute's president, argues that the elimination of the young-child supplement, which is approximately $249 annually, 'makes the inequality gap between the child-care allowance benefits for low- and modest-income families and high-income families all the wider, because the low-income families are losing that $249 annually whereas higher-income families never got it' (Galloway, 2006: A1). In its report, the Caledon Institute also indicated that the families who will benefit most from the Conservative policy will be those families earning $200,000 a year or more and have one parent who stays at home. These families will retain $1,076 of the $1,200 allowance whereas families with two working parents with a combined income of $30,000 will only keep $199 of the allowance due to the loss of other social benefits (Galloway, 2006: A7).

Coming at the same time as Canadian governments at all levels are enacting legislation to allow same-sex couples to marry or, at least, to join together in civil unions, the national debate over child care as an essential element of family policy has more importance than ever before. Effective family policy, especially child care now preoccupying federal, provincial, and territorial jurisdictions, needs to reflect the emerging reality of family life in Canada. Viable options for creating such policy are available. For instance, the renowned family sociologist, Margrit Eichler (1997), charges that family policies have not kept up with the dramatic changes that have occurred with Canadian families. Specifically, she argues that the **individual responsibility family model**, which has shaped many of our family policies since about 1970, is inappropriate and needs to be abandoned. In part, this family model views fathers and mothers as equally responsible for the economic well-being of their families and for providing care to those family members who need it. The state takes on these responsibilities only when a husband/father or wife/mother is not present or cannot fulfill his or her responsibilities.

Eichler proposes that more efficient family policies will result once the individual responsibility model is replaced by a **social responsibility model** of the family. Under this model, there is a concerted effort to minimize stratification on the basis of sex,

while legal marriage is considered an option rather than being privileged over other types of relationships. Parents are responsible for their children's economic well-being whether they live with their children or not. Thus, residency is not a requirement for parental responsibilities. Importantly, the care of dependent children is the responsibility not only of the parents but also of society. In this way, the state no longer distinguishes between same-sex couples and heterosexual couples; regardless of their sexuality, couples/parents are entitled to the same state benefits.

Conclusion

Although the state in Canada has had decided influence in determining marriage and in intervening in some family issues, such as the neglect or abuse of children, it actually has had a minimal role in overall family policies. The essential reason for this course of events resides in Canada being a liberal welfare state, something compounded by the fact that in a federal polity different levels of government have defined roles in handling family issues. None of this is to say that federal, provincial, and territorial governments have abdicated their responsibilities towards families. Initiatives over time, such as paid maternity leave, child and family benefits engineered through the taxation regime, and the plan for 'A Canada Fit for Children', show that the state has sought to help families. But for every advance, there have been failures—the abortive Canada Child Care Act in 1988 and the Liberals' national child-care program in 2005 are cases in point.

The problem for Canadians is that there has never been a comprehensive national family policy. Instead, a piecemeal set of programs and policies has emerged that either directly or indirectly affect families. In an important sense, the state lags behind in coming to grips with social and economic changes that affect families. The issue of child care is a telling example. Despite some difficulties, only Quebec has managed to provide an effective child-care system. The rest of Canada now has an opportunity to use and build on Quebec's example; to do so will take more than public money. It will also take intergovernmental co-operation and the construction of policy based on a realistic understanding of contemporary Canadian families. Producing an effective family policy is a challenge of immense importance facing the state in Canada and the people who give it legitimacy.

Notes

1. The term 'state' refers to the federal and provincial governments, and, in the present context, to institutions/agencies that are directly involved in family life (for instance, social services).

2. The exception is the Quebec government, whose family policies will be discussed later in this chapter.

Study Questions

1. What challenges does Canada face in developing a cohesive national family policy?
2. What are the strengths and weakness of both targeted and universal family policies?
3. Why will a better balance between employment and family responsibilities facilitate gender equity?
4. Discuss why a social responsibility model of the family should improve family policies.
5. Do you think that child poverty can be eradicated by the construction and funding of a comprehensive national policy? Explain.

Glossary

Family policy An array of policies and programs that directly relate to families with children under the age of 18 years.

Individual responsibility family model A family model premised on gender equality whereby there is no distinction between married and common-law partners, and the state is not responsible for either economic well-being or the provision of care as long as there is a husband/father or wife/mother present.

Liberal welfare state In most areas of political, social, and economic endeavour, individuals have greater responsibilities for their life than government; government intervention and benefits in regard to family policy tend to be minimal since it is thought that individuals bear the responsibility to have and raise children.

Maternity leave benefits Assistance to women in balancing family and employment through (1) financial support when they take time away from their employment to have and care for their newborn; and (2) protection of their jobs by ensuring that they can return to the same or an equivalent position upon their return to their employment.

Parental leave benefits Paid leave that enables fathers to take time away from their employment so that they can participate more fully in their newborn's life.

Pro-natal policies Policies aimed at maintaining or raising fertility. Conversely, anti-natalist policies are those aimed at bringing down high birth rates (i.e., 'family planning policies').

Social democratic state One in which there is greater emphasis on government involvement in society and the economy—the raising of children is thought to be a collective responsibility, and consequently there tend to be more state government intervention and more generous benefits than in a liberal welfare state.

Social responsibility family model Characterized by a concerted effort to minimize stratification on the basis of sex without distinguishing between types of relationships such as legal marriage or same-sex couples; they are all considered types of relationships where one is no more privileged than the other. The well-being of dependent children is the responsibility of parents and society; thus, all families are entitled to be supported by the state.

Further Readings

Baker, Maureen, and David Tippin. 1999. *Poverty, Social Assistance and the Employability of Mothers: Restructuring Welfare States*. Toronto: University of Toronto Press. An examination, from a feminist and political economy perspective, of cross-national differences in restructuring social programs for low-income mothers in four liberal welfare states: Canada, Australia, New Zealand, and the United Kingdom.

Eichler, Margrit. 1997. *Family Shifts: Families, Policies and Gender Equality*. Toronto: Oxford University Press. A great source to see how families and family policy have changed over the past century in Canada. Eichler offers policy-makers a more realistic and improved family model from which to build future family policies.

Evans, Patricia M., and Gerda R. Wekerle, eds. 1997. *Women and the Canadian Welfare State: Challenges and Change*. Toronto: University of Toronto Press. An informative collection of interdisciplinary papers focusing on how the relationship between the welfare state and women has changed, how the policies and benefits of the welfare state impact women's basic freedoms, and how women can be active in shaping future policy.

Gauthier, Anne Hélène. 1998. *The State and the Family: A Comparative Analysis of Family Policies in Industrialized Countries*. New York: Oxford University Press. A discussion of how family structures have changed over the past century and the various family policies adopted by 22 different countries in response to these changes. Based on the differences found among these countries, the book concludes with an informative typology of models of family policy.

Marshall, Dominique, and Nicola Doone Danby. 2005. *The Social Origins of the Welfare State: Quebec Families, Compulsory Education, and Family Allowances, 1940–1955*. Waterloo, Ont.: Wilfrid Laurier University Press. A detailed, well-written history of Canada's welfare state with a particular focus on the development of social policies in Quebec.

Websites

www.vifamily.ca/about/about.html
The Vanier Institute of the Family's website offers a range of research publications, public presentations, media interviews, and speeches on an array of issues that affect families.

www.ncwcnbes.net/index.htm
The National Council of Welfare is a citizens' advisory body to the Minister of Social Development Canada on matters of concern to low-income Canadians and on social and related programs and policies affecting their welfare. The website contains published reports pertaining to poverty and social policy issues.

www.irpp.org/indexe.htm
The Institute for Research on Public Policy, an 'independent, non-partisan think-tank', has as its mission the advancement of new ideas to 'help Canadians make more effective policy choices'. Its website contains numerous publications that assess existing family policies while offering new policy initiatives for future policy-makers to consider.

www.oecd.org/topic/0,2686,en_2649_33933_1_1_1_1_37419,00.html
The Organization for Economic Co-operation and Development's social policy website offers statistics, publications, and assessments on social and family policies for each of the OECD countries. Their purpose is to identify policies that assist families in reconciling work and family life.

www.cprn.org/en/index.cfm
The Canadian Policy Research Network is one of Canada's leading think-tanks. Its website offers access to much of its research on a wide array of policy issues that impact families in Canada, Europe, and developing countries.

References

Armitage, Andrew. 2003. *Social Welfare in Canada*, 4th edn. Toronto: Oxford University Press.

Baker, Maureen. 1994. 'Family and population policy in Québec: Implications for women', *Canadian Journal of Women and the Law/Revue Femmes et Droit* 7: 116–32.

———. 2001. 'Definitions, cultural variations, and demographic trends', in Maureen Baker, ed., *Families: Changing Trends in Canada*. Toronto: McGraw-Hill Ryerson, 3–27.

Baril, Robert, Pierre Lefebvre, and Philip Merrigan. 2000. 'Quebec family policy: Impact and options', *Choices: Family Policy* (IRRP) 6, 1: 4–52.

Beauvais, Caroline, and Pascale Dufour. 2003. 'Articulation travail-famille: Le contre-exemple des pays dits "libéraux"?', Canadian Policy Research Networks Family Network. At: <www.cprn.org>.

Behiels, Michael D. 1986. *Prelude to Quebec's Quiet Revolution*. Montreal and Kingston: McGill-Queen's University Press.

Canadian Council on Social Development (CCSD). 2004. *One Million Too Many—Implementing Solutions to Child Poverty in Canada: 2004 Report Card on Child Poverty in Canada*. Ottawa: CCSD.

———. 2005. *Decision Time for Canada—Let's Make Poverty History: 2005 Report Card on Child Poverty in Canada*. Ottawa: CCSD.

Canadian Policy Research Networks (CPRN/RCPP), Family Network. 2003. 'Unique Quebec Family Policy Model at Risk', 26 Nov. At: <www.cprn.org>.

CBC News. 2004. 'Canada's child care will impove, Dryden insists', 25 Oct. At: <www.cbc.ca/story/canada/national/2004/10/25/childcare_041025.html>.

———. 2005. 'Day care in Canada', 9 Feb. At: <www.cbc.ca/news/background/daycare/index.html>.

Comeau, R. 1989. *Jean Lesage et l'éveil d'une nation: les débuts de la révolution tranquille*. Sillery, Que.: Presses de l'Université du Québec.

Dandurand, Renée B., and Marianne Kempeneers. 2002. 'Pour une analyse comparative et contextuelle de la politique familiale au Québec', *Recherches sociographiques* 43, 1: 9–78.

Eichler, Margrit. 1997. *Family Shifts: Families, Policies, and Gender Equality*. Toronto: Oxford University Press.

Evans, Patricia M., and Gerda R. Wekerle, eds. 1997. *Women and the Canadian Welfare State: Challenges and Change*. Toronto: University of Toronto Press.

Galloway, Gloria. 2004. 'Ottawa, provinces agree on child-care principles', *Globe and Mail*, 3 Nov., A11.

———. 2005a. 'Dryden leaves the door open for separate childcare deals', *Globe and Mail*, 11 Feb., A4.

———. 2005b. 'Money comes with no strings attached', *Globe and Mail*, 24 Feb., F3.

———. 2006. 'Child-care proposal gives least to poorest', *Globe and Mail*, 26 Apr., A1, A7.

Gauthier, Anne Hélène. 1998. *The State and the Family: A Comparative Analysis of Family Policies in Industrialized Countries*. New York: Oxford University Press.

Globe and Mail. 2005. 'Harper's prescription for choice in child care', 6 Dec., A22.

Government of Canada. 2005. *Employment Insurance (EI) and Maternity, Parental and Sickness Benefits*. Ottawa: Department of Human Resources and Skills Development. At: <www.hrsdc.gc.ca/asp/gateway.asp?hr=en/ei/types/special.shtml&hs=tyt#Maternity3>.

Government of Quebec. 1999. *Report of the Auditor General to the National Assembly for 1998–1999, Summary*. Quebec City, ch. 4.

Hamilton, Graeme. 2004. 'Quebec's sacred cow has quality issues', *National Post*, 9 Dec.

Hamilton, Roberta. 1995. 'Pro-natalism, feminism, and nationalism', in Francois-Pierre Gingras, ed., *Gender and Politics in Contemporary Canada*. Toronto: Oxford University Press, 135–52.

Jensen, Jane. 2002. 'Against the current: Child care and family policy in Quebec', in Sonya Michel and Riane Mahon, eds, *Child Care Policy at the Crossroads: Gender and Welfare State Restructuring*. New York: Routledge, 309–30.

———. 2003. *Redesigning the 'Welfare Mix' for Families: Policy Challenges*. Ottawa: Canadian Policy Research Networks.

——— and Sherry Thompson. 1999. *Comparative Family Policy: Six Provincial Stories*. Ottawa: Canadian Policy Research Networks.

Krashinsky, Michael. 2001. 'Are we there yet? The evolving face of child care policy in Canada', *Transition* 31, 4: 2–5.

Krull, Catherine. 2003. 'Pronatalism, feminism and family policy in Quebec', in M. Lynn, ed., *Voices: Essays on Canadian Families*, 2nd edn. Toronto: Nelson Thomson, ch. 11.

Laghi, Brian. 2005. 'Poll finds gender gap on daycare', *Globe and Mail*, 8 Dec., A4.

Langlois, S., J. Baillargeon, G. Caldwell, G. Fréchet, M. Gauthier, and J. Simard. 1992. *Recent Social Trends in Québec, 1960-1990*. Montreal and Kingston: McGill-Queen's University Press.

Lavigne, Marie. 1986. 'Feminist reflections on the fertility of women in Québec', in Roberta Hamilton and Michèle Barrett, eds, *The Politics of Diversity: Feminism, Marxism and Nationalism*. London: Verso, 303–21.

Lefebvre, Pierre, and Philip Merrigan. 2003. 'Assessing family policy in Canada: A new deal for families and children', *Choices: Family Policy* (IRRP) 9, 5.

McCloskey, Donna. 2001. 'Caring for Canada's kids', *Transition Magazine* 31, 4: 1–2.

McKeen, Wendy. 2001. 'Shifting policy and politics of federal child benefits in Canada', *Social Politics* 8, 2: 186–90.

Maroney, Heather J. 1992. 'Who has the baby? Nationalism, pronatalism and the construction of a "demographic crisis" in Quebec, 1960–1988', *Studies in Political Economy* 39: 7–36.

Matas, Robert. 2005. 'Questions of funding dog talks on national child-care program', *Globe and Mail*, 12 Feb., A6.

Maximova, Katerina. 2004. *Memorandum for the Minister—Family-Friendly Policies in Quebec*. Ottawa: Government of Canada, Social Policy Research.

Ministère de l'Emploi, de la Solidarité sociale et de la Famille. 2005. 'Financial support for childcare'. At: <www.messf.gouv.qc.ca/Index_en.asp>.

Ministère de la Famille et de l'Enfance du Quèbec. 1999. *Family Policy: Another Step towards Developing the Full Potential of Families and Their Children*. Quebec City: Les Publications du Québec.

National Council of Welfare. 2004a. *Welfare Incomes 2003*. Ottawa: Minister of Public Works and Gov-ernment Services Canada. At: <www.ncwcnbes.net/htmdocument/reportWelfareIncomes>.

———. 2004b. *Poverty Profile 2001*. Ottawa: Minister of Public Works and Government Services Canada, Catalogue no. SD25–1/2001E–PDF.

OECD, Directorate for Education. 2004. *Early Childhood Education and Care Policy. Canada: Country Note*. Paris: OECD.

Office of the Prime Minister. 2004. 'Speech from the Throne' and 'Reply to the Speech from the Throne', 5 Oct. At: <http://pm.gc.ca/eng.ftddt.asp>.

O'Hara, Kathy. 1998. *Comparative Family Policy: Eight Countries' Stories*. Canadian Policy Research Networks, no. 15734. Ottawa: Renouf Publishing.

Régie des rentes du Québec. 2005. 'Family Benefits'. At: <http://www.rrq.gouv.qc.ca/an/famille/10.htm>.

Ross, Jonathan. 2006. 'Get real about child care: Why Harper feels he can go to the polls on the issue.' *The Tyee*, 20 Apr. At: <http://thetyee.ca/Views/2006/04/20/Real ChildCare>.

Séguin, Rhéal. 2004. 'Quebec to assume control of parental-leave program', *Globe and Mail*, 20 May, A12.

——— and Gloria Galloway. 2004. 'Some provinces skeptical about federal daycare plan', *Globe and Mail*, 2 Nov., A6.

Thompson, Elizabeth. 1999. 'Daycare woes ignored: Auditor report blasts lack of supervision', *Montreal Gazette*, 10 Dec., F7.

Thomson, Dale C. 1984. *Jean Lesage and the Quiet Revolution*. Toronto: Macmillan.

Vincent. Carole. 2000. 'Editor's note', *Choices: Family Policy* (IRRP) 6, 1: 2–3.

Wyatt, Nelson. 2005. 'Quebec to operate parental leave plan', *Globe and Mail*, 2 Mar , A5

CHAPTER 15

The Past of the Future and the Future of the Family

Margrit Eichler

Learning Objectives

- To learn about the various bases on which predictions can be made.
- To appreciate the inherent difficulties in making predictions.
- To place the family into a societal context.

Introduction

Making predictions is a risky business—they may come back to haunt one. My first reaction was dismay when I was invited to contribute a chapter to this book on the future of the family—on what basis could I possibly make any sensible predictions? Then a colleague suggested that I look at past predictions.[1] This has turned what might have been a very difficult and ultimately self-defeating undertaking into an instructive and enjoyable exercise.

I decided to restrict my review of old predictions to those published at the latest in 1975, meaning that a minimum of 30 years had passed since their publication. This is certainly enough time to judge whether the predictions made came true or not.

Family sociology within Canada is a relatively young subdiscipline. The first monograph on the family in Canada was written by Frederick Elkin and published in 1964 (Elkin, 1964). In her overview of the development of family studies in Canada, Nett identifies the 1970s and 1980s as the 'period of Canadianization and policy concerns' (Nett, 1988: 9), but publishing really only took off in the 1980s. My search for older sources therefore netted primarily American and some British authors. The oldest source I found is from 1930.

The search for old predictions turned up some very surprising results. Most prominently, the time at which a prediction was made bore no relation to its accuracy. Some older predictions are much more accurate than some that were made significantly later. This being the case, I discarded the notion of ordering the predictions in terms of the time at which they were formulated.

It did not seem advantageous to group predictions in terms of their accuracy or inaccuracy, since I found some of both on virtually every theme. I finally decided to group predictions by topic to avoid repetition and allow for a comparison between successful, unsuccessful, and partially successful predictions under every heading.

This paper is therefore organized in three parts. First, I examine past predictions about the future of the family, then I consider the basis on which such predictions are made and attempt to determine which bases seem to yield more solid predictions, and third, I engage—with hesitation and much trepidation—in the risky business of making some predictions myself.

Past Predictions about the Family

The observations of Baber on marriage, from over half a century ago, still seem relevant today:

> There are three types of opinion on marriage: (1) the opinion held by those who consider monogamic, indissoluble [heterosexual] marriage the only divinely sanctioned form and therefore the only one that can ever be tolerated; (2) the opinion held by those few sophisticates at the other extreme that not only is the usefulness of marriage past but also it is now doing a

genuine disservice to the family and should be immediately abolished; (3) the opinion held by the vast number of persons in between these extremes that marriage performs valuable service in regularizing sex relations and stabilizing the primary group in which children are reared and that it should be not indissoluble but subject to correction and improvement. The latter are not willing to say that monogamy must always prevail, but only that at present it fits into our total culture pattern better than any other form. It is conceivable that a condition might arise that would call for some other form of marriage. (Baber, 1953: 681–2)

Correspondingly, we have a slew of predictions, from sociologists committed to Baber's second opinion concerning marriage, that the family is dead or dying, and opposing views by those who hold to one of the other opinions.

The Future of the Family/Marriage as an Institution

Predictions that the family is about to disintegrate and disappear seem as old as the family itself. Between 1930 and 1970, there was a lot of concern with the 'disintegration of the family'. Paul wrote in 1930 in Great Britain that 'the disintegration of the family is going on, and something will have to take its place' (Paul, 1930: 38). In the United States, Sorokin thought in 1941 that the family had 'passed from mere instability into the process of actual disintegration' (cited after Baber, 1953: 678). In 1947, Zimmerman suggested that 'the family system will continue headlong its present trend toward nihilism' (Zimmerman, 1947: 808).

In 1949[2] and again in 1959, Anshen commented that in the US 'the present collapse of marriage and the family is a perverted triumph of a profaned passion which in truth now largely consists in a reversion to abduction and rape' (Anshen, 1959: 512). This is a particularly interesting comment, since the 1950s are often held up as the golden age of the family in North America.

This negative view of the future of the family could easily be carried forward into modern times. Nimkoff replies to the authors who argue that the family is a dying institution that the same arguments used to demonstrate the collapse of the family can be used to support precisely the opposite. 'The issue may be stated thus: Does the individual exist for the family, or the family exist for the individual?' He suggests that '[t]he totalitarian family organization is as real as the totalitarian state' (Nimkoff, 1947: 603). In his time, family subservience had given way to individualization—which he by and large saw as a positive development, but which authors who subscribe to marriage as a monolithic, indissoluble institution interpret in wholly negative terms.

By the same token, others have argued that marriage and the family are ongoing concerns that have adapted to very different circumstances for a very long period of time and that they would continue to do so. Linton, an American anthropologist, after reflecting on this issue, concluded simply: 'The ancient trinity of father, mother, and child has survived more vicissitudes than any other human relationship. It is the bedrock underlying all other family structures' (Linton, 1959: 52). He would probably not insist that the father has to be the biological father of the child.

Cavan concludes her book as follows:

> The exact form of family that will emerge cannot be fully predicted, but present research indicates the need for a family that is flexible, with leeway for individual development; adjustable to external social conditions, keyed to mobility and social change; interdependent with other institutions; and ready to accept important though limited functions, such as meeting personal and sexual needs, giving emotional security, and rearing children for life in an industrialized, urban society. (Cavan, 1963: 533)

Ten years later, Bernard asked rhetorically 'does marriage *have* a future?' and answered with an unequivocal 'yes', although both its name and form might change. She adds, 'I do not see the traditional form of marriage retaining its monopolistic sway. I see, rather, a future of marital options' (Bernard, 1972: 301–2)—which is, of course, what we find today in Canada: legal and common-law marriages, dual-earner couples, traditional breadwinner couples, and some non-traditional breadwinner couples in which the wife is the breadwinner and the husband the stay-at-home parent and spouse.

COMMUNAL FAMILY STRUCTURES/ GROUP MARRIAGES

The authors cited above who are predicting the disappearance of the monogamous, nuclear family see this as a negative, terrible event, threatening the very existence of civilization. By contrast, by the late 1960s and early 1970s a considerable number of intellectuals and authors believed that this form of the family was basically passé and that alternative structures were needed. This was the time of the hippie movement; significant numbers of communes had sprung up in its wake, and various authors had created attractive fictional accounts of communal families (e.g., Skinner, 1948). The women's movement had become a major social force, voicing clear dissatisfaction with the patriarchal nuclear family: 'our American family model, with its emphasis on "success" on the one hand and "domesticity" on the other, appears to be actually a model for marital misery' (Howe, 1972: 13). The **zero population movement** had been spawned by the environmental movement, and there were conflicting views on fertility (see below).

This put the family high on the political agenda. A number of symposia and conferences looked at the future of or alternatives to the family and resulted in publications (e.g., Barbeau, 1971; College of Home Economics, 1972; Elliott, 1970; Farson et al., 1969; Goode, 1972; Otto, 1972). In Canada, the report of the Royal Commission on the Status of Women was released in 1970. Questioning the role of women inevitably led to a discussion about the future of the family, since

until that time women had been largely relegated to and identified with the family.

Monogamous marriage, and the family based on it, was seen as 'grim, lifeless, boring, depressing, disillusioning—a potential context for murder, suicide, mental human decay' (Greenwald, 1970: 63). Contemporary marriage was described as 'a wretched institution' that turns beautiful romances into a bitter contract and a relationship that 'becomes constricting, corrosive, grinding and destructive' (Marvyn Cadwaller, cited in Otto, 1970: 3). In short, the consequences of 'continuing family structures as they exist now' are 'fearful' (Stoller, 1970: 145).

Having established that it was dangerous to continue to support the nuclear family of their day, a considerable number of authors proposed and some predicted some form of communal or tribal family, or various forms of group marriages (Downing, 1970; Gerson, 1972; Goode, 1972; Hochschild, 1972; Kanter, 1972; Kay, 1972; Orleans and Wolfson, 1970; Platt, 1972; Schulz, 1972).

An interesting feature of these discussions is that they focus primarily on the adults, ignoring the raising of the children—certainly one of the reasons why this has not become a significant subform of the family. An exception to this is Levett, who develops a model where every boy has a third parent, 'a male figure educated, trained, and equipped to serve the socializing needs of male children' (Levett, 1970: 162).

Thamm saw the move towards a communal family as the outcome of a linear development: stage 1 was characterized by the consanguine family, stage 2 by the conjugal family, which at his time (1975) was in the process of dissolving, thus leading to stage 3, the communal family, which will have wonderful consequences: 'The individual and the collectivity will be merged. Conflict and competition will yield to relations of cooperation, and jealous possessiveness will evolve into a loving concern' (Thamm, 1975: 128–9).

A particular version of some form of communal living was the suggestion of polygyny for people over the age of 60. Kassel argued that 'the need for polygyny is obvious: there just are not enough men. Therefore, any man over age sixty could marry two, three, four, or five women over sixty' (Kassel, 1970: 138). He listed the benefits of such an arrangement, which included a better diet, better living conditions, help in illness, help with housework, sex, better grooming: 'when there is a choice between uninterested, dowdy, foul smelling hags [i.e., widows who did not find a man to remarry], and alert, interested, smartly dressed ladies [the lucky co-wives], the selection is obvious' (ibid., 141).

Since the women in this scenario continue to do all the cooking and other housework, it is not clear why they need a man to achieve all these benefits—they could simply live together. The only activity which is reserved for the man is sex, and here again the women might be content with each other.

By contrast, Rosenberg concludes that while polygyny would make sense, given the 'ever growing surfeit of old widows' (Rosenberg, 1970: 181), this is unlikely to actually happen due to the existence of a counter-ideology—the ideology of the nuclear family.

Gender Roles

One of the most important axes of discussion turns around gender roles,[3] specifically, women's roles. Among the more spectacularly wrong predictions we can count those of Parsons and Bales, who argue that the patriarchal family[4] is a *sine qua non* for the welfare of the United States. This includes very specifically that women not be active in the labour force, which, on the one hand, accomplishes the maintenance of the household and child care and, on the other, 'shields spouses from competition with each other in the occupational sphere, which, along with attractiveness to women, is above all the most important single focus of feelings of self-respect on the part of American men' (Parsons and Bales, 1955: 264–5).

Given that the labour force participation of women is almost equal to that of men today and that the US and Canada have continued to exist and even flourish, clearly the patriarchal bread-winner family is not necessary to the continued survival of these societies. The fact that Parsons and Bales talk only about the self-respect of men, ignoring what women might desire, lies obviously at the root of some of their misperceptions.

At around the same time, Cavan (1963: 515) suggested that the major contribution of the feminist movement, which 'has spent its force', has been the transition from the patriarchal family to 'the present-day ideal of the partnership family in which husband and wife share equally in rights and responsibilities'. It was, of course, precisely the *failure* of the family to live up to this ideal that generated some of the harshest critiques of the second-wave feminist movement—which at that point was readying itself to re-emerge.

Pollak, reflecting on the consequences of **women's lib**, suggested that 'partly due to genetic endowment, partly due to shifts in employment policies, women will prove to be frequently more successful in the role of earner than their husbands. The consequence will be power shifts. Women will gain power, men will lose power, and where power is lost, functions will have to be redefined. Unavoidably under such conditions, fathers will be called upon to assume a greater share in child rearing than in the past' (Pollak, 1972: 71). This has been borne out to a very modest degree only. While fathers *do* participate more in rearing their children, the lioness's share is still carried by mothers (des Rivières-Pigeon et al., 2002; Haddad, 1996; Hossain, 2001; John and Shelton, 1997; Kitterod, 2002; Sanchez and Thomson, 1997; Shelton and John, 1996; South and Spitze, 1994).

Winch predicted that husbands would fail to participate more in housework as their wives become more active in the labour force. However, he then also predicted that we would therefore 'presently be returning toward a norm that will give increasing emphasis to the differences between the sexes' (Winch, 1970: 14) and that we would hence presumably return to the traditional division of labour—something that has not happened.

In spite of the fact that most men are not at this point doing their fair share of housework, the *norms* have changed. Today, 99 per cent of respondents of a national Canadian sample agreed with the statement that 'Parents need to take equal responsibility for raising children' and 94 per cent agreed that 'Couples should share household duties equally' (Bibby, 2005: 6). This suggests that we will continue to move gradually towards a more even balance with respect to housework and care work.

Eichler noted in 1975 that there 'there is no equalitarian family in existence in Canada at the present time. . . . It is clear that equality in the family can come neither quickly nor easily, nor in isolation from far-reaching changes in the legal, economic, educational and political systems' (Eichler, 1975: 230).

SEXUALITY

Many authors—besides those who argue for alternative family forms—have reflected on the nature of sexual relations within and outside of marriage, although this is almost uniformly restricted to heterosexual relations. Except for one side comment (Schulz, 1972: 420), no one predicted that we would have same-sex marriages in Canada or North America by now. Nonetheless, numerous authors predicted the loosening of restrictions on non-marital sex. Ogburn and Nimkoff predicted that due to technological innovations sexuality would be separated from procreation, and that 'the sex act may occur for pleasure rather than for procreation' (Ogburn and Nimkoff, 1955: 308). This, of course, would require 'a disappearance of moral and legal sanctions against extra-marital sex' (Winch, 1970: 12). This has certainly happened.

Davids predicted that 'the law will accept abortion, all forms of birth control will be seen as medical problems, free of any statutory limitation' (Davids, 1971: 190–1), both of which have happened in Canada.

DIVORCE AND COHABITATION AS ALTERNATIVES TO PERMANENT MONOGAMOUS MARRIAGES

In a 1967 journal article on the future of the family, Edwards argued that:

Economic overabundance . . . in the long run will have a repressive effect on the rate of marriage. The recognition of alternatives to wedlock, as that concerning alternatives to premarital chastity, will not occasion sudden behavioral consequences. But change is overdue. When women, already imbued with the economic ethos, fully realize their equality in this sphere, much of the *raison d'etre* of marriage will no longer be present. . . . Women will no longer find economic dependence a virtue and worthy by-product of marriage, for, given the opportunity, they will succeed for themselves as ably as any male might. (Edwards, 1967: 510)

Hobbs notes that '*we are in the process of abandoning the permanence of marriage, while maintaining* (in law and in principle, even if less in reality than ever before) *its sexual exclusiveness*' (Hobbs, 1970: 37, emphasis in original). He then suggests that we should turn this around.

Winch (1970: 15) also predicts a decrease in marriage (which has happened) as well as in birth rates (which has also taken place), as do the Birds: 'with fewer mutual responsibilities, these marriages, we can expect, will have less permanence as their goals and interests change, so will their choice of mates' (Bird and Bird, 1971: 6). However, they assume that cohabitation will increase because there will be more free time—while in fact the amount of time people in North America spend on their paid work has increased, not decreased.

Cohabitation has increased, as predicted by a number of people, including the Canadian sociologist Whitehurst who dealt with the topic by calling it 'Living Together Unmarried' (LTU). He suggested that LTU 'will come to be seen as a kind of period like engagement is today, a trial period in which it becomes (legally or informally) possible to try out one or two live-in situations before making a commitment to long-term marriage' (Whitehurst, 1975: 441). In fact, cohabitation in Canada today exists in three forms: as a premarital arrangement, as Whitehurst suggested, as a permanent alternative to legal marriage, and as a type of post-divorce union. It is particularly prevalent in Quebec and in the northern territories, which have a high proportion of Aboriginal people (Wu, 2000: 53).

FERTILITY AND FERTILITY CONTROL

The issues around fertility are particularly interesting. Writing at almost the same time, some authors fear that we are moving towards extinction because women do not have enough babies, while others are concerned about overpopulation and fear that women have too many children. Zimmerman writes about the 'sit-down strike on having and rearing children' (Zimmerman, 1947: 793) due to a drop in the birth rate. This, he argues, is particularly problematic because 'the sources of immigration (what the Romans called the "good barbarians")' are now exhausted. 'Between 1820 and 1920, the United States imported forty million immigrants from Europe. These are now no longer available.' When the surplus population of the Mexicans and French Canadians are exhausted, 'almost the only fertile peoples of the western world now available to us— we too will begin the grand finale of the crisis' (ibid.). People from non-Western countries he apparently did not see as a viable source for immigration. Nimkoff went even further in his projections. He worried about 'the problem of the maintenance of the population'—which could, he feared, lead to the extinction of the human race if it declines over a sufficiently long period of time (Nimkoff, 1947: 604).

In contradistinction to those who worried about humanity dying out because of the lack of children, others worried about overpopulation. Goode, for instance, noted that the population in the US was still increasing while they were using proportionately much more of the world's resources than anyone else. Since most of the children were wanted, he saw no easy solution to this problem, except for one he judged destructive but helpful in the population crisis: 'to focus our lives away from the family itself. Totally free abortion, late marriage, all women working, no tax benefits for children, and so on' (Goode, 1972: 123).

Motivated by a similar fear of overpopulation, the Canadian sociologist Davids suggested:

> There will be public control of reproduction— less than 1/3 of marriages will produce children, would-be parents will be strictly screened and rigorously trained in a large number of subject areas, with examinations and a license for parenthood at the end. The age difference between husbands and wives will disappear, childbirth will be delayed into the middle and late thirties. (Davids, 1971: 190–1)

Davids was not alone in proposing/predicting a regulatory approach to population control. Paul E. Ehrlich, Garrett Harding, and Kenneth E. Boulding also put forward this proposition (Blake, 1972: 59), in line with the zero population movement. He was, however, accurate in predicting the postponement of childbirth into the thirties, though certainly not under the conditions he proposed. 'Nearly one-half of the women who gave birth in Canada in 2003 were age 30 or older' (Statistics Canada, 2005).

NEW REPRODUCTIVE AND GENETIC TECHNOLOGIES

Ogburn and Nimkoff anticipated in the mid-1950s much of what actually happened with respect to new **reproductive and genetic technologies** in the 1980s and later. On the basis of scrutinizing animal experiments, they predicted the widespread use of birth control pills, increased artificial insemination, in vitro fertilization, use of donor eggs, sex selection of fetuses, Viagra and its female equivalent, hormone replacement therapy, longer life expectancies.[5] Their view is a rare exception compared to that of others, the vast majority of whom ignored evidence pointing in these directions.

On the basis of these predictions, they suggest 'when the procreational function is modified by biological research, the effect will be considered revolutionary' (Ogburn and Nimkoff, 1955: 307). Among other things, they argued that the status of women within the family would rise, for one, because women would no longer be blamed for 'barrenness', for the other since the various factors would likely result in a decrease of the birth rate, which, in turn, would lead to encouraging child-bearing (fostered by nationalistic-militaristic elements) and hence to an appreciation of motherhood. The latter part, of course, did not materialize—most likely due to the fact that immigration levels have continued to be high in the US (and Canada, as well). They also predicted a refocus on eugenics, which has certainly occurred in the guise of prenatal and pre-implantation diagnoses, although they did not foresee the plotting of the genome and hence assumed that the 'hereditary endowment' of an individual would not be easy to establish.

UNANTICIPATED TRENDS

Overall, then, there have been a number of spectacular misprognoses as well as some surprisingly accurate predictions. In addition, some trends have taken place that no one predicted. Among these is the return of young people to living with their parents for longer periods of time. In 1981, 27.5 per cent of persons aged 20–9 lived with their parents in Canada, and by 2001 the figure had risen to 41.1 per cent—a tremendous increase in a rather short time (Beaujot, 2000: 15). Even more dramatically, if homosexual relations were dealt with at all it was under the heading of sexual deviance. No one anticipated same-sex marriages. With the exception of Ogburn and Nimkoff, sociologists did not foresee the emergence of the new reproductive and genetic technologies and the moral, legal, and social dilemmas they would generate (Basen et al., 1993). No one assumed that people would spend more time working in their paid jobs—if the issue of leisure was considered, the general assumption was that there would be a need to educate people to deal with their ample free time.

The Various Bases for Making Predictions about the Family

In 1964, Reuben Hill identified four methods to predict the future:

1. extrapolation from trends into the future;
2. projection from generational changes;
3. the impact of inventions;
4. the family specialists' future family.

To this we can add Goode's criterion:

5. identifying societal changes and reflecting on their importance for the family (Goode, 1972).

All of the authors I examined used one or more of these methods to come up with their predictions.

1. Extrapolation from trends into the future. Looking at each of these methods, Hill, along with other authors, realized that extrapolation can only go so far. He judged this 'an exciting but dangerous method' (Hill, 1964: 21) because some trends are short-term or not linear, and because assumptions about the social and economic circumstances would need to be crystal clear since predictions were based on them.

2. Projection from generational changes. Hill refers to this method as carrying the same hazards but worth attention. It involves studying three generations of the same family, determining consistent differences that persist through the three generations, and projecting on the basis of trends observed in the youngest married-child generation. In another context, Goode (1972: 125–6) makes a comment that is pertinent to this method of prediction. Parent–youth conflicts, he suggests, have probably always existed, but parents at least used to know what a child is like at that age because they, too, were once that age. He goes on to note that 'when the whole era changes, that similarity no longer exists' (ibid., 125).

The rate of technological and other change has accelerated enormously over the past few decades. Young children today grow up in a world that is in important ways very different from the one their parents and certainly their grandparents grew up in. The Internet shapes their world view; photos on electronic cameras are instantaneous—whenever someone takes a photo of my grandson he begs 'let me see, let me see' and he finds it incomprehensible if the photo is not available for immediate viewing. Most teenagers have cellphones. Children grow up playing computer games and watching TV and DVDs, and they engage in less physical exercise than a generation earlier.

On the dark side, Canadian high school students are growing used to electronic monitors in their schools, and youth and parents fear weapons and murders as well as drug dealers in high schools. The tsunami that hit the coasts in South Asia in December 2004 was documented daily on TV, chronicling the devastation of human life and of the landscape in graphic detail. Pictures of war are continuous TV fare. AIDS is ravaging large parts of sub-Saharan Africa while SARS and other infectious diseases, it is feared, will sweep the globe. The 'war on terrorism' keeps awareness of the possibility of acts of violence at the forefront of the collective consciousness.

Never in the history of humanity has the gap between the haves and the have-nots been as great as today. In North America, rampant consumerism has to a large degree displaced the values formerly preached by organized religion.

This shrunken and fragile world is qualitatively different from the world even three decades ago. On this basis, it may be very perilous to assume that children today experience the world as similar to the one their parents experienced when they were their age.

Mothers are predominantly in the paid labour force. In Canada, as in the world at large, child poverty is a fact of life. In 2001, 15.6 per cent of Canadian children under the age of 18 lived in poverty (National Council of Welfare, 2004: 9). Counter to predictions that we would not know how to use our free time, young parents in particular experience a lack of time to accomplish all that must be done. Counter to their parents, most children have no or only one biological sibling, although more have stepsiblings.

Given these factors, it would seem promising to use projections from generational changes as a basis for making predictions. There are two problems with doing so, however. First, such data are not presently available for Canadian families. Second, the social and technological changes in the past 20 years have been more rapid and more far-reaching than ever before. I would expect this pace of change not only to continue, but perhaps even to accelerate (see below). This would mean that the next generation would likely face conditions very different from those experienced at present by their parents. Hence the behaviour of their parents may not be the best guide for predicting the future behaviours of the next generation.

3. The impact of inventions. A number of authors look at technological inventions to predict the future of the family. Hill calls this method 'exciting but hazardous' (Hill, 1964: 24) and argues that we have overestimated the speed with which certain inventions would be merchandised. This seems less of an issue today, but he restricts his analysis to household conveniences. If we extend this approach to look at all technological inventions, this is certainly an important part of the world that impacts on the family. Ogburn and Nimkoff's predictions concerning the new reproductive and genetic technologies provide a startling testament to the efficacy of the approach.

4. The family specialists' future family. This method looks at the type of family advocated by family professionals through their writing and publishing. Hill characterizes this method as novel, interesting, but leading to normative statements rather than predictions. This is very evident in the large spate of predictions and prescriptions around 1970 about communal replacements of marriage and the family.

5. Identifying societal changes and reflecting on their importance for the family. Goode argues that all family issues are structural and what we really need to know if we wish to predict how the family will change is how society will change. This seems to me the most promising but also the most difficult method.

Some Tentative Predictions about the Future of Canadian Families

Given the assessment of the various methods of how to predict what will happen with respect to future families, I am here concentrating on projected societal changes in my attempt to look into the crystal ball.

WORLDWIDE CHANGES

Unfortunately, the future promises major challenges. At the global level, **climate change** is undoubtedly the single most important issue confronting humanity. Although the Kyoto Accord came into force in February 2005, its provisions may not be strong enough to prevent further climate change. The United States—the world's greatest contributor to greenhouse gases, being responsible for a quarter of global emissions (Gordon, 2005: A3)—has not ratified the Kyoto Accord. And Canada's newly elected Conservative government declared in 2006 that Canada will pull out of the Kyoto Accord.

Already, the rate and severity of natural disasters have increased manifold in the early twenty-first century. The severe effects of disasters have much to do with human-generated changes to the environment. For instance, the destruction of much of the mangrove forests on the South Asian coast that was most affected by the tsunami that ravaged this area in December 2004 removed a protective wall that would have greatly diminished the devastating effects of the tsunami. Where the mangroves remained intact, the villages also remained intact (Thekaekara, 2005).

We can thus expect more severe natural disasters, such as the record-breaking hurricane season of 2005 in the Caribbean and Gulf of Mexico, and more sudden swings in climate, with negative effects on the world's crops. If the polar ice caps keep melting, some currently inhabited land may disappear into the oceans. At the same time, more topsoil and forest cover are lost every year, while water tables are falling (Brown, 2003).

Climate change is a legacy of the exploitation of natural resources by the world's richest countries (which include Canada), of over-consumption, the reckless burning of fossil fuels that, among other things, power an ever-increasing number of cars, exploitation of resources that would have been renewable if they had been used in a sustainable manner (such as fish in Newfoundland), deforestation, and other factors.

Worldwide, the division of people into haves and have-nots has never been as great as it is today. The personal wealth of a few individuals is almost unimaginable. In 1997, *Forbes Magazine* estimated that the world's three richest people have assets that exceed the combined GDP of the 48 least developed countries and that the world's 225 richest people have a combined wealth equal to the annual income of the poorest 47 per cent of the world's people (UNDP, 1998: 30). Millions of children in low-income countries grow up malnourished; millions of people die of malnutrition, starvation, and diseases brought on by poverty every year while obesity is recognized as the new epidemic in North America. Even within rich countries, and certainly within Canada, there is a sharp divide between the rich and poor. Homeless people are a common sight today in Canada's big cities.

The production of oil has likely peaked,[6] and as it becomes more and more expensive, current differences between rich and poor will be further exacerbated unless governments take decisive actions to prevent this. At the moment, such a process has not started. The United States is now the only superpower in the world, and it has taken on the role of enforcing its will on the world. The Iraq war may be only one in a series of wars that are fought—rhetoric notwithstanding—around safeguarding access to oil resources.

The cumulative effects of the various trends are likely to result in ever-increasing international turmoil, as the countries that have benefited least from the 'progress' of the last century pay the highest price. As a consequence, I would expect anti-American sentiment to increase sharply in the future because of the dominant position of the United States in the world and because it is likely to serve as a symbol and flashpoint for a way of life that has advantaged the few and disadvantaged the many. As this anti-American view starts to affect the US economy, it will have a strong negative effect on the Canadian economy as well because the latter is tied so strongly to the former.

To this mix we must add the uncertain dangers posed by **genetically modified (GM) crops**. While resistance to GM crops in Europe has been very strong, Canada sees biotechnologies as an important growth area and is committed to develop this sector further. On the other hand, McCain Foods is refusing to use GM potatoes for its potato chips and Prince Edward Island is debating whether or not it should declare the whole province a GM-free zone.

It is not clear what the long-term effects of these technologies will be. To provide just one example, Monsanto has developed the so-called 'terminator seed', which is sterile in the second generation, so that farmers cannot use part of their own crops for replanting but must buy new seed from the company (Kneen, 1999; Shiva, 2000). This is a very troubling situation in its own right. It becomes completely frightening if such genetic traits are able to wander into other crops. Such an effect could have catastrophic consequences for the world's food supply.

The overall effects of these trends are likely to be global economic, social, and political turmoil.

Effects of World Developments on Families

MORE THREE-GENERATION FAMILIES

Unhappily, if these predictions are right, the pressure on Canadian families is likely to increase significantly. Economic uncertainties may result in people moving together in larger units, thus reversing the trend of shrinking household size. We have already seen that young people live longer with their parents than they used to. We may experience a modest trend to more three–generation families. This might happen partially because of economic uncertainties generated by worldwide political, economic, and environmental instability, as well as by increased immigration from countries in which three-generation families are still the norm.

DECREASE IN LIFE EXPECTANCY

I expect life expectancy to decrease. Just as oil production is likely to have peaked, so increases in life expectancy may have peaked. The people whose lifespan has been expanding over the past century grew up in a period where pollution levels and other environmental stressors were considerably lower. Today, many people have compromised immune systems. This means that at a time in which environmental stressors are likely to be greater, the physical capacity of people to deal with them will be lower. There is a constant stream of information about newly identified problems. For instance, flame retardants (PBDEs) are now commonplace in the breast milk of Canadian mothers (Picard, 2005a). In addition, lifestyles of both children and older people have resulted in a sharp increase in obesity, which will likely result in more health problems. Furthermore, obese mothers are more likely to give birth to babies with health problems than are non-obese mothers (Picard, 2005b: A15). It may be that the life expectancy of people who are quite old will continue to increase for a while, while that of people born later may be curtailed at the same time. If this were the case, a trend towards lower life expectancies might not show up in general statistics for a while. To check the accuracy of this prediction, we would have to examine cohort-specific mortality rates.

In Africa, life expectancy at age 15 has decreased by nearly 7 years between 1980 and 2001, and in the former Soviet countries of Eastern Europe it has decreased over the same period by 4.2 years for males and 1.6 years for females (Global Forum for Health Research, 2004: 56–7).

If this also happens in Canada, we will be faced with a combination of lower life expectancy for young people who married later and had children later. One of the effects would be that fewer children would have all their grandparents alive, and fewer parents might receive help from their own parents. For the older people it would, of course, mean that fewer of them would be alive to enjoy their grandchildren.

LOW FERTILITY COUPLED WITH HIGH IMMIGRATION RATES

I expect the fertility rate to remain below replacement values, as it is at present. Worldwide, fertility decreases as women attain higher levels of education and take on paying jobs. At present, more Canadian women than men attend university. We will therefore have a highly educated group of women in child-bearing age. At the same time, the pressure for people to immigrate to Canada for political, economic, and, increasingly, environmental reasons is likely to increase. If Canadian immigration policies will admit such immigrants, Canada will significantly increase its proportion of people of colour, since these are the people who will most likely wish to immigrate. Provided Canada manages to overcome its current racism (Henry et al., 2000), this may become its saving grace. People who grew up in countries that have suffered from the economic and environmental policies of past and current times may be more likely to support strict environmental regulations and more just external policies. If a sufficiently large proportion of the population supports stronger environmental protection and more egalitarian social and foreign policies, they might conceivably exert enough pressure on governments to achieve real policy change.

SEXUALITY

At the time of this writing, same-sex marriage is legal in Canada, although the newly elected Conservative government has promised to hold an open vote in the House of Commons on whether to re-establish a traditional definition of marriage as a union between one woman and one man. The prediction is that the new definition of marriage as a union between two persons will win by a narrow margin (Valpy et al., 2006).

Regardless of the outcome of this debate I expect an increase in openly gay and lesbian unions, whether legally married or cohabiting, and a corresponding decrease in homophobia. More people will personally know lesbians and gays, simply because more of them are likely to be 'out', and this should lower resistance to homosexuality.

NEW REPRODUCTIVE AND GENETIC TECHNOLOGIES

The new reproductive and genetic technologies as applied to humans have developed extremely rapidly. They have fundamentally changed, indeed, revolutionized how reproduction is considered within society. Mass media have popularized alternative forms of conception such as in vitro fertilization (IVF). Nevertheless, only a minority of people are directly affected by such techniques, while almost all pregnant women are offered various prenatal diagnostic techniques. Since the intent is usually to abort the fetus if a characteristic perceived as undesirable is detected, this is a form of eugenic gatekeeping. This is currently being challenged by disability rights activists (Wolbring, 2001). It is unclear what will happen. If religious fundamentalism were to rise in Canada, this practice may diminish. On the other hand, strong economic pressures may keep the practice alive.

GENDER ROLES

Women in the past 30 years have taken on most of the roles that men used to play, but men have not taken up women's roles to the same degree. Nevertheless, men do contribute a bit more to housework and to child care. I would expect that trend, modest as it has been, to continue into the future, on the basis that normatively almost all Canadians—male and female—agree that housework and child care should be shared (Bibby, 2005). Even though the behaviour lags behind the norms, one would expect that there will be some move to reconcile the two.

Divorce and Cohabitation as Alternatives to Permanent Monogamous Marriage

At present, the trend towards cohabitation as a precursor and alternative to marriage as well as a post-divorce form of union seems strong. If economic uncertainties develop in the direction predicted above, and if fertility remains as low as it is at present, then cohabitation will likely become even more popular than it is today, but I would not expect it to displace legal marriage altogether. In times of political and economic uncertainty, more people may turn to more fundamentalist forms of religion. For this part of the population, at least, marriage would retain (or regain) a religious value, and therefore I would expect marriage to continue to keep an important place in Canadian culture.

It is possible that my predictions about the future of Canadian families may be as wrong as those of so many eminent sociologists before me. Indeed, I hope so. However, even if the events predicted do occur in their broad outlines, there could potentially be some positive outcomes, if governments and people seize the opportunities.

Strangely enough, if oil—and therefore fuel for cars—becomes significantly more expensive, this may have significant positive effects besides the negative effects that it will undoubtedly have. If cars become too expensive to drive for trivial purposes, this may eventually turn suburbs into genuine neighbourhoods. Corner stores would become profitable, more cultural events would likely happen locally, leading to a market for local artists. Local production of produce would receive a boost. Population density would need to increase in the suburbs, which would make it possible to introduce better mass transit services. If people started to walk and cycle more, obesity would certainly diminish, thus reducing the importance of one of the factors cited above for lower life expectancy. Pedestrian traffic also increases possibilities for more interaction between neighbours, thus potentially setting the stage for a more robust civil society with more citizen involvement, which, in turn, could result in positive political changes.

Conclusion

In this chapter, we have looked at a number of predictions that were made about families from 1930 to 1975. Some of these predictions were spectacularly wrong; others were surprisingly accurate. The time at which predictions were made was not a predictor of their accuracy. Instead, the important aspect seemed to be the basis on which they were made: those predictions based on societal or technological changes were more likely to be accurate than those based on extrapolation of trends or predictions of family experts. A fifth method, projection from generational changes, was not employed by enough people to gauge its effectiveness.

Given these findings, I have identified some changes that I anticipate for the future, in particular, climate change and the peaking of oil production. If these two things occur, I expect the future will see a modest trend towards three-generation families as one response to economic uncertainties and political turmoil, a decrease in life expectancy, continuing low fertility with high immigration, less homophobia, a continuing slow erosion of strictly defined gender roles, and a continuing diversity of unions, including common-law and legal marriages and same-sex marriages.

In other words, families will continue to exist—some will prosper, others less so—and children will continue to be raised within family settings, which will probably be even more diverse than at present.

Notes

1. I owe the idea to Patrizia Albanese, who also lent me some of her old family sociology textbooks and gave me feedback on this paper. Lingqin Feng found a number of old articles and books for me. I would like to thank Gregor Wolbring and David Cheal for helpful comments on the paper. My sincere thanks go to all of them.
2. In the first edition of the book. I am using the second edition.
3. I have consistently opted to use modern terms when discussing phenomena, but it needs to be noted that the term 'gender roles' only started to be used in the mid- to late 1970s.
4. This is not a term they use, but it is certainly an accurate one.
5. I am using modern terms. For the most part this does not reflect the language employed by the authors, but the phenomena under discussion are the same.
6. This point is made very forcefully in the film *The End of Suburbia: Oil Depletion and the Collapse of the American Dream*, DVD2004, The Electric Wallpaper. See <www.endofsuburbia.com>.

Study Questions

1. Select a basis on which to make predictions, choose one significant trend (e.g., birth rate, divorce rate, labour force participation of women), and predict how this trend will develop within the next 20 years. Explain why you make this prediction.
2. What are some of the societal factors that affect your own life course and that of one other family member of a different generation?
3. What might the situation of your family be if you were living in another country? Pick a specific country and explain the reasons for your statements.

Glossary

Climate change Long-term change in the weather pattern of a specific region or for the planet as a whole.

Genetically modified (GM) crops Plants created for agricultural purposes by humans through the combination of genes from different and frequently entirely unrelated species that are more resistant to disease and/or more productive.

Reproductive and genetic technologies The use of birth control pills, artificial insemination, in vitro fertilization, use of donor eggs, sex selection of fetuses, Viagra and its female equivalent, hormone replacement therapy.

Women's lib Early name for second-wave feminism, which started in the 1960s.

Zero population movement A social movement that started in the late 1960s advocating that the number of births should be restricted so that the human population would not outstrip the capacity of the earth to sustain humanity.

Further Readings

Todd, Nancy Jack. 2005. *A Safe and Sustainable World: The Promise of Ecological Design*. Washington: Island Press. Written in a personal style, this is a report of various very impressive successful experiments and projects, using ecological design, to lessen humanity's negative impact on the earth.

Alternatives Journal. This periodical provides background analyses as well as positive examples of how to deal with environmental problems. The website of the journal is <www.alernativesjournal.ca>.

Websites

www.insnet.org
An excellent weekly electronic newsletter with articles on issues of environmental and social justice concern.

www.childcarecanada.org
The Childcare Resource and Research Unit (CRRU) at the University of Toronto is a policy and research-oriented facility that focuses on early childhood education and care.

www.policyalternatives.ca
The *CCPA Monitor* is the monthly newsletter of the Canadian Centre for Policy Alternatives and is available at this site. It takes an integrative social justice/ecological approach to problems and contains thoughtful analyses of current social and environmental issues.

References

Anshen, Ruth Nanda. 1959. *The Family: Its Function and Destiny*. New York: Harper.

Baber, Ray E. 1953. *Marriage and the Family*. New York: McGraw-Hill.

Barbeau, Clayton C. 1971. *Future of the Family*. New York: Bruce Publishing.

Basen, Gwynne, Margrit Eichler, and Abby Lippman. 1993. *Misconceptions: The Social Construction of Choice and the New Reproductive and Genetic Technologies*, vol. 1. Hull, Que.: Voyageur.

Beaujot, Roderic. 2000. *Earning and Caring in Canadian Families*. Peterborough, Ont.: Broadview Press.

Bernard, Jessie. 1972. *The Future of Marriage*. New York: Bantam.

Bibby, Reginald W. 2005. 'Future families: Surveying our hopes, dreams and realities', *Transition* 35: 3–14.

Bird, Joseph, and Lois Bird. 1971. 'Marriage: A doubtful future', in Barbeau (1971: 1–10).

Blake, Judith. 1972. 'Here and beyond—the population crisis: The microfamily and zero population growth', in College of Home Economics (1972: 55–68).

Brown, Lester R. 2003. *Plan B: Rescuing a Planet under Stress and a Civilization in Trouble*. New York: Norton.

Cavan, Ruth Shonle. 1963. *The American Family*. New York: Thomas Y. Crowell.

College of Home Economics, Iowa State University. 1972. *Families of the Future*. Ames: Iowa State University Press.

Davids, Leo. 1971. 'North American marriage: 1990', *The Futurist* 5, 2: 190–4.

des Rivières-Pigeon, Catherine, Marie-Josèphe Saurel-Cubizolles, and Patrizia Romito. 2002. 'Division of domestic work and psychological distress 1 year after childbirth: A comparison between France, Quebec and Italy', *Journal of Community & Applied Social Psychology* 12: 397–409.

Downing, Joseph J. 1970. 'The tribal family and the society of awakening', in Otto (1970a: 119–36).

Edwards, John N. 1967. 'The Future of the Family Revisited', *Journal of Marriage and the Family* 29, 3: 505–11.

Eichler, Margrit. 1975. 'The equalitarian family in Canada?', in P.S. Wakil, ed., *Marriage, Family and Society: Canadian Perspectives*. Toronto: Butterworths, 223–35.

Elkin, Frederick. 1964. *The Family in Canada: An Account of Present Knowledge and Gaps in Knowledge about Canadian Families*. Ottawa: Vanier Institute of the Family.

Elliott, Katherine. 1970. *The Family and Its Future. A Ciba Foundation Symposium*. London: J.&A. Churchill.

Farson, Richard E., Philip M. Hauser, Herbert Stroup, and Anthony J. Wiener. 1969. *The Future of the Family*. New York: Family Service Association of America.

Gerson, Menachem. 1972. 'Lesson from the kibbutz: A cautionary tale', in Howe (1972a: 326–40).

Global Forum for Health Research. 2004. *Monitoring Financial Flows for Health Research*. Geneva: Global Forum for Health Research.

Goode, William J. 1972. 'Social change and family renewal', in College of Home Economics (1972: 116–33).

Gordon, Sean. 2005. 'Kyoto enforcement may vary, Dion says', *Toronto Star*, 17 Feb., A3.

Greenwald, Harold. 1970. 'Marriage as a non-legal voluntary association', in Otto (1970a: 51–66).

Haddad, Anton. 1996. 'The Sexual Division of Household Labour: Pragmatic Strategies or Patriarchal Dynamics: An Analysis of Two Case Studies', Ph.D. thesis, York University.

Henry, Frances, Carol Tator, Winston Mattis, and Tim Rees. 2000. 'The ideology of racism', in Henry et al., *The Colour of Democracy: Racism in Canadian Society*. Toronto: Harcourt and Brace Canada, 15–34.

Hill, Reuben. 1964. 'The American family of the future', *Journal of Marriage and the Family* 26, 1: 20–8.

Hobbs, Edward C. 1970. 'An alternate model from a theological perspective', in Otto (1970a: 25–42).

Hochschild, Arlie Russell. 1972. 'Communal living in old age', in Howe (1972a: 299–310).

Hossain, Ziarat. 2001. 'Division of household labor and family functioning in off-reservation Navajo Indian families', *Family Relations* 50, 3: 255–61.

Howe, Louise Kapp, ed. 1972a. *The Future of the Family*. New York: Simon & Schuster.

———. 1972b. 'An introduction', in Howe (1972a: 11–24).

John, Daphne, and Beth Anne Shelton. 1997. 'The production of gender among black and white women and men: The case of household labor', *Sex Roles* 36, 3 and 4: 171–93.

Kanter, Rosabeth Moss. 1972. '"Getting it all together": Communes past, present, future', in Howe (1972a: 311–25).

Kassel, Victor. 1970. 'Polygyny after sixty', in Otto (1970a: 137–44).

Kay, F. George. 1972. *The Family in Transition: Its Past, Present and Future Patterns*. Newton Abbot: David and Charles.

Kitterod, Ragni Hege. 2002. 'Mothers' housework and childcare: Growing similarities or stable inequalities?', *Acta Sociologica* 45, 2: 127–49.

Kneen, Brewster. 1999. *Farmageddon: Food and the Culture of Biotechnology*. Gabriola Island, BC: New Society Publishers.

Levett, Carl. 1970. 'A parental presence in future family models', in Otto (1970a: 161–82).

Linton, Ralph. 1959. 'The natural history of the family', in Anshen (1959: 30–52).

National Council of Welfare. 2004. *Poverty Profile 2001*, vol. 122. Ottawa: Minister of Public Works and Government Services Canada.

Nett, Emily M. 1988. *Canadian Families, Past and Present*. Toronto: Butterworths.

Nimkoff, Meyer F. 1947. *Marriage and the Family*. Boston: Houghton Mifflin.

Ogburn, W.F., and M.F. Nimkoff. 1955. *Technology and the Changing Family*. Boston: Houghton Mifflin.

Orleans, Myron, and Florence Wolfson. 1970. 'The future of the family', *The Futurist*: 48–9.

Otto, Herbert A., ed. 1970a. *The Family in Search of a Future: Alternate Models for Moderns*. New York: Appleton-Century-Crofts.

———. 1970b. 'Introduction', in Otto (1970a: 1–9).

———. 1972. 'New light on human potential', in College of Home Economics (1972: 14–25).

Parsons, Talcott, and Robert F. Bales. 1955. *Family, Socialization and Interaction Process*. New York: Free Press.

Paul, Eden. 1930. *Chronos or the Future of the Family*. London: Kegan Paul, Trench, Trubner and Co.

Picard, Andre. 2005a. 'Flame retardants building up within us', *Globe and Mail*, A19.

———. 2005b. 'Obese moms risk having babies with birth defects', *Globe and Mail*, A15.

Platt, John. 1972. 'A fearful and wonderful world for living', in College of Home Economics (1972: 3–13).

Pollak, Otto. 1972. 'Family functions in transition', in College of Home Economics (1972: 69–78).

Rosenberg, George. 1970. 'Implications of new models of the family for the aging population', in Otto (1970a: 171–86).

Sanchez, Laura, and Elizabeth Thomson. 1997. 'Becoming mothers and fathers: Parenthood, gender, and the division of labor', *Gender and Society* 11, 6: 747–72.

Schulz, David A. 1972. *The Changing Family: Its Function and Future*. Englewood Cliffs, NJ: Prentice-Hall.

Shelton, Beth Anne, and Daphne John. 1996. 'The division of household labor', *Annual Review of Sociology* 22: 299–322.

Shiva, Vandana. 2000. *Stolen Harvest: The Hijacking of the Global Food Supply*. Cambridge, Mass.: South End Press.

Skinner, B.F. 1948. *Walden II*. New York: Macmillan.

South, S.J., and G. Spitze. 1994. 'Housework in marital and nonmarital households', *American Sociological Review* 59, 3: 327–47.

Statistics Canada. 2004. 'Births', *The Daily*, 19 Apr.

Stoller, Frederick H. 1970. 'The intimate network of families as a new structure', in Otto (1970a: 145–60).

Thamm, Robert. 1975. *Beyond Marriage and the Nuclear Family*. San Francisco: Canfield Press.

Thekaekara, Mari Marcel. 2005. 'Weakened coast was prime target', Manchester *Guardian Weekly*, 8.

United Nations Development Program (UNDP). 1998.

Human Development Report 1998. New York: Oxford University Press.

Valpy, Michael, Caroline Alphonso, and Rheal Seguin. 2006. 'Same-sex vote likely to be tight', *Globe and Mail*, A1, A4.

Whitehurst, R.N. 1975. 'Alternate life styles and Canadian pluralism', in P.S. Wakil, ed., *Marriage, Family and Society: Canadian Perspectives*. Toronto: Butterworths, 433–45.

Winch, Robert F. 1970. 'Permanence and change in the history of the American family and some speculation as to its future', *Journal of Marriage and the Family* 32, 1: 6–15.

Wolbring, Gregor. 2001. *Folgen Der Anwendung Genetischer Diagnostik Fuer Behinderte Menschen*. Enquete-Kommission des deutschen Bundestages: Recht und Ethik der modernen Medizin. Calgary: University of Calgary.

Wu, Zheng. 2000. *Cohabitation: An Alternative Form of Family Living*. Toronto: Oxford University Press.

Zimmerman, Carle C. 1947. *Family and Civilization*. New York: Harper & Brothers.

Index